CHRIS ANDERSEN

THE SNIPER

HUNTING A SERIAL KILLER - A TRUE STORY

ISBN 978-1-09830-382-2 eBook 978-1-09830-383-9

CONTENTS

INTRODUCTION

This is a true story of a crew of serial killers whose specialty was robbing armored trucks and how they were ultimately undone.

Unique to this particular robbery crew was its paramilitary-type operational sophistication and their use of a sniper hidden within a specially modified vehicle. After months of preparation, the sniper would shoot the targeted armored truck guard/courier from a distance once they had left the safety of their bulletproof armored vehicle to make a money delivery. Once the courier was killed, then other members of the crew would move in to empty the armored truck of its contents or grab the courier's money bags.

In an around-the-clock, high-risk surveillance operation—which lasted over three months, with many twists and turns, utilizing covertly mounted vehicle tracking devices, hidden cameras, cell phone analysis, shadowy informants, and a wiretap—a small, elite undercover police tactical unit along with its attached federal agents and prosecutors all worked together to stage a decoy operation that stopped these criminals moments before they were planning to kill yet another courier with their sniper.

This is also the story of the same undercover police tactical unit assigned to develop a new methodology to dismantle violent commercial business robbery crews (High Risk Surveillance). Intermixed with all of its surveillance operations, police shootouts, and resulting political intrigue, this same mysterious sniper-initiated robbery crew with ties to the black supremacy movement had been working in the shadows for close to four years.

Starting in 2014, the proliferation of these crews was responsible in making Houston the robbery capital of the United States. These armed suspects were almost exclusively black males with street gang affiliation, who were also sometimes responsible for the murders of innocent citizens—many of them black—during the course of these same robberies.

At the time this new anti-robbery initiative was being implemented, the United States was experiencing a wave of civil discontent regarding the unwarranted shootings (either true or perceived) of black men by law enforcement (the Black Lives Matter era).

The robbery initiative, by using advanced technical surveillance techniques, was an unqualified success. By the end of 2016, the commercial business robbery rate crashed by 80% while the murder rate fell by 58% on the north side of Houston, where this tactical unit was assigned. It was unquantified how many innocent citizens were also saved as a result of their operations! But, because of the surveillance tactics being used, this same small police tactical unit often came into direct confrontations with these violent street gangs while in the actual commission of takedown robberies. As a result, more than a few of these armed suspects were shot and killed. The killing of black men (even armed violent criminals) was something the upper police administrators (the politicians) wanted to avoid at all costs, to not agitate black activists. To accomplish this, the police upper administration then tried to coerce the leadership of this undercover surveillance unit to incorporate tactics that would lessen the possibility of having to shoot robbery suspects, while significantly increasing the chances of an innocent person being killed or seriously injured.

This unrecognized form of police corruption, in my mind, had the sole purpose to pander to black political activists and their followers.

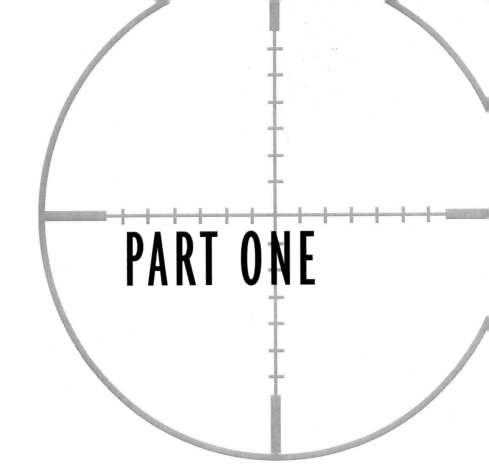

PART ONE

PROLOGUE

I was born in 1960 on Long Island, just outside of New York City. After I was born and after the birth of my brother John and sister Karen, my parents moved the family to the end of Long Island (the North Fork) to the "country" and as far away from New York City as possible—in Southold, NY.

In the 1970s, the area was rural, covered by potato farms attended to almost exclusively by Polish-descended farmers whose last names I could not pronounce. The area was interspersed with sections of heavily wooded areas. More significantly, the North Fork was surrounded by water. On one side was the Long Island Sound (on a clear day you could see Connecticut), on the other side the great Peconic Bay.

My mother insisted that every year I attend swimming lessons. Swimming lessons in that era was more of a swim camp held for a few weeks each year in June. As you got older and as your proficiency grew, you would progress to a higher level of "swim class" until, at the completion of the course(s) over the years, you would emerge as an efficient swimmer.

Of much greater interest to me was the woods and the great out-doors. My friends and I spent most of the time outside, where we acted out our favorite scenes from the popular movie *Jeremiah Johnson,* a fictional account of a loner mountain man in the 1800s, living in the wilderness, who fights hostile Indians and eventually earns their respect.

As I got older, playing Jeremiah Johnson gave way to hunting. My father was an enthusiastic bow hunter (archery) and a disciple of Howard Hill, Fred Bear, and Saxon Pope— well-known archers/bow hunters from earlier in the twenty-first century famous for their shooting exploits. I became a bow hunting enthusiast—so much so, that we kept a few hay bales in the backyard, where I would practice nearly every day in anticipation of the upcoming deer or small game season. Later in life, I would lose all interest in hunting (although I don't fault those who do) and now hold the view that there should be a more valid reason to kill animals other than the "thrill of the hunt" or for a "trophy."

I hated school. I found high school in particular to be confining and boring—and for the life of me could not understand the relevancy of algebra in relationship to my dream of being a New York State Conservation Fish and Game Officer. This job was where I could fulfill my life's destiny of always being outside, in the wilderness, and engaged with the activities I enjoyed. To say I was a marginal student was an understatement and I did just enough to get by.

Throughout high school and into college, I worked various part-time jobs. The first was as a farm hand, at $1.83 an hour. Later, I was a carpenter's helper (for slightly more an hour), which was hard physical labor, particularly when trying to navigate large sheets of ¾ inch plywood onto construction sites and then hand nailing them into position (there were no pneumatic nail guns then). I have to admit that I relished neither job's hard physical labor, particularly in the heat of the summers or in the bone-numbing cold of those windy Long Island winters.

But there was a much better job available to me—LIFEGUARD! The North Fork of Long Island was a summer mecca for tourists from New York City. The reason the life guarding gig appealed to me: GIRLS. Now, usurping my desire to be a modern reincarnation of Jeremiah Johnson and live a hermit's life in the wilderness, I discovered that I found the company of attractive women much more interesting. A lifeguard's job would surely provide many opportunities to meet those attractive, cosmopolitan, young, Greek, Jewish, and Italian girls from New York City. But first I had to pass the dreaded Open Water Life Guard Test—a series of tests of various swimming proficiency skills. You had to pass each test to get your Life Guard certification, which would be your pathway to a "better tomorrow." I passed. I received my Life Guard certification and soon after the town hired me as an open water lifeguard.

One high school program I was involved in was Navy Junior Reserve Officer Training Corps (NJROTC). This program taught leadership and good citizenship, as well as stressing United States Navy history, tradition, and indoctrination. I entered the program on the off chance that if I couldn't be a conservation officer, then maybe I could serve on a submarine.

The United States Navy's primary East Coast submarine base was across Long Island Sound in New London, Connecticut. The Brooklyn Navy Yard, farther up Long Island Sound in New York City, was where, in the 1970s, navy ships were still being repaired. My father recalled during World War II, as a kid, he'd seen heavily damaged ships being towed into the navy yard after having been torpedoed by German U-boats (submarines). As a NJROTC cadet, I could take tours of both bases as well as the major surface combatants moored there.

I graduated high school in 1978, majored in gym, study hall, and skipping school. My only extracurricular activities were on the wrestling and the small bore (.22) rifle team. I can remember bringing my rifle and ammunition and storing it in my school locker. I am sure this would never pass muster in this day and age.

After graduating from high school, I applied and was accepted (I think everyone who applied was accepted) to Suffolk County Community College, where I would pursue an associate's degree in criminal justice, this being somewhat related to my intentions of becoming a conservation officer.

I did well in community college (it was interesting and relevant to my career goal).

Surprisingly, I made the dean's list and received my associate's degree in criminal justice in 1980. While in community college, a harsh reality began to emerge. Two factors were conspiring to derail my conservation officer ambitions: during the presidency of Jimmy Carter, there was an oil embargo, and the Northeast was in a deep economic recession. There were few jobs available and the State of New York had no immediate plans to hire many conservation officers in the near future. In addition, this was also the era of affirmative action and there was a great overabundance of white males seeking these types of jobs.

I realized I would have to reframe my career path to something more readily available: a position in a municipal or state law enforcement agency. As soon as I was able, I began taking the Civil Service Exams for the Suffolk County Police and New York City Police Departments, as well as the New York and Connecticut State Police. Back then, most of the departments used a "three list" civil service system: one list for white males, one for females, and one for blacks. Then, depending on how you scored on the testing (primarily the written test), you were on one of three lists, according to your gender and/or ethnicity in rank order. During the hiring process, if the department wanted a black male, they would go to that list and hire the top name on the list, and so on.

I learned that because of the fierce competition among white males, I would most likely have to get a perfect written score besides having the maximum number of veterans credit points added to my raw score (military veterans received a certain number of points depending on their length of military service) and high school NJROTC did not count. But a black male only had to pass the civil service test to be hired. It was a dawning reality that, as a white male, living in the Northeast during the late 70s, getting a law enforcement civil service job would be difficult. Although I did well on the various civil service exams, there would not be any job offers forthcoming.

During the fall of 1980, upon receiving my associate's degree, I then entered the State University of New York at Brockport, a college in Upstate New York, near Buffalo and the Canadian border. It was here I was to work on my bachelor's degree in criminal justice. I lacked motivation. There were no jobs to be found and I was going into heavy debt. My family was not wealthy and I had to fund my college education by taking out government college loans and supplementing that money with part-time jobs. I could not see a path forward and again had to redefine my career path.

The answer appeared to be the Army ROTC program that my college offered. By joining this program, the Army would pay for the lion's share of my tuition and, in return, I would be committed to several years of active duty service upon the completion of my four-year degree. Of great interest to me was the program they were pushing forward—a bit of a bait and switch— in which I could, if qualified, become a warrant officer/helicopter pilot. I talked to my father about this and he discouraged me from this career path: "You would be an idiot." My family does not have a military or law enforcement service tradition. My father was drafted during the Korean War and served as a forward artillery observer in post-World War II Germany; he did not see the military as a good career path for his son. Remember, this was not too long after the Vietnam War and the United States military was perceived by many to be in disarray and disrepute.

One day, my college roommate told me that a recruiter from the Houston Police Department was on campus and that Houston was actively recruiting "us" (white college boys). I headed to the Criminal Justice Department where the recruiter had been, but missed him. Fortunately, he left several thick recruiting packets, which consisted of a multi-paged application and a thorough questionnaire about one's personal life—including questions such as "list below everything that you have ever stolen" (I listed unpaid overdue library fines). I was excited and thought this was a possibility to a real job and career. After reviewing all the material and filling it out and being honest and transparent on the questionnaire, I mailed it to the Houston Police Department's Recruiting Division.

A few weeks later, I received a form letter from the Recruiting Division. I had passed the first hurdle (if I had been honest in the application and questionnaire) and I was to call a recruiter for further instructions. Upon contacting the recruiter, he told me that if I wanted to move forward with the application process, it would be necessary for me to travel to Houston (at my expense), where, over a three-day period, they would conduct the following testing:

Written Exam

Physical Exam

Physical Agility Test

Credit History Check

Polygraph Exam

Oral Interview

Psychological Exam

Failing any of the tests would prevent you from going to the next one and it disqualified you from any further consideration. If you passed all the testing, at some point, the department would conduct a background investigation. If you passed this last hurdle, then a job offer might be given. This opportunity was unique. There was a lack of interested qualified applicants in the Houston area because the local economy was booming and the jobs in the oil sector were high paying. The department, in its quest for qualified applicants, would pay the cost of sending an investigator back to the applicant's hometown, often across the country, to determine whether he or she would be a good fit. What was encouraging was, although they preferred minorities, all were welcome to apply as there were that many positions available.

In the late fall of 1980, after scraping together the money for a round-trip air flight ticket to Houston, I made the journey. It was a rough start. I panicked that I would miss my flight as my Ford Pinto had disappeared in a snow drift overnight; even if I could locate it, I would not have been able to dig it out in time to make the flight. I hitchhiked to the airport and, as fortune would have it, made my flight. This was the first time I had ever flown.

I did not know what to expect when I landed in Houston. My expectations were stereotypes of Western movies. I expected to see desert, tumbleweeds, and everyone looking like extras from the movie *Urban Cowboy*. This was not the case. Houston was heavily wooded (not desert) and not everyone was dressed like a cowboy/cowgirl. I noticed that the weather was much warmer than northern New York. And the women were, mostly, much more attractive (very interesting). This observation was not an unfounded opinion on my part; in later conversations with other displaced Yankees, they also made the same observations.

I took a cab, which delivered me to a downtown hotel. I was to report to the Houston Police Department's Recruiting Division to begin the selection process. The next morning, I sat in a room with all the other applicants who would start the three-day process with me. They all seemed older, bigger, and more capable then I was. Even though I was now twenty and a strapping 5'8" and maybe 143 pounds, I looked more like I was fourteen or fifteen and had some doubts that, even if I passed all the testing, the department would consider hiring me.

By the third day, they had eliminated about half of our group. The biggest obstacle was yet to come, this being the polygraph test, or the lie detector test. The guy who examined me was some old white guy, with a flat-top haircut and a gruff and unfriendly disposition. The first thing he did was to have me fill out again the same lengthy personal questionnaire (list everything you have stolen in your life, how many times have you had sex with an animal, what illegal drugs have you taken, etc.). The polygraph examiner told me that this time when I filled out the questionnaire, I had to be totally honest; if I lied, he would detect it and I would be disqualified.

I realized at this moment that if I documented anything different on the second identical questionnaire as compared to the first that this would be tantamount to falsifying my application and they would disqualify me. Fortunately, I had been transparent while filling out the first questionnaire and I wrote out the same answers. Wow! He was not happy with this. After I had finished the second questionnaire, he pulled out the first question-naire from a folder and compared the two. He yelled at me, cursed me, and said he knew I was lying, and that before we started the actual test, he was giving me one more chance to tell the truth or else! I didn't budge.

I maintained my composure and assured him I was telling the truth.

They hooked me up to the polygraph machine and we went through the entire questionnaire. On some of the responses to the questions I gave, he said he was "getting a reading" and that I was being deceitful. I maintained my innocence. At the end of the examination, as I was being unhooked from the machine, I asked whether I had passed the test. The examiner wouldn't tell me. He instead told me to report for my final inter-view and I was to tell the interviewer(s) that "I was a queer" and "smoked marijuana"!

As I walked to the Recruiting Division building for my final inter-view, I realized I had passed the polygraph test because I was advancing to the next hurdle; they wouldn't be wasting the time or effort had I failed the polygraph test. When I sat down for the final interview, I was introduced to a lieutenant and a sergeant. The lieutenant then asked me, "How did the polygraph test go?" I then told him with a straight face that the "flat-top guy" told me to tell you I was a queer and smoked dope! They smiled and laughed. The rest of the interview was relaxed. I had passed!

Later, back at the airport, waiting for my flight back to the land of snow and ice, I ran into some of the same guys I had met on the first day and would have expected to have been shoo-ins and passed. All of them had been eliminated, one of whom was emotional. They had eliminated most of them at the polygraph test, having made contradictory statements. I didn't tell them I had passed and kept quiet, feeling their pain.

Between Thanksgiving and Christmas 1980, the Houston Police Department sent a background investigator to my college, where he interviewed me as well as interviewing several of the other residents who lived with me in my dormitory hall. Some of my neighbors were "enthusiastic connoisseurs" of marijuana and also die-hard Jimmy Morrison fans. Morrison, the lead singer of the Doors, had died of a drug overdose in 1971. I am sure the investigator was not so impressed. After visiting my college, the investigator then flew to my hometown to finish his investigation. The next day, my mother called me in a panic. She told me that the interview had gone well, but…she admitted that she had been nervous as this was the first Hispanic American she had ever spoken to. She said that our family dog had sensed something wasn't quite right and had attacked him, biting him in the leg and drawing blood. She didn't know whether the dog attack would prejudice him against me and hurt my chances for the job.

It didn't. Just after Christmas, I was notified by mail that I had been accepted as a police trainee and instructed to call the Recruiting Division as soon as possible. When I called, my designated handler confirmed that I had been accepted and was assigned to Class #95, which was scheduled to start on January 12, 1981. He told me they expected me to report by January 8 for orientation, less than two weeks away. I asked whether they could slot me to a later class, telling him that moving to Houston in that short a time frame would be difficult. He brusquely said, No! The job offer was only good for Class 95—did I want it, yes or no? I said I did and told him I would report to the orientation before Friday the 8th. He also told me that our academy class would be the first class to start at the newly constructed Houston Police Training Academy and that it was on the far north side of Houston, near the Intercontinental Airport. He also recommended that I get an apartment in the Greenspoint area, which would be close to the new academy.

Several days later, having packed up my Ford Pinto with all my possessions (there weren't many), I drove to Houston, Texas over two days. When I arrived, I went straight to the north side, located an apartment finder and within hours signed a lease for a small one-bedroom apartment in a brand-new complex near the intersection of Greens Road and Imperial Valley. Years later, the Greenspoint area would see a dramatic reversal of fortunes and would be renamed "Gunspoint" by both cops and civilians because of the unprecedented level of crime and violence. But in January of 1981, it was a great place to live.

Upon reporting for orientation, I learned, contrary to what I had been told just days before, the new training facility was not ready and that we were to report for cadet training at the Central Police Station in downtown Houston. This was a formidable undertaking for me. To arrive at the Central Police Station in a timely fashion (tardiness was not tolerated) for the morning roll call, it would require navigating the unpredictable morning rush-hour traffic. No easy task for someone like myself who came from a town with but one traffic light. The first day at the academy was stressful enough, and it first started with a crazy morning commute.

CHAPTER 1

THE HOUSTON POLICE ACADEMY

The Houston Police Department is a paramilitary organization; police cadets are at the bottom of the barrel. The academy was eighteen weeks long, and it would not be a gimme. To graduate, you would have to apply yourself. But presumably, because of the selection process, there was some expectation that everyone should pass and graduate. Ultimately, this was not the case. Several of the cadets in my class washed out. Some because of academic failure, some for injuries, and some for discovered character flaws. As an example, one cadet was caught drinking on duty. Apparently he was an alcoholic. One instructor smelled alcohol on his breath and unceremoniously removed him from the class and we never saw him again. Other cadets disappeared when the staff determined that although they were passing academically, they were lacking a "certain presence," "command bearing," "basic common sense," or, in short, "something was wrong." These missing attributes are hard to define but are clear when they are not possessed. They were "squirrels."

In the vernacular of the Houston Police Department, a squirrel is a person who doesn't quite get it, has a personality quirk, something is not right, or is just plain weird! He is the guy who, later in his career, had never really developed a relationship with any of his peers; he's hyper-aggressive, overly passive, abusive, arrogant, a sex pervert, etc. He is the cop other cops dread making their scene because although you have it all under control, as soon as he arrives, he will say something to piss off the citizenry and it will be a fight—or an Internal Affairs complaint.

According to a wise old seasoned street cop, who was assigned to cadet training and who we called Old Man Witcher (behind his back), squirrels are the bane of the Houston Police Department. He postulated that many of the problems between the police department and the community were directly proportional to the number of squirrels in our midst (in later years, I would observe firsthand how much grief and harm that would come to many because of the actions of squirrels). Mr. Witcher would also regale us with stories of his police experiences going back some thirty years to drive home the points he was trying to make. He also told police stories that had occurred in Houston going back long before his time, these being a collective institutional memory.

I remember that many of these stories were not pretty. That policing in those days was harsh and brutal (although accepted by the community) and vigilante justice was not uncommon. I remember him telling me about what he had been told about the Camp Logan Riots of 1917, when black United States Army soldiers billeted in Camp Logan (now Memorial Park) rioted over mistreatment with racist overtones by some members of the Houston Police Department. In the ensuing riot, five police officers were killed and, according to Mr. Witcher, several of those killed were mounted officers pulled off their horses and bayoneted to death. Later, after a military trial, nineteen soldiers who had taken part in the riots were executed by hanging.

Mr. Witcher did not tolerate squirrels and I have personal knowledge that he identified several, who he removed from the classes he was responsible for (a cadet or probationary police officer is an "at-will" employee and does not enjoy civil service protection). Unfortunately, many squirrels are attracted to police work and Mr. Witcher felt that they needed to be aggressively ferreted out, preferably right at the beginning before they could harm the department.

The police academy provided the raw basic knowledge necessary for the job. It also served as an introduction to the culture of the department. The instruction that I enjoyed the most was Officer Safety and Survival and Firearms Training. There, we were told repeatedly that the most important thing was that we, as police officers, come home safely from our shifts each night! In the weeks of our academy training, we were told that after our graduation they would assign us to the Field Training Program, where we would pair up with experienced officers who would train and document our performance in the real world. The Field Training Program was another hurdle that we would have to pass before becoming "real" police officers. Then, assuming that we had graduated the academy and successfully completed our field training, we would then get to select our permanent Patrol Division (all new officers start in the basic function of the Houston Police Department—uniform patrol) depending on our overall class standing and where the positions were being allocated. The officer who explained the process then gave us a rundown on the personality and culture of each patrol division and her assessment of each one's desirability. I remember how she relayed that Beechnut, Central, and Northwest Patrol Divisions were "good" patrol divisions because they were not so "busy" (minimal violent crime) as some other duty stations. In fact, back then, the Northwest Patrol Division was called the Ponderosa because it was so quiet and serene. She admonished us to avoid assignment to either the Northeast or the North Shepherd Patrol Divisions because they were so "busy" and "crazy." These high-crime areas had a lot of "knuckle heads." Many of the members of my academy class took this information to heart and underwent great pains to be sure they were assigned to the quiet stations, while a few of us opted for the busiest stations where all the action supposedly was. I chose North Shepherd, because not only did it have the reputation, I also liked the sound of the name—it sounded cool!

I graduated from the Houston Police Academy on May 16, 1981. I was twenty, not even old enough to buy ammunition for my .357 revolver. Crazy—too young to buy ammunition, but old enough to be a police officer. What was the administration thinking by hiring people so young and with few life experiences!

Houston is large in area, much like Los Angeles. The police department is decentralized, with the uniform patrol divisions being scattered across the city at various substations. The bulk of the department's investigative divisions and support units were housed in a single building in the downtown area. The Command Staff was also housed downtown, this being the very upper management for the department: the deputy chiefs, assistant chiefs, and the chief of police. The North Shepherd Patrol Division was the first of the outlaying police substations and was known as Station One.

My first impression of the station was of a rundown facility that smelled funny. It had its own small jail facility for holding suspects for minor crimes (Public Intoxication, Loitering, etc.) before they were transported to the Central Jail in groups. Back then, the division had nearly 400 officers/sergeants/lieutenants spread across three shifts for twenty-four-hour coverage and a captain, who was the division commander and was ultimately responsible for everything.

The academy staff was right. North Shepherd was "off the hook" busy, more so than I ever imagined. The first shift that you were assigned to during the field training program was the day shift, which was quieter than the other shifts. There, the probationary officer could start off slow and get used to handling the more mundane calls, mostly investigative report calls. It was also easier to orient yourself to the driving conditions during the daylight. Most of the calls I handled were "after the fact" —report calls.

It also bears noting that at this time, per capita, Houston was the Murder Capital of the country. The year before, there were over 700 murders. Those murders were not spread out evenly over the city; most were in the North Shepherd and Northeast Patrol Divisions. When working day shift, it was common for some citizen to discover a body. The victim, having been murdered the previous night, was only found at first light when the general, "normal" population was up and about. Back then, "Mexican Cantinas," which catered to illegal aliens, were notorious for violence and the proprietors disdained any police involvement. There would be some disturbance inside the club, which would then degenerate into a stabbing or shooting. The suspect would flee; the staff (many times illegal aliens themselves) would drag the victim— either dead or dying while still inconveniently inside the club—out of the bar, into the parking lot. Then they would lock the business up and go home. No ambulance or police called— nothing. These cantinas usually had dirt or gravel parking lots and the next morning you could see the drag marks where their bodies had been dragged out the front door and unceremoniously dumped. I suspect that few or any of these types of crimes were solved. The suspect, the victim's family, and the witnesses wanted no contact with the police, presumably because of their immigration status.

The evening shift was the second phase that you worked while on the Field Training Program. This was the busiest shift. Most of the calls were disturbance related (domestic disputes). Unlike the day shift, frequently you were interacting with citizens in the moment of a major life crisis, and this was another level to your training. You quickly learned as a young police officer to compartmentalize, to emotionally distance yourself from the drama, to put it in a box and not to be drawn into it.

One evening, my field trainer and I received a call regarding an unknown disturbance/medical emergency at a family residence. We arrived after a Houston Fire Department pumper truck had. This was not uncommon, as there were often not enough emergency medical technicians (EMTs) available and a fire pumper crew would be sent to assess

17

or triage the victim until the more highly trained or equipped unit could arrive on the scene. I knew the scene was going to be bad because as my trainer and I were getting out of our police car, a fireman suddenly burst out of the front door, the outer screen door flying off its hinges. He then stumbled a few steps and began vomiting uncontrollably on the grass of the front yard. The rest of the fire crew was outside and had not gone inside, awaiting our arrival to render the scene "safe." Apparently one member of the pumper crew had decided not to wait and went inside to "do the fireman thing."

My trainer and I went inside. The house was dark and, because it was daylight, I had not thought to bring my flashlight. As I searched the house, calling out "Police," something or someone bumped into my shin. I froze! My trainer turned on the light and there was a human form—a man, on his hands and knees. What was so horrific—some catastrophic event had removed his entire lower face, including jaw, nose, and one eye. They were all gone! Yet he was still alive and the only way for him to clear his airway and breathe because of the pulverized flesh and flowing blood was to be on his hands and knees. There was nothing we could do. First-aid class in the police academy never covered this.

The first paramedics arrived and later a Life Flight helicopter crew landed and did a commendable job of keeping the guy alive. I watched as the doctor performed an upside down tracheotomy after propping the faceless guy up over a coffee table, again to keep the "breathing hole" open where his face had been. The "victim" was more the suspect. He had been sexually assaulting his daughter for years and she had told him that today was the day that she was telling her mother and the authorities what he had been doing. He then decided to commit suicide (before the wife got home) and botched it. He had sat on the toilet, placed a 12-gauge shotgun to his chin, and pulled the trigger. The shot load and expanding gasses had literally blown his face off but his brain was still intact. Later, I heard that while still in the hospital some weeks later, he was able to "more successfully" commit suicide.

Experiencing these types of traumatic events was common to any street cop who works in a busy urban department, particularly one that was then labeled the Murder Capital of America.

It changes you.

It was not uncommon for some initially idealistic young police officers to quickly realize that they don't have the stomach for the streets and as quickly as possible seek an assignment as far removed as possible from the unpredictable violence and ever-present danger of being the "point of the spear." In the lingo of the Houston Police Department, they became "secretaries with guns." Although they might wear a uniform, carry a gun, and have some war stories to tell their civilian friends, they were pretenders and had little interest in protecting and serving.

Not a pretender: Ray Alexander.

One night, in the early 1980s, rookie Officer Raymond Alexander was driving his private vehicle to work. Ray was assigned to the night shift at the North Shepherd Patrol Division. As he drove south into Acres Homes on Veterans Memorial Drive, toward the station, he observed a masked man committing a robbery in a small convenience store. Ray pulled in and ended up confronting the suspect in the parking lot. The suspect had a 16-gauge sawed-off shotgun wrapped up in a jacket. Before Ray could react, the suspect shot him at close range. The shotgun was loaded with bird shot and blew off a considerable amount of flesh from Ray's left forearm and continued on, penetrating deep into his abdomen. Ray then emptied his .357 revolver at the suspect.

When I arrived on the scene, the paramedics were already there, working on Ray. It appeared the suspect was dead. When I walked over to secure the body (handcuff it), I noted that the suspect was still very much alive. One round Ray had fired had hit the suspect in the shoulder and the other had center-punched him right through the forehead. When I pulled off his ski mask, it was evident that the round that hit him in the forehead had not penetrated into the suspect's brain but rather traversed, along the skull, under the skin, and exited on the side of his head near his left ear. Both Ray and the suspect survived. Even though Ray had been badly wounded, he recovered and continued working in patrol. He ultimately retired many years later as a sergeant, still working at North Shepherd, still a conscientious, hardworking employee.

One of the highest compliments street cops can pay to another is "he's not scared."

After successfully completing the Field Training Program, I was assigned to the North Shepherd Patrol Division's swing shift. This was a unique patrol shift that straddled the busiest call for service load for the north side: 7 p.m. to 3 a.m.. This was when most of the crime occurred. It was not atypical to take several shooting calls in a single shift, intermixed with burglaries of businesses and/or robberies in progress. You pretty much ran from one call to another. The pace of work was quick, and the experience obtained was unprecedented. I imagine that there are only a few places in the country where such an intense amount of high crime drama can be experienced in such a short time. Every night, there were foot chases, high-speed vehicle pursuits, shootings, stabbings, and fights. It was all interesting and exciting for a young officer. Not only was the work stimulating, but the shared experiences and bonds you made with other officers was rewarding. This camaraderie was one of the most attractive aspects of the job.

My family and civilian friends don't understand this camaraderie, or even why I or others would want to do such a dangerous job that most of the population wanted no part of. The short answer was that the danger and camaraderie made the job interesting. It was also a job that we all felt was important. I know it's a cliché, but for some of us, we felt we were making a difference.

There was also quite a cultural change for me. I was a born and bred Yankee from New York and was quite an oddity for the officers who were native Houstonians. That I was a Yankee was clear because of my accent.

Most of the officers I worked with were Texans and they were proud of it. I was in for quite a bit of good-natured ribbing because of my accent and origins. A topic of several conversations seemed to revolve around the American Civil War—or, as some referred to it, the "War of Northern Aggression"!

Texans are enormously fond of their state.

I was fortunate to emerge unscathed from my time as a young officer. One night, my partner and I observed what appeared to be an illegal alien (Mexican) sleeping on a bench in front of a movie theater on North Main Street. We decided to wake him up and move him on. As I walked up to him, I subconsciously noted that, "Man, he is big for an illegal." I then tapped his feet with my nightstick, which I held in my right hand, while my left held my flashlight. The guy woke up. Before I could react and while he was still lying flat on the bench, he punched his right hand forward toward me with what later turned out to be a .44 caliber Charter Arms snub-nose revolver. In that split second, I remember thinking, *Damn—he is going to shoot me*. He would have, if not for the guy I was riding with.

Dwight Whitehead was a much older cop and a former M-60 Marine Corps machine gunner who served during the Vietnam War. As the suspect brought the gun up, Dwight jumped on him and got both of his hands on the suspect's gun hand. The fight was on. We wrestled the gun away from the suspect and after much physical interaction, got him handcuffed and under control. Later, after bringing him up to the Homicide Division, where he was interviewed by a Spanish-speaking investigator, we learned that the suspect was not Mexican. He was a "Marielito," a Cuban who Fidel Castro had released from one of his prisons to emigrate to the United States. The Marielito confessed to being a career criminal in Cuba before being forcibly deported by Castro and was making his way in the United States by robbing Mexicans in Houston before his chance encounter with us.

In patrol, a violent encounter could come when you least expected it. Often, over just what appeared to be mundane calls. One night, a wrecker driver called in to the police dispatcher about a drunk driver passed out in his vehicle, blocking a moving lane of traffic. When we got there, the driver awakened and in his drunken, paranoid-fueled state somehow decided that it would be a good thing to shoot at the nice police officers (us) with his semiautomatic pistol and was not deterred until I hit him with a load of number four buckshot from the Remington 870 12gauge that I kept up in the front seat of my patrol car.

I guess, as an omen of things to come, the first police vehicle that I was regularly assigned to drive (known in Houston Police slang as your "shop") had two deep furrows laterally across the engine hood, the result of a gunfight involving another patrol officer and an aggravated robbery suspect. I was never sure whether the furrows were incoming or outgoing but remember that the involved officer had been wounded in the leg and survived.

Much of the violence we observed and experienced was robbery related.

As a young officer, I had other "exciting" moments, like when with a rookie police officer (I was now a Field Training Officer), we were frantically flagged down by a citizen who blurted that the Burger King up the street was being robbed. As we pulled into the parking lot, I could see a masked man inside the restaurant with a double-barrel shotgun, pointing it at a terrified clerk behind the register with hands up. As I pulled in through the parking lot, the suspect spotted us and ran into the back of the restaurant, probably heading for the back door. I quickly positioned our patrol vehicle to cover the back. My rookie ran to the far side of the building, out of my sight, to cover that avenue of escape. As I pulled out my Remington 870 shotgun, I heard two muted gunshots and assumed that the suspect had gone out the other side and shot my rookie. But now running in my direction was the suspect, with a shotgun in one hand and a Burger King paper bag filled with money in the other, running straight at me. I threw up my shotgun, racked a shell into the chamber, placed the bead on his chest, and pressed the trigger.

Nothing happened! Back then, we were trained to always carry our shotguns with the safeties off and the chambers empty. Then, when engaging a threat, to simply rack the slide and pull the trigger. Somehow, the safety had been bumped into the "safe" position, preventing the gun from discharging. Because we were never really trained at length (muscle memory) to automatically and subconsciously manipulate the safety, I didn't quickly realize what the problem was. I didn't shoot—not because I didn't want to, but because my shotgun wouldn't. The suspect didn't shoot me, but ran past me and was quickly arrested when a responding police unit ran him over as he continued to run through the parking lot. My rookie was not hurt. The suspect, while still in the store, had decided to not run out the back door but while out of my sight had turned around and came out the front door, but not before he emptied both barrels of his shotgun into the menu hanging above the cash registers. I guess to keep everyone's head down.

In the early 1980s, there were many police officer-involved shootings with robbery suspects in the north side of Houston. In the vast majority of the cases, they ended poorly for the suspects. I would say that these shootings happened frequently enough that no special notice was made of them. It was just part of the job. After all, Houston was the Murder Capital of the country.

CHAPTER 2

SERGEANT EXAM

After a certain number of years as a Houston police officer, anyone aspiring to become a sergeant was eligible to take the Civil Service Written Exam, and depending on your score plus seniority points (up to ten), you were rank ordered. The person with the highest civil service written score plus seniority points was number one and so on. The list was in effect for a year and the number of sergeants promoted depended on how many positions became available either through attrition or that were newly created. Basically, a test date and a book list were announced ninety days in advance. If eligible and you had the desire, you would register for the test, buy the books, and began studying. To score high enough, you had to memorize the books from cover to cover, because those sneaky test makers in civil service asked such pertinent, relevant, police questions like "What is the Library of Congress Control Number for the book *Patrol Procedures*?"

I was single, did not have a family, and devoted myself to preparing for the test, especially considering I only had the minimum of seniority points. The test was given in December 1984. I did well, scoring number six out of approximately 600 test takers, and was to be promoted to sergeant in March 1985. I was twenty-four.

Just prior to my promotion, I was "invited" to meet with the captain of the Homicide Division. It was intimidating to be summoned to speak with a captain, much less the captain of the Homicide Division, particularly when you're a young Yankee patrol officer.

Captain Adams was of the old school and got to the point in his gruff, no-nonsense German heritage manner. "Boy, how would you like to be a big-city homicide investigator?" He explained that several of his night shift detectives had gotten into big trouble. Apparently, one night, while on duty, several of them had engaged in an impromptu drinking party. One detective who got "out of his mind drunk" had fired several shots from his handgun into the Houston Police Officers' Union building on State Street. The next day, the then-president of the Houston Police Officers' Union, not knowing the true source of the bullet holes in the building, had speculated to the news media that the shots were fired and resulting damage was caused by antipolice members of Houston's gay community. At that time, gay rights had become a contentious issue in the recent mayor's election. Kathryn J. Whitmire, the mayor, was unpopular with the members of the Houston Police Department. Mayor Whitmire was a strong advocate for the gay community and enjoyed their total support, whereas the Houston Police Officers' Union was in fierce opposition to the mayor, mostly because of her fiscal policies.

Eventually, it all came out. One detective who had been at the party made the truth known and a major scandal erupted. They demoted the lieutenant, several of the detective sergeants received significant discipline, and the actual shooter was fired, or in the euphemism of the department, "indefinitely suspended."

Captain Adams wanted me to take the position of the sergeant who was being fired as soon as civil service completed his termination. He theorized that because I had a squeaky-clean reputation, I would be low maintenance and not subject his division to any more scandals. I was also an outsider, not part of the "good old boy" system that sometimes operated in the department (people got their positions and assignments by who they knew, not necessarily by merit). Normally, newly promoted sergeants (absent the "good old boy" system) were first assigned to the less desirable positions within the department, namely Jail or Dispatch. To be invited to come straight to the Homicide Division, bypassing all the more senior sergeants on the transfer list, was a great honor and I said yes!

Being a Homicide detective is not glamorous…perhaps prestigious, but definitely not like what is portrayed in Hollywood. In Houston, because of the number of murders, the Homicide Division was separated into three shifts: day, evening, and night. Most of the true "whodunit" follow-up investigation was done on the day shift (these being the more experienced investigators), while the evening and night shift processed the initial murder scenes. If the case could be quickly cleared, the evening and night shift would complete it. Otherwise, it would be passed to the day shift for more long-term investigation. It was unfortunate, but back then, because of the large number of murders and the overworked status of the homicide investigators, many of the cases were not adequately investigated and never cleared. The families never received closure and justice was never served.

In a death investigation, typically, patrol officers made the initial call. If they determined a murder or the death was under suspicious circumstances, they would then call the Homicide Division's front desk, where the determination was made to send or not send homicide investigators. If the scene warranted it, then two homicide investigators would be sent. Mostly, we had regular partners, and it was a team effort by you and your partner. One guy would handle the scene while the other would interview the witnesses and/or suspects. The initial scene investigation and interviews could take many hours depending on its complexity. After completing the initial scene investigation, you would then travel to the Harris County Institute of Forensic Sciences and examine the body (which by then had been transported from the scene to the morgue). After obtaining your information, your partner and you would then go back to the Homicide Division and in excruciating detail document—in writing—everything! You didn't go home until the initial investigation was done. Working twenty-four hours straight was not uncommon.

After the initial investigation was done, you and your partner might have some down time till you were "next up" and were assigned to the next investigation. Sometimes, on a busy Friday or Saturday night, you might catch two murder scenes.

I can't remember to this day how many death scene investigations I made. They all sort of blurred together and only the ones that were unique or different now stand out. At a certain level, the human brain suppresses these memories and puts them in a lockbox where they all live and don't come to your conscious memory unless sufficiently prodded.

Besides all the death scene investigations, we also made all the law enforcement officer-involved shootings, in which a suspect was wounded or killed, or occasionally when a police officer was wounded or killed. We would be the primary or lead investigators in these types of incidents because of our expertise in homicide investigations. However, both the Houston Police Department's Internal Affairs Division and the Harris County District Attorney's Office, Civil Rights Division would run parallel investigations, sending investigators to the crime scene to coordinate with us and monitor our investigation.

I remember all the death scenes involving children.

One of these was of a young black girl, a child who had been murdered. My partner and I were called to a hospital emergency room where she had been transported and pronounced dead. She was a victim of blunt force trauma. Her ex-felon stepfather was the last person to be with her and the likely suspect. He was in custody by the responding patrol officers and we had him transported to the office for interrogation. I interviewed him, first reading him his legal warnings and then asking the usual questions.

The interrogation in this case was critical. There was a lack of physical evidence and witnesses. If the stepdad had killed the little girl, then it would only probably be solved with his confession. The suspect waived his rights; he was cooperative, and we were talking. He had not yet confessed, but I was reasonably confident that the longer we talked, the greater the likelihood that he would admit to having killed her, albeit some self-serving statement (*She made me do it, etc.*).

Then, while talking to the suspect, I was called out of the interrogation room by a high-ranking member of the Houston Police Department, who told me that the suspect's lawyer (just hired by the suspect's family) was waiting in the lobby and that the lawyer wanted to talk to his new client. Apparently, the lawyer was somehow known to the upper management of the Houston Police Department and he was pulling strings to intervene in the interrogation before the client, whom he had never met, confessed. I was furious and pointed out that the suspect had voluntarily declined to have one present! The lawyer did not have a right to have a client! I also pointed out that it would be better to get a confession, even if the possibility existed that it might be later suppressed in court, than to never get it. It didn't matter! I was ordered to let the lawyer contact the suspect. The stepfather, on the wise advice of this lawyer, immediately stopped cooperating. The case was then passed on to the day shift. My partner and I began catching other homicide scenes and the murder of this little girl was never solved. It still makes me mad to this day.

I would like to say that my partner and I, while in Homicide, solved a lot of whodunits, but this just wasn't the case. We were more the first part of an assembly line that processed death scenes.

One case does stand out and in my mind represents the high water mark of my tenure as a big-city Homicide detective. One afternoon, my partner Lynn Dollins and I were sent out to make the scene of yet another murder. The victim was a cab driver. That day, I handled the witnesses and Lynn had the crime scene. When we arrived, I interviewed a witness who said that while he was driving down the street (just east of downtown Houston) he saw a cab, suddenly veer off the road and come to a halt. Shortly afterward, he saw a black male get out of the cab, walk down the street, and go up on the porch of a residential house, briefly talk to the people who were there, and then walk off. The witness said that he then lost sight of the guy but that he was older and looked like a "black Ronald McDonald" because he had an afro but was bald on top. Lynn determined that the dead man, the cab driver, had been shot several times in the back of the head. Lynn also noted that it appeared that robbery was the motive, because the pants pockets of the victim, Nathan Oakley, were pulled inside out. The suspect, after killing Mr. Oakley, had searched his body, presumably looking for any money. In Texas, a murder committed during a robbery is a Capital Murder and the punishment was either life or death. The Harris County District Attorney's Office back then was not reticent about seeking the death penalty.

The only lead was the citizens on the porch.

I went to the porch and talked to two young males, who were uncooperative—didn't know anything, about anything! Also on the porch, however, was an elderly black woman, named Ms. Anderson. I started to talk to her at length and was gentle, spending time to make a rapport. We talked about the Bible and Jesus. I asked her about the man who had come up on the porch. She said yes, a man had come up to the porch, and she gave me a detailed description, which was close to the description as described by the first witness. She also said that the man in question had asked about the metro bus schedule and then had walked off. Something clicked in my head. I then asked her, "Do you know the man?" Ms. Anderson hesitated; she didn't want to answer. I pressed her. She still hesitated, and I could see the indecision on her face. I then appealed to her faith and doing the right thing before God. She then loudly exclaimed, "Lordy, Lordy, it was Jerome Butler. I haven't seen him in years!" I thanked her and then escorted her to our office for a sworn statement.

Within an hour or two, Lynn and I started to connect the dots. A Jerome Butler had been recently paroled to Houston after serving a lengthy prison sentence for murder. He had also spent time in New York (for attempted sexual assault and robbery) and was incarcerated there in Attica Prison during the time of the 1971 prison riots, when ten correctional officers and thirty-three prisoners were killed.

I pulled Butler's mug shot and noted that he was bald. We showed a photospread to Ms. Anderson and the original witness—both gave positive identifications.

Two uniformed patrol officers who had made the original scene and transported the original witness were in the office with us. They were eager to help, and watched and listened as the case unfolded and we developed a suspect. As always, my next step was to get an arrest warrant. Immediately, I was on the phone with the district attorney, laying out my probable cause for an arrest warrant.

As I was talking to the district attorney, explaining the situation, my two new uniformed "friends" disappeared without saying a word.

About half an hour later, one of the uniformed guys called the office and asked for me. I took the phone, and he excitedly told me he and his partner had left the office and "just happened" to drive by the house where Butler had been paroled to and low and behold, there in the front yard, was Jerome Butler. They immediately arrested him.

I was a little upset. This was a Capital Murder, and I didn't want any complications. I wanted all the legal niceties in place—like an arrest warrant! It was what it was. We made our way to the arrest scene and there was Butler in the back of a police car, in handcuffs. And yes, he looked like a black Ronald McDonald. I had the well-meaning officers transport Butler and book him into the downtown jail, while Lynn and I tried to figure out how to legally get into the house he was living in, to search for the murder weapon or any other evidence.

I knocked on the door and talked to the woman who owned the house, Ms. Jones. She, like Ms. Anderson, was elderly and also wanted to be helpful. I explained our purpose and talked about the murder of Mr. Oakley. Ms. Jones stated that she rented a room to Butler. I asked permission to search her house, and she readily agreed and signed the Consent to Search form. The problem was, although I had permission to search the house, Ms. Jones could not give effective consent for me to search Butler's room, where presumably any pertinent evidence was located. Lynn and I walked through the house and noticed nothing that seemed relevant to the investigation. I asked Ms. Jones, "Do you have any guns?" She said that she had two revolvers, which she kept under her nightstand in her bedroom. "May I see them?" I asked, and she pointed me to them. I pulled both of the revolvers from under the nightstand. They both looked ancient, in poor condition. I didn't think either of them worked, and didn't seriously consider that either of them could be the murder weapon. I was even contemplating not taking them as evidence to not inconvenience Ms. Jones. About that time, Ms. Jones's phone rang, her phone being on the nightstand where the guns had been located. In our presence, Ms. Jones had just received a phone call from Butler, who was in the city jail and had been afforded his one phone call. I couldn't hear what Butler was saying, but I heard Ms. Jones's side of the conversation: "Now, Jerome, these are my guns and if I want to let these nice police officers have them, that's my business." It was evident that Butler was calling his landlady to admonish her to not let us search the house or let us take possession of her guns.

I decided that maybe these old guns might be important after all. After Ms. Jones hung up the phone, I politely asked her whether I could take possession of her guns. She agreed and even provided me the receipts from Wolf's Pawnshop to show that she had legally bought them and she was the owner.

Lynn and I returned to the Homicide Division. We submitted Ms. Jones's revolvers to the Firearms Lab for ballistic comparison. Bullets would be fired from the revolvers to then be compared to bullets recovered from Mr. Oakley's cranial vault during autopsy.

I then pulled Butler out of his cell, took him to the interview room, and read him his legal rights (Miranda warning). I told him not to say anything but to listen to what I had to say. I summarized his criminal career, that for most of his life he had been in prison, talked about all of his arrests and convictions, and, most importantly, that he was on parole for murder. I then talked about the evidence showing that he had killed Mr. Oakley during the commission of a robbery and we would charge him with Capital Murder and he would either get life in prison or the death penalty. Given his lengthy criminal record, I told him there was a good chance he would be executed by the state.

I told him I would testify in court about this exact moment—I could tell the judge and jury that he confessed and showed remorse, or that he was a stone-cold killer and showed no remorse and killed Mr. Oakley for a few dollars. It was his choice.

Butler showed no remorse.

A few days later, the lead Firearms Examiner for the Houston Police Department called me and told me that one of the revolvers we had recovered from Ms. Jones was the murder weapon.

At trial, Jerome Butler was found guilty. During the punishment phase, when the jury was deciding life or death, I testified that Butler showed no remorse. He was given the death sentence.

Unlike other death row inmates, Butler didn't want his lawyers filing any appeals (although there is an automatic one). However, to have his conviction classified as non-capital and thwart the death sentence, he made it known through his lawyer he had killed Mr. Oakley, but had killed him because he recognized Oakley as the man who had allegedly raped his daughter many years before. The State of Texas was a little nervous about executing Butler because the only evidence indicating that the murder occurred during a robbery was our report and crime scene photos showing that Mr. Oakley's pants pockets had been pulled inside out and there was no cash or his wallet to be found. The Harris County District Attorney's Office sent a special investigator to California to interview Butler's daughter, who now lived there. She affirmed that yes…she had been raped as a young girl, but that the person who had raped her was actually her father—Jerome Butler!

The Texas Supreme Court also decided that based on Mr. Oakley's pants pockets being pulled inside out, it was reasonable to assume that the defendant had removed his wallet or other property and thus the murder could be classified as Capital, upholding Butler's death sentence.

About three and a half years after his conviction, in Huntsville, Texas, Jerome Butler was executed by lethal injection. I hope that Ms. Robbie Oakley, Nathan's widow, received some closure. The *New York Times* reported that Butler's last words were: "I just want to say I wish everybody a good life and things like that." I have it on more reliable authority that his last words were actually, "See you in Hell!"

My time in the Homicide Division was actually a period of loneliness for me. I was young and single; the other detectives were older, with wives and children. We were all in different places. I had no family in Houston and my friends were, mostly, all assigned to the North Shepherd Patrol Division. All the death scene investigations were a grind. I also had a hard time letting go of some investigations and was unable to sleep as alternate theories about unsolved murders marched through my head. What was worse, because I did not have any children, my well-meaning lieutenant would assign me to many of the evening shift incoming death scene investigations involving kids. He did this to spare the fathers in the unit any additional psychological trauma, as dead children tended to break through that armored psychological bubble that every seasoned homicide investigator had. His reasoning was that because I had no children, these types of scenes would be easier for me. I am not so sure about that, but I understood.

One day, Lynn and I were assigned to another death scene investigation. A work crew had been opening up and inspecting the manhole covers for a drainage system of an unfinished residential subdivision. The streets and all the associated infrastructure was completed but because of a downturn in the economy, no houses had yet been built. At the end of the drainage system, parts of a human skeleton were observed at the bottom of the last manhole cover to be opened, at the end of the line. The remains sat at the bottom of a ten-foot shaft; visible from the top was a skull and some larger bones in a shallow depression filled with water. What was worse, the body had putrefied in the water, and the flesh and organs had sloughed off the bones in some jellified mixture of stinky yuck.

This is why death scene investigation is not glamorous! To do a thorough investigation, it was necessary to recover all the bones and all the rest of the soft body parts. There was no easy way. I volunteered and went down into the hole. Lynn lowered a bucket to me on a rope and I then scooped the human remains onto it. He then hauled the bucket up and dumped these remains onto a screen so the water could drain off and then packaged it all into big trash bags to haul to the Harris County Institute of Forensic Science's office. There, the medical examiners could "put the pieces back together" and try to identify the person and a cause of death.

It was while Lynn was pulling up the bucket we were using to transport the goopy putrid human remains and chunks of jellified flesh up to the surface that the bucket tipped on its journey and the contents poured out on top on me.

I had a eureka moment. I decided that maybe I really didn't want to be a "big-city homicide investigator" anymore.

By looking at missing person reports and comparing skeletal records, we determined that the human remains found in that drainage system was that of a young Vietnamese woman who, within her community, was a person of some fame, being an accomplished singer and who toured the country, singing in clubs that mostly catered to Vietnamese immigrants who had come to the country at the end of the Vietnam War. Her husband was insanely jealous of her success and was a "bit mental." We brought him in for questioning by an investigator who spoke Vietnamese and whose nickname in the department was Luke the Gook. The husband did not confess. Our theory, based on the totality of the evidence, was that he had thrown her alive into the storm system and sealed up the cover; she had crawled to the end of the line, trying to find a way out but had died of exposure, starvation, or dehydration. Her location was so isolated that no one heard her screams for help. The case is still unsolved.

It took me a few weeks to steel up my courage and in one of the hardest things that I have had to do, because I respected him so much and because of the faith he had placed in me, I told Captain Adams that I wanted to transfer back to North Shepherd as a patrol sergeant.

I would say that overall I worked and learned from the best and most experienced investigators in the Houston Police Department. But I knew that something had to change in my situation. The only eligible "nice" girl I met in those years was the one who I met one night while at the morgue. I was examining the body of a recent murder victim as part of one of my investigations and struck up a conversation with an attractive woman who was in the room with me, cutting out the corneas on the recent dead for transplant.

To this day, over thirty years later, I still have a recurring nightmare that I am some serial killer and in my backyard I have buried and hidden several bodies. But over time, some bones of the victims have risen to the top of the ground. Then the dream flashes to homicide investigators who are now searching my property and processing the scene, looking for the bodies. The dream is enough to wake me up and for a few terrible minutes, it seems very real. Although I am now grateful that over the years, the dream comes less frequently.

God bless the men and women assigned to the Homicide Division. Unless you have been there, you can never fully appreciate the job they do.

Particularly when, in their humanity, they also identify with the families of the victims and share their pain.

CHAPTER 3

BACK TO NORTH SHEPHERD

I went back to the North Shepherd Patrol Division as a sergeant assigned to the 7 p.m. to 3 a.m. shift. I was also given the assignment of the Field Training Sergeant; besides the normal duties of a field supervisor, I also supervised the officers who were assigned to train and evaluate the flow of probationary officers who recently graduated from the Police Academy. My job was to ensure that the training was unbiased, that the new officers were fairly treated, and that their training documentation supported either their advancement to police officer and resulting civil service protection, or termination and separation from the department.

It was about this time that the Texas sodomy laws were struck down and homosexuality was no longer considered a hiring disqualification. Sometimes I would receive a call from the upper management giving me a heads-up that probationary Officer "Jones" was gay and to make sure they were fairly treated. Management presupposed that because most of the officers assigned to the North Shepherd Division where white males (as was most of the department at that time) that the influx of minority officers or "sexually diverse" would be discriminated against.

This stereotyping by upper management was not the reality, in my experience. Mostly, the only thing that mattered for the busy, hardworking officers at North Shepherd was more if you were a good, dependable cop. Again, just like in the academy, if you were identified as a squirrel, other officers avoided you or, if possible, you were shown the front door. Your color or sexual preference just didn't matter.

These years flew by and I can't recall all the high-risk vehicle pursuits, in-progress calls (murders, robberies, burglaries) that I was involved in. They are all a blur, but it was considerable. The other "active" sergeants and I became adept at crisis management and developed formulas for dealing with most of the critical incidents that we frequently handled.

In April and May 1992, the "Battle of Los Angeles" was raging. There was public outrage and then rioting over the acquittal of several Los Angeles police officers for excessive force in the arrest and beating of Rodney King, a black man, who received abusive treatment by uniformed police officers at the end of a high-speed vehicle pursuit. Much of the resulting outrage and rioting was felt and/or precipitated by black citizens. Los Angeles burned. Sixty-three people were killed and over 2,000 injured.

April and May in Houston is a time of potentially heavy rain downfall. Houston, known as the "Bayou City," has numerous bayous that all drain out to the Gulf of Mexico. Normally, the bayous are shallow and slow moving. But with heavy rain, the bayous can sometimes become treacherous white-water rivers because of all the rainwater that runs off and drains into them.

While Los Angeles burned, Houston experienced an unusually heavy rainstorm.

Predictably, the bayous turned into raging rivers. I was working overtime and riding with another sergeant, when an excited voice on the police radio announced that a child who had been playing near one of the bayous had fallen in. Also, an unknown uniformed Houston police officer had jumped in, trying to save this same child and pull him out to safety. The officer was unable to and now they were both being swept helplessly downstream.

As fortune would have it, a police helicopter (known in HPD as "Fox") was in the immediate area. The pilot adjusted his course and was soon directly over the bayou, following the officer and kid as they were being swept along. The observer began advising over the radio their exact location, as the pilot carefully followed the waterborne path of both victims as they were swept downstream.

I was driving the patrol car and knew this particular bayou pretty well. I looked to my north and there I could see the police helicopter crabbing sideways, flying but a few feet above the water. The pilot, despite the danger of striking nearby trees, was trying to position the landing skids of the helicopter where maybe either victim might be able to grab on. But they were unable to.

Soon, the victims in the bayou, and the police helicopter overhead, were about to pass my position. I had just enough time to drop my handheld radio and heavy Colt 1911 automatic pistol and jump into the bayou with them. After all, I used to be a lifeguard and my mom hadn't sent me to all those swimming lessons for nothing.

I recognized the other officer as Fred Mullins. Fred was a big man and although brave, maybe was not a proficient swimmer. He was in a bad way, floating a few feet behind the kid as they both moved pretty rapidly down the bayou. Fred was just trying to tread water and keep his head above water. I heard him cry out, "Jesus, help me!"

When I hit the water, I was not happy. The water was cold, just like the North Atlantic in June. I knew I could not help Fred—he was too big—and felt it was more important to save the innocent citizen. I made my way to him and tried to put him in a cross chest carry. When I say kid, he was almost as big as me (even though he was thirteen). He was wide-eyed with panic as he flailed in the water, trying to keep his head up. I couldn't get him into position; as soon as I got close, in his panic, he tried to climb on top of me so he could better breathe. As he did this, I would then be forced under and then I would have to fight my way to the top for air. Eventually, I began to tire and gave up trying to get him into a cross chest carry where I could better manage him. I was also having some difficulties myself: I was in uniform, wearing body armor, with heavy combat boots on. So I settled on holding him at arm's length, with my strong hand, while he flailed about. I then could leverage his head out of the water so he could breathe from time to time, although when I did this, it would force my head under.

We were all in a bad way. In the part of the bayou we were in, the sides were steep concrete walls and there was no climbing out. All we could do was ride the white water and try to keep our heads above water and not drown.

But I realized that something much worse was coming and I would have to make a hard decision soon. I knew this bayou system. After an upcoming railroad bridge, it would soon go underground into the storm tunnel system that ran under a Houston freeway interchange system. The tunnel system ran for maybe a quarter of a mile. If we were swept down into it, there would be no surviving. The tunnels would be full of water and there would be nowhere to catch a breath of air, not to mention it would be devoid of light. We would all drown.

I couldn't do anything for Fred, and I wasn't strong enough or a good enough swimmer to pull the kid to safety. I made the conscious decision that at the railroad bridge, which was almost upon us, I would have to let the kid go and try to save myself. I was not going into the tunnel system! I know that Fred and the kid probably didn't realize what fate awaited them around the corner.

The railroad bridge was in sight. I was trying real hard to pull the kid to safety, yelling to Fred it was now or never—but we couldn't get out of the bayou; it wasn't going to happen.

I was just about to let the kid go. Yes, I knew he would drown, but there was nothing I could do.

But! Providentially, we all were suddenly no longer being dragged against the concrete that lined the bayou; the concrete wall suddenly ended, and because of high water, we were now floating among small trees and the bushes that lined that part of the bayou. I could finally pull the kid to safety and Fred could get out himself. Soon, other police officers were helping us out and paramedics arrived. We were all suffering from the ill effect of swallowing a lot of polluted water. While at the hospital, Fred had to be placed in a warming tent because he was suffering from hypothermia because of the cold water. I was sick for weeks with some lower intestinal infection, but I was alive!

I give credit to Officer Fred Mullins. He jumped in to save a child and I learned in later conversations that he was not a great swimmer and was also a recent cancer survivor. Whereas I was much younger, healthier, and had spent most of my life around and in the ocean and even at one time had been a certified open water lifeguard.

It just so happened that the kid we saved was black.

Shortly after the rescue, the mayor of Houston and the Houston Police Department's Command Staff gave Fred Mullins and me a hero's welcome at City Hall. Mayor Bob Lanier gave a speech, part of which was that in Los Angeles the police were known for beating black citizens, but in Houston the police were known for risking their lives to save black citizens.

Fred and I were both ill at ease during the assembly. We were gratified to receive the recognition, but felt that our recognition was more about political leverage to help ward off any potential local civil disruptions that might occur in Houston because of what was occurring in Los Angeles.

The Houston Police Department awarded us the Medal of Valor.

Fred Mullins deserved it more than I did!

Late in the 1980s and early 1990s, the north side of Houston, particularly within the black communities, was plagued by the crack cocaine epidemic. There were many locations where street-level dealers congregated to sell "rocks" to prospective customers. Back then, many of the patrol divisions had "tactical units," these being small units with a mix of undercover and uniformed officers who addressed specific crime problems within their respective districts. The tactical units were "tools" that the commanders—"captains"—of each patrol division could use to "solve problems" within their areas of responsibility.

Congruent with the formation of Division Tactical Units (DTUs) was also the federal government's "War on Drugs" and a lot of federal funding in the form of grants (to be used for overtime pay and equipment) was funneled down to these tactical units for the "war."

In the early 1990s, they assigned me to the North Shepherd Division's Tactical Unit. We exclusively worked street-level dope, combating the crack cocaine epidemic. Our operations boiled down to several basic tactics.

The first operation was known as the "buy-bust." We would have one or two of our undercover officers (often minority officers) in a plain vehicle drive up and solicit crack dealers who were selling on the streets. The undercover officer would seek to buy a rock or two of crack cocaine, paying with discreetly marked department-provided monies. As these undercover officers approached a prospective dealer, other undercover officers would attempt to keep the interaction between the buyer (undercover officer) and dealer (suspect) under observation for the safety of the undercover officers doing the buying, and for evidentiary and coordination purposes.

In addition, a small hidden audio recording device, a "wire," was secreted on the person of the undercover officer posing as the drug buyer, so we could monitor the communication between the suspect and the undercover officer in real time. Historically, there were several officer-involved shootings where a suspect who was purported to be a narcotics dealer actually instead intended to rob at gunpoint potential buyers, who, in our case, were actually undercover police officers.

Attached to this operation was also a nondescript van occupied by several officers, who were heavily armed, wearing light body armor and police raid jackets. These officers were known as the takedown or the raid team. These officers were foremost there to rescue the undercover officer who was doing the buying in case he or she was imperiled. Their secondary function was to effect the arrest of the seller or dealer after a successful narcotics transaction had been made, after the undercover officer had bought the dope.

Working in coordination between the raid team and the officers buying the dope were one or two secondary undercover surveillance officers, whose job was to keep "eyes" on the interaction between the buyer and the dealer. Then, if all went well, as soon as the transaction was complete and the buying undercover officer drove away from the scene with dope, these other surveillance undercover officers alerted the raid team, who were waiting, lurking, a few blocks away, monitoring the conversation, just out of sight from the dealer, in our plain, unmarked, nondescript van.

As everybody monitored the wire and a successful "hand-to-hand" was made, the buying undercover officer (with the dope for evidence in their possession) drove off and left the immediate area. The other surveillance undercover officers, who still hopefully had eyes on the dealer, "talked in" by radio, the raid team guiding them to the exact location of the dealer.

This is where it became interesting. The van with the raid team then began their approach, trying to get as close to the dealer as possible while trying not to alert him. The strategy was to "slow roll" right up to the suspect, slide open the van's side panel door, and rapidly disembark the raid team. The goal was to catch the suspect by surprise and make the arrest without incident.

We conducted "buy-bust" operations multiple times a week, and it was not uncommon to have several foot chases and subsequent "wrestling matches" with suspects every time. The recovery of our marked money from the dealer and the submission of the cocaine bought from him by the undercover officer would then become the basis for a charge against the suspect for Delivery of a Controlled Substance (Crack Cocaine).

I was almost always assigned to the raid team in the van. It was always nice to know as we headed in to make an arrest that the targeted dealer was fat or old, hopefully not swift of foot!

The suspects and the local community knew the officers in the van as the "jump out boys."

SURPRISE, SPEED, AND VIOLENCE OF ACTION!

The second operation we crafted was designed to take down the many crack houses in our area. We maintained a criminal informant fund and by various means, citizens from the community, who often were themselves of dubious character, provided information or helped facilitate operations against these crack houses. These criminal informants (CIs), while under direct observation and direction by our undercover officers, would buy illegal drugs from the occupants inside a targeted crack house. This might be done several times. Each time a buy was to be made, the CI would be given departmental monies and after making the buy (again, ideally under observation by us), the CI would directly deliver the dope he had bought back to the undercover officer who was handling him. After making a few such buys and gaining the confidence of the suspects in the crack house, it was hoped that the CI could then introduce an undercover officer to the sellers/suspects in the crack house. The undercover officers would then start making buys, eventually without the presence of the CI (to protect his identity in any later court proceedings).

After the undercover officer had made a few such buys at the crack house, the next step was to get a narcotics search warrant based on the buys the undercover officer made.

Often, a narcotics search warrant would have a "no-knock" clause: a door to the crack house would be immediately breached (no-knock) by a breaching team, wearing heavy armor and using a "battering ram" (entry tool)—or, in the lingo of the Houston Police Department, a "Moby."

In these types of operations, there were no niceties, no prior announcement of, "Police— open the door!"

Once there was a successful breach, the entry team, which was "stacked" immediately behind the breaching team, would rapidly enter the crack house. The objective: by maintaining surprise, speed, and violence of action, they would "lock down" the crack house and its occupants before they had time to react and/or destroy the illegal narcotics.

Executing no-knock warrants, also termed "dynamic entry" in police lingo, was deemed to be high risk and for me (at that time), it was also stimulating. In my ignorance, I loved doing them.

Regarding narcotics operations: years later, my thinking transformed as to the appropriateness of conducting dynamic entries and no-knock warrants, particularly on residential houses. Basically, we were trying to "rescue dope," which was stupid. The risk to the involved officers and innocent citizens was far too great for what we were trying to accomplish (save the dope from being flushed down a toilet). Often, besides the suspects, children and other uninvolved innocent persons were also in these houses. I remember one time, being the first one in (the point man of an entry team) after a front door was just successfully breached, having to jump over a small child who was strapped into a baby carrier and who was left lying on the floor in the hallway just inside the doorway. Also, over the years, several Houston police officers have been critically wounded or even killed while conducting these types of operations, mostly because they lost the advantage of surprise, speed, and/or violence of action that these types of high-risk operations require.

I also believe that in some of these cases where officers were shot, the offending suspects may have thought the people crashing through the door were other criminals intent on stealing drugs or drug money. This was a real concern for the dope dealers as they were sometimes preyed on by others who impersonated a real police narcotics entry team. In the lingo of the streets, this was a "dope rip."

I later found out (in my next assignment), more shockingly, corrupt police officers conducted some dope rips, whose objective in the raid was to steal money and/or drugs to enrich themselves.

It became my view that a police tactical unit doing a no-knock dynamic entry on a dope house to "save dope" was a really terrible idea. Dynamic, no-knock police entries are perilous and should only be reserved for hostage rescue or active shooter situations, where innocent lives are in imminent danger. Starting in about 1999, this concern was readily voiced to the Houston Police Department's Command Staff, mostly by us in the tactical operations community. But nothing changed for over twenty years.

The Command Staff of the Houston Police Department periodically moves its division commanders to different assignments, usually to meet the needs of the department or to account for attrition as other captains are promoted, retire, etc. But sometimes these movements are done because a captain has fallen out of political favor and/or made a misstep. Sometimes, a newly promoted captain might prove to be a squirrel; the common saying back then was that the department did not have enough "squirrel cages" (backwater-type assignments where they could do no harm) to put all the squirrely captains in.

A few times, captains were seemingly moved to undesirable positions because they were men or women of high integrity. Depending on the position they took on various issues, they might find themselves at odds with the Command Staff, because they wouldn't "play ball" or do the bidding of these higher entrenched police administrative-political establishment types. These captains wouldn't violate their own personal moral code. These same captains would then find themselves transferred to the Jail Division or other crappy assignment—"for the good of the department."

For a good number of years, the captain of the North Shepherd Patrol Division was David Massey. Under Captain Massey's leadership, the division was mostly happy and content (we were a big family). We all perceived him as a caring and effective leader.

Eventually, the Command Staff decided to "shuffle" division commanders and Captain Massey was transferred to the Narcotics Division, which was good for him as it was seen within the department as a desirable position.

Unfortunately, for the men and women of the North Shepherd Patrol Division, the new division commander, who had just recently been promoted to captain, was "difficult." Perhaps he was still finding his management style, as years later he was able to redeem his reputation to some degree. It could be he was under considerable self-induced stress; he eventually had a heart attack, which he survived. It was only after this heart attack that his management style changed for the better. But initially, after being promoted to captain, I would term his leadership style as toxic. In a relatively short time, the supervisors and officers at North Shepherd were no longer focused "outward"—doing their job, serving and protecting the citizenry—but were focused "inward" on all the internal drama this new leader created. It became so bad that members of the Command Staff had to leave the Ivory Tower (their downtown office) and come physically meet with the supervisors at North Shepherd and quell a mutiny.

Most of the lieutenants at North Shepherd transferred out during this time because of the new captain and his toxic leadership, including my supervisor, Lieutenant Donald Curry, who then went to the Internal Affairs Division.

Because of the reputation of the North Shepherd Division's new captain, no lieutenants in the department wanted to transfer in and work for him. As a result, they made me the acting lieutenant and for a period of nearly six months performed both my job as well as Lieutenant Curry's former duties. It was as stressful as it was impossible to meet this new captain's expectations. Much worse for me, when a newly promoted lieutenant was finally transferred in to take over Lieutenant Curry's position, I found this person to be someone I could not work for, finding his primary motivation in life was all about money.

One of the first things he required was that all the officers and sergeants who were assigned to him sign a written "Oath of Loyalty," pledging fidelity to him alone. I refused to sign his loyalty oath, thinking it was outrageous.

This lieutenant also didn't tolerate any divergent opinions from his own and I had many.

I was on my way out.

Fortunately, Lieutenant Curry heard of my plight and, in an act of compassion, "put me out of my misery." He made sure I was transferred—rescued—out of the North Shepherd Patrol Division and to the Internal Affairs Division.

CHAPTER 4

THE INTERNAL AFFAIRS DIVISION

The Houston Police Department's Internal Affairs Division is a fairly large division composed of investigative sergeants who investigate internal complaints against department employees, where criminal conduct or serious misconduct is alleged. These complaints are normally generated by citizens, other officers, or are initiated by the chief of police. For example, all officer-involved shootings where injury or death occur are automatically adopted by the chief of police and are always investigated.

Most of the sergeants assigned to Internal Affairs conduct standard reactive investigations (after the fact) and serve strictly as fact finders; i.e., collecting evidence, interviewing witnesses, and getting written statements from the involved officers and citizens, etc.

All of this information is processed into a detailed report, which is then submitted to one of several lieutenants within Internal Affairs, who then reviews the report, writes a synopsis, and then draws a conclusion based on these facts. The Internal Affairs lieutenant also specifically comes to a conclusion for every allegation of wrongdoing that are alleged and/or "discovered" during the investigation conducted by the Internal Affairs sergeant. The investigative conclusions are Sustained, Not Sustained, Unfounded, or Exonerated.

Sustained: The evidence is sufficient to prove the allegation.

Not Sustained: The evidence is insufficient to either prove or disprove the allegation.

Unfounded: Allegation is false or not factual.

Exonerated: Incident occurred, but was lawful and proper.

Presumably, the Internal Affairs investigative process is supposed to be nonpartisan, above reproach—a police officer's due process insulated from internal and outside influence that might try to sway the investigation. This, I found during my tenure in Internal Affairs, was not necessarily the case. Particularly in investigations that might have political overtones or were high profile.

In some internal investigations, the Internal Affairs lieutenants were told "what their conclusions would be" by members of the Command Staff or by the lawyers in the department's Office of Legal Services. These pressured and altered outcomes often were done for political reasons or to protect the department and Houston from possible civil litigation. The unspoken departmental strategy seemingly was that the very upper management, for the good of the collective, thought it was sometimes necessary "to throw rank-and-file employees under the bus, to protect the city"— and, vicariously, their own positions. To their credit, some lieutenants in Internal Affairs who found themselves in these ethical dilemmas refused, as a matter of conscience, to alter their findings and concede to the desires of the Command Staff or department lawyers. Sometimes Internal Affairs Division lieutenants, of conscience, found themselves under considerable career pressure.

All the sergeants and lieutenants assigned to Internal Affairs have to serve a tour of at least two years but no more than five. If the Command

Staff was pleased with your performance in Internal Affairs and after your minimum of two years, they might reward you in that your next assignment would be a "good" one. Conversely, if you were not perceived as a "team player," your next assignment could be night shift in the Jail Division!

After the Internal Affairs lieutenant wrote his synopsis, the investigation then moved up the chain of command, ultimately being reviewed by the lawyers assigned to the department's Office of Legal Services. Finally, if the investigation had sustained allegations, which might cover the whole disciplinary range from minor discipline to termination of employment, the investigation would then be sent to the employee's assigned division, where the employee's supervisors, including the division commander, would make discipline recommendations based on the prescribed ranges of punishment. From there, the investigation would move to the Discipline Review Committee, where recommendations were also made. Ultimately, the chief of police made the final decision about discipline. However, because of all his or her responsibilities (there was no time for the chief to read each investigation), a decision would be made with great weight being given to the recommendation by the lawyers in Legal Services.

My first assignment in Internal Affairs was that of a traditional reactive investigator. Most of the complaints I investigated while in "reactive" were Use of Force type complaints where citizens alleged that during some interaction with a Houston Police officer, too much or inappropriate force had been used against them. Many of these investigations were concluded as "Unfounded" or "Not Sustained." But not all!

One morning, my lieutenant assigned me a Use of Force complaint. What made this case unusual was that the individual making the complaint was a Houston Police officer, specifically a female officer who was still on probation, having just graduated from the police academy. The rookie alleged that another female officer (a senior officer) had beat a female complainant in the head with her police flashlight, causing trauma (open wounds). She also indicated that the citizen who had been victimized had initially contacted the police, because she had been beaten by her husband (domestic violence) and when responding officers arrived, she was hysterical and couldn't or wouldn't coherently answer the questions as to what had occurred to her. Then, according to the rookie officer, for unknown reasons, the senior female officer had—perhaps out of frustration—struck the hysterical woman several times in the head with her flashlight, causing injury. The hysterical woman who had initially called the police was then arrested and charged with Assault on a Police Officer.

There was a racial component to the investigation. The rookie female officer was black, the hysterical woman who was allegedly beaten was black, while the senior female officer who allegedly did the beating was white, as well as several other officers who checked by.

Initially, after reviewing the complaint and other documentation, I thought perhaps the rookie officer was overreacting or had misinterpreted what had occurred. I presupposed this because she was a rookie and perhaps unfamiliar with the realities of policing (sometimes police work is not pretty).

I called the rookie officer down to my office so I could interview her and get a detailed written statement. Her statement was consistent with her initial complaint. When I broached the subject that perhaps because of her lack of street experience she had misinterpreted what had occurred, she was not happy.

She then gave me a lecture. She explained that she was not naive; she had grown up in the hood and been a teacher in the Houston Independent School District prior to joining the department and had much inner city life experience. She looked me in the eye and said what happened out there was WRONG! That senior female officer had beat that poor woman in the head with a flashlight for no reason other than she was hysterical and wasn't answering questions! I believed her.

Before questioning the suspect officer or interviewing the other officers who were out on the scene, I "dumped" all the mobile data terminal

(MDT) information from all the patrol vehicles that were dispatched to or had "checked by" that night. Every marked patrol unit had a MDT, which allows the officers who ride that vehicle to make various computer inquiries, such as on license plates of vehicles or outstanding warrant checks. Besides being an integral part of the computer-aided dispatch (CAD) system, these MDTs also allowed patrol officers to send private messages to each other, without using the radio, specifically to the MDT in that respective patrol vehicle.

These messages were archived, and I was able to retrieve the private MDT messages between all the involved police units/officers who had been present at the incident that night. What I was interested in was what the officers who were not directly involved, but physically present, said to each other about what had occurred after leaving the scene.

The retrieved MDT messages between the officers who had checked by on the scene were an eye-opener!

"I can't believe she did that."

"Did you see the way she beat her."

"I am glad I didn't tell the dispatcher that I was checking by."

"She did it again."

The MDT messages indicated that police brutality had occurred. I had the "witness officers" in my office as soon as possible, with a list of questions about what they had observed. Initially, before asking questions, the narrative they wanted to put forward was "they hadn't seen anything"! I then gave them a list of questions, provided copies of their MDT transcripts, and asked that they carefully think about their answers considering their comments to each other that night via their MDT units. I also suggested it might be important that they consult with their lawyers before submitting their formal statements.

Later, the answers were in. Everything the rookie officer told me was true. In addition, it was also revealed that this wasn't the first time that the suspect officer had engaged in police brutality. Further investigation revealed that it was a regular pattern of behavior on her part.

I saw that the charges against the victim were dismissed. The suspect officer was charged with Aggravated Assault (Deadly Weapon). They fired her from the department. Instead of going to trial, she accepted a plea bargain offer from the Harris County District Attorney's Office and pled guilty to Official Oppression, received a probated sentence and had to surrender her Texas Police Officer license.

I didn't spend a long time on the reactive side of Internal Affairs.

Administratively attached to the Internal Affairs Division is a small, elite, and secretive unit, composed of one lieutenant and eight sergeants. Some rank-and-file officers of the department don't even know that this unit exists. It is housed in a non-police affiliated building and there are no signs to show its presence. The members of the unit are all undercover and drive nondescript rental vehicles. They "live apart" from the rest of the department and their identities are obscure. The unit is known as Proactive Internal Affairs and is charged with conducting surveillance and sting operations against the most corrupt members of the department. Most of its mission tasking is to conduct operations against police officers involved in narcotics trafficking. The unit also conducts operations against officers suspected of stealing money from citizens or prisoners, and also those using their official positions to commit sexual assault, or any other criminal activity.

An example: A citizen reports and files a complaint stating that during a traffic stop, Officer X fondled her. A traditional reactive investigation is conducted and because of a lack of evidence, the investigation is stalemated to an impasse: he said/she said. The investigation is concluded as "Not Sustained" as the evidence is insufficient to either prove or disprove the allegation. Then, suppose sometime later, another citizen reports and files a complaint stating that during a traffic stop the same officer, Officer X, fondled her. The two citizens are unknown to each other, but are making similar allegations against the same officer. This is a red flag! However, much like the first traditional reactive investigation, this investigation will also most likely be concluded as "Not Sustained." Also, even where there might be some circumstantial evidence to add credence to the allegation, the Harris County District Attorney's Office is reluctant to prosecute "weak" criminal charges against police officers as juries are mostly reluctant to find the defendant officer guilty unless there is overwhelming evidence.

This investigation then might be sent to the Proactive Internal Affairs Unit, which would then craft and develop a sting operation to catch the suspected officer in wrongdoing and thus prove the allegation. In this example, it would mean using an undercover female officer (usually from another agency) who bears or purports to have physical and/or life status similarities to the alleged victims. Then, while the decoy is under extensive surveillance and during a tightly controlled undercover operation, it would be arranged for the suspect officer to contact the decoy under similar circumstances as described by previous alleged victims.

To protect the decoy and get the necessary evidence to get criminal charges against the suspect officer, many resources would be brought to bear, including but not limited to vehicle tracking devices, pole cameras, discreet audio and video recording devices, fixed wing surveillance aircraft, and the SWAT Detail—the members of which had been sworn to secrecy—standing close by, immediately ready to intervene and protect the decoy and to also effect the arrest of the suspect officer.

I guess because of my previous experience in Homicide and in a Tactical Unit, they invited me to become a member of the Houston Police Department's Proactive Internal Affairs Unit.

I spent several years in Proactive Internal Affairs. My specialty and developed area of expertise were the dope rippers.

In the world of mid-level and upper-level narcotics trafficking, large amounts of crack cocaine is produced in Mexico, Columbia, etc. This cocaine is then smuggled into the United States. Houston, because of its location, is considered a hub and this cocaine (mostly) is bartered and sold by kilo amounts to a buyer, who then sells them down the line until ultimately it reaches the street level, where it is sold to the individual consumer.

As contacts are made and developed, these multi-kilos are sold to prospective buyers. Often the buyers and sellers will meet at a public or neutral location, like a Walmart parking lot, where they will conduct their prearranged transaction. The seller might deliver multi-kilos of cocaine, each kilo being worth, depending on black market fluctuations, over $20,000. So it was not uncommon for the buyers to be coming to the location with several hundred thousands of dollars in cash.

Criminals are much more opportunistic and crafty than what the public thinks. They also regularly steal from each other, if given the opportunity. Mid-level narcotics dealers (sellers and buyers) are not above setting up the other side for a "thug rip." In a pre-planned armed robbery, instead of buying or selling, they would—by force—steal the shipment of cocaine or money from the other side. However, in doing this, there is the potential for extreme unpleasantries.

Retaliations would often occur between these groups and would be seen on the nightly news as a "drug-related murder/shooting, etc."

A thoughtful and enterprising trafficker of narcotics came up with a brilliant plan. Instead of having his boys rip the dope or money (because the other bad guys would know they were set up), he would recruit and have a uniformed police officer, driving a marked police vehicle, perform a "routine traffic stop" on the driver and vehicle of the "load car" just prior to the scheduled transaction, as it travels to the meet location. This targeted vehicle "load car," usually was the one transporting the multi-kilos of cocaine (or the money) to the prearranged location to "consummate the deal." This police officer, during the "routine" traffic stop, will then "discover" the contraband and seize it. No arrests would be made and the driver and vehicle would be released. The corrupt officer then, instead of submitting the money or narcotics to the crime lab or property room, delivered it to the mid-level dope dealer he was in cahoots with. The involved officer would be handsomely rewarded in cash.

The beauty of this type of rip is that the side being ripped can never be sure whether it was a setup or a legitimate routine traffic stop, which gives the mid-level dope dealer, who masterminded the rip, the plausible deniability to say that he was not involved and thus avoid future violent retaliations from the other side. In fact, he might still do future "legitimate" dope business with them.

A few of Houston's mid-level criminal narcotics dealers had several corrupt police officers on call, working for them. When the time was right, these narcotics dealers would "activate" one or more of their corrupt officers and they would rip another dealer for his money or dope.

This bad-guy, out-of-the-box thinking even morphed into home invasions. Police officers or a mix of police officers and civilian suspects (dressed in police raid gear), pretending to be a legitimate police narcotics raid team, would force entry into a house to steal large amounts of narcotics or money.

There is much money to be made in rips by corrupt officers working with or for mid-level narcotics dealers.

Unfortunately, the Houston Police Department has, in my estimation, several police officers at any given time working for drug dealers.

From time to time, information would come forth—usually from informants—that provided glimpses into this reality. Often the informant himself had been caught trafficking illegal narcotics and was now under contract by investigators in the Narcotics Division or the Drug Enforcement Agency (DEA). A contract means that to mitigate their sentencing, they had to provide information—"tell us everything about everything"—or help facilitate sting operations against other narcotics dealers they might be associated with. Sometimes these "contract informants" had knowledge of police officers who in the past had partaken in the drug trafficking industry by taking part in dope rips or had even guarded shipments of illegal narcotics passing through Houston.

Mostly, these bits of information were unsupported and were being made by an individual who was not necessarily credible, often had a significant criminal history, and whose motivation was to fulfill his contract in any way possible. We documented this intelligence on police corruption in an "Information File," the content only accessible to members of the Proactive Unit and the chief of police. It was only when information was current and of "actionable intelligence" that a sting operation was put into action.

I preferred to work with "paid informants," who were generally more reliable and who were at that moment ideally positioned to help facilitate a sting operation. Normally this type of informant was only paid at the conclusion of a successful operation. During my tenure in Proactive Internal Affairs, we paid several informants large sums of money for facilitating sting operations that resulted in the arrest and indictment of Houston police officers for serious drug trafficking charges. Often, we would have to brief the chief of police of credible or significant information prior to implementing any sting operation in which there was a likelihood that a member of the department would be arrested.

For example, a criminal informant who worked as an exotic dancer in one of Houston's high-end topless clubs connected me with one of her coworkers, who had been dating a Houston police officer and who, according to the informant, was "crooked." The officer's ex-girlfriend, Mary, was furious with the officer she had been involved with. She wanted to marry him; he had made some promise but had decided to instead marry another girl he was dating and who was pregnant with his child. Mary was a woman scorned. She was mad and wanted revenge.

According to Mary, she had first met the officer at the club where she worked. He frequented it often with his friends (other police officers) and they knew him as a big spender. They had dated for several months, and he had lavished her with gifts and money. During this time, he had confided and bragged to her he was a big player in the drug trafficking industry.

I developed a professional relationship with Mary and listened to all her problems, but was careful to bring another member of the unit anytime we met face-to-face. Eventually she agreed to work with me; she reestablished her contact with the officer and began recording their phone conversations. It was during these conversations that sometimes she would bring up his alleged drug trafficking business and he would talk about it in generalities. However, I was not sure whether he was corrupt or just telling tall tales to impress a woman who appeared to be intrigued by this lifestyle. There was no corroboration of this criminality. Even his financial records appeared within bounds of his salary as a police officer.

I was getting ready to close out the investigation into an Information File, when a narcotics investigator contacted me, saying that an informant of his had just been approached by a "black Columbian" who lamented that while delivering a multi-kilo load of cocaine, he had been stopped on a traffic by a uniformed Houston Police officer and that the officer had taken his load of cocaine and released him. According to the Columbian, he believed that the officer who stopped him was corrupt and kept the cocaine for himself. The Columbian was in dire straits because he was on the hook to his bosses for the multi-kilo load and they were already threatening to kill his grandmother back in Columbia if he didn't make good on the loss. What the Columbian wanted was a "crooked cop" to help him find the other "crooked cop" who stole his load of cocaine and recover it for him!

We arranged a meeting with the Colombian; one member of our unit who spoke fluent Spanish posed as a corrupt police officer willing to help him with his problem.

We monitored the meeting and recorded the conversation. I almost felt sorry for the Colombian. He was beside himself about the loss of the shipment and seemed to genuinely fear severe retaliation. Our "crooked cop" interviewed the Colombian, who said that he was driving a rental car with six kilos of cocaine in the back of it; he was going to meet and sell the load to a guy by the name of Paul. He said that the officer who stopped him on traffic was black and told him he had pulled him over for a minor traffic offense. The officer put the Colombian in the rear of the patrol car and then searched the rental vehicle. The Colombian said while the officer was searching his vehicle, he had tried to escape the patrol car by attempting to pop out the rear and side widows, but was unsuccessful. Eventually, after seizing the cocaine and putting it in the trunk of the patrol car, the officer then released the Colombian.

We arrested the Colombian the next day, after the meeting, on some relatively minor drug charges. He agreed to cooperate for consideration on his sentencing. I am not sure whatever happened to his grandmother.

I did an MDT dump on all the department's mobile computers for the day that the Colombian said he had been ripped. I was fishing to see whether anyone had made a computer inquiry on the license plate of the rental vehicle that he had been driving on the day in question.

Bingo! One of the department's MDTs had been used to run the Colombian's license plate, and the date and time matched. More interestingly, the officer assigned to that patrol car was the same officer who had been romantically involved with Mary and whose recorded phone calls I had been reviewing!

Using the pretense of vehicle maintenance, we had a trusted contact in the department bring us the patrol vehicle that had been used for the alleged rip and had it secretly processed for fingerprints, specifically in the rear seat area (prisoner compartment). Just as he said, the Colombian's fingerprints were found in the locations as he described. That added credibility to his story.

The suspect officer was Donald Sutton, who was assigned to the South Central Patrol Division. I had been the original case officer on Sutton, but now that he had become a high priority, Sergeant John William

Belk—Billy—was also assigned to the case with me. Billy, a longtime Homicide and Sex Crimes investigator, was intelligent and capable.

Although we had the help of the other members of the unit, it was now up to Billy and me to prove the criminal allegations against Sutton or, if that were not possible, to find provable just cause to have his employment as a Houston Police officer terminated. Much of the information that we had, including Mary's testimony, was undiscoverable (could not be revealed in a criminal trial or even in a civil service hearing).

The Proactive Internal Affairs also works closely with the Harris County District Attorney's Office Public Integrity Division. As previously mentioned, there needs to be a mountain of evidence for juries to convict police officers of criminal acts. The testimony from an admitted drug trafficker would not be nearly enough. What they needed was to catch the officer in the commission of a crime, where proactive internal investigators were the eyewitnesses and, if possible, everything was recorded and thoroughly documented.

Over the next few months, Officer Sutton became our primary focus. In addition, other information came in and the dots were connecting. In one of Sutton's recorded conversations with Mary, he had alluded that his "business partner" was a man named Paul—the same name of the guy the Columbian was supposed to be selling the load of cocaine to when Sutton ripped him. Mary was also able to glean that Paul drove a black Lexus.

Then the FBI called a meeting to tell me that Sutton had been overheard talking to a suspect in one of their investigations on a "T3." A T3—or Title III—is a warrant authorized by a federal judge so that the FBI could monitor and record private phone conversations between individuals as part of a criminal investigation. The only thing the FBI agent said, or was authorized to tell me, was that Sutton was not the initial target of their investigation but he had been communicating with the primary subject of their investigation and that the communication was deemed "suspicious." In addition, they also told me that the overall federal investigation was regarding illegal narcotics trafficking. Much more of a problem for me was, by law, the FBI was required to make notification to any individuals whose conversations they had intercepted. I knew that if Sutton was informed that he had popped up on the FBI's radar, he would probably lie low and our chances of facilitating a sting operation against him would be slim. I asked the FBI agent to coordinate with me and my investigation and that we could share information. The FBI said no!

Remember, this was in the days before September 11, 2001 (World Trade Center attacks) and the various federal law enforcement agencies were not known for sharing intelligence and coordinating operations with other agencies. This was one issue being pointed out in the post-investigation of the terrorist attack; had there been more cooperation and information sharing between various agencies who held various pieces of intelligence information, someone might have been able to connect the dots and possibly saved many lives. After the World Trade Center attacks, the federal government's law enforcement agencies provided greater cooperation and more information sharing, particularly with local law enforcement.

Even though I had asked them to stall until my investigation was done, just days after our meeting, the FBI alerted Sutton that private phone conversations of which he was a party to were monitored and recorded pursuant to a federal criminal investigation!

Shortly after he was notified by the FBI, Sutton called Mary and told her how the FBI was on to him and that he would have to be extra careful. Sutton was making plans for the future.

He now indicated to her that he was going to form and equip his own home invasion robbery crew, composed of several, presumably criminal, gang members who he would equip with police raid gear. They would purport to be a legitimate undercover police narcotics unit and would then do home invasions on residences where he suspected large amounts of narcotics and money might be located.

Interestingly, the patrol station where Sutton was assigned was experiencing a higher level of administratively reported lost or stolen police property by the officers assigned there.

These items included official police identification(s) and jackets marked "Houston Police."

Sutton was getting married. He was planning a large bachelor party and would rent out a large room at an area motel. He was also hiring many topless dancers and other women we suspected would provide prostitution services. Unknown to Sutton, two of the girls who were going to "dance" at the party were also police informants (mine). I am not sure how much it cost Sutton to put on this grandiose event but it was considerable. Billy and I estimated that over sixty men attended, many of whom were law enforcement officers from Houston and other area agencies. Sutton funded the entire party. He paid for the alcohol, the room rentals, the DJ, and—probably what was most expensive—for all the aforementioned women, which all required payment for whatever "services" they would provide to the partygoers. These women were not the common streetwalker types or who danced at the less expensive exotic clubs but rather were of the "high end," providing the more expensive variety of "male entertainment."

While the party was going on, Billy and I drove through the parking lot and recorded every vehicle and license plate parked at the hotel. Of particular interest to us were any black Lexus; there were two.

I began running the license plates of the vehicles that I had documented while in the parking lot and one black Lexus was shown to be registered to a "Paul." This particular Paul also had a lengthy criminal history, for narcotics trafficking.

Had we found Paul?

In my mind, Paul would be key to the investigation and any future sting operation.

Very early the next morning, after the bachelor party had broken up, Billy and I debriefed our two topless dancer girls (informants) who had been hired by Sutton to perform at his party.

They both reported that Sutton and some of his buddies had engaged in group sex with a woman who was known to be a high-end prostitute and that while doing so, they had been smoking marijuana.

Now another opportunity immediately presented itself to rid the department of Sutton.

Reliable and credible informants had told us they had observed Sutton and presumably other Houston police officers smoking marijuana. The Houston Police Department has a zero-tolerance policy when it comes to illegal drug usage by its employees. It also has a specific drug testing protocol to enforce this policy. As soon as possible, we alerted the chief of police of what we suspected, asking whether he would authorize a drug test for Sutton.

The answer was yes. In addition, we were also directed to identify and have drug tested all the Houston police officers who we had documented as being at Sutton's bachelor party.

To Billy and me, this was a win-win situation. Sutton, as a condition of employment, would have to take the test and we were confident that he had been smoking marijuana. If he refused the order to submit to the test, he would be administratively charged with insubordination. Either way, his employment with the Houston Police Department would be terminated.

The problem was we had to get the help of the investigators on the reactive side of Internal Affairs, to mask that Proactive was involved. This required that Sutton had to be located and verbally ordered by a reactive IAD sergeant to report to the testing facility and submit a urine sample. There was a specific protocol to follow and no one could locate Sutton as he was on his regular days off and was taking some scheduled time off for his wedding. It was almost a week after the party and after the time that he had smoked marijuana before he was located and ordered to report to Internal

Affairs. Upon reporting to IAD, they ordered him to submit to a drug test. Initially he refused and when informed that he would then be charged with insubordination, he asked the investigator whether he could call his lawyer. In the presence of the reactive IAD sergeant, Sutton called his lawyer and asked him what he should do. His lawyer gave him good advice: take the gamble, take the test; if you refuse, you will be fired for sure.

Sutton then submitted to the urine test and all the proper procedures were followed.

A few days later, the drug test was in. Sutton had passed! It had taken us too long after the time we suspected that he had smoked marijuana to have him tested; there was not enough "marijuana stuff" in his system. There was a "positive" for marijuana, but the amount for an "official positive" had not been reached or exceeded.

We were back to square one. But, because of the bachelor party, we were now certain we knew the identity of "Paul," who we suspected of being Sutton's criminal business partner.

We then began an extensive surveillance operation on Paul, utilizing all the surveillance equipment at our disposal, including pole cameras and vehicle tracking devices.

A pole camera is a video camera disguised to be a normal part of either a streetlight or part of the electrical power system that is strung across poles that services nearly all residences and buildings. The placement of the cameras is accomplished by a specially trained crew of undercover law enforcement officers who pose as employees of the electric company. They install these covert cameras, utilizing a bucket truck, and appear to be performing routine service to the aboveground electrical infrastructure, but in fact are installing cameras which would allow investigators (Billy and me) to monitor, in this case, Paul's house to observe remotely the happenings there. The cameras can be utilized without a court order and because they "tap into" the existing electrical system can operate indefinitely.

Another mainstay for surveillance was our mobile vehicle tracking devices. These were more complicated and required a certain expertise to operate. A court-approved warrant had to be written and signed by a district court judge. And at least until 2012, the level of proof that needed to be articulated to be able to obtain the warrant was "reasonable suspicion." After 2012, the United States Supreme Court ruled that for most part (there were exceptions) because of the expectations of privacy, the standard for obtaining a tracking warrant was upgraded from "reasonable suspicion" to "probable cause." Once a vehicle tracking warrant was obtained, we would be able to covertly (usually in the middle of the night) place a tracking device on Paul's vehicle. The tracker had a self-contained battery and a finite life. The trackers we used back then were fairly bulky. After we located the vehicle (parked), and it was safe to do so, someone would have to crawl underneath it and place the tracker, which had strong magnets on one side, to a solid metal part of the undercarriage of the vehicle.

It is possible for a team of trained undercover officers to do "rolling surveillance" (keeping a targeted vehicle under surveillance while it is being driven—without using a tracker). But because of the heavy traffic in Houston, it is difficult. Frequently the vehicle is lost by the surveillance team. Using a tracking device enhances the surveillance operation, and I came to rely on them in all of my surveillance and sting operations.

It didn't take long to figure out Paul's daily routine. I noted he consistently frequented the same high-end nightclub, being a regular fixture there.

We planned to catch Paul "dirty." We would stage a criminal sting operation, targeting Paul. If we could then arrest him in a significant criminal law violation, the prosecutors we worked with (Harris County District Attorney's Public Integrity Unit) would then offer him a "contract" to assist us in consideration for a reduced sentence. If successful, and if Paul agreed, he would become my criminal informant and would then help us in our investigation against Sutton, even testifying against him in court. To make this happen, to catch Paul in a criminal act, Billy and I needed help. Fortunately, the Houston Police Department Narcotics Division had just the people we needed. Put on special assignment and assigned to Billy and me were two black undercover officers: Jim and Fred.

There was initially a lot of second-guessing regarding the wisdom of bringing Jim and Fred into the unit on temporary assignment and making them privy to all we knew. But, if it were not for these two officers, the investigation against Sutton would have been stymied. The short story was that Jim and Fred had contacts and could go to locations and operate in places within the black community that the rest of us in the Proactive Unit could not. Yes, we had black sergeants assigned to the unit but they did not have the "right look," the experience, and/or mindset to do this undercover work.

Billy and I gave Jim and Fred the assignment to undo Paul. It took them about two weeks! For them, it was simple. They began going to the same nightclub as Paul. They also "planted" one of their trusted informants within the club, with orders to "hang out with Paul." Eventually the informant and Paul were introduced. The informant purported to be a "high roller" and spent a lot of money in the club and more importantly, bought Paul drinks. Paul and the informant talked! The alcohol—bought with monies from my departmental expense account—probably loosed some lips and facilitated the goodwill between them. All along, Jim and Fred's informant kept alluding to Paul that he was some "big time dope dealer" looking for business.

Paul took the bait. He told Jim and Fred's informant that they should do business together. Paul told the informant he had some "laws" working for him and if he (the informant) set up a large narcotics delivery with one of his contacts then he (Paul) would have one of "his" police officers rip the dope shipment during a routine traffic stop, while it was being transported to the meet location. Then they (Paul and the informant) would sell the "stolen" shipment (without paying for it), and split the proceeds. Jim and

Fred's informant agreed to the arrangement and told Paul he would soon be in contact with him to coordinate and make arrangements.

When Billy and I debriefed Jim and Fred, we were ecstatic. This was great news! But I had assumed that Paul was exclusively working with Sutton. In his conversation with the informant, Paul had alluded to having more than one police officer working for him. Who were the others? Or was Paul bragging? We didn't know.

It was all hands on deck. We were setting up a dope rip targeting Paul and "his" police officer(s). I hoped that Paul would use Sutton for the rip. Sutton was the guy I had been working on for nearly six months.

All the members of the Proactive Unit were now fully engaged. All the other cases we were working were now on the back burner. There was much coordination that had to be accomplished. We had to bring into the "circle of trust" a few members of the Houston Police Department's SWAT Detail, as well as coordinate aerial surveillance, both helicopter and fixed wing. The chief of police had to be briefed. We also had to locate an undercover officer from an outside police agency to pose as the drug courier.

Most importantly, I had to get five or six kilos of real cocaine. One does not just saunter down to the crime lab and sign out six kilos of cocaine (previously seized and slated for destruction) for a sting operation. I had to meet with the highest levels of the leadership of the Harris County District Attorney's Office and promise, cajole, and explain why it was necessary. I had to make many assurances that the cocaine would not be "lost" and let back out into circulation on the streets. If the cocaine was "lost" and it became public, it would embarrass the involved agencies.

I got my court order, picked up the cocaine, and wrapped all the kilos together in multiple layers of plastic wrap so the bundle could not be easily pulled apart and the kilos separated in the sting operation. In the middle of the bundle, I added a "dummy kilo," which contained one of our tracking devices so presumably I could track the entire load and not lose it.

As soon as possible, a few days later, we sent word to Paul via our informant that he had set up a multi-kilo cocaine buy and that a courier would bring in the load from out of town. We had the informant give only the basic information to Paul, the approximate meet time and location, but not the description of the load vehicle that our courier was driving, which would be hauling all the dope.

Paul told our informant that he would be ready and would have one of his "laws" in the area in a patrol car to intercept the courier. Paul reiterated to the informant that as soon as it was known, to tell him the description of the load vehicle so he could relay it to his officer. He also said that he would be in the immediate area and shortly after "his" officer ripped the dope, it would be delivered to him. Then, soon after, he would meet with our informant to split the load of cocaine. Paul also said that he paid the officer in cash, so he should get a bigger part of the load because he had "overhead costs."

The day came. All our surveillance was in place. We had two teams of SWAT officers in uniform in patrol vehicles for the arrest and take-down of Paul and the corrupt police officer he was working with. We had undercover surveillance, all the sergeants in Proactive Internal Affairs, as well as Jim and Fred. A fixed wing surveillance airplane was flying at high altitude over the area, and a police helicopter stood by. More worrisome for me (I was the case agent) was several members of the Houston Police Department's Command Staff as well as representatives from the Harris County District Attorney's Office who were monitoring the operation from our office, which also served as our command post.

True to his word, we identified Paul inside his personal vehicle, standing by in the parking lot where the drug transaction was scheduled to take place. Also parked close to the location was a marked Harris County Constable patrol car, which was occupied by a single occupant. Could this be the corrupt police officer Paul would use?

I was with the informant, who had cell phone communication with Paul.

We called Paul: Are you ready? Paul responded he and his "law" were in the area and that "she" was ready.

SHE!!!

Donald Sutton was not a she!

Quickly, I had one of the undercover officers get "close eyes" on the marked constable patrol car. Sitting inside was a female sergeant in uniform. My heart sank. I hoped that Paul would bring out Sutton for today's rip but had brought an officer from another agency.

Billy and I decided to "queer the deal" for that day. Often in the narcotics world, deliveries are postponed and transactions often don't happen on schedule. It's called "turd time." I wanted to set up the deal a day or two later, hoping that Paul would bring out Sutton for the rip. Also, I was not feeling good about letting the rip go down just yet and felt there were still weak spots in my plan and was afraid of losing the dope. I wanted more time to polish the cannon ball. I had a "loud" telephone discussion with the prosecutors from the Public Integrity Division back in the command post about delaying the operation, but ultimately I was the case agent and it was my decision.

We stalled. I had the informant tell Paul that something had come up and that the shipment coming in from out of town was delayed. Maybe in a day or two. Paul said no problem, just let him know—he would be ready!

I drove up to the constable sitting in her patrol vehicle and pretended to be some random regular citizen who was lost and needed directions. She was most helpful. I turned the charm on, and we engaged in small talk. She was by no stretch of the imagination a "looker" and I think she genuinely appreciated the male attention. Before I left, she thoughtfully gave me her business card with her telephone number written on the back! Very convenient!

Late that night, after obtaining a court order, Billy and I snuck in and placed a tracking device on the "take-home" patrol car of the female constable sergeant, which was parked in her residential driveway. We did not alert her supervisors (yet) because we did not know whether they could be trusted.

A day or so later, through the informant, we called Paul. The shipment was really, really, coming in, no more delays...are you ready?

Paul was ready. He would be back in the area, waiting with one of his officers the next morning.

I was still hoping that Sutton would be the next officer "up" on Paul's rip rotation. But we quickly learned, without even having to get eyes, it would be my new friend the female constable sergeant—as we tracked her marked patrol vehicle right into the same spot she had parked last time.

We were ready. All the assets were in place and now we pumped the last bits of information to Paul: the description of the drug courier (who was actually an Austin-based Texas Department of Public Safety [DPS] undercover narcotics lieutenant and who was playing the role of our "mule") and also the description of the vehicle he was driving. Inside the rental vehicle were "my" six kilos of cocaine.

As our undercover mule drove the load car past the female constable, she pulled in right behind him and turned on her overhead lights. As planned, she was conducting a traffic stop.

As planned, she seized the whole load of dope and told our undercover officer to leave the area.

As planned, we tracked her and our load of dope for approximately half an hour.

As planned, we watched as she met with Paul and passed the dope shipment off to him and watched as he appeared to pay her.

This is what we wanted. The constable sergeant had just ripped a multi-kilo cocaine shipment, from our mule. The street value of these drugs was well over $100,000. This law enforcement officer had just delivered these "seized" illegal drugs to an unauthorized civilian (Paul), who, in this case, we believed to be the ringleader and the central person to this entire nexus of police corruption.

As planned, the constable sergeant and Paul separated and drove their separate ways.

When they were several miles apart, I called for the takedown of the involved vehicles: the one Paul was driving (which contained my dope) and the marked Harris County Constable Precinct 7 patrol vehicle driven by the female sergeant. The SWAT officers moved in; Paul surrendered and was arrested without incident.

What was not planned? When the SWAT officers who were driving marked Houston Police patrol vehicles attempted to pull over the sergeant driving a marked constable's office patrol vehicle, she ran. A high-speed vehicle chase ensued. Several Houston police cars and a police helicopter chased this constable vehicle, everyone involved in marked police cars. Eventually, the constable spun out into a ditch and then bailed out of her vehicle, while in uniform, and ran on foot. Bad decision. The pursuing officers were all SWAT and were in top physical shape. They ran her down and after a short struggle had her disarmed, in custody, and handcuffed.

When we searched Paul's vehicle, we found only part of our shipment of cocaine. The packaging had been cut open and two of our real kilos were missing. Fortunately, the other two were found in the trunk of the constable's vehicle. We surmised what had happened. Thieves, even those in collaboration with each other, will, if given the opportunity, steal from one another. The constable, besides being paid approximately $10,000 by Paul (we recovered the money from her) for stealing the load, had also prior to meeting him "pulled off" two kilos of cocaine for herself from the original load and secured them in the trunk of her patrol car. Not only did she make money from Paul, but apparently had a way and/or a contact to sell the two kilos she had just held back. The two kilos were worth over $40,000. So for a few minutes of work, she had potentially made $50,000!

Later, Billy and I read the constable her legal rights and she (as expected) immediately evoked her right to not self-incriminate herself (she didn't want to talk). We didn't tell her much and released her. Even though it seems counterintuitive, we were confident that she would not tell anybody about the incident and her arrest. We also knew that she was a "separate cell" to Paul's operation and would not be able, even if she wanted, to warn the other officers (HPD) about what had occurred. We would simply obtain a Two Be (2B) Arrest Warrant at a later date when the rest of the sting operations we envisioned were completed and again arrest her and then formally charge her.

Paul, however, was a chatterbox! He agreed to cooperate fully, to tell everything he knew and even to help facilitate future sting operations against "his" corrupt police officers. All this was done in the presence of Harris County prosecutors, who then drew up a contract offering him "consideration" on any future sentencing related to his conspiracy with area police officers who were involved in the trafficking of illegal narcotics.

We had a problem. Paul's contract would not happen overnight. It would have to be approved by higher authorities within the district attorney's office. The weekend was upon us, so the earliest we could expect approval and signatures was sometime Monday, which was several days away. We couldn't book Paul into any jail facilities. He was already alluding to multiple Houston police officers who were at his beck and call. If we booked him, any police officer could make a simple computer inquiry and discover that he was in jail. Even if we released him later, it would be a red flag and it would be suspected that Paul was compromised and now under contract. Paul also couldn't go "dark." He was connected with many movers and shakers in the narcotics industry as well as corrupt police officers. He had to make and receive calls on his cell phone to appear that all was good, still business as usual.

73

Across from our office was a hotel. So Billy and I, along with the other members of the unit, rented a room and spent our time with Paul, babysitting him. Paul was actually personable and charismatic, and Billy and I enjoyed conversing with him, learning everything we could about his business. It was nice to know that many of the theories that we had developed over the months were true.

First thing Monday, we had Paul down at the district attorney's office and his contract was approved and signed. Billy then sat down with Paul and got a detailed statement about his dope ripping business. Paul had three Houston police officers in his employ and the constable was the last one he had recruited (a total of four law enforcement officers). All three of the HPD officers (including Sutton) worked at the same police station, on the same shift, and were known to each other and corroborated together in the rips. As we suspected, because the FBI had informed Sutton that one of his phone conversations with a "highly placed narcotics trafficker" had been intercepted, all the HPD officers had shut down their corrupt activities for the time being.

I was curious about the individual the FBI was targeting on their T3—was it Paul? I made a discreet inquiry and was told, "Sorry, we cannot deny or confirm." I believe it was.

Because it appeared that the FBI had screwed our operation, we settled on another course of operation. Because Paul was fully cooperative, we would have him meet with Sutton and the other officers and in casual conversations have them talk about their previous narcotics rips together. The prosecutors felt that with Paul's statement, recorded conversations between Paul and the police officers talking about their crimes, as well as any corroborating evidence Billy and I could develop, it would provide for a sustainable criminal prosecution against the officers. It was not optimum but perhaps sufficient. Again, there was always the problem that if we went to a jury trial, there is a built-in bias for police officers (citizens just didn't want to believe that police officers could be so corrupt).

Over the next few days, while we had him under surveillance, Paul met face-to-face with the involved officers or talked to them on his cell phone. They all made incriminating statements that corroborated Paul's written statement. We recorded all the conversations. We had Paul try to talk them into doing another dope rip with him, but because of the FBI T3 debacle, they were not going to do it. Sutton indicated that he was putting future efforts into his creation and the outfitting of a counterfeit police raid team and even talked about getting a nondescript white van to use as a transport and raid vehicle for his "boys."

We were gathering evidence and getting close to where the prosecutors felt comfortable in obtaining probable cause warrants against the involved corrupt officers. However, there was still lingering doubts and everyone wanted the "smoking gun": a sting operation, with Proactive Internal Affairs members as the witnesses, fully documented with video and audio surveillance.

But it did not look like it would happen, even with Paul, my new best friend!

Manna from Heaven! One morning, while in our hotel room (it was my turn to sit with Paul), Paul's cell phone rang. It was Sutton. I began recording the conversation. After talking about women and sex, Sutton got to the point and asked Paul, "Can I buy a white girl from you?" A "white girl" for this group of criminals was code for one kilo of cocaine. As soon as Sutton asked Paul for a white girl, Paul looked at me with a quizzical look on his face. I quickly nodded yes. Paul then told Sutton that he would hook him up with a white girl and they negotiated a price—20K. Sutton explained that he was helping his younger brother in his dope business and they had a buyer on the East Coast they wanted to start dealing with. They wanted to establish a relationship with the East Coast buyer and then maybe do a money rip at a later date when the "pot" was full. Sutton said that his brother would be the mule and would transport the white girl up to the East Coast. Paul then told Sutton (under my direction) that he would bring him the white girl the following day; they agreed on a location on the south side of the city at a popular restaurant.

Our unit worked fast. I had to obtain another court order and "borrow" another kilo of cocaine from our crime lab. All the logistics were worked out: undercover surveillance, aerial surveillance, tracking devices on the involved vehicles, SWAT standing by to make the arrest, Command Staff briefed, etc.

The next morning was anticlimactic. Paul, while under our direction, in a public place and under our surveillance, met Sutton. Paul gave him a white girl (my kilo of cocaine). Sutton paid Paul $20,000.00 in cash. They separated. While we still had Sutton under surveillance, the bust signal was given. SWAT moved in rapidly and arrested Sutton without incident (and recovered my kilo of cocaine). We met with Paul and recovered the money Sutton had used to pay for the white girl.

We had Sutton dirty; not only were we going to prove the historical dope rips and the conspiring to conduct home invasions with police imposters, but now we would add this whole side business of the trafficking cocaine to the East Coast.

Billy and I took Sutton back to the office. We attempted to interview him but he invoked his right to not self-incriminate.

In the weeks following, we were able to "roll" the other Houston police officers up and charge them with the historical crimes. All the HPD officers were fired (or resigned) and received prison sentences. Also charged and convicted were the constable and several other civilians.

We had made a deal with the devil, and Paul was not charged in any of the crimes as per the spirit of his contract. We all felt it was necessary; for the greater good, it was more important to get the corrupt officers.

Not long after this operation, Paul was arrested and charged in another case for Aggravated Robbery. He, along with several other gang members, had orchestrated the robbery of a pharmacy where they attempted to get a large amount of narcotics. He was convicted and sent to prison for several years. I wish he had turned his life around. He was intelligent, personable, and if he had applied his skill sets and energy in a legitimate business enterprise, he could have done well.

Sutton was criminally charged and fired from the Houston Police Department. When he was sentenced to state prison, the Texas Department of Corrections intended to incarcerate him in its facility exclusively for ex-police officers or other offenders who might be endangered by the general prison population (former police officers in prison are often targeted for abuse). Sutton was adamant he didn't want to go to the "special prison, for special prisoners." He wanted to be incarcerated in the general prison population "with his home boys" (other black men). I guess his lawyer helped facilitate his request because he got his wish.

Years later, after Billy earned his law degree and retired from HPD, I ran into him at the post office downtown. We shared stories and caught up on our families, etc. Billy then relayed to me that recently Sutton had sued the State of Texas, alleging that the state had failed to protect him (as a former police officer) from harm by incarcerating him with the general prison population. The lawsuit alleged that because Sutton was an ex-HPD officer, he had been brutally targeted, on many occasions, by other prisoners who had anally sodomized him so often that his sphincter muscles had been permanently damaged. Billy said that the lawsuit was eventually dismissed. If the story is true, I guess that Sutton was probably wishing that he had opted for the special prison for special prisoners after all. Or maybe it was just another one of his get-rich scams.

During the next several years, the Proactive Internal Affairs Unit was able to do several similar sting operations targeting corrupt police officers. This was made possible not by running countless hours of surveillance on the suspected officers hoping to catch them in a crime, but by targeting their civilian coconspirators and covertly turning them into our agents—a double cross. Houston's Chief of Police Sam Nuchia authorized Billy and me to pay the key informant who gave us Paul and ultimately Sutton and the other "dirty cops" $20,000, in department monies.

This large sum of money (for the 1990s), became the standard amount that we in Proactive Internal Affairs would pay out to these types of well-placed informants who were uniquely situated to not only provide key information but could help us facilitate sting operations against corrupt cop-dope rippers.

Billy and I joked that we were making Houston safe for drug traffickers to ply their trade without fear of police rips.

Before my tenure in the Proactive Unit was over, the Command Staff asked that I investigate the backgrounds and recruiting files of several of the officers I had arrested. They were looking for any commonality. Were there any indicators of possible future criminal activity? In every case, there were red flags! Particularly in their pre-hire background investigations. Such as, close family members being identified as part of the Houston narcotics trafficking infrastructure or failed or inconsistent responses during the polygraph examination. Some of these people were hired despite these obvious red flags to meet minority recruiting goals (not to say that every corrupt Houston Police officer was a minority—this was not true). More disturbing was that in at least one case, the officer I had arrested had been hired (despite red flags) because of nepotism. A ranking member of the department had intervened in the hiring process because the initially declined applicant was then engaged to his daughter and it appeared that he would be his new son-in-law. I received no feedback from the Command Staff regarding my analysis.

If I could have, I would have stayed my entire career in the Houston Police Department's Proactive Unit investigating and orchestrating sting operations against corrupt police officers.

But a sergeant's tour of duty in the unit was limited to no more than five years.

I gained a lot of experience during this time. However, in my IAD dealings, I became jaded about the integrity and character of some members of the department's Command Staff and the departmental lawyers who advised them. I suppose it's true in every organization, but the hypocrisy, nepotism, incompetence, politics, and sometimes just plain indifference was difficult for me to stomach. Because of my position within Proactive Internal Affairs, I had a ringside seat to much of the inner workings of the department and was often not impressed with the integrity and capabilities of our leaders.

Some in the Command Staff had no real-world police experience. It was evident that all through their careers they had gravitated to administrative assignments rather than criminal investigations and not to patrol, where bad things can happen. During this part of my career, someone asked me, as a favor, for a three-week period to temporarily perform the administrative duties of sergeant in one of the offices of an assistant chief. The permanently assigned sergeant was taking off to study for the lieutenant's exam. It was the longest three weeks of my career! It was filled with meetings, memos, reading IAD cases, phone calls, all the while trapped inside an office deep within the "ivory tower." It was not my cup of tea and frankly I couldn't understand why any police officer would want the job. It was monotonous, tedious administrative work that seemed more suited to a civilian employee rather than a sworn, presumably highly trained police officer. At the end of the three weeks, when the regular administrative sergeant returned (he didn't do well on the test), I asked him why he wanted this assignment.

His response spoke volumes and is true for some officers, supervisors, and Command Staff in the Houston Police Department. Initially they might have been attracted to police work for noble reasons. But after a short time of working the streets, they discovered it was not their cup of tea. They didn't want to subject themselves to the dangers, liability, and career-threatening instant decisions that had to be made, particularly in the patrol setting or in any "point of the spear" type job in the department.

There was a wide chasm in the department between police officers. There were those officers who sought the low-key, safe, administrative type assignments as opposed to those who preferred the more dangerous, "guardian of the public" type position. The same sworn officer whose sole function—throughout their career, decade after decade—was to hand out the radios and keys to police vehicles at the beginning of a patrol shift received the same pay and retirement benefits as the undercover narcotics officer or the patrol officer working night shift in the worst part of the city. Worse, often these same administrative types—the "radio hander outers" or "secretary with a gun" type —were the ones who continued to keep being promoted and eventually years later ended up in top Command Staff positions.

We called them the "anything but patrol" people. Although a cursory review of their departmental resumes might seemingly reflect, on paper, real police experience, they didn't have any (at least in depth). It was also frustrating to talk to them about issues regarding field operations, investigations, or how sting operations were conducted and to see blank, uncomprehending looks on their faces. Sadly, even though they were in top leadership positions, they rarely knew what we were talking about. They were foremost administrators (paper pushers) and often (if they didn't have large egos and were open to it) you would have to spend a considerable amount of time trying to explain to them the hows and whys of criminal investigations—particularly, complicated undercover sting operations or other proactive operations with a lot of moving parts—so hopefully they could make an informed decision.

Some of these people had spent their entire careers figuring out how to get ahead by determining which way the wind was blowing so they could "fly their flag" the same way. They were the worse type of careerists! Some of these same careerists were also promoted to Command Staff positions, because they filled a certain racial, gender, or sexual orientation demographic! They were not necessarily advanced because they were leaders or made good decisions or were even competent, but for the political optics.

POLITICAL ACTIVISTS!

Every city has its political activists for social change. Back then and to this day, Houston has individuals who are the informal, but the recognized leader of certain special interest groups—the black activist, the Hispanic activist, the gay activist, etc.

Initially, probably a sound idea, was that each informal activist leader would have a point of contact within the Houston Police Department's Command Staff. Deputy Chief X would be the point of contact with Mr. Boney the black activist, Deputy Chief Y was assigned to be the point of contact with Mr. Hill the gay activist, etc. This was all fine and good, as these points of contact were probably first envisioned to solve problems and smooth over potential friction points between the police department and the respective activists and their constituents. What was not good was that sometimes there was a little more information sharing and corroborating than appropriate, with the appearance of the motivation being for personal enrichment. Specifically, some members of the Command Staff appeared to be concerned about their career advancement (looking good to the community and politicians) and were using their influence with these activists to back-channel confidential departmental information, such as ongoing police investigations, to the detriment of the department and the police mission.

It also appeared that the motivation of some upper Houston Police leadership was to curry the favors of these activists with tidbits of information and departmental gossip to actually create controversy, or a crisis between the special interest group and the police department! When the activist had "discovered" this information and then made it public, it would generate interest or an uproar with the community. Then the same Command Staff member, who leaked the information, could step in, with foreknowledge, bring calm to the situation, solve the problem, explain the department's position, recommend policy change, etc. Both the activist and the involved member of the Command Staff would then get credos and enhance their standing with their respective audiences. It was the old political game of "you rub my back and I will rub yours." I believe that the motivation of some members of the Command Staff was to also one-up other Command Staff members to better position themselves for the ultimate appointed position—Chief of the Houston Police Department.

This close, interdependent relationship between the Command Staff and activists could take on what was regarded by most of the department as "abhorrent decision-making" by the upper echelon, on behalf of the activists and to the detriment of individual rank-and-file officers and sergeants.

For example, earlier in the 1980s, the primary black activist leader in Houston was a man named Jew Don Boney. Mr. Boney was an outspoken and controversial ordained Baptist minister. A man who members of the Houston Police Department's Command Staff kept an open line of dialogue and communication with and maybe tried to appease to keep his goodwill. Unfortunately, Mr. Boney, besides having been previously arrested for Possession of a Controlled Substance (Cocaine) which was later dismissed because of a mistrial, also had an open arrest warrant charge related to his failure to appear at a child support hearing. In 1989, a uniformed Houston Police Department patrol sergeant by the name of Don Harford arrested Mr. Boney for this outstanding warrant. Apparently, Mr. Boney enjoyed special status in the eyes of the upper leadership and politicians, and Sergeant Harford was in trouble. An Internal Affairs investigation was initiated, and he was given several days off without pay for making the arrest. I believe the department cited him for "failure to use good judgment," which is a catchall to use where there is no applicable law or Departmental General Order or rule that fits. Don Harford didn't take it lying down and appealed his suspension, and after a long fight had it overturned.

Again, not all the Houston Police Department's Command Staff were incompetent, career-opportunist politicians who were seemingly willing to prostitute their integrity to get ahead and score political points but some, in my mind, were. To those who were not of this ilk and were willing to make moral, sound, politically unpopular decisions (despite the reality that the decision was not best for their career enhancement), you have my respect. That's true leadership!

DEPARTMENT LAWYERS!

There is a saying that the Houston Police Department is run by the lawyers (Office of Legal Services). They appear to hold considerable sway and influence over some members of the Command Staff. To the rank-and-file, their primary consideration in decision-making is to avoid lawsuits and avoid having to pay money out in settlements. We joked that if the lawyers had it their way, police officers would make no arrests and would sit at the station, be dispatched to a call, return to the station, write their report—then repeat. That police officers should be more like security guards—only there to observe and report, while creating a perception of security to the public. One executive assistant chief once explained to me that his job was not to protect the officers or employees, but the entire department. The individual employee's career (in the tide of perceived public opinion) was ultimately expendable for the collective good of the department— even if he or she had done no wrong!

Sometimes the lawyers came up with unfathomable decisions or gave advice that adversely affected the department, causing us to shake our heads in bewilderment.

For example, while assigned to Proactive Internal Affairs, we were contacted by supervisors in the Vice Division. One of their undercover officers had made telephone contact with a man who was advertising to "meet someone" in a local newspaper classified ad that was known to be a front for the solicitation of prostitution. Later, after making contact and during the initial phone conversation with the prospective john, he made it known that he wanted to dress up like a woman and then be bent over and sodomized with a device wielded by the prospective prostitute (the undercover Vice officer). The customer went into great detail about how

83

he wanted the experience to transpire and that he kept his "costume" and other equipment in the attic of his house where his wife wouldn't find it. The Vice officer, feigning great interest and excitement in being able to participate in this "adventure," then inquired whether he would pay for the services, as she was a working girl. John said yes! He would pay $250.00 for her services (a criminal offense—Solicitation of Prostitution). Then the kicker! During their phone conversation, in the background, the undercover officer heard transmissions over a police radio and immediately recognized it as being Houston Police Department radio traffic. She then asked, Are you a police officer or a fireman? He responded that he was a policeman, and that she didn't need to worry about being arrested, because he was not a Vice officer!

We were able to identify the john. He was a Houston police officer and, at the time of his call with the female Vice officer, was on duty. The undercover Vice officer had also recorded the call, and we met with the prosecuting attorneys in the Public Integrity Division. They said under normal circumstances they might accept criminal charges, but because the suspect was a police officer and the subsequent difficulties in prosecution, they wanted a sting operation where the prostitution of solicitation would be face-to-face and also clandestinely videotaped and documented by our Proactive IAD Unit to have overwhelming evidence if there were a jury trial.

Fair enough!

Next Friday night, we arranged a meeting with John through our undercover Vice officer.

They were to meet at a local hotel. But he was a no-show.

We had our Vice officer call John the next day, and he made some plausible excuses (needed a babysitter) but he still really, really wanted this experience and again offered $250.00 for this sex act, plus some extra money for her inconvenience.

The next Friday night, we tried one more time and John was again a no-show.

We eventually figured out or suspected that John was only interested at the present time in talking about the experience that he was fantasizing about. He was not quite ready to actually bend over and go through with it.

The unit got busy with more actionable intelligence regarding police officer dope rippers and we broke contact with John and moved on to other investigations. However, several months later, he was back at it again and we had another Vice officer in our office with a voice recording where John was soliciting for a certain sexual experience (it was the same as before) and how much money he would pay for it.

So maybe, we thought, our friend John was now serious and ready to bring his sex fantasy to fruition and we could then satisfy the evidentiary concerns of the prosecutors and make the criminal case. The next Friday night, just like before, we arranged a meeting at another local hotel, with the undercover female officer. And guess what? He was a no-show!

My lieutenant was not having it and in consultation with the Internal Affairs captain, directed us to bring John in, relieve him of duty and write up an administrative case against him for Engaging in Criminal Activity. Even though the Harris County District Attorney's Office had cold feet about filing the actual criminal case, John was guilty of Solicitation of Prostitution, an offense that many citizens in Houston are prosecuted and convicted for in monotonous regularity.

John's administrative case went up the chain of command. All the mid-decision makers recommended that his employment should be terminated, because while on duty he had engaged in criminal activity (soliciting a prostitute). But not the department's lawyers! Upon reviewing the case, they got worried, concluding (by themselves) that John might have some gender identity issue/crisis and if he were fired, it might open the department up to a potential lawsuit. At that time, discrimination against transgender or "gender confused" persons in the workplace was just becoming a hot-topic issue. Never mind that John had, many times, even while on duty, solicited the services of a prostitute. Or that if he had been an ordinary citizen, he would have been arrested and probably convicted. John was ultimately cited and given a minor reprimand for "Conducting Personal Business While on Duty" and was quickly returned to active duty status. It was awkward over the years when I would see him at department gatherings. Years later, I heard he had gone AWOL from the department (no longer bothered coming to work) and had left his wife for a man.

The issue was not John's sexuality, gender confusion, or unusual kinks (all of this was none of our business). The issue was that, while on duty as a police officer, he was engaging in criminal activity, by soliciting the services of a prostitute. But the department lawyers were afraid of a lawsuit and thought it better to sweep John's criminal conduct under a rug.

Before my five years in Proactive Internal Affairs was up, my stars lined up and I was reassigned me to a highly sought-after position in the department. Before I left for my new assignment, Billy and I received an award for our work in the dismantling of several "nests" of corrupt Houston police officers who were engaged in the dope ripping business. Because of the semisecret, classified nature of our work, the award was given to us by the chief of police in the privacy of his office, with only a few high-ranking members of the department present.

For several years after leaving Proactive Internal Affairs, they called me back from time to time to help facilitate sting operations, or just so they could pick my brain.

CHAPTER 5

SPECIAL WEAPONS AND TACTICS (SWAT)

So many times in the Houston Police Department, your career path depends on timing. For me personally, that was while I was in Proactive Internal Affairs. Only a few of the mid and upper managers even knew about the intricate sting operations we were doing and the success we were having. Unfortunately, for some in the department, the knowledge that you were assigned to the unit could also be a career hindrance. Some departments' mid and upper managers had skeletons in their closets and if you had been a sergeant in Proactive Internal Affairs, you might know all their "secrets" and they preferred not to have you assigned to their division(s). For instance, one individual who I conducted a criminal investigation against was a close friend of an assistant chief. At the conclusion of the internal investigation (he knew I was the investigator), the district attorney's office declined to accept criminal charges, and the department proceeded with the administrative case and began termination proceedings.

He was ultimately not fired, but received rather light discipline in the form of several days off. Later, he was promoted to lieutenant and assigned to the Narcotics Division, where he remained for many years. Because of my previous investigation and knowledge of his personal affairs, I never considered seeking an assignment in that division for fear that I might end up being his subordinate. It would not be good!

Again, timing is everything. Unlike many police departments, the Houston Police Department's SWAT Detail is a full-time assignment (there is also a part-time team to serve as an adjunct). Its members are on call twenty-four hours a day, seven days a week, for special threat situations: hostage situations, barricaded suspects, or for planned high-risk warrant service or unique operations such as when we used certain squads to help facilitate the arrests of corrupt police officers while I was in Proactive Internal Affairs.

SWAT at that time had three sergeants assigned to it because the detail was split up into three sections. There were two "assault teams" and another team of "snipers" (the more politically correct term was "marksman").

One assault team sergeant was transferring out and if I wanted the job, it was pretty much mine. But I still had to pass all the testing, which would not be easy. There were written and psychological tests, and an oral interview. But the biggest hurdle was the physical test—very competitive and not fun! A two-mile run for time (under 16 minutes was the minimum time), as many sit-ups you can do in two minutes (50 minimum), and as many push-ups in two minutes (50 minimum). All the push-ups and sit-ups had to be done with perfect form.

However, just doing the minimum on the physical test would not cut it. Fortunately, I have always been a physical fitness enthusiast and when the test was announced, I was trained up and ready to go. I think I ran the two miles in under 14 minutes and did over 100 push-ups and 100 sit-ups.

I got the assignment.

A part of me didn't want to leave Proactive Internal Affairs. I really enjoyed "connecting the dots" and setting up sting operations and arresting corrupt police officers. But I couldn't stay indefinitely.

However, I was disconcerted when I spoke with the SWAT sergeant I was replacing. We had lunch a few times while we were waiting for our respective transfers to be approved. The reason he was leaving was because of his intense dislike of the captain of the Tactical Operations Division, who was over the SWAT Detail and mostly made all the decisions while the detail was deployed in a special threat situation. The sergeant who was leaving was well respected within the department, but told me he would have to leave before he was forced out by this captain. His criticisms were that over the past few years, during domestic violence-type hostage situations, when opportunities arose to save hostages (innocent lives), the captain—out of an abundance of caution (department civil liability)—would not allow police intervention or a hostage rescue. Unless the hostage taker could be "talked into surrendering" by the Hostage Negotiation Team, no hostage rescue or "preemptive action" (sniper shot) would be entertained. The officers assigned to the SWAT Detail referred to their acronym "SWAT" as meaning Sit, Wait, And Talk.

The departing sergeant also gave several specific incidents where there had been opportunities to save innocent lives but the captain would not authorize a rescue; members of the SWAT Detail had to stand down while hearing shots being fired in the objective (house they had surrounded), as the suspect began killing the hostages. Apparently, there was one notorious incident in Katy (a small city to the west of Houston) where Houston SWAT had been called out to and when negotiations failed, the suspect shot and killed several children. The SWAT officers listened outside as the shots rang out and were not allowed to enter and intervene. It was something that the public knew nothing about, having been carefully swept under the rug.

According to the sergeant, the mind-set of the SWAT captain was better the hostage(s) die by the suspect's hand than to risk a rescue and have the Houston Police Department's SWAT incur any civil liability by using deadly force.

This was a "dirty" secret not well known, even in the department, and the morale of the detail "behind the veil" was low because of it. Most SWAT officers were highly disciplined and motivated individuals and took much pride in their assignment. Secretly, they despised the captain who they saw as slovenly, sloppy, and more concerned about keeping his position. Under his leadership, the unit was not shooting many suspects—although not saving any innocent lives either. What also didn't help was the appearance that he spent most of the workday sleeping on the couch in his office, having worked his extra jobs (security consultant) late the previous nights.

The departing sergeant said that his relationship with the captain had recently gone from bad to worse. He referred to a recent hostage scene in the Greenspoint area of the city. A male suspect in an apartment was holding an infant hostage. The suspect was armed with a large knife and threatening to cut the throat of the child, apparently upset with the child's mother (his ex-girlfriend). Maybe in the mind of some male suspects, there is no better way to inflict great emotional harm on a mother than to kill her child or children.

The situation was tense. Several SWAT officers were actually in the apartment, only a few feet from the suspect who had a knife to the throat of the baby. A hostage negotiator was trying to talk the suspect down—but it wasn't happening.

The sergeant explained to me that on this particular scene, he was running the command post. The intelligence officer had determined the suspect's name and a quick computer check had shown that he had been arrested for numerous violent crimes. Since the captain was in the command post with him, the sergeant began arguing that there was at present an opportunity to safely kill the suspect and save the child. It would not be difficult. The suspect was stationary, at close range, and a precision shot could be easily fired into the suspect's cranial vault (to pierce the medulla), which would then instantly incapacitate him. If the situation continued, this opportunity could be lost and there was a great likelihood that the suspect would do exactly what he was threatening to do—kill the child! Much like what had supposedly happened at other SWAT scenes with this same captain, a fierce argument ensued within the command post. The sergeant was threatened with insubordination and the captain was adamant: no rescue, no shot would be taken!

Fortunately, the hostage negotiators did indeed talk the suspect into surrendering and no one was hurt. The sergeant told me he was looking for a new job somewhere in the department before they pushed him out.

This departing sergeant warned me about taking the SWAT Detail assignment, saying that in the long run I would be sorry and encouraged me to take a position in the Narcotics Division, where I had a standing invitation. But like I said, I didn't want to take a chance of having to work for one lieutenant assigned there who had been the subject of one of my investigations.

I went to SWAT.

Being assigned to the Houston Police Department's SWAT Detail is a unique assignment. The workday consisted of a lot of physical exercise to maintain oneself in top physical training (some guys took this more seriously than others). Also, perhaps not daily, but frequently, maintaining shooting proficiency with our various weapon systems. In the assault teams, this was with handguns (your choice) and the M4 carbine, while the snipers used various .223 rifle systems configured with telescopic sights (usually a Trijicon ACOG), and a bolt-action .308 with a higher magnification variable power scope. The .223 sniping systems were used more for close-range deployments, like within an apartment complex, while the .308 systems were used for longer range, where more precision and/or penetration was anticipated.

The only problem was when I got there, the M4 carbines that we had just bought from Colt were unreliable and frequently jammed. The guns were failing to extract, leaving an empty cartridge in the chamber while the bolt came back. Then, as the recoil spring overcame the inertia and went forward as normal, it stripped off a loaded round from the top of the magazine and then rammed the unfired cartridge nose-first into the rear of the fired empty cartridge left in the chamber. As soon as a jam occurred, the only thing to do was to transition immediately to your handgun. The guys were trying everything to solve the problem: different magazines, changing ammunition, meticulous cleaning, blowing out the gas tubes, etc. Nothing worked.

It was such a serious issue that, almost as soon as I arrived, I was sent off to a Colt Armorers school being held in San Antonio to learn all about our primary weapon system to be able to fix our guns.

After the school and as soon as I got back to the detail, I could diagnose the problem. When Colt manufactured this lot of guns (it must have been a Monday), they shipped them all with the wrong extractor springs. The extractor springs that were installed were too weak and during the extraction cycle, the extractor was slipping off the rim of the spent cartridge case.

After we installed the correct springs, our M4s ran just fine.

Most days, after physical training, the guys disappeared from the office. We were on an electronic tether (our pagers) and if needed, could be called out twenty-four hours a day, seven days a week for a special threat situation, which seemed back then to occur only every few months. The only semi-regular field operation(s) was high-risk warrants, usually narcotics related, where a "positive breach" was necessary because the doors of the crack house were believed to be fortified or the suspects inside were believed to be heavily armed. In these cases, we would use the "Beast," an armored vehicle (supposedly immune to most small arms gunfire) produced by Cadillac Gage with a heavy hydraulically operated arm up front and a large cylindrical steel bar mounted vertically at the end. When extended, this arm could then be used along with the forward momentum of the vehicle to easily force open fortified doors or rip down the exterior walls of houses or buildings—all to facilitate warrant service or to uncover an armed suspect hiding in a structure.

But even these high-risk warrants were far and few between. Mostly, when a division (like Narcotics) requested the services of the SWAT Detail for a planned operation, the division making the request was also on the hook for the overtime (it came out of their budgets). Back then, it was a moneymaker (along with special threat situations) for many guys in the unit and for the supervisors. So even though the actual operation might have only required a small team to clear the objective, often the entire detail was utilized, so everyone got a piece of the pie! The cost for using SWAT in these high-risk warrants became so expensive that some divisions were reluctant to use us because of the strain on their budgets and resented the appearance that the supervision in SWAT was gaming the system to make extra money in overtime.

One week of every month was devoted to training. There were multiple lesson plans that were regularly updated and each month during the training week, usually in sequential order, a lesson plan would be utilized as the basis for that month's training week; Monday through Thursday (Friday was always gun cleaning day). For example, one month's training week cycle might be Maritime Operations, the next month's training week, Dynamic Entry and Room Clearing, the next, Vehicle Assaults, etc. In addition, during the year, the detail would also put on schools, mostly high-risk warrant type training for other HPD units and/or other police departments.

I have to give the Houston Police Department SWAT Detail credit. Most of the internal training within the Houston Police organization is geared or dumbed down to the lowest dominator—even the most dim-witted, least motivated, least capable Houston Police officer can pass; pretty much all that is required is a heartbeat. Not so in the schools SWAT puts on. The SWAT Basic School was a physically grueling, six-day school designed (within the limits of civilian law enforcement) to see whether the student had the prerequisite foundations (physical fitness, mental toughness, decision-making, ability to take criticism, etc.) necessary to be assigned to SWAT. The school sucked and to do well, you had to physically train for it. One just didn't show up and go through it. Those who were not prepared flunked out, injured themselves, or just didn't show up the next day. In other departments, the SWAT Basic School is more of a "gentleman's" course and far more benign. Not Houston's!

Still, I imagine military special forces training was much more difficult and intensive than SWAT's. By day two of my stint going through Houston's Basic SWAT School, we had been running hills, crawling through bayous, and doing wind sprints all while carrying our rifles, wearing heavy armor, and with our gas masks on, etc., for hours. While we were about to transition to another training evolution, I was making small talk with another participant who had just a few years before been a United States Navy SEAL. I asked him how Houston's SWAT Basic School compared to the Navy's Basic Underwater Demolition/SEAL Training—"Hell Week." He just smiled and laughed. I forgot about all that swimming in cold water! He was a good guy with a great attitude.

After flying through the SWAT Basic School, the ex-Navy SEAL was not selected for the full-time SWAT Detail. Sadly I noted, particularly in later basic schools, several veterans who had also previously served in highly regarded "high speed" military units breezed through the training course but were not selected. I realized that some leadership within the SWAT Detail had a bias against ex-military Special Forces members and appeared to be threatened by them (*they might know more than we do*). Mostly, back then, it was harder for previous military members to get a position within Houston's SWAT Detail. Successfully passing the SWAT Basic School was not a guarantee; rather, there was a *very* subjective evaluation of your overall personal attributes, which was the real hurdle to being hired to either the full-time or part-time team. One former Green Beret who, when asked by another SWAT supervisor which one was harder—the SWAT Basic School or the United States Army's Special Forces training—answered that his special forces training was much more difficult; it didn't even compare! This applicant was then blackballed. They deemed him "cocky" and dropped from consideration.

One of my all-time favorite members of the SWAT Detail back then was Patrick Straker, affectionately known to all as "Hootie" because at one time he sang lead in a Country and Western band. Over the years, Pat's path and mine would intersect frequently in dramatic fashion. I learned much while assigned to SWAT and talked to an experienced former SWAT sergeant from the Los Angeles Police Department (LAPD), Ron McCarthy. As many people know, the LAPD was credited with the concept of these types of special teams back in the 1960s. One thing I learned from Ron was an easily understood and remembered mantra that he taught regarding threat/risk assessment as it applied to police tactical operations:

You Risk a Lot to Save a Lot!

You Risk a Little to Save a Little!

You Risk Nothing to Save Nothing!

The concept is simple. It applies to the saving of innocent human life. For example, as a sworn police officer, you should be prepared to personally risk your life and (if a supervisor) even those of your subordinates; to place yourself or them in personal danger if the need arises to protect innocent life. As police officers, you took a solemn oath to be the guardians and protectors.

This simple concept was actually at odds with my training as a police cadet and what was espoused in later years within the Officer Safety Unit of the Houston Police Department. The mind-set that the only thing that was important (in the context of police officers performing their sworn duties) was that you (the police officer) come home safe at the end of your workday.

For example, you're a SWAT supervisor at a hostage scene. The suspect is the ex-husband. He has a gun. He is threatening to kill the kids. From inside the objective, shots ring out and screaming is heard. At the first inkling that a shooting had taken place or even before the shots were fired (depending on a totality of the exigent circumstances), the hostage rescue should be ordered and the tactical officers should endeavor to get between the suspect and his intended victims and neutralize the suspect ASAP. This direct action puts the involved officers at great risk, but because of their training (surprise, speed, and violence of action), equipment (heavy body armor, ballistic helmets, shields, etc.) and their mind-set, there is a high probability that no officers will be injured and innocent life will be saved.

In these types of situations, hard decisions have to be made quickly by law enforcement, particularly the supervisors and commanders. All the officers assigned to the Houston Police Department SWAT Detail at the time had the requisite personal qualities such as great courage and the skill sets to perform such a mission. Not so much for some supervisors.

Conversely, if you're a SWAT supervisor on the scene of a suicidal person (or any barricaded suspect) who is armed with a firearm or other credible weapon, but with no hostages and who will not exit a residence or a building, then there is normally no reason to make entry or for any police officer to place themselves at risk. The fact is that there is no innocent life to save. Let the hostage negotiators try to talk the barricaded person into exiting or surrendering. We're not going to go in after them! At worst, if the situation becomes protracted and it calls for it, shoot tear gas into the objective and force him out into the open where he doesn't have any cover or concealment and we (SWAT) have a much superior tactical advantage!

As a side note, we found that, not infrequently, barricaded suicidal individuals were intending to "commit suicide by cop" and were maybe unsure just how proficient the first responding uniform police officers would be in accomplishing this. So they would wait till SWAT arrived on the scene and then start a confrontation by exiting (while brandishing a weapon), and approach a SWAT officer who would be in a position manning the inner perimeter. They were probably thinking the SWAT officers would do the best job in killing them as compared to the average patrol officer. Very sad but true; if they were armed with a firearm, then either the engaged SWAT officer or the sniper covering that area would have to use deadly force, because of the imminent threat.

Upon arriving on a scene with a barricaded suicidal person, one of the first things to do if it was both safe and feasible, before the Hostage Negotiation Team (HNT) arrived and set up shop, was to actually tie off, with rope, the outer doors of the objective (most outside doors except those on trailers open inward) to prevent the suicidal person from easily exiting the building and confronting officers. One basic tactic that HNT used in these situations to deter suicidal persons from committing suicide by cop (if they got out of the objective) was to establish communication and articulate to them that SWAT would *not* kill them, but because SWAT officers were so highly trained, if they attempted to confront them (suicide by cop), then a sniper would just wound them by shooting them in the knee with a .308 rifle. The wound would be extremely painful, but not fatal! Usually HNT was good about getting the suspects to surrender, but not always. Sometimes the suicidal person ultimately died by their own hands. And with those seeking suicide by cop, if they were motivated enough and had a credible weapon, it could end in a tragedy, despite the best efforts of HNT.

Suicide by cop is quite a problem, and tactical units with trained counselors/communicators (HNT) are best equipped to handle these scenes.

Sadly, the philosophy of You Risk a Lot to Save A Lot—You Risk Nothing to Save Nothing was not yet mainstream in the police tactical community, before the massacre at Columbine High School in 1999. Two students went on a murderous spree inside their high school, killing twelve students and faculty members and injuring twenty-one others. Eventually, the two suspects killed themselves. What is not widely known is that that the police doctrine at the time called for the initial responders (patrol officer) to such an incident to surround the location, not to go inside, and to wait till the SWAT Detail and supervisors arrived to handle it! At Columbine, this is exactly what happened. As innocent children were being shot and killed inside the school, the responding patrol officers did exactly what they had been trained to do. They set a perimeter outside the school and they didn't engage the suspects. They waited for the area SWAT Detail. By the time SWAT finally entered the school, the killing was long over and so was the dying. There is evidence that wounded innocent victims bled out and could have otherwise been saved if they received medical intervention in a timely fashion. Because even after the killing stopped, nothing was done quickly to stop the dying. How many innocent lives could have been saved—risk a lot to save a lot! Sadly, the responding police uniform units were just following the standard training protocols at the time.

The Columbine massacre was a pivotal moment for many police administrators. It was suddenly realized that when seconds count, SWAT is a half hour away. With the rise of active shooter events, many police departments embraced this new reality and began developing policy and commensurate training: rank-and-file patrol officers were no longer to wait for SWAT but to go in and "neutralize" the active shooter immediately!

It would seem obvious but this was a radical new way of thinking for some police trainers and administrators, particularly for administrators with no real-world police experience.

Many police departments (including Houston's) had preached in ongoing annual police training and as well as to their police trainees that the most important thing in a police critical incident was *you*, and that *you* be able to go home to your family that night! That above all things, don't do anything or take any action where you might get hurt; take cover and don't leave it! For a brief time, the Houston Police Academy taught cadets that if you, as a police officer, could not react at a critical incident (frozen in fear), then just endeavor to be a "good witness!"

The problem with this doctrine of "me first" was that if correctly applied, no police officer would ever risk his life to save an innocent person. There is no reason to go into the school building and confront the bad guy(s) killing all the kids—he might shoot *me*!

After the Columbine massacre and advent of active shooter training, the principle adopted by many (not all) police officers was it is my sworn duty to protect innocent life. The life of the innocent was more important than our own—we will engage!

Unfortunately, some police officers are not of that ilk and will not place themselves in danger when appropriate. There is no way to predict how an officer will react in that ultimate crisis moment. Later, when I became an Active Shooter Instructor for HPD, we endeavored to train the entire department in this new mind-set, while also providing good, solid tactics. The other instructors and I were sometimes disheartened to overhear comments made by some officer/students: "I will never go in" or "They don't pay me enough to do that." Sadly, this is probably true in any large police organization. There are always those who lack "something" and should have probably sought some other career choice. I was also suspicious of the "macho cop" who displayed an overabundance of bravado. I suspected that this over-hyped bravado was false and he or she was overcompensating for something they were lacking internally.

In my experience, some police administrators are perhaps still ignorant or don't embrace the principle of the lives of innocent citizens being the most important for police tactics/doctrine. They are more concerned with the special interest group perception, politics, or potential civil actions against the city.

The unnamed sergeant who I had replaced in SWAT had warned me; he was not lying!

On the west side of Houston, a drama was unfolding. A woman who had lived in another part of the county had fled to Houston to escape her unstable and violent ex-husband. She had come to Houston to start a new life. Until she could afford her own residence, she was staying at a girl-friend's apartment. Her ex-husband learned where she was seeking sanctuary and drove all the way to Houston.

He found her.

He confronted her in the apartment complex parking lot, where she was living, at about 2:30 p.m. They were arguing and people were watching. During the argument, he pulled a .45 caliber pistol out of his waistband and shot her in the upper thigh. She went down screaming (wounded but at the time very much alive). He then grabbed her by her long hair and, while she was still screaming, dragged her caveman style into the apartment where she had been staying. He then slammed the door shut. They were both inside. Patrol officers quickly arrived at the scene and the call for SWAT went out immediately. Since it was at the end of the workday (SWAT's normal duty hours) we were still on duty and close by; unlike most callouts, we were at the scene in a short time. I was the first to arrive.

Knowing that the hostage was seriously wounded and time was of the essence, I decided that as soon as enough members of the detail arrived, we were going in. We would start an immediate hostage rescue, to save her life, before she could succumb to her wounds (bleed out). Other members of the detail soon arrived and we were forming up, only moments away from breaching the front door and rescuing her.

Then the captain of Tactical Operations and the SWAT Detail walked up to my position.

"What do you think you are doing?" he asked.

I gave him the scenario. "We still have time to save her!"

I looked to my breaching team as they waited for the nod of my head to start the hostage rescue.

Then the captain said, "No, you're not!" And added, "She's probably already dead. Stand down!"

We knew she wasn't dead—we could still hear her moaning!

I argued.

Then I was given a direct order: no rescue attempt!

Approximately twelve hours later, the hostage negotiators were able to talk the gunman into surrendering; he exited the apartment and was taken into custody. As soon as he exited and was handcuffed, the SWAT commander allowed us to go inside the apartment and "rescue" the hostage. When we found her, she was dead. Predictably, while we waited impotently outside and HNT talked, she had lost consciousness and bled to death.

I was beyond words! The other members of the detail were not surprised—it was what they were used to. It was business as usual! What was important, apparently for the captain, was that the unit he was responsible for had not been put into a position to have had to use deadly force and maybe kill a suspect. I perceived his attitude toward the death of this innocent hostage as one of general callous indifference!

One patrol officer who had made the original call and was still on the scene lost it! I didn't blame him. He vented on me—a sergeant and supervisor of the SWAT Detail—"FU...K YOU GUYS!" Jabbing his finger at me, he continued on a rant, cursing us (HPD SWAT) and questioning why the department even bothered having a SWAT Detail. "What the *FU...K ARE YOU GUYS GOOD FOR!*" He shouted that he was sorry that he had even called for us! Had he known we would not do anything, he and his fellow patrol officers would have taken the initiative, gone in and tried to save her!

Twenty years later, thinking about that innocent woman lying there in that apartment— dead, covered in blood, her lifeless eyes still open with her mouth agape—still makes me sick with emotion.

There is little doubt in my mind that we could have saved her.

We should have gone in. Maybe I should have had the personal courage to disobey the captain in that moment and just nodded my head to give the go signal to the breaching team to proceed with the rescue. But I didn't.

I vowed to myself to never let it happen again.

RISK A LOT TO SAVE A LOT!

I was not a good fit in the Houston Police Department's SWAT Detail. I was a workaholic and the detail only trained about four to six days of the month, besides each member's personal fitness training. The callouts to special threat scenes and high-risk warrants were infrequent back then.

I was bored and had a bright idea. I always had a lot of respect and affection for the average patrol officer. These men and women were often the unsung heroes of the department; they were the ones who were really the department's "point of the spear." They were also, mostly, the ones most at risk for being injured or killed.

I thought SWAT officers were being underutilized and had more to offer the department, particularly in helping the patrol officers. With the approval of my lieutenant, I pushed forward a program where instead of disappearing after the morning workout, the SWAT officers would get into marked police vehicles and back up patrol officers in high priority calls, particularly robbery in-progress calls. Historically, many robbery in-progress calls occurred during the day shift when the commercial businesses were open. It was in responding to these types of dangerous in-progress calls where your average street cop could easily be killed or wounded by bad guy gunfire.

Why not have the most highly trained and presumably most motivated officers and sergeants in the department run or at least back up the patrol officers in these most dangerous of calls?

It didn't go over well. Although some younger SWAT officers wanted to contribute more to the "mission," some more seasoned members (the informal leaders) were much opposed. The other two sergeants in the detail also wanted no part of it.

For so many years, the Houston Police Department's SWAT Detail had been run like a country club. A previous member of the Command Staff had been a big sports enthusiast and saw that many of the "athletes" from the department's softball and basketball team were placed on the detail as a reward. He had also "promised them" that because they were on call all the time, they were not expected to do such things (run patrol calls) during their regular duty hours.

I was in trouble. The informal leaders didn't like the direction I was pushing the detail in and the other sergeants were not supporting me. Worse, as the weeks went by, members of the Command Staff received anonymous letters, complaining about the new direction of the detail, the resulting bad morale and that I was the cause (they were right). I suspect that I also didn't have the support of the captain who had the "don't create any waves, just maintain the status quo" sort of mentality. He also probably knew that I didn't hold him in high regard.

After a few years, I was "pushed" out of SWAT and headed back to my home at the North Shepherd Patrol Division.

In retrospect and fairness to HPD SWAT, there were several (particularly the younger) operators who were both highly motivated and talented in the detail back then. Maybe because being on call twenty-four hours a day, seven days a week is such a stressor, I was wrong. Maybe it would have been best to not push so hard to fill the normal uncommitted workday of SWAT by riding around in marked units, running dangerous calls. But then again, I was a workaholic.

And that was a problem!

CHAPTER 6

NORTH PATROL DIVISION

It was good to be back to my old home, North Shepherd Patrol!

In the years I had been gone, the North Shepherd Patrol Division had been renamed and had physically moved to a purpose-built facility in the heart of the Acres Homes community. Now it was known as "North Patrol." Although I had been gone for a long time, I was still well remembered by many of the officers and sergeants still assigned there.

It was refreshing to no longer be on call 24/7 like in SWAT or to have the burden of being the case agent of a significant police corruption investigation. Every day as a sergeant in patrol was a new day. You did your eight hours and dealt with whatever happened, and the next day would be a new day. Also, there was a lot of camaraderie at North and the morale was high.

But it became clear to me personally, that in my careerism and tendency to be a workaholic, I had neglected my wife Samantha (Sam).

We had lived in the same apartment complex; after noticing her at the pool, one day we were introduced. We started casually seeing each other while we both still dated others.

Samantha was a catch. Not only was she beautiful, but she was a woman of great character, besides being a lot of fun to be around.

She was way out of my league.

Samantha and I were married in June 1989. I still don't know why she married me, but am eternally grateful that she did.

Now, Sam had a career and made nearly as much money as I did. But being a career woman was not her desire: she wanted children; she wanted to be a mother! I knew of her desire but really didn't seriously consider it and perhaps saw fatherhood as a potential hindrance and a distraction to my career. I really didn't entertain her desire.

I was selfish—my life was all about me.

Early in our marriage, Sam had become pregnant. We didn't know, but it was a tubular pregnancy and eventually the tube ruptured. One morning, Sam was in terrible pain and I rushed her to the nearest hospital emergency room, where I watched as the on-duty doctor examined her. In a short time, Sam was in emergency surgery. She was saved. The baby she was carrying was dead.

In the years after that terrible day, we had the usual tests done by fertility specialists. The consensus was we could not conceive a child. The only option was in vitro fertilization. The doctor warned that the procedure was to implant several eggs to increase the chances of one being viable; however, if too many of the implanted eggs became viable, then it would be necessary to perform selective abortion to limit the number of developing children in her womb. We both were strongly opposed to abortion and could not in good conscience take that chance or even consider doing this.

After the fertility tests and consultation(s), we had talked about adoption. Not only would it give us the opportunity to have a family, but we felt that as pro-life Christians, we should put our lives and money where our faith was, if the situation arose to adopt children who would have otherwise been aborted. Yet, while I intellectually subscribed to this ideal, it still came in as a distant second place to my career. All the while, my wife waited patiently for me to get my "mind right."

I was getting close to being forty, and now decided to actively pursue parenthood. In October 2000, I gave Samantha the green light.

Samantha started researching and sending out applications to area adoption agencies. We also attended several adoption seminars.

In December 2000, out of the blue, Samantha got a phone call. A small adoption agency in a neighboring city had a newborn baby girl they were trying to place. Samantha had only sent the agency a preliminary application, and we weren't even on the list of prospective eligible parents. But, there was a caveat—a major complication. The birth mother was a registered Cherokee Indian and the Cherokee Nation had considerable say over who would be able to ultimately adopt the child. The entire process with the Cherokee Nation would take months and there was no guarantee that even if Samantha and I took the child into our house and began the adoption process that we could make her a permanent part of our family. Also, even though it would be a closed adoption, the birth mother had a say in the process and whichever couple(s) agreed to begin the adoption process would have to be "approved" or selected by her.

Samantha and I had to make a fast decision that would have profound consequences in the lives of many people. That same day, we called back the adoption agency and told them we were willing to adopt the child, knowing that from the beginning it was not a sure thing and that the Cherokee Nation had the final say.

Everything now went into hyperdrive. The State of Texas required a home study by a licensed social worker to make sure we were suitable parents. There were documents to be submitted and paperwork to be completed before we could take custody of this newborn baby girl. We had not even been to the adoption agency. Heck, we were not even set up with a baby room and all the "equipment" and support systems that were apparently necessary for the induction of a baby into a modern household.

About a week later, the preliminary paperwork was completed, as well as the "rushed" home study. We drove to the adoption agency, picked up the child, brought her home, and named her Rebekah.

It was a battle to keep Rebekah. The Cherokee Nation wanted her to go to another family who were registered members of the nation. A lawyer had to be hired to represent Rebekah and to protect our interests. We had bonded with her, as she had with us. Ultimately, some ten months after I first held her, we were able to formally adopt her as our own. The Cherokee Nation asked that we register her as a member of the tribe and that we raise her with the knowledge of her ancestors.

Samantha was a mother, and I was a father. Life was no longer about me.

Being a father changed my life. I fell in love with Rebekah shortly after we adopted her and can't imagine loving her anymore even if she were our natural child. Soon Samantha was working only part-time at her job and transitioned to being a full-time mom. Losing her income was significant, and we struggled. To pay for the costs associated with adopting Rebekah, we went into debt and times were tough. But that was okay.

A year after adopting Rebekah, I wanted to do it again—adopt another child before Samantha and I were too old. We had a few promising leads on newborn babies but they all fell through.

I wanted to adopt from China, to be part of the solution of the failed "One Child" policy instituted by Mao Zedong (Chairman Mao) in post-World War II. I found the story of baby girls in China tragic. Because of the cultural preference for male children, baby girls—if born, if unwanted—sometimes "disappear" (gendercide) or are abandoned.

In retrospect, part of my rationale for being such an advocate for adoption was because it really made a difference in the life of a human being. Again, it was about innocent life.

Samantha was initially unsure about adopting from China. Fortunately, a couple visited our church who had recently adopted a little girl from China. Samantha picked their brain about the China adoption process. She was won over; we would try to adopt from China.

It took time to process all the paperwork for a Chinese adoption (all the forms and documents had to be converted to Chinese). But once submitted and after months of waiting, we received a referral (a child assigned to you) from the Chinese government. We received a picture of a beautiful little girl, perhaps three or four months old, who had been found abandoned in Fuzhou City (Jiangxi Province) and placed in an orphanage. All the information we received was the picture, and a one-page form letter (in Chinese) indicating that her health status was "normal"; the administrators in the orphanage had named her Fu Zong Fang and estimated her date of birth. We were directed to check one of two boxes: "We accept the child mentioned above" or "We cannot accept the child mentioned above." It was a no-brainer—we accepted.

Shortly after "accepting" and making the travel plans, we were in China. After navigating all the government red tape, we flew home with another child. We named her Rachel.

Samantha and I now had a family! I affectionately referred to my kids as "the big noisy one" (Rebekah) and "the little Chinese" one (Rachel).

For nearly the next ten years of my career, I kept an assignment in the department that would no longer require being on call 24/7 or running investigations and sting operations, which would keep me from my family days on end. Whereas before I had been all about the job, now it was more about raising two little girls and being a part of their lives.

As a patrol sergeant, I had a steady schedule: the same days off, the same duty hours. I left for work at the same time and returned at the same time. It was good.

But assignments in Field Operations (patrol) are not without personal risk and often it's the most dangerous place in a police department to work. What makes patrol so dangerous is the unexpected, the unknown: The 911 hang-up call you're dispatched to and when you arrive, you find an estranged husband cutting up his wife's body for easy disposal. The traffic stop for a routine violation that turns into a gunfight. One moment, you're driving down the street, trying to decide where to eat that day; the next moment, you're watching as several heavily armed suspects are robbing a bank.

Some field sergeants didn't lead from the front and spent most of their time hiding in their office, playing or watching videos on their computers. These same sergeants would also overcompensate, most notably in their radio communications, to create the impression of being involved and always working. They were often "Johnny on the spot" when it came to authorizing or making mundane, easy decisions related to their job, such as "I need a supervisor's approval to tow this abandoned vehicle from a moving lane of traffic." This type of sergeant would quickly answer with his unit numbers and give his permission. This breed of supervisor would, mostly, make it his or her habit to instantly answer the radio on inconsequential matters. They majored in the minors. They were pretenders, not leaders, and lived out their careers terrified of having to make a hard decision.

When patrol officers were yelling on the radio because they needed help, because they had a "crazy naked guy" who was armed with a machete running around the neighborhood threatening to kill everyone, that sergeant wasn't budging from his office, wasn't about to get on the radio, and for sure would not arrive on the scene until way after the drama had unfolded and the dust settled. He would let other sergeants handle it. When questioned by his peers about where he was, there was always a barely plausible excuse. After all, didn't he usually always answer his radio promptly and wasn't his paperwork submitted on time!

During my time in patrol, I was asked to teach newly promoted sergeants, heading to patrol, about managing the critical incident. One of the first things I would talk to the class about, particularly if they didn't have a strong background or affinity for patrol work, was to not be "that" sergeant.

In a large organization like the Houston Police Department, many of the officers promoted to sergeant are first assigned to patrol. Some of these newly promoted sergeants headed to patrol are stressed with the impending responsibility because they never were good patrol cops or had spent much time in a uniform field assignment. Fortunately, the Command Staff, seeing this pitfall in the promotion system, implemented a training program for newly minted sergeants, which then helped many of them to adapt, to give them the confidence and skill sets so they would not be "that" sergeant. I enjoyed mentoring these newly promoted "rookie sergeants." Most of the men and women who had spent years in patrol as officers already had the requisite skill sets and were "immediately good to go." Others who had spent years in investigative divisions might be a little rusty on patrol procedures and just needed some help to get up to speed.

I was really impressed with and learned much from several of the newly promoted female sergeants who had spent years in the Juvenile Division as Child Abuse or Child Sexual Abuse investigators. What a tough job!

Then there were some newly promoted sergeants who unfortunately were just plain lazy, incompetent, or just didn't have the right people skills. The ones of this ilk upset the troops every time they opened their mouths (yes, they had always been squirrels but now they were sergeant squirrels!).

As a patrol sergeant, you're always attached to your radio and monitoring the communications, making scenes that might turn into a critical incident, backing up officers in emergency calls, or just being ready to help solve problems or misunderstandings between the police and the citizens.

Listening to the radio became an ingrained subconscious habit; you were always evaluating the calls and the radio chatter. Over time, you became familiar with the voices of other officers and supervisors who you regularly worked with and could normally identify anyone, even if they only "broke the air" for but a word or two. This ability was important in an emergency, particularly if the involved officer needing the help and making the transmission garbled his unit identification numbers (very common in stressful situations). For instance: "6B ...ASSIST THE OFFICER!" As an experienced sergeant, you could often identify the involved officer by just briefly hearing part of his radio transmission. Then you could immediately inquire with the dispatcher, "Where is 6B12, Officer Baldwin, located?" Then assistance in the form of other officers or paramedics could be sent immediately to his location.

This "radio communication acuity" was important, particularly when working with older, experienced officers and sergeants who were not prone to excitement and were level-headed. It was sometimes hard to tell that they were in a dire situation when they were communicating over the radio, perhaps requesting backup. But if you knew the individual officer well enough, you could often detect a subtle change in the tone of their voice, over the radio, that would immediately catch your attention; something was not right, the involved officer was stressed.

One morning, an experienced officer was dispatched to an unknown disturbance at a business. The business was an importing company that brought sporting goods in from China, which then shipped these goods to retail stores across the country. Most of the front of the business was office space with many workstations for the administrative staff, which were located in cubicles or private offices. The rear of the building was comprised of a large warehouse.

I didn't think much of a citizen's call about some disturbance at the location. It amounted to an "unknown disturbance" type call, these being mundane and common. The dispatched officer arrived on the scene and soon got on the radio and in a low, even, unexcited voice, asked for more units to check by. I was familiar with the officer; he never got excited, but I noted a subtle difference in the tone of his voice. I sensed something bad was happening. I told the dispatcher to send the backup units—"Code 1" (emergency, lights, and sirens)—as I headed to the scene.

Soon I arrived.

It was bad.

A crowd of employees from the business gathered in the front parking lot, surrounding the officers who had just arrived. Some civilians were hysterical. There was a lot of pointing, gesturing, screaming, and yelling. Soon enough, we could decipher a rough picture; it was one of the worst-case scenarios. There was an active shooter inside the business; shots had been fired and were still being fired. An unknown number of employees inside had already been shot and their conditions were unknown. Other employees were still inside, presumably hiding in their offices or cubicles and they were being hunted down by the gunmen.

What to do?

We (the uniformed officers) acted immediately, within seconds. I took the "pick of the litter": the officers who were of known quality, clear thinking, and who were wearing body armor. We formed up, went in, and moved swiftly to the sounds of the gunfire and commotion. I was the only one with a long gun: a Benelli semiautomatic 12-gauge shotgun, loaded with rifled slugs. I took center, another officer covered to the left, another to the right, and another acted as the rear guard. We moved fast. We went past people cowering under their desks, past bullet holes in the wall, past a dead body lying on the floor. We moved around a hard corner and there, about ten yards away, was my active shooter: a small Asian woman, armed with a Glock pistol.

We were close (I was easily within her kill zone).

I wasn't waiting and didn't give any commands. I brought the Benelli up from the low ready while pushing off its safety, settled the front sight on her chest and hesitated for a split second. *Were there any innocent citizens downrange in my zone of fire?* My field of fire was clear of innocents. I began my trigger press and just before a one-ounce,.73 caliber lead slug ended her life, she dropped her gun and was no longer a threat. I didn't have to shoot her, and we easily took her into custody.

Only one person was killed. The shooter had just discovered that her sister was having an affair with her husband. They all worked together at the business. In addition, she had also learned that her coworkers knew about the ongoing affair, but had not told her. The affair and her ignorance of it had become a running joke and the center of gossip within the workplace. The body that we had passed was that of the suspect's sister. We had emergency medical services standing by, but nothing could be done; she was deceased. One bullet that her sister had fired had penetrated her cranial vault into her brain and she had died instantly. The suspect had also fired several other rounds inside the office, but fortunately no one else was injured.

Maybe we saved some lives on this day.

The department later gave the four of us Meritorious Service Medals.

It wasn't really a hard decision. There are many men and women in the Houston Police Department who have internally reflected on what they would do in a similar situation and have already concluded that the lives of innocent citizens come before their own. But not all!

RISK A LOT TO SAVE A LOT!

During my time back in patrol, I began working with Kenneth Bounds, who went by the name Heath. Heath had just been promoted to sergeant, and we found a commonality in that we liked to work and had a strong affection for the rank-and-file police officer who were assigned to field operations (patrol) and for all the risk and burdens that entailed. Heath and I had a lot of similar ideas about how to make patrol a safer place to work and together we pushed those ideas up the chain of command for consideration by the Command Staff. Over the next few years, we format-ted these ideas into written proposals in "official" formal correspondence(s) and sent them to the chief of police via our chain of command. We would then also pitch the proposal to the Houston Police Officers' Union, which was the majority bargaining agent with the city and presumably would be another interested party in making Field Operations (patrol) a better place to work for the officers.

The ideas we formally pitched to the Command Staff included:

New Uniforms: Dark navy-blue with an option for body armor worn on the outside to be more comfortable and increase the likelihood that officers would wear armor (back then, the wearing of body armor by patrol officers was optional). Even when the wearing of body armor eventually became mandatory, many supervisors and officers still ignored it. Unless you have worn body armor in July, August, or September in Houston, Texas, you will never realize just how uncomfortable and hot it can be. At that time, the uniform shirts were a light-baby blue color, which in most of the country was the color of a security guard's uniform. The dark navy blue was more universally known as the uniform color for police officers. Citizens mistaking police officers for security guards can be an issue and can lead to serious misunderstandings, with potentially tragic results.

While I was in the academy, Officer Witcher told me that at one time, one member of the Houston Police Department's Command Staff, one of the deputy chiefs, had a side business running a security guard company. His security guard service watched over and provided private security for the River Oaks community, a very influential area in Houston where the wealthiest citizens live. The deputy chief wanted to blur the lines between the real police and his security guards; by utilizing his official position and influence, he was able to change the uniforms of Houston police officers so they bore a remarkable resemblance to the employees of this security guard company. I guess that many citizens, when making contact or seeing his security guards in this rich neighborhood, assumed that they were police officers.

Weapon Mounted Lights: Some more tragic officer-involved shootings that have occurred in the history of the Houston police department involved officers killing unarmed citizens when the officers incorrectly perceived what was in a citizen's hand, thinking they had some weapon. Over the years, there were several shootings where it was thought that the suspect was brandishing a weapon when in fact he was trying to discard incriminating evidence like a short piece of glass pipe commonly used to smoke crack cocaine with. Many of these shootings occur in diminished light or in darkness. It is difficult to fire a handgun one handed, while holding a flashlight in the other. It's also almost impossible to successfully manipulate a long gun (which requires two hands) and a light at the same time. At the time Heath and I started pushing this technology, the police use of weapon mounted lights was becoming mainstream with more progressive police agencies. But not the Houston Police Department, which had more of a "years of tradition unencumbered by progressive thinking" sort of mentality.

In particular, Heath and I saw the adoption of weapon mounted lights as a big issue, particularly as it struck at the heart of not shooting someone who didn't need to be shot! One night, Heath and I checked by at the aftermath of a vehicle pursuit. The suspect had stopped in the driveway of a residence and was not complying with the commands of the officers, who correctly had not approached him and maintained their positions of cover behind their police vehicles. As we arrived and during the process of talking the suspect out of his vehicle, he was observed to have something in his hand. Heath initially perceived it to be a handgun and nearly shot the suspect, but didn't when the suspect brought the object up to his ear and Heath realized that it was a cell phone. The suspect was drunk, had ignored the officer's commands, and was calling his mother to come help him. Heath, an experienced police officer, was shaken by what had nearly occurred and firmly believed that if he had a weapon mounted light, he would have more quickly identified the item in the suspect's hand as a non-weapon and not come as close as he did to a needless tragedy. He had almost killed a man who was not a threat.

We also pushed other ideas forward: Gunshot trauma kits in all the police vehicles to provide lifesaving medical aid to both innocent citizens and suspects in the event of a shooting or traumatic injury, to be used when emergency medical technicians were not immediately available. Breaching kits in all the patrol supervisors' vehicles, to be used when a forced entry was needed such as in an active shooter event, when moments counted, to save innocent lives. Aimpoints on patrol carbines, to enable more precision shooting so that innocent bystanders were not endangered.

The Houston Police Department's Command Staff ignored us and all these ideas. Their prevailing attitude was "it's not a good idea until it's our idea!" Apparently we were creating work for them with these ideas and they were content with the status quo. In the Houston Police Department, requests or ideas coming from the bottom of the organization (in this case from mere sergeants) was not appreciated. We sometimes ran into open hostility and severe criticism from the upper management (Command Staff), whereas we had the support of the mid-managers like the lieutenants and captains. Heath and I were openly disparaged because we wanted to change the color of the uniforms. Members of the Command Staff didn't want to consider changing because it was "departmental tradition," or they would get on a soapbox and talk about how proudly they had worn this uniform for the last thirty years and that officers had died wearing this uniform. In the culture of the Houston Police Department, changing the color of the uniforms was a huge deal and highly divisive. Heath and I were the evil instigators.

The biggest trouble came with the weapon mounted lights. We thought it was a no-brainer—it would help prevent some needless shootings (did the suspect have a gun or a pen in his hand?). By this time, the Houston Police Officers' Union had appointed me as their representative to various Houston Police Department committees, including the Uniform, Weapons, and Critical Incident Committees, where I had frequent "discussions" with the Command Staff. The subject of weapon lights blew up. After we brought it up and kept pushing for their widespread usage, a new General Order was issued that weapon mounted lights (and electronic sights on carbines) were expressly prohibited!

The Houston Police Officers' Union, Heath, and I pushed back. Why, we wanted to know.

We got our answer. The Command Staff, in conjunction with the department lawyers, were afraid that there might be some idiot patrol officer out there, who, lacking a proper handheld flashlight, would use his weapon mounted light to direct traffic or use it to illuminate a traffic citation so a citizen could sign it. The obvious answer to this was that the vast majority of officers had the good common sense to use this tool appropriately (also why we have training) and if we had an isolated incident, then discipline the squirrel who did it! If, because of weapon mounted lights, we saved one innocent life, did not shoot just one suspect who did not need to be shot, wouldn't it be worth it? I was upset and wrote a formal letter up the chain of command and also "ghost wrote" an article for the police union's monthly newspaper. In both, I denounced the new policy and called it *ill conceived*!

Maybe I shouldn't have used the word *ill conceived*.

It didn't go well. I hurt some feelings. Shortly after my correspondence went up the chain of command and the article was published in the union newspaper, I was summoned to the office of a Command Staff member, one of the assistant chiefs rumored to have been appointed to his position, not so much on ability, but because of the department's need for a specific minority representative. I sat in his outer office for approximately half an hour before he decided that he was ready to "receive me." Then, after I was allowed into his presence, I was the recipient of a "very vigorous butt chewing." The central theme to my butt chewing was "WHO DO YOU

THINK YOU ARE!" It was implied that, I—a lowly sergeant— should not have the audacity to ever criticize the decision-making of the Command Staff, the lawyers, and/or the chief of police, etc. After the session, I expected him to file a formal Internal Affairs complaint. But he didn't. I suspect it was because I was acting in concert with the Police Union and it would have been "complicated."

Eventually, all the ideas that Heath and I had pushed forward and fought for were adopted and implemented by the Houston Police Department. Mostly, they occurred when the Command Staff saw other large police agencies adopting them and then suddenly our ideas became their ideas. Heath and I never received credit, nor did we care. We just wanted to see them implemented, to make the job easier for patrol officers.

We both laugh to this day when, on rare occasion, we go to the police academy and see the new cadets who are now being issued holsters that are specifically designed to be used with lights mounted on handguns and wearing all navy-blue uniforms.

Heath and I experienced much career stress, even ridicule for step- ping out of line as sergeants and advocating so strongly for our "radical, crazy" ideas.

I guess we had become nuisances and were viewed as thorns in the side of the Command Staff.

Heath and I liked to work and frequently rode together. We both really enjoyed working at North Patrol and with rare exceptions connected with the officers who were assigned there. We saw the officer's job as more difficult than ours and wanted to assist any way we could. We advocated a servant-leader mentality and when making a scene or checking by, the first thing we would ask was "How can we help?"

How I led always depended on the situation. Most times, my style was what was termed in the police supervision books as "laissez-faire" in that I was permissive and, time permitting, would let the involved officer figure out the solution for themselves. Often the solution that they might come up with was not the exact way that I would have done it, but as long as it was legal, moral, and fell within department policy, I was good with it.

However, if it was a critical incident and there was no time for discussion or explanation, I switched gears and became an "autocrat" and made fast decisions, giving out assignments I expected to be done immediately. One technique, time permitting, for critical tasks was to tell the officer what to do (give direction); then I would have him repeat it back to me so I was sure he understood it correctly. This "sliding" leadership style worked very well for experienced patrol officers. The officers knew, understood, and appreciated that I would only micromanage them if it was a critical incident. Sometimes, other supervisors would micromanage all the time, even with mundane matters; others were indecisive, not taking charge and responsibility of the scene when it mattered. Of course, this type of supervisor would probably avoid making the scene of a critical incident, at all costs, so as not to have to make a decision.

Sometimes during critical incidents, even the best tactics and strategy could still end in tragedy. One afternoon, Heath and I were riding together. As usual, I was driving. Information started coming through the dispatcher's office and was then being broadcast for all the North patrol units. The Texas DPS, which is the state police agency for Texas, reported that they had just received a letter from one of their civilian employees who had been recently disciplined and may now be going through some psychotic episode or crisis. The employee had left a note on the desk of a DPS sergeant indicating that it was their intent to "go postal" and do a mass shooting at the regional DPS headquarters in the north side of Houston. DPS supervisors thought the threat credible enough that they immediately alerted all the area police departments. Not long after the initial alert, other information was forthcoming about a pickup truck that the suspect was driving and that they might now also have a hostage.

We had a bad feeling about the whole situation. This was way out of the ordinary and the DPS supervisors who knew the initial facts were concerned and taking every precaution to notify all the other law enforcement agencies in the region. In about fifteen minutes, Heath and I positioned patrol units to observe and to intercept along the roadways that the suspect might take to the DPS office, while we took up a position closer along the most likely route. As a precaution, Heath got his AR-15 carbine out of the trunk because he was the passenger.

We didn't have to wait long. A patrol unit soon spotted the suspect's vehicle, and the officer was now following. There were two individuals in the truck; presumably the suspect was driving but we were not sure. We fell in behind the suspect vehicle. Other patrol units stacked up behind us. A police helicopter was now overhead. At the opportune moment, I had all the units turn on their emergency equipment (lights and sirens) to initiate a high-risk vehicle stop.

The suspect driver didn't comply and a high-speed chase ensued.

Other units and agencies were headed to the scene. Heath and I were the primary unit and were immediately behind the suspect vehicle while the observer in the overhead police helicopter called the chase out over the radio. Up ahead, a Harris County Deputy Sheriff (HCSO) had pulled off into the median; as we raced by his position, he deployed spike strips to flatten the tires of the suspect's truck to end the chase. As the deputy threw the spike strip out into the roadway, the suspect veered either to avoid the spike strips or to run the deputy over (the deputy had to jump out of the way and was nearly hit) or both. The left front and rear tires of the truck ran over the spike strip and started to deflate.

But the chase went on, although now much slower. Through the back window of the truck, Heath and I could see some physical struggle going on between the suspect and the hostage. I did not know it but later found out that the suspect was the driver and was holding a loaded pistol in their right hand, pointing it at the hostage. When the tires deflated, the suspect could no longer steer the vehicle (it was pulling hard to the left) with only one hand and had placed the gun under their right thigh to use two hands to steer. At that moment, the hostage had seized her opportunity and grabbed for the gun and now, even though the chase was still going on, they were both fighting for possession of it.

The suspect made a hard right turn into the parking lot of a gas station and came to a stop. The struggle inside the cab was still going on. Heath and I stopped short and exited our vehicle to begin the high-risk vehicle stop and to try to "call out" (voice commands) the suspect from inside the vehicle. At the same time, we kept cover behind our patrol vehicle in case the suspect started to shoot at us.

Suddenly, the hostage, who had apparently kept control of the pistol, tossed it out of the passenger side window. It hit the pavement and skidded to a stop about twenty feet from the truck and maybe forty-five feet from us.

In that second or so, I remember thinking, *good—problem solved!* The gun had been taken out of the equation, which would now make our job in arresting the suspect much safer.

In that moment, before Heath and I could do anything, the suspect opened the driver's side door of the truck, jumped out, and sprinted to where the gun was laying. The suspect picked it up and began to orient the gun in our direction.

We had no choice.

In a split second, before the suspect could push the safety off the loaded pistol, we both fired approximately nine times each, Heath with his rifle and me with my semiautomatic pistol.

Every round struck home, and the suspect was dead.

Even though the suspect was originally intent on shooting up the DPS Headquarters, at the end it was probably suicide by cop.

Just to show how divisive our push for change had become within the department and the pettiness of some people, an older officer in the SWAT Detail, who I had not gotten along with when I was assigned there years previous, took it upon himself to write a formal correspondence regarding our shooting (he wasn't even there) and forwarded it to one member of the Command Staff. In his letter, he pointed out (correctly) that in the shooting of the would-be DPS headquarters mass shooter, Heath had used a rifle equipped with an Aimpoint, which was true. He then postulated that because the Internal Affairs investigators had not made an issue of the presence of the Aimpoint, Heath must have removed it from his weapon so that its existence would not be discovered prior to IAD's arrival at the scene. This SWAT officer then pointed out that Heath was guilty of a felony crime, in that he had "Tampered with Evidence." He then implied that because I was with Heath and also involved in the shooting, I must have had knowledge and was also a party to it.

Fortunately, the shooting occurred at a time when the Houston Police Department's Firearms Policy neither allowed nor disallowed the use of Aimpoints or electronic sighting devices on rifles. It was before the new "ill conceived" policy, which forbade weapon mounted lights and Aimpoints, was issued. Which was eventually superseded years later by yet another policy that permitted weapon mounted lights and Aimpoints!

The assistant chief who received the letter of complaint (he showed it to me) did not initiate an investigation. He saw it for the silliness that it was.

In SWAT, or in some other departmental assignments I had, I never really felt any personal danger while on the job. But I did in patrol. Often you were alone and what first appeared to be ordinary situations quickly turned dangerous. Sometimes you could feel the hair literally standing up on the back of your neck when you got that "this is going to be bad" feeling.

Over the years, several of my friends and associates in the Houston Police Department met violent deaths, often alone. All them were dedicated officers and were not the type to seek administrative assignments within the department strictly for their personal safety.

On Sunday, December 7, 2008, while teaching an adult Bible study at my church, I received an urgent call from a coworker. That morning, a few minutes earlier, Officer Tim Abernethy, who worked at my station, had just been murdered. Tim was alone and went to pull over a vehicle during a routine traffic stop. The driver evaded arrest and bailed out of his vehicle. Tim chased him on foot into an apartment complex. The suspect ambushed Tim and shot him numerous times and had then escaped. Good citizens in the complex tried to render first aid, but Tim was dead. Heath and I headed into work and by the time we got there, the Harris County Sheriff's Office had connected the dots and arrested the suspect. We assisted the Homicide investigators in the witness canvass and searching for the murder weapon.

In Tim's autopsy, it was determined that the fatal round had been a bullet that had penetrated through his head. Witnesses said that the suspect had stood over Tim while he was down, wounded and still alive, and fired the fatal round. This bullet was not recovered and presumably (if the witness statements were true) was embedded deep in the ground after passing through his head. After being shot, Tim had been immediately transported to a hospital by EMTs and no one was exactly sure where he was laying when the final fatal shot was fired. What was important was that if the fatal bullet were recovered, it would show the callousness of Tim's murder. He was executed!

The next day, Heath and I, along with several patrol officers (who were also friends of Tim) and a crime scene investigator, dug up the ground in the area where we believed Tim had been killed. We dug and sifted through the earth, looking for that fatal bullet. It took hours, but we finally found it. At his trial, the suspect was found guilty and received the death penalty. I made it a point to go to every Houston police officer's funeral whose death had occurred in the line of duty—too many to count. I don't know why but Tim's affected me more than all the others. What got me the most was the pain felt by his family, particularly his children!

It might be a lack of character or a weakness on my part, but Tim Abernethy's funeral was the last line of duty funeral that I went to. It just became too much for me!

Both Tim and his wife as well as Tim's father were veterans of the United States Navy. Tim had served on submarines. At the time of his murder, Tim's son was deployed on a nuclear-powered fast attack submarine, serving in the United States Navy just like his father had. The Navy was gracious enough to "retrieve" his son so he could attend his father's funeral.

Eventually, as a tribute to Tim's service, his ashes were "spread" (fired out of a torpedo tube) by the crew of one of America's submarines, while submerged, out on patrol, somewhere in one of the world's vast oceans.

In about the thirtieth year of my career, I was assigned to the North Patrol Division's day shift Tactical Unit (NDTU). The NDTU was under the umbrella of the North Division's Tactical Section, which included a day shift and an evening shift Tactical Unit(s), a Divisional Gang Investigation Unit, a Crime Analysis Unit, and a newly formed unit, a Warrant Execution Team (WET), which Heath would run and supervise.

The crime-fighting theory behind WET is simple. In Houston, there are many, many suspects who have "open" warrants for their arrest. They are charged with crimes, or are in violation of their respective parole or probation. Mostly, there are no dedicated units within HPD actively trying to locate and arrest these fugitives. There is also presumption within law enforcement that a significant number of these wanted suspects, who are not yet in custody, may very well be committing other crimes. The theory follows that if a diligent effort is made to arrest these wanted suspects and they are then in custody, they cannot commit more crimes.

Ergo, the overall crime rate will be lowered.

When a criminal investigator (detective) files an arrest warrant against a suspect who is not in custody, the warrant is known as a Two Be Warrant or a "2B." The Harris County District Attorney's Office maintains a database of all outstanding felony and misdemeanor 2B warrants within its jurisdiction. Because of their heavy caseloads, frequently, the investigator, assuming he has "solved the case," would file a 2B warrant against the perpetrator of the crime and would then move onto his next assigned investigation. Because of the volume of crime and the resulting high caseload in Houston, it's an assembly line process. Most of the time, the HPD investigators really don't have the time to go out into the field to locate and arrest these wanted suspects (even more so for the Harris County Sheriff's Office Robbery detectives). Also, assuming that the investigators had the time and the inclination, the execution of arrest warrants should not be done by a lone investigator. They also rarely have the prerequisite "polished" tactical skills (their skill sets are as reactive investigators). The execution of outstanding warrants is best handled by a team of tactical officers trained specifically for the mission. It can be a dangerous assignment, for obvious reasons.

Lacking any dedicated team actively searching for these wanted individuals, often the only way these fugitives are apprehended and taken into custody is if they have a future random encounter with law enforcement and the involved police officer(s) then conducts a computer inquiry on the name and date of birth that the suspect provides. It's not uncommon, in Houston, for wanted suspects charged with serious crimes such as Aggravated Robbery and even Murder to not be taken into custody for months or even years! There are many wanted suspects and unfortunately there is often no one in HPD actively looking for them.

On the north side of Houston, in particular, there are thousands of wanted suspects on the lam. They are wanted for a wide range of crimes from murder to minor misdemeanors and everything imaginable in between. There were so many wanted suspects that the North Patrol Division's newly formed WET only had time to concentrate on the fugitives wanted for felonies. Even then, they would average 60-90 apprehensions a month for suspects who might otherwise not have been taken into custody and who were often involved in other ongoing criminal activity. Almost all of them were not first-time offenders and had already been arrested many times by law enforcement. It was not unusual to see fugitives with over thirty previous arrests!

Before the team went out into the field for their shift, the members of the WET would research and "pull" all the newly filed felony warrants for the north side. The research would focus on developing locations where the suspects might be found but also locations where family members or associates of the fugitive might be interviewed. The team would then "launch," running together in three or four marked two-man units. They would plug in the closest researched location into their GPS navigation systems (often a residence or apartment), drive to the location, surround the house, knock on the door, and then talk to the occupants.

Sometimes, if you were fortunate, one initial researched location was good and the suspect was promptly found and arrested. If the suspect was inside the location and was uncooperative, it also might require making forced entry—"knocking down the door." Forced entry was only contemplated if the legal requirements were met. After entering the residence, the team would then conduct a methodical search to locate the fugitive, who might hide anywhere in the house, many times in a closet or up in the attic. Sometimes, as the entry team was going through the front door, the suspect would try to escape, usually out the back door, hopefully into the arms of the officers manning the perimeter.

Most of the wanted fugitives would not be at the location the earlier research had developed. The team would then hopefully be able to interview someone who knew the fugitive and more times than not, information would be provided that would later lead to an arrest.

During these interviews, it was important to build trust or some connection with these citizens, and tactical officers with a John Wayne or Clint Eastwood persona were not usually successful in getting cooperation.

Often this cooperation was quickly forthcoming when you made it known that the providing of information that led to the arrest of a wanted suspect could lead to the potential of reward money under the Crime

Stoppers Program. This program was a telephone tip line administered by representatives of the various area law enforcement agencies, wherein tipsters could phone in anonymously and if the information proved helpful, in solving a crime or arresting a fugitive, the tipster would then receive a cash reward.

For example, the WET might go to a residence looking for a fugitive, but the suspect is not there. At the residence is Grandma, who then tells you that the wanted suspect (her grandson) no longer lives at the location and she is not sure where he is to be found. You spend a little time talking to her, then mention Crime Stoppers and the money she can make if she can provide helpful information that leads to her grandson's arrest. You also emphasize that her grandson will never know that she was the "snitch." Low and behold, sometimes, as soon as later that same afternoon or in the following days, a "tip" is forwarded to the team via Crime Stoppers that the grandson (your wanted fugitive) "lays his head" (lives) at apartment so-and-so in the Greenspoint area. Early the next morning, the WET then goes to the apartment and arrests the fugitive. WET then reports back to Crime Stoppers that the tip was good and provides the relevant information. Crime Stoppers then pays the tipster—in this case, Grandma—whatever the going rate is for that sort of tip, usually several hundred dollars.

Another successful tool for apprehending fugitives was the "Cell Phone Track." If the fugitive could not be readily located and if the apprehension of the fugitive was important enough, there was sometimes an opportunity for a last-ditch effort. If during your research and investigation, you could establish the number to the cell phone that the suspect uses and presumably keeps on his person (maybe ask a cooperative family member), then a warrant could be obtained to track the fugitive's cell phone signal, using advanced triangulation technology, which analyzed the signal of the suspect's cell phone as compared to the way it interacted with multiple area cell phone towers. The technology for this cell phone tracking is not the domain of the WET but requires the services of specially trained and equipped officers from the Houston Police Department's Criminal Intelligence Division (CID).

The short story is that after WET obtained the required warrant, the guys in CID could then "press a button" (there was a lot more to it than that) and, depending on the cell phone carrier, could determine from subsequent analysis where the phone "lived." Assuming that your suspect was still using that phone and it was in his possession, a successful cell phone track could then direct the WET to exactly where the fugitive was located. The incoming, "almost real time" information from CID was slightly delayed; if the suspect was mobile, you would have to be patient and wait until the signal was stationary. Often, the NDTU would assist by placing undercover surveillance officers at the indicated location, to get "eyes" on the fugitive before the WET, which was standing close by, made their "run in" to make the apprehension.

Cell phone tracking was time-consuming and also required the cooperation and assistance of other units. But usually this tactic had a good chance of success.

Unfortunately, in the past few years, your savvier and more experienced career criminal became aware of cell phone tracking and also how even the historical locations of their cell phones could be retrieved by law enforcement (which might then link them to crimes they previously committed, yet are still unsolved). Some of these criminals knew that they could thwart this historical cell phone analysis by switching out their personal cell phones regularly.

Imagine the stars don't line up for a serial residential burglary suspect, and he is caught by patrol officers who happen to be passing by and are flagged down by witnesses. The officers capture the suspect red-handed. The patrol officers, while booking the suspect into jail, take the initiative. Instead of placing the suspect's cell phone in his "prisoner property bag" (this being property he receives as soon as he is released or bonds out), the officers, thinking the suspect's cell phone might be important, take the extra time and effort to "tag" his cell phone into the Police Property Room. There, the phone can only be released back to the suspect by approval of a supervisor or the involved detective investigating the burglary to which the suspect was initially arrested for.

Let's assume the burglary investigator is dedicated, thorough, and his caseload allows it. He takes note that in the weeks previous to the suspect's arrest, there was a rash of residential burglaries in the same neighborhood where he was arrested. The investigator then submits the suspect's cell phone for analysis and, low and behold, a few months later when the analysis is done, it shows that this same cell phone—which was probably in your suspect's back pocket at the time—was in the same geographic location(s) on the same dates and times as all the other burglaries. This would be a clue! Subsequent investigation could then lead to many other charges and the suspect—who is now probably out on bond, committing other burglaries, who only thought he was facing one Burglary of a Residence charge—now faces seventeen others. All these other charges will be filed as 2B warrants. If found guilty, his sentence might be considerably enhanced.

It was also common for the more "tier one" type criminals who were involved in planned serial criminal enterprises—for example, bank robbery crews—that might require coordination between criminal associates to use burner phones. These are phones that the suspect(s) don't normally use in their day-to-day lives and are phones only used to help facilitate that specific criminal operation. After the criminal operation was completed, these phones are then quickly discarded or hidden away. These burner phones are used to prevent law enforcement from linking their normally used (and known) cell phones to the location, date, and time of the bank robbery, which would then implicate them in that crime.

If it can be shown in a trial that a phone in the defendant's possession is "his" phone—a cell phone number he has used for years, the one that he uses to call his mom and girlfriends and his buddies, etc.—and if in the reactive investigation the phone is triangulated in a historical analysis to show it had been present in the area at the same date/time that the robbery occurred, this is big! Alone, it might not be enough to get a guilty verdict, but together with other evidence, it was the stuff juries loved to hear! Or that plea bargains were made of! But, to historically triangulate a particular cell phone to a crime scene, you had to have a place to start; you needed the cell phone or number that the suspect was using. So first you had to have an idea who your suspect(s) were; you needed names!

The WET was, physically and mentally, a grueling job. Particularly considering, under the color of law, you were entering citizens' private residences whether or not you had their permission. You dealt with many irate citizens who were sure their rights were being violated and as much time as you spent trying to explain the law to them, they were never satisfied.

About two years after North Division's WET was up and running, the unit was using a phone track to locate a wanted felon on the north side of Houston. This suspect was a black man and based on the phone track, the WET ended up at a house where the historical information indicated the suspect had been recently. What Heath and the officers in WET didn't know was that this wanted fugitive and his family members were well connected with an assistant chief within the Houston Police Department's Command Staff. After checking several locations, trying to pin the suspect down, the unit received a phone call from the assistant chief, who lambasted the members of the unit and Heath for *going around, kicking in people's doors for no reason.* Heath was able to connect the dots. These records showed that shortly before he received the call from the angry assistant chief, the suspect's cell phone (the one they were tracking) was used to call the very same assistant chief!

It got much worse for Heath. This assistant chief also sat on the Houston Police Department's Personnel Concerns Committee. This committee was empowered to place "problem employees" on a fast track for termination from the department. If the employee was placed on the program, it was for six months. It was highly structured and required much written documentation by the affected employee's supervisor. If an employee "didn't get his mind right" and didn't successfully complete the program, he or she could be fired. Heath's name was submitted to the committee for inclusion in the program. Inside information was when the committee voted on whether Heath should be placed on Personnel Concerns, the vote was not to. The regular members of the committee, being a cross section of the police department, realized that Heath was doing a difficult job and operating well within the law. However, somehow (draw your own conclusions) despite the committee's recommendations, a member or members of the Command Staff placed Heath in the Personnel Concerns Program anyway despite the recommendation!

Placing Heath on the program reeked of political correctness and was seen by the rank-and-file as an appeasement to some radical members of the black community and members of the Command Staff.

Back at the North Division's Tactical Section, we were all outraged and thought Heath being placed in the Personnel Concerns Program as yet another example of racial game-playing within the department. It was looking like a racial political witch hunt, with Heath now in the cross hairs. Now, if during the six months, another citizen complained about him and/ or WET, it was possible that radical factions within the Command Staff could lobby to have his employment terminated.

So, because in my assignment (sergeant over the NDTU) the chances of being a recipient of citizen complaints was much less likely as compared to Heath's and with the approval of our lieutenant, Heath and I switched jobs for the time being. I ran his WET for six months and he ran my DTU; then we switched back. Heath survived the Personnel Concerns Program ordeal, and I was careful in my supervision of the WET. One way to ensure my personal career survival was to volunteer the WET for one of the prototype body camera studies that the department was then undertaking. I and the other members of WET wore body cameras and recorded all of our interactions with both citizens and suspects while we executed felony warrants. At the end of six months, there were no complaints. And if any high-ranking member of the department had questions about our tactics or how we treated people, they only had to review our archived video recordings.

In my estimation, Heath and his WET were effective, as a way of reducing crime and making Houston's north side neighborhoods safer. But this estimation is hard to quantify as there are many reasons for crime. What we knew was that the convicted criminals who were being paroled out of state prison did not want to be paroled to the north side of Houston. The word was out: if they violated parole, Sergeant Bounds and his team would come for them. Better to be paroled somewhere else!

In 2018, the Houston Police Department's Command Staff disbanded all the department's Warrant Execution Teams. My understanding was that they wanted fugitives arrested on "more neutral ground." The rank-and-file of the department interpreted this to mean that the upper leadership of the department didn't want—or wanted to at least minimize—the "heat" they were taking from minority political activists that sometimes resulted from police tactical units making entry into the homes of minority residents looking for wanted felons, even if it was under the color of law. The "optics" of this aggressive law enforcement maybe was perceived as detrimental to some Command Staff member's long-term political survival. All the Command Staff positions—the chief of police, executive assistant chiefs, and assistant chiefs—are all appointed and subject to the approval of the mayor of Houston—an elected politician.

Overall, the operational tempo of the NDTU was the same as when I had been assigned there years before, primarily narcotics and prostitution enforcement—what the guys in the unit referred to as "dope and whores"— predictable operations with not too many challenges.

In the morning, we would all head out of the office as a unit. Most of the guys would be undercover, driving cars from our fleet of beat-up, ragged, dissimilar vehicles that were mostly castoffs that no other division or unit wanted. We counted ourselves fortunate if our vehicles had running air-conditioning. Summers in Houston are tough and fatigue from heat stress sometimes became a real issue. The undercover vehicle issue for the department DTUs was a significant ongoing problem. Most of our undercover vehicles were in such poor condition that it became common for officers to perform maintenance on them themselves and pay for some repairs out of their own pockets. When a vehicle finally gave up the ghost and it was sent to the scrapyard, we would have no replacement until, sometime in the unknown future, yet another marginal piece of junk was handed down to us. It was always a great source of irritation for us to see other units in the department—who did not do the heavy lifting, who were more administrative or whose officers served in support roles—driving much newer, department-issued vehicles with actual working air-conditioning—while year after year the NDTU's undercover vehicle fleet looked more like some gypsy caravan arriving from a third world country. The vehicle situation was not the fault of the patrol lieutenants or captains; they had no say in the matter. But we placed the blame squarely on these individuals in the very upper leadership of the department who did not place a high priority on the department's "point of the spear."

These Command Staff might have all the right, soothing, empathetic words when we brought the vehicle issue up to them time and time again, but no solution would be forthcoming. By their lack of action (reallocating resources from those who were supporting the mission to those doing the mission), they appeared to be indifferent to actually reducing crime.

Our undercover vehicle fleet was my ongoing headache.

There was always a bit of excitement and gratitude within the unit when our lieutenant or captain were able (sometimes through the department's quasi-black market "good old boy network") to find and snag a serviceable undercover vehicle for our use.

One of the few "new" undercover vehicles that the NDTU ever received during the period from 2011 to 2018 was a silver, Toyota Corolla with but a few hundred miles showing on its odometer. The department had initially purchased it for exclusive use by the administrative and clerical personnel working for the Command Staff. For whatever reason, they (the secretaries) never drove it and it had sat idle for nearly a year, "forgotten" in the expanse of the department's multi-level parking garage downtown. One day our lieutenant realized its existence and "appropriated" it. When I asked Lieutenant Garza how she found it and got it assigned to our unit, she sort of smiled and just said, "Don't ask!" I suspect that it was probably an "in house" auto theft on her part. We really appreciated her for "stealing" it.

Maybe, partly because of its dubious and mysterious acquisition by Lieutenant Garza, the Toyota Corolla was thought to be "jinxed" and soon earned the nickname the Silver Bullet—and for good reason! In but a few months, after receiving it, our undercover officers killed two suspects, in separate incidents, all while conducting narcotics surveillance from it.

The first shooting was when a Hispanic gang member with a criminal history for aggravated robbery tried to carjack the undercover officer who was driving it. The officer (Arnold Chapa) was parked at the time, sitting in the Toyota, watching an apartment complex for reported narcotics trafficking. Fortunately, Arnold spotted the suspect approaching the Silver Bullet from behind with a pistol already in hand. Arnold beat the bad guy to the draw, shooting him several times and killing him.

A few months later, the Silver Bullet was again being driven by Arnold, but this time Ben "White Chocolate" LeBlanc was seated in the front passenger seat. Both undercover officers were assigned to conduct narcotics surveillance in the Acres Homes community and were watching a reported crack house. During their surveillance, a suspect approached the driver side and assaulted Arnold. Before the two officers could react, the suspect stabbed Arnold in the left arm with a knife. Immediately, before the suspect could stab Arnold again, Ben, from the front passenger seat, pinned Arnold back into his car seat with his left hand, to get a clear shot at the suspect with his pistol in his right hand. Ben killed Arnold's assailant by firing several shots into the bad guy's chest with his .40 caliber Glock.

The guys in the NDTU were not necessarily superstitious, but the Silver Bullet had a dark history. Besides the shootings, there was other violent drama, all involving this one vehicle.

About a year after recovering from his wound, Arnold Chapa transferred to a quieter assignment. He had done his part!

Most of my DTU undercover officers were in plain clothes and driving undercover vehicles. I would then also assign a few (two or three officers) to drive marked patrol units. The officers driving them either wore uniforms or were in clearly marked police raid gear.

The flow of our operation was best pictured as a big octopus. We would go into an area or neighborhood that was experiencing street crime (prostitution and narcotics trafficking), and my uniform units would conceal their presence in the area by parking behind a warehouse or a strip center, out of sight. The undercover units would fan out a mile or so in all directions from the hiding uniformed officers, looking for criminal activity. Our priority was "dope and whores." When an undercover spotted something suspicious, like a suspected street-level narcotics dealer, then the other undercover officers would slowly work into positions where they also could get surveillance on whatever activity was occurring. We called this "getting the eye." Depending on what was occurring, we would wait till we were certain that we saw a drug transaction between the dealer and a potential customer (usually crack cocaine). We called this a "hand-to-hand."

When we saw a hand-to-hand, then our uniform units would roll in and try to take down (arrest) both the suspected dealer and the customer, both of whom were likely to have possession of crack cocaine. As the uniform units made their approach, the undercover officers would direct them, by radio, play-by-play, till the uniformed units had the suspect(s) in sight; they would slowly make their approach to try not to spook them into running, trying to look like a regular beat cop making his routine rounds, with no clear agenda. To facilitate these types of operations, we used a "back channel"—a radio channel dedicated to our own use—as these operations required a lot of communication to coordinate both the surveillance and takedown. Hopefully the arrest was made with no drama, but once or twice a week we might have a foot chase or have to fight a suspect who decided he didn't want to go to jail that day.

Arresting the prostitutes was icky. Usually in the same area as the street-level narcotics activity, there also would be street-level prostitutes—both male and female. There is nothing glamorous about street-level prostitutes on the north side of Houston. In the hierarchy of prostitution, it looked like this: A top-tier prostitute might be some fitness model who works by word of mouth, with an exclusive clientele and who might charge hundreds or thousands of dollars for sexual services (price often determined by type of sex act to be engaged in and/or the time of the "rental") to the rock-bottom tier (north side streetwalkers) where oral sex could be gotten for as little as five or ten dollars—or even a pack of cigarettes. Most often, these north side streetwalkers were not wearing anything flashy but were presumed to be working depending on the area they were walking in. If you watched for just a short amount of time, you would notice that they had no clear destination and frequently made eye contact with the drivers of the vehicles that passed his or her location.

Once a suspected "working girl/boy" was spotted, one of my undercover officers would "roll in" and approach them in his vehicle, roll down the window and make conversation. At the same time, other undercover officers would keep eyes on the interaction to both protect the involved officer and facilitate the prostitution case. If the conversation went well—"Hey, baby, do you need a ride or are you working?"—the prostitute would then get into the undercover officer's vehicle with him and they would drive off. Over the radio, one of the covering undercover units would announce, "They just loaded." Then, while the undercover officer who had "loaded" the suspected prostitute was driving around, he would work the conversation between them into a solicitation of a sex act for money. If he or she agreed—sex for money— then the elements for the crime of prostitution would be met. The undercover officer, making the deal, would then covertly give a signal to the other undercover officers who were following, unbeknownst to the prostitute with him in his front seat, like tapping the brake pedal so the rear brake lights blinked several times, or leaving one vehicle turn signal light on. This would be the "signal" of an agreed upon prostitution transaction, i.e. a "bust signal." The trailing undercover officers would see the covert signal and announce over the radio to the uniformed units, "It's a good deal," at which time a uniformed unit would pull the undercover officer over as if it were a routine traffic stop and then arrest the prostitute.

In a short time, when all the backseats of my patrol units were full of prisoners, I would have them all transported to the city jail and everyone else in the NDTU would head back to the office to do the paperwork. The writing of the offense reports and filing of the various criminal charges, we called "cleaning up." Often the suspects we arrested were also wanted for other offenses and had open 2B warrants on them. Again, these warrants could cover the gamut from murder to minor offenses. We considered these open warrants to be a bonus. At the end of the month, all the arrests were tallied up; this was known as the "duck count." In an average month, there might be thirty felony ducks and twelve misdemeanor ducks. The statistical breakdown of this monthly duck count would then be forwarded to our division commander, who would forward them to the Command Staff so that in future meetings with the citizenry, they could have talking points about all the arrests that had been made by the DTUs on behalf of the community.

Unfortunately, these types of arrests (prostitution and drugs) were just a big revolving door. As these people went into the criminal justice system, they would serve a short sentence and would soon be back on the streets, doing the same thing. Mostly, they were unemployable, with no job skills, long criminal records, addicted to crack cocaine, or mentally ill. All they knew to do was be a whore or to sling dope. We, in the DTUs, thought there had to be a better way to deal with the problem. I suppose we were a deterrent and probably kept a lid on the problem so it didn't explode out of control. But day after day, it was "dope and whores." This was our assignment, and it was all about the numbers (how many arrests were made.) We knew that a lot of these type of arrests kept the Command Staff happy.

When I joined the Houston Police Department in 1981, one of the most active locations on the north side of Houston for this type of street crime was the area surrounding Airline Drive and Crosstimbers Road. Nearly forty years later, after all of that enforcement work, after an untold number of arrests, Airline and Crosstimbers remains a dope dealing, prostituting hub. Nothing has changed, only the names and faces of succeeding generations of prostitutes and dope dealers. There has to be a better way! We in the NDTU held no malice against the prostitutes; in many ways, they were victims themselves. We had much empathy for "our" north side street prostitutes and would much rather have somehow gotten at the pimps who capitalized on them, not to mention the johns.

On a lighter note, sting operations against prostitutes could provide humorous events that only cops can appreciate (cop humor). One story that sticks in my head is that of Officer David Smith. Dave worked for me the entire time I was supervising the NDTU and was one of my older, more experienced guys. Dave had a knack for getting things done. There was a connection I had with Dave and it might have been that back in the 1980s I worked with his father, who was also a police officer but who died at an early age from a heart attack. Dave was good at picking up and making cases against the street prostitutes, whereas some guys couldn't pick up a whore (male or female) no matter how hard they tried.

One morning, Dave loaded a rather large, muscular male streetwalker who was poorly camouflaged as a female. The "shemale" got into Dave's truck and another guy in the unit had the "eye." The undercover officer who had the eye was Mark Smith, who we nicknamed Muscles. Anyway, Dave drove around a while, with his new friend, while Mark monitored, the rest of the unit being fairly close by. Suddenly, Dave came to a halt in the middle of the roadway and stuck his left hand out the window and frantically started motioning "come on." Dave had not given the usual bust signal, so Mark, perplexed and wondering whether the person in the car with Dave had spotted him following, announced over the radio, "I guess Dave wants me to go around." So Mark did just that: he bypassed Dave and the male prostitute, leaving the area.

Dave was not signaling for Mark to bypass him, but rather, "I NEED HELP!" Dave had made a tentative agreement to be the recipient of a sexual act from the man whore. Before he could give the bust signal, the man whore had, with practiced skill, swiftly undone Dave's pants. Mr. Man Whore took much enthusiasm in his job and was with great vigor and clear excitement pulled down Dave's britches with a single-minded determination to consummate the deal. Dave vigorously protested and tried to back out, to cancel, and to somehow re-negotiate the terms of their arrangement. Dave repeatedly said, "NO!" but it was to no avail. His pleas fell on deaf ears. The man whore was totally engrossed and, being bigger and stronger than Dave, was not effectively deterred. They were both now rolling around in the truck's cab in a desperate tug-of-war over Dave's britches. From all accounts, it appeared that Dave was in real danger of being raped.

No means no!

Fortunately, Kelly Huey, one of my uniformed guys that day and who has a good radar for "bad things happening," swept in and intervened before Dave completely lost his pants and was violated. I suspect that the cross-dressing guy that we then arrested and who had tried oh-so-hard to "do" Dave was not interested in the money, but was acting out some weird, kinky sex fantasy and was carried away with the thought of being able to bring his dreams to fruition. He wasn't a "for real" street prostitute.

Just another day on the streets for the NDTU!

Police officers have a strange, twisted sense of humor. After what happened with David, there would be payback.

A few weeks after David Smith's near-rape experience, the unit started receiving complaints from business owners about an obvious and flagrant male prostitute who was aggressively soliciting johns and scaring off legitimate business customers. Of course, we could never locate this particular prostitute, so I set up a system where the offended business owners could call me directly, if this notorious man whore showed up again. Sure enough, my cell phone rang and a business owner had the prostitute, in sight, at that moment, in front of his business.

Immediately, I sent my undercover officers out to the location and there was Mr. Man Whore, in all of his glory: long-haired wig, skin-tight short shorts, and a spandex pink muscle T-shirt tied up in such a way to expose his midriff. The suspect was easy to spot because when the boys got there, he was sashaying and dancing in the middle of the street (we call that a clue!).

Mark Smith promptly volunteered and "rolled in." The man whore immediately accepted Mark's "invitation" and jumped into the passenger seat of his undercover vehicle; off they drove. The man whore apparently was easy to negotiate with and Mark quickly made a deal—sex for money—and immediately gave a discreet bust signal to the other members of the NDTU watching out for him.

Mark pulled into a parking spot where supposedly their sex transaction could be acted out. But unknown to the prostitute, before the sex act would occur, the uniformed units were going to (or were supposed to) arrive and make the arrest because Mark had given the bust signal.

The other undercover officers remembered what happened to Dave. They saw Mark pick up the male prostitute, give the bust signal, and then pull into the parking spot. The rest of the undercover officers were in proximity and all had "eyes," including Dave Smith. But no one announced it was a bust or moved in to arrest the man whore and presumably pull him out of Mark's lap. Minutes went by and now everyone could see Mark frantically giving all the bust signals he knew to give: stomping on his brakes, causing his rear brake light to blink on and off, turning his signal light on—both left and right, etc. But it was to no avail. No one budged.

Over the radio, I could hear one of my guys nonchalantly say, "Gee, I am not sure if he's made a case or not—let's wait a while longer and see what happens!" Still, no one announced a bust or moved in. The rest of the UC (undercover) NDTU officers had Mark surrounded. He was not in any danger. The other UCs were in their respective vehicles, parked in a semi-circle only fifty yards away from Mark, with the uniformed units just out of sight behind them. Another minute or two went by and now Mr. Man Whore was done with the small talk. Or maybe it was that Mark ran out of words and didn't know what to say to postpone the inevitable. The male prostitute was now moving in on Mark, trying to invade his very personal of personal spaces, eager to perform his side of the bargain. Mark was not so eager. Just about the time I arrived on the scene, Mark jumped out of his car as if it were on fire, apparently because Mr. Man Whore was getting "hands on."

The uniforms finally moved in, making the arrest and ending Mark's "big adventure."

Mark was a little shaken having been touched by another man, but regained his composure and his unique brand of "redneckness" by pulling out his ever-present can of chewing tobacco, which he always kept in the back pocket of his jeans. He snapped the can against the side of a marked police car to sift the tobacco inside "just right." Then he pulled out a big pinch of chew and stuck it in its usual spot between his lower front teeth and gums.

After getting his fix of tobacco, Mark was good to go! But I couldn't help noticing the beads of sweat running down the sides of his face.

Everybody, including Mark, had a good laugh.

Sometimes, at church my fellow congregants ask me, "Anything interesting happen at work last week?" I always tell them, "Just the usual."

They tended not to understand police work or police humor! I didn't even try to explain.

After I was reassigned to the NDTU, a big problem arose. One member of the unit was suspected of stealing money from citizens and prisoners. Being a police officer can lead to much temptation. This is one reason I believe police departments should invest money and resources into the background investigation of potential police trainees before they are hired, to have a better chance of eliminating these potential applicants with discoverable character flaws. So often the best indicator of future performance is previous performance.

A Hispanic man had come to the North Station to complain to the desk sergeant. He alleged that a uniformed police officer (one of my uniformed units) had pulled him over on a routine traffic stop and then, during the stop, the officer had stolen a fairly large amount of cash from him and then released him. An Internal Affairs complaint was initiated and subsequently assigned to a normal reactive IAD investigator. The investigation ran its course, and the investigation was classified as "Not Sustained" (insufficient evidence to either prove or disapprove the allegation).

But after the investigation, the investigating IAD sergeant sought me out and asked to talk to me privately. Although he couldn't prove it, there were—in his words—"big red flags" and he believed that the involved officer was guilty of stealing the money. He told me that the Hispanic man was not a citizen of the United States and was undocumented. We both knew that undocumented aliens, particularly Hispanics, were often targeted by criminals because of their reluctance to report crime to the police for fear of deportation. They didn't want any interaction with law enforcement. However, this man was angry enough about being victimized by a police officer that he was willing to risk official police entanglements to seek justice. The investigator also relayed to me other interesting information that he had discovered during his investigation and I agreed with him that there was much for me to be concerned about.

The lieutenant over the North Division's Tactical Section at this time was still Rachel Garza. Lieutenant Garza was competent and well experienced. She had a reputation for fairness and looked after her subordinates; we all enjoyed working for her. She, like me, had also completed a tour in the Internal Affairs Division and we both had similar jaded views of the Command Staff and Legal Services (we both had stories). I told her about my private meeting with the IAD investigator and his concerns. She took it all in and we decided to surreptitiously closely monitor the involved officer for any other additional allegations. It was not long coming.

A few weeks later, the NDTU had a foot chase with a suspected street-level narcotics dealer. Eventually, he was captured and taken into custody. The uniform officer who had been the target of the initial theft complaint was also the one who ran down and arrested the suspect. This officer then passed the prisoner off to a second uniformed officer, who was already going downtown to book another prisoner into jail.

An hour later, the transporting uniformed officer called me and told me that while he was booking the street-level narcotics dealer and counting his money out for him, the prisoner told him that several hundred dollars was missing. Street-level narcotics dealers often have a lot of cash on their persons (from selling drugs) and these criminals are sometimes the targets of other criminals, who will rob them of their drug sale proceeds—or perhaps, in this case, by a police officer. Both the citizen and police criminal think because of the victim's lack of credibility (drug dealer with criminal history) that legitimate law enforcement will not believe the victim, or the victim will not even bother to report the theft or robbery.

I told the transporting/booking officer to tell no one about the allegation and I reported the information to Lieutenant Garza. We knew if we made a formal IAD complaint and it was handled on the reactive side, the resulting investigation would most likely end up in another "Not Sustained" and we would still have a criminal in our unit. We stepped outside the usual protocol. I called the lieutenant of the Proactive Internal Affairs Unit, who

I had known since he was a rookie. In my mind, a sting operation against "my" officer would be fairly easy to orchestrate and would also serve as an integrity test.

The lieutenant of Proactive IAD was probably not the best man for that job. Although he was administratively competent, an experienced reactive investigator, and a friend, he had little or no experience in conducting sting operations and doing undercover police work. I tried to help him with the planning and crafting of an operation, but he just seemed to have problems envisioning it and began bemoaning all the what-ifs.

I then politely suggested that he seek the assistance of my former Proactive IAD lieutenant (who was now assigned to the Narcotics Division), Dennis Gafford, to help him in the facilitation of the sting operation. The two lieutenants got together, set up a scenario in which narcotics investigators had supposedly arrested a suspect (actually another undercover officer) in a hotel room, and needed the assistance of a uniformed member of the NDTU to transport the prisoner and help process the scene. Because I was "in on it," I sent my suspected thief to assist the Narcotics Division in their investigation.

Unknown to the suspected officer, the hotel room to which he was sent to assist the Narcotics investigators had hidden cameras set up in it (everything was staged). During the subsequent processing of the scene for evidence, my suspected thief/employee stole money that was laying out in plain view within the hotel room. Proactive IAD was able to record the theft with their hidden cameras and when the officer didn't later place the money into evidence, it being clear that he was keeping it for personal use. He was arrested.

It was a sad day for the NDTU when one of its members was arrested for being a common thief! But, Lieutenant Garza and I were satisfied with the outcome. The involved officer was subsequently found guilty of Official Oppression and fired from the Houston Police Department. Several years later, he was arrested yet again, this time as a citizen, when he became ensnared in a prostitution sting operation. Good riddance!

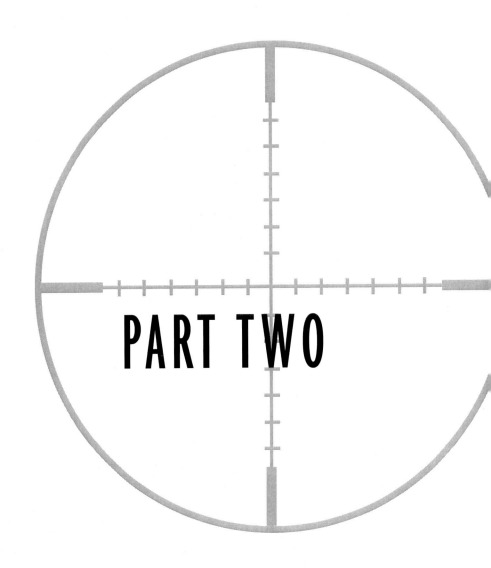

PART TWO

CHAPTER 7

THE RISE OF THE ROBBERY CREWS

In early 2014, all the supervisors of the various Houston Police Department Tactical Units were called together for a meeting. The subject was the significant rise of commercial business robberies and other violent crime in the city. The meeting was held by two members of the Houston Police Department Command Staff, Assistant Chief Donald McKinney and Assistant Chief Mark Eisenman. Their overall tone and message to the supervisors of the departments tactical units was: do something about violent crime, especially the increasing number of aggravated robberies and particularly those of commercial businesses, which were overwhelming the city.

In the Texas Penal Code, Aggravated Robbery is a First Degree Felony (imprisonment no more than 99 years or less than 5 years). Aggravated robbery amounted to committing a theft and the suspect also did the following: caused serious bodily injury to another or uses or displays a deadly weapon. If during the aggravated robbery the victim was killed, then the offense becomes Capital Murder, which could land the defendant on Texas' Death Row or life in prison with no possibility of parole. In the Houston metropolitan area, a significant number of Capital Murders occurred during the commission of Aggravated Robberies.

Many of these suspects committing these aggravated robberies and targeting commercial businesses almost always used a firearm as their deadly weapon of choice. They were mostly armed with handguns, but there was also a worrisome number of long guns being used. It was not uncommon to view security videos in the aftermath of these robberies, and note that the suspects were using AR-15s and AK-47s.

During Chief McKinney's and Chief Eisenman's meeting with the department's tactical units, they offered no definitive direction or strategy that we were to use, other than "help" the Robbery detectives! It was clear we, the NDTU, were to tackle the robbery epidemic. But no one was sure how we were to do so, only that we were to do "something."

Apparently, the driving force for this meeting was that the FBI's Uniform Crime Report (UCR) had recently been made public and Houston had the highest number of Aggravated Robberies (Commercial Businesses) in the entire nation! This was bad enough. What was maybe even more worrisome for the department's Command Staff was that the *Houston Chronicle* (a major newspaper/outlet in the Houston area) had published a feature article alerting the citizenry to this and it looked bad!

Commercial Business Robberies:

Houston - 1,400

Los Angeles - 1,100

New York - 800

Chicago - 800

Philadelphia - 400

Source: FBI Violent Crime Task Force

These statistics were only for commercial business aggravated robberies and did not even include the aggravated robberies of individuals.

To give even more perspective on how serious and pervasive the number of commercial business robberies had become in Houston, it became even more evident when compared to the approximate populations in these same cities.

New York - 8.5 million

Los Angeles - 4 million

Chicago - 2.7 million

Houston - 2.3 million

Philadelphia - 1.6 million

The Houston Police Department's Command Staff was right to be concerned about the number of commercial business robberies in the city, particularly compared to the numbers in cities like Chicago, which was reputed to be a much more violent and dangerous city.

The other sergeants at the meeting figured that the Command Staff were again posturing and grandstanding for the sake of their political survivability and noted how no real direction or strategy was being offered as to just how a tactical unit was to combat violent crime, particularly the commercial business robberies.

Whereas most classified positions/jobs within the Houston Police Department are protected by civil service, this is not true for Command Staff positions (chief of police, executive assistant chief and assistant chief of police). All these positions are political in that the mayor of Houston, who is an elected official, appoints the chief of police and ultimately, by extension, the executive and assistant chiefs. These appointments are also approved by the city council (other elected officials). All these Command Staff positions are "at-will" and unlike other positions in the police department, the people appointed to these positions must be astute at navigating the political minefield of urban policing, within Houston, to survive and keep their jobs. These positions all have significant salaries, perks, and other benefits.

After the meeting between the Command Staff and the tactical units, I met with the members of the NDTU and we discussed at length what had been said at the meeting with the assistant chiefs. The overwhelming consensus was that the meeting had been for show and we had all been down this same road before. As soon as the unit's monthly number of felony arrests (dope and whores) dropped because we were helping Robbery detectives conduct their reactive investigations (showing photo spreads, getting statements, etc.), then there would soon be a clamoring from these same assistant chiefs for "numbers" (more felony arrests—dope and whores). The meeting with the assistant chiefs was so they could go back to the community and announce how the department was taking a "redirection" and was now serious about doing something about violent crime. It was all smoke and mirrors!

Ultimately, the Command Staff also had a fallback position they could use to defend their inabilities. If the robbery/violent crime rate went off the charts (as it had) and they began to feel heat from the citizenry, then the police department higher-ups could deflect any criticism of their crime-fighting strategy—using the old argument "we just don't have enough police officers" or "if only we had more police officers then we could really do something"—rather than take ownership of any leadership deficiencies or crime-fighting strategies on their part.

Although the Houston Police Department was definitely under-staffed and it could only be good to have more police officers, the more important and relevant issue was how the officers we had now were being deployed. Were the resources of the department really going to the "tip of the spear," to those units that have the most impact in making Houston neighborhoods safer? In the history of the Houston Police Department, it often appeared as hiring increased and more police officers became available, the many non-essential departmental units (not core to the mission), or some Command Staff member's "feel-good pet project" (the ones least likely to make Houston neighborhoods safer) swelled and became "fatter."

The next important question, besides police staffing, was what tactics and strategies were being utilized? Mostly, it was the same tactics and strategies that had been used for many years. It was more about the numbers of tickets and arrests rather than real solutions.

Initially, the NDTU did nothing about the commercial business robberies and went back to dope and whores. After all, wasn't it really what the department wanted? Dope and whores was politically safe; it was what we were good at and it was our comfort zone. Wasn't it about the number of arrests?

The Command Staff said nothing. Like times before, their talk about doing something about the robberies was just for show!

Nothing really changed—years of tradition, unencumbered by progressive thinking!

In late April 2014, the North Patrol Division was assigned a new commander and the men of the NDTU—and I—were in for a rude awakening!

Immediately prior to April 2014, the overtime budget for the North Patrol Division was in disarray. The previous captain, although a nice enough guy, had just retired and had not done a diligent job in keeping the division's overtime budget in line. This was a big problem. The division was significantly "over" and now the Command Staff was looking for a new leader who first and foremost could fix it, and who could manage such a large division.

The problem was that there was not a lot of good, competent captains eager to volunteer to take on the North Patrol Division. Besides the budget problems, the division led the city in almost all crime categories. Because it was one of the biggest as well as the busiest of all the patrol divisions, it also had more than its fair share of internal issues and Internal Affairs Division complaints, all of which can sap much of a division commander's time and energy. Also, within the geographical borders of the

North Division were several vocal neighborhood civic groups, who were sometimes perceived as "high maintenance." These civic groups, who were often politically connected and whom the Command Staff wanted to keep happy, could be demanding of police resources. They often petitioned for increased police action within their respective neighborhoods, often to enforce minor nuisance-type crimes—or, more accurately, the vigorous enforcement of various city ordinances. This enforcement had little impact on violent crime or of the safety of the general citizenry on the north side.

In the North Division's area of responsibility, there were a lot of "squeaky wheels" demanding a lot of oil, and the go-to guy was the captain. It is not an easy job to be the commander of a large patrol division.

One captain volunteered to take on the North Patrol Division: Larry Baimbridge. A few Command Staff eyebrows were raised when he asked for the assignment; mostly, no captain volunteered for North! There were so many easier assignments for captains, with far fewer headaches. Why go there?

But many of us knew why. Captain Baimbridge was like us—someone who had a long history with North Patrol and who felt a strong loyalty and connection to both the community as well as the officers and sergeants who spent their police careers there. He, like many of us, had also been friends with Tim Abernethy.

Captain Baimbridge was not assigned to the North Patrol Division at the time of Tim's murder, but he had gone immediately to the hospital where Tim's body was initially transported. There he comforted Tim's widow and "made the mistake" of viewing Tim in his bloody police officer's uniform.

In later conversations with Captain Baimbridge, I found that one of his motivations for coming back to the North Patrol Division was not only out of loyalty for the men and women who worked there, but because he wanted to help "heal" the division. What stuck in Captain Baimbridge's craw was that the captain who the Command Staff had assigned to North

Patrol at the time of Tim's murder had a poor reputation within the department. Throughout this man's career, many rank-and-file considered him a "problem": a pathological liar, an egotist, and a racist. The perception was that because of his race and rank, he had the status of a "unicorn" and therefore was protected and shielded by members of the Command Staff who overlooked his character flaws for political considerations. In the days just prior to Tim's murder, this captain had allegedly been harassing Tim, making his life difficult and was forcing him out of his assignment, to make way for one of his favorites. Tim's difficulty and the perceived unfairness with this captain was well known to some of us. Tim had approached both Heath and me, looking for advice on how to handle the situation, the week before he was killed.

It was no small matter when at Tim's funeral, which was attended by thousands of police officers—some from around the country—Tim's widow and family politely refused the consolation of this captain, despite Houston Police Department protocol and tradition. The feelings were so bitter that during the ceremony the family did not even want this man to present them with the American flag that had been draped over Tim's casket. This honor was instead given to a previous North Division commander, Captain Randy Ellen.

To Captain Baimbridge—like it was to others, like it was to me—the Houston Police Department's North Patrol Division was home.

Captain Baimbridge arrived and soon began putting the division back in order. I will have to be transparent here: I thought I was in for an easy time. I knew the new captain and although we were not necessarily social friends, we had a similar work ethic. Unlike many who are assigned to patrol, we were both fortunate to have worked in many other assignments within the department: Homicide, various tactical units, and even Proactive Internal Affairs. The opportunity to have worked so many diverse assignments gave us both a unique, broad view perspective of policing, and we both saw the potential of "paradigm shifts" in police strategies and tactics.

I also knew him as a man of faith who had quietly and generously helped fund a church mission trip to Honduras that I had overseen.

Where I had never even taken the lieutenant's test, he had quickly climbed the promotion ladder even though he was nearly twelve years my junior. He was well received by all, having previously established an excellent reputation as a hard worker within the North Division, first as an officer and then years later as a lieutenant, who had also helped to establish the division's Warrant Execution Team, which was seen by many as the best one in Texas. He was approachable, considerate, and fair, definitely not a pushover! He also wanted to get things done and could be demanding.

Whereas earlier in my career I had embraced change and liked to implement new ideas, the Command Staff's reticence to listen to the rank-and-file had beaten me down and I was now stuck in a rut. My intent was to finish out my career "going with the flow" and "flying below the radar." All I had to do was keep up the NDTU's number of "dope and whore" arrests for a year or two and then I would retire. I didn't want any more departmental drama; I just wanted a low-stress assignment with fairly regular hours so I could spend quality time with my wife and daughters.

As Captain Baimbridge retrenched himself in the North Patrol Division, he slowly made changes. Because the Command Staff was most concerned with the budget, this was the first area to be addressed and corrected. Slowly he worked his way through other deficiencies he perceived within the division. Some changes he made were initially unpopular with the rank-and-file. But later, after the drama and emotionalism had subsided (officers and sergeants don't like change), it was realized, by most, that the change was needed and the North Division was more efficient and provided better service to the community because it.

Eventually, the North Division Tactical Unit came under Captain Baimbridge's scrutiny.

Captain Baimbridge and I had a few meetings, and I was transparent (I like to lay it out like it is) and didn't try to sugarcoat and spin it otherwise. The NDTU's mission for the last thirty years had been "dope and whores," with only an occasional tasking to other operations, such as decoy or high-profile fugitive apprehension where undercover surveillance would be beneficial. I also conveyed to him that there was now a parasitical type relationship between the North Division Tactical Unit and the Narcotics Division. The NDTU went out each week, and because of our surveillance expertise and intimate familiarity with the area, we could make as many narcotics-related arrests as we wanted—almost effortlessly. We would often then call narcotics officers to the scene, who would tag the dope into the crime lab and who would also write the offense report (so we didn't have to). The NDTU would then transport the suspect(s) and book them into jail. This "arrangement" mostly benefited some narcotics officers, who didn't have to go out and make their own cases—"find their own dope and make their own arrests." Both the NDTU and Narcotics Division then received credit for the arrest and for the dope recovered. This arrangement with Narcotics officers was not limited solely to the NDTU, but was practiced widely throughout the department by other tactical units and Narcotics squads. Basically, you had two department entities (tactical units and street-level narcotics units) doing the same work and carrying the workload that was intended for but one!

I thought Captain Baimbridge would be content (like all the previous captains) with his tactical unit doing "dope and whores"; after all, at the time, we led all the other departments DTUs in the numbers of felony arrests. However, he was not impressed nor satisfied.

We met again privately. Captain Baimbridge explained that the NDTU and I were no longer to conduct Vice and Narcotics operations. He wanted the Vice and Narcotics Division to deal with the problem like they were supposed to. And just to give me no wiggle room, so there was no doubt, he told me that the only exception to our conducting Vice or Narcotics operations was if he authorized it.

Captain Baimbridge explained that the mandate of the NDTU would change dramatically. I was told to focus all of my attention and efforts to do something about the problem of aggravated robberies in the North Division's area of responsibility. He also wanted, in my efforts in dealing with the aggravated robbery problem, to not merely replicate what Robbery Division investigators did (traditional reactive type investigation: photo spreads, witness statements, etc.) but to think outside of the box and come up with another way to dismantle the robbery crews. As far as he was concerned, he didn't care about the number of felony arrests we made. The way we would be evaluated—the new yardstick for the NDTU—would be how much we could reduce the commercial business robbery rate in our area.

He also politely let it be known to me that if I couldn't do it, then he would find a sergeant who could! I asked if this new mandate had been his "marching orders" when the Command Staff assigned him to the North Division. To which he responded that when he was reassigned as the commander of North Division by Executive Assistant Chief Michael Dirden, he had voiced no concern about the violent crime and robberies on the north side of Houston but instead wanted the division's budget fixed.

Captain Baimbridge explained that not only did the Houston metropolitan area have the greatest number of commercial business robberies in the entire country, but that the north side of Houston (his area of responsibility) was the highest in the Houston area for the number of both commercial business robberies and robberies of individuals.

Simply put, the north side of Houston/Harris County where the NDTU operated was the epicenter for commercial business aggravated robberies in all the United States and my captain, out of his own personal convictions, wanted something done about it.

I needed a plan. Fortunately, some ideas had been percolating in the back of my brain for many years about how to deal with the aggravated robbery problem in a new way (at least new to the Houston Police Department). I had never implemented or tried to push forth this new way of doing things because either the needed technology was immature, was not readily available, or, most importantly, there was no mandate from my superiors. But now that had all changed. The technology was there and more significantly, I was being told to do something!

There were some obstacles to overcome. This tactic or strategy would be new and had not yet been vetted by the Houston Police Department's Command Staff. Ideally I would want clear, written guidance from the top of my organization! I also knew that the Houston Police Department's Command Staff was not good at "new."

Although this new idea had the potential to be successful, it also had great potential liability.

Some hard operational decisions would have to be made. It would be imperative that the Command Staff be involved and provide definitive direction on how to proceed. Would they even want to embrace a new proactive approach to the commercial business robbery epidemic?

Would they tell me where the "lines were drawn," so I could "drive" right down the center?

Maybe the risk was not worth the potential rewards. Maybe in the minds of the Command Staff it was better for Houston to be the nation's commercial business robbery capital, even with all the resulting murders of innocent people that came with it.

I was concerned, because of my previous personal experiences (and observations) with the department's Command Staff overall mind-set being "if it's not our idea, then it's not a good idea"—or its institutionally engrained, agonizing slowness and reluctance in wrapping their minds around new ideas. Particularly if it was a new idea arising from the bottom of the organization (from a mere sergeant). The old cliché "paralysis by analysis" was very applicable, with the typical endless committee discussions with the resulting infinite loop; no one made a decision, until the idea died a slow death and was conveniently forgotten.

Before putting my thoughts into a written proposal and a plan of action, I conducted research and had several discussions with the officers and sergeants assigned to gather street gang intelligence or to conduct reactive robbery investigations. Through these interviews, I came to understand that the high number of commercial business robberies on the north side of Houston and Harris County were mostly committed by the various criminal street gangs that populated the area. In particular, the north side Acres Homes and Greenspoint areas. One gang intelligence officer famously quipped that aggravated robbery was the "cottage industry" for these north side street gangs and was fueled by the following factors:

- Lax prosecution of defendants accused of Aggravated Robbery by the Harris County District Attorney's Office and the judiciary.

- Low bond amounts for defendants accused of Aggravated Robbery.

- Higher standards in eyewitness/suspect identification.

- Glamorization of violent takedown-type robberies as compared to street level narcotics trafficking within these criminal street gangs.

- Large cash amounts obtained in commercial business robberies.

- Social media hype: "Look at me—I am a gangsta with a gun, look at all my money, etc."

- Police enforcement resources focused primarily on street-level drug trafficking and prostitution activity (it was about the number of arrests).

I also identified the general method of operation (there are variations) the criminal street gangs employed in conducting these robberies.

- Scout and/or reconnoiter the commercial business to be robbed— preferably one where there is the potential of significant available cash.

- Placement of a lookout(s) in the parking lot of the business, who would then call in the robbery crew at the opportune time—the shot caller(s).

- Robbery crew consisted of several armed men (usually handguns; sometimes long guns), all with masks and gloves.

- Often, immediately before the planned robbery, steal a vehicle (the "lick" vehicle) and make use of it before it was reported stolen and the vehicle information was entered into law enforcement databases such as the National Crime Information Center (NCIC) or Texas Crime Information Center (TCIC).

- Robbery crew using the stolen vehicle pulls up to the targeted business; suspects rapidly exit the vehicle and "take over" the business: attempting to force the employees to open the safe, etc.

- After committing the robbery, the crew would escape in the stolen vehicle, travel a short distance, and then abandon the stolen vehicle and be immediately picked up by another vehicle—the "switch" vehicle—that would wait a short distance away.

I concluded that it was not a lot of suspects committing a few robberies but a few suspects (criminal street gang members) committing a lot of robberies!

Also, these commercial business robberies were almost all being committed by black men. My biggest concern was this was almost certain to bring political correctness into the equation.

CHAPTER 8

HIGH-RISK SURVEILLANCE

After receiving the mandate by Captain Baimbridge and conducting my research, I decided on an overall strategy to deal with the issue. As per Captain Baimbridge's orders, the NDTU would now be totally given over to dealing with the commercial business robbery problem and would no longer be guided by how many crack pipe and/or prostitution arrests could be made.

The NDTU would first seek to partner with other law enforcement agencies to obtain as much intelligence about active robbery crews and get any assistance they were willing to offer. In addition, to facilitate this cooperation, the NDTU would be available to assist these other agencies in the dismantling of these robbery crews, even if the only known incidents were outside the NDTU's geographical area of responsibility. The presupposition was "your crooks are our crooks" and the next robbery they commit might very well be in our area.

The primary focus of the initiative would be to identify a vehicle that a serial robbery crew was using to facilitate their criminal activities. Contrary to the stereotype of these criminals as not being imaginative or intelligent (common among some police administrators who do not have extensive backgrounds as criminal investigators or street cops), some of these street gang members were running fairly well-thought-out operations, which had more moving parts than anyone previously imagined.

I came to believe that the Achilles' heel in their operations were the vehicles they were using.

Normally (but not always), the vehicle they used to actually commit the robbery (the lick vehicle) was stolen or as I came to call it, "not repeatable." Once the stolen lick vehicle was used directly in a robbery, it was often immediately discarded. Not uncommonly, the lick vehicle sometimes was a rental vehicle. The rental was through a legitimate car rental agency, but was rented by a female proxy only distantly connected to the members of the robbery crew. Often, this was an uninvolved woman who would rent the vehicle on behalf of the crew and might later report it "stolen" just prior to the planned robbery ("*I came out of my apartment and it was gone*") while in fact she had delivered the rental vehicle, as previously agreed upon, to the robbery crew for their use.

What I was looking for were the vehicles that were "repeatable," i.e., used again and again by the robbery crew in a secondary role to criminal operations. I wanted to track the vehicles that the members of the crew were using to support and somehow indirectly facilitate robberies! For example: Identify and track a vehicle that was being used to steal other vehicles; these other stolen vehicles were then used to commit the actual robbery. Identify and track a vehicle that was reported as being suspicious by a business owner and was believed to be scouting the business prior to a planned robbery. Identify and track a vehicle that was in the parking lot prior to the actual robbery and believed to be occupied by the "shot caller" (a member of the crew who had surveillance on the business to be robbed and by cell phone, calls in the robbery crew waiting in proximity for the opportune time to strike). Or, which happened the most frequently, identify and track the vehicle that was being used to pick up the robbery crew as they abandoned the stolen or rented lick vehicle immediately after the robbery.

Once a vehicle was identified as having been used to facilitate, in some fashion, commercial business robberies, I presupposed that there was a likelihood that the robbery crew would use it again in that same support-type capacity. After the vehicle was identified, then a court-approved vehicle tracking order would be obtained and the NDTU would covertly place a mobile global positioning tracking device on the vehicle in question. By virtue of being able to track the support vehicle, vital intelligence could be obtained. Which would lead to a dismantling of the entire robbery crew. It sounded simple and intuitive but actually it wasn't. It had never really been done before in Houston on a widespread, consistent basis.

The members of the NDTU would have to develop a capability to quickly gather intelligence and identify the gang members' support vehicles via their license plates. This would require daily reading and compilation of police offense reports for aggravated robberies, from multiple law enforcement agencies, looking to identify and link these incidents to a specific robbery crew. Not only that, but the NDTU might have to canvass the area immediately after a commercial business robbery for witnesses or to get any surveillance video from the surrounding area, looking to identify the support vehicles that the crew might have been using.

I have a saying, when it comes to the timeliness of tactical operations, "windows open and then soon shut." When the window of opportunity opens, you need to immediately be prepared to capitalize on that opportunity before that window (of opportunity) closes and is forever lost.

Once the guys in the NDTU identified a support vehicle, the intelligence pieces having come together and having a good license plate number, I would immediately begin writing a court order (Application for Mobile

Tracking Device), laying out my probable cause and linking the vehicle to being used in serial crimes and my rationale for wanting to track it. This order was then reviewed and if approved, signed by a State of Texas district court judge.

Ultimately, the NDTU streamlined the writing of these orders to the shortest time possible. I would begin writing the order, in a Word document template, as soon as one of my guys started to develop clues about a support vehicle being used by one of the crews. As these bits of information trickled in, they would make me aware of the nuances so I could make fully informed decisions on how to proceed and, if applicable, plug the information into the draft of my tracking order. I had the full expectation that soon my guys could find the critical piece of information that gave us the license plate. As soon as that last piece of critical information was found and we had met the standard of probable cause to track that vehicle, I would complete my document and email it to the Harris County District Attorney's Office, Special Crimes Division.

Their prosecutors, I knew, would quickly review it, tweak it, and print the document.

At the same time, one NDTU member who was intimately familiar with the investigation would hightail it to the district attorney's office, where he would pick up the printed order and take it posthaste to a district court judge for approval. The whole process was so streamlined that often as soon as the vital piece of information was gotten, the tracking order could be approved and signed by a judge in an hour or less! We acted immediately and because of our pre-planning and timely intelligence gathering, along with our good relations with "our" attorneys in the Special Crimes Division, we could obtain court-approved vehicle tracking orders in record time!

Another piece of the puzzle had to fall into place. If we had a vehicle identified and were in the process of or had already obtained a tracking order from the judge, the next question was: Where does this vehicle live?

When the robbery crew was not using the vehicle in their criminal operations or it was not being used, where was it parked? It was a crucial part to the puzzle. Because as soon as we had the tracking order and knew where the vehicle was kept by the bad guys, we would then try, as soon as possible, to sneak a team in, unobserved, and place a small mobile tracking device on the undercarriage of our target vehicle. The tracking device, once installed, would be hidden from view—only discoverable if the vehicle was placed on a lift where its underside could be easily viewed.

My first problem, as we were preparing to begin the initiative, was where was I going to find the vehicle tracking devices? The Houston Police Department's CID had a few of them. But when we started the initiative, CID was not user friendly. It usually went like this: You had to have the tracking order signed by a judge. Then fax a copy of the order over to CID's office in downtown Houston. Then, *if* they had a tracking device available, they would decide on a day or night that they would come out and try to install the device on our target vehicle. When dealing with CID, it often seemed there was no urgency to their attempting to get the tracking device on our target vehicle and they manipulated their work schedule in such a way that they were only coming out of the office if they would make paid overtime.

I wanted to get the tracking device on in minutes—or at most, hours—from the time the order was signed, not days or weeks later when it was convenient for CID to make overtime money. One element that I believe is important in small unit police operations is "ownership." The guys in CID did not have any real ownership in the investigation or the operation. It was just a job and a way for them to pad their pockets (with but a few exceptions, at least that's how it appeared to us).

We (the NDTU) needed to gain access to many tracking devices that we could directly control and manage. Tracking devices that the NDTU could deploy in the shortest time available. The answer to this problem was not going to be with HPD. I had already applied and received a modest federal grant for nearly a hundred thousand dollars, mostly to cover some overtime costs associated with the projected surveillance on the vehicles we anticipated tracking. But not all of this money was designated for overtime; some was earmarked for equipment. My plan initially was to use these other designated monies to buy tracking devices solely for the use by the NDTU.

The problem was, if I purchased tracking devices, they would become HPD property and only a few units in HPD (outside CID) could run their own tracking devices (for example, Proactive Internal Affairs). If I used the grant monies to buy tracking devices, then they would have to be possessed and ultimately managed by the folks in the CID. This would be a problem. Based on previous experience, if the window of opportunity opened to covertly mount a tracking device on a vehicle, CID would not be willing or able to act quickly enough and the window would shut. Having to use CID only created another level of bureaucracy in which the investigative operational momentum would be lost or stymied. To the administrators who wrote the General Order stipulating that only CID could control, manage, and possess HPD-owned tracking devices, I am sure that it sounded reasonable and doable. But for us who were to conduct the operations, it was a deal breaker.

But if I could solve the "tracker" problem so we could quickly and efficiently get a tracking device on a vehicle that the gang was using, then the NDTU could conduct long-term undercover surveillance on the identified vehicle to facilitate the reactive criminal investigation and/or direct action enforcement activities against the robbery crews to utterly dismantle them indefinitely.

Looking outside the box, I reasoned there might be other law enforcement agencies who were well-funded and equipped—who might help.

So, the NDTU would seek to partner with the federal government, in particular the Federal Bureau of Investigation (FBI) or the Bureau of Alcohol, Tobacco and Firearms (ATF) to obtain technical assistance, primarily mobile vehicle tracking systems, but also maybe pole cameras, cell phone interception technology, etc.

Also perhaps, if there was a partnership with the "Feds," this would also facilitate prosecution of these serial commercial business robbers/ criminal street gang members in the federal justice system.

In conducting my previous research, I heard about a large Northeast city that had some years before been able to drastically decrease its rate of commercial business robberies. The success was attributed to the federal prosecution of the suspects rather than local or state prosecution. When the word got out among the robbery crews or potential future robbery crew participants that the federal government was involved and that stiff sentences were being handed out—with no possibility of parole—suddenly, committing aggravated robberies of businesses was not so attractive and the criminals sought some other avenue rather than participating in this violent crime.

What is the advantage of federal prosecution? It's big! Under the Hobbs Act, there is a presupposition that you are interfering with interstate commerce when one commits a robbery of a commercial business: Interference with Commerce by Threats or Violence (18 USC 1951). There are also significant penalty enhancements for the use of a firearm— Carrying, Displaying or Discharging of a Firearm in Criminal Conduct (18 USC 924c). Not only that, there is strict sentencing guidelines that the federal judge has to follow, by law. So even if you end up in the court of the most liberal federal magistrate, there is little or no wiggle room in the sentencing. If during an investigation, John Doe, a member of a serial commercial business robbery crew, is arrested and successfully prosecuted federally and two or more of the robberies he participated in are proven up and that he used a firearm in the commission of these robberies, the minimum sentence that he can get is 32 years in federal prison, with no real chance of parole. The sentencing, mostly, is "day for day." If, however a defendant cooperated with investigators and if he or she pleads to the charged offense(s) and tells "everything they know about everything," which then leads to even more indictments against other members of the crew, they might receive some leniency from the court.

Compare and contrast that with the Harris County judicial system wherein the same suspect, under the same circumstances, facing the same charges, would often receive probation, or a light prison sentence—a slap on the wrist.

Moreover, under the state and local system, criminally charged, but not convicted defendants, normally have the right to bond. The defendant's family or friends would go to a local bond service company and put down 10% of the actual court-decreed bond amount, or they might even pay this 10% off in monthly or weekly installments. Sometimes arresting one or two members of a robbery crew and filing state charges, wherein the judge saw fit to give them the opportunity to make bond and "bail out," created more robberies! The other members of the robbery crew, who had not been arrested and charged, were then under an informal obligation or previous tacit agreement to get the monies to bail out their buddies. Guess how they would do that? They commit more aggravated robberies.

Not so in the federal system. You rarely get bail when charged with violent crimes (you're a danger or threat to the community). Instead, you're remanded into the custody of the United States Marshals Service until your case is disposed of! To a lesser extent, this same draconian position to violent crime was also true in some criminal justice systems, in the counties adjoining Harris County. These counties having elected conservative judges and prosecutors. Generally, the robbery crews from Houston were reluctant to "do licks" in these more rural, conservative Texas counties (such as Montgomery County to the north of Harris). The bond amounts were much higher and the prosecutors, judges, and juries would tend to "hammer them" if they went to trial and were found guilty.

For the commercial business robbery initiative to be most effective, it was of critical importance to get the partnership of the ATF and FBI, whose agents would then be the conduit to the federal prosecutors and the federal government's judicial system with its more "zero tolerance" of violent crime. After several robbery crews were dismantled and handed severe prison sentences under the federal system, with no possibility of parole, then committing aggravated robberies in Houston and Harris County would not be so attractive. The word would go out!

It was also my experience that the criminal street gang members gained certain "street credentials" and gained standing with their peers when they were arrested and prosecuted on the state side. It was not, after all, going to be a big deal. In their minds, they would not receive a significant prison sentence (if any), particularly if they were younger and played the plea bargain system. It was all part of that "gangsta" or "thug" persona that some young black men in the city were trying to develop and enhance. I am not sure of the socioeconomic reasons this persona was so attractive; I only knew it existed.

I hate to say this, but there was not so much of a "fear factor" among the street gangs when it came to the local police, prosecutors, and judges. The involvement of the federal government was an unknown factor that these street gangs had to now consider; right or wrong, federal government agents, prosecutors, and judges were much more feared and/or respected by the criminals than local authorities.

The members of criminal street gangs don't want any federal government entanglements.

Providentially, the NDTU received the help it needed to make the initiative work and the pieces rapidly fell into place.

In the earliest days of the transition, when the NDTU was still formulating its plans, I attended a meeting with Robbery detectives from the Harris County Sheriff's Office. As I alluded to previously, the north side of Harris County was being inundated with aggravated robberies and, ominously, most of the unsolved homicides were characterized as "stranger on stranger"—many of the murdered presumably victims of robberies that had gone awry. At the end of the presentation, I introduced myself to the audience and briefly talked about how the Houston Police Department's NDTU was being tasked solely with commercial business robberies and how I was trying to facilitate communication and a partnership with the sheriff's department and other area law enforcement departments to facilitate intelligence gathering, specifically to identify the vehicles that the crews were using to support their operations. One talking point I used was "your crooks are our crooks."

After the meeting, Special Agent Dominic "Dom" Rosamilia, who was assigned to the ATF, approached me. Dom had a distinct accent; he had grown up in New York, just as I did. His partner, Special Agent John "Big John" McDonald, was originally from Michigan. Both men were assigned to the Houston's ATF Regional Office, specifically the Violent Crime Group. We talked at length about the NDTU's envisioned commercial business robbery initiative, the surveillance, mobile tracking devices, vehicle tracking, pole cameras, and ultimately federal prosecution as a new way to handle business. We recognized that up to that point, both Houston and Harris County had only primarily utilized two "tools" to dismantle the crews. The first was the unplanned random chance encounter between uniformed patrol officers and the robbery crews during the commission of the actual robbery or if the reported getaway vehicle was spotted by patrol officers immediately after. The second tool was the old school reactive investigative techniques (detectives in suits and ties) developing leads from incident reports, developing names, showing photo spreads, filing 2B warrants, etc. Both traditional mainstays were not proving sufficient to handle the problem and now the NDTU would bring forward a third way!

Big John and Dom wanted to help, to be a part of the initiative. And they did, in a big way! The ATF had plenty of global positioning system (GPS) mobile tracking devices. After they called and conferred with their supervision, it was decided that NDTU could take possession and use these tracking devices as long as they were used under the ATF umbrella.

Fortunately, because these devices did not belong to HPD, I could in good conscience skirt the whole HPD CID fiasco.

One morning, a day or so after our initial conversation, Big John walked into my office with ten Sendum mobile GPS vehicle tracking units for the NDTU's use. I felt like a kid at Christmas! I didn't think HPD's CID had more than three or four trackers to service the entire department! I also learned that if we needed to borrow more trackers or if a unit malfunctioned, all Big John had to do was make a call to ATF Headquarters in Washington DC and whatever we needed would be sent to us via FedEx the next day.

It got even better!

Shortly after this, Dom called me and asked that I attend a meeting at his office; he wanted to introduce me to someone. When I got to ATF and sat down with Dom, I was introduced to Richard (Rick) Hanes, an Assistant United States Attorney (AUSA), a federal prosecutor with the Southern District of Texas. At first, I didn't speak in the meeting. From the flow of the conversation, I realized that Dom was trying to convince Rick to adopt our (NDTU's and ATF's) future investigative cases and prosecute the members of these robbery crews under the federal government's Hobbs Act. The conversation went well. Dom did most of the talking. Initially, Rick was hesitant, but said he was bored prosecuting dope cases and was looking for a challenge and maybe doing something about violent crime. At the end of the conversation, Rick was on board and would help us.

I had been naive. I didn't realize how important a federal law enforcement partnership would be. Our working hand in hand with a federal law enforcement agency such as ATF would be the path for securing federal criminal charges and prosecution against our robbery crews. Dom and Big John knew the federal judicial system and could adopt our criminal cases and write them in the format and style germane to the "language" of federal prosecutors. I also realized that as our surveillance operations began,

Big John and Dom would have to be with us every step of the way to ensure that all the evidentiary and/or necessary documentation was accomplished.

After Rick made known his support for our planned initiative, he later introduced me to Heather Winter, an AUSA who worked with him out of the same office and who also wanted to help prosecute these cases.

Over the next few years, Big John, Dom, Rick, and Heather would become invaluable to the NDTU.

Big John and Dom knew I had another problem: the age-old problem of undercover vehicles for HPD's DTUs. Without good undercover vehicles, we could not do effective surveillance. ATF could not just "give" us vehicles; they tried (God bless them) but there were insurmountable insurance and liability issues. So instead, with the approval of their bosses, Dom and Big John pitched the idea of making two members of the NDTU official ATF Task Force Officers (TFOs). Simply put, a TFO is a local law enforcement officer who, after being thoroughly vetted, is deputized as a federal agent (of sorts) and works closely with the parent federal law enforcement agency—in this case, ATF. If two of my guys were made ATF TFOs, then ATF could assign them permanent undercover vehicles for their exclusive use—vehicles that they could use 24/7 and would ease the unit's overall undercover vehicle problem.

Normally, police officers from HPD's Divisional Patrol Tactical Units are not made TFOs with federal law enforcement agencies; it was initially pretty much unheard of. Usually, TFOs almost always came from the suit-and-tie sort of traditional detective divisions; normally they got these coveted positions. This was something new and different. I didn't have the authority to authorize any of my officers to be TFOs (*oh boy, the Command Staff was going to love this one*) so I punted it up my chain of command directly to Captain Baimbridge, who quickly said yes! I suspected that unlike other division commanders, he often never asked permission from the Command Staff for such new ideas; he just took the "better to ask forgiveness than ask for permission" sort of mind-set and gave me his blessing.

Before the commercial business robbery initiative first started, the NDTU was actually comprised of two different squads: a day shift supervised by me and an evening shift supervised by Sergeant Hilario "Lalo" Torres. Captain Baimbridge and Lieutenant Garza, to facilitate this new initiative, combined both squads into one, to be supervised by two sergeants. They did this so there would be enough staff to conduct the anticipated surveillance operations and also foster a spirit of team unity. It turned out to be a good match. Lalo was an experienced sergeant, a former United States Marine whose father had been a longtime arson investigator for the Houston Fire Department. Lalo also possessed a good look for undercover work; he was of Mexican ancestry, bald-headed, thick of stature, with a long mustache and beard. Sometimes we would put him in a beat-up old truck, throw a few lawnmowers in the back and he would be able to nonchalantly drive through any neighborhood, with the window down, puffing on a big cigar, looking for all the world like "El Jeffe" going to pick up his lawn-cutting crew.

Lalo had the younger officers (evening shift) and I had the older guys (day shift) and now we merged the two squads into one big happy family.

Lalo and I offered two of the guys of our new squad to be ATF TFOs who were not only top rate undercover officers, but who had also in the past showed a knack for investigative work (they had sharp, inquiring minds). I recommended David Smith, a longtime officer adept at ferreting out clues.

Also recommended to be an ATF TFO was Justin "Red" Williams. Justin was much younger than David and had worked previously for Lalo. He was also not your stereotypical police officer. In high school and college, he was—or appeared to be—some long-haired grunge rock-and-roll guitar player, and possessed an eccentric flair. His father was Guy Williams, the retired sheriff of Montgomery County. When Justin graduated college, he got married, cut off his hair, and joined HPD.

At first, I was unsure about him being a TFO. I didn't know him and he was…well, different. But Lalo was adamant; Justin was the guy for the job. Lalo was right. I am not sure what Justin's IQ is but it must be off the chart. When he began thinking hard, his mind would go to overdrive, racing and processing information like some super computer. While his mind was kicking into warp drive, Justin would start vocalizing his thoughts and the information would flow faster and faster until you would have to tell him to stop or slow down. He was brilliant, although, like I said, he was different than your average cop—which, in my mind, made him interesting.

In the spring of 2015, just as the NDTU transitioned to commercial business robbery crews, our lieutenant, Rachel Garza, transferred to the Narcotics Division, something she had wanted for a long time. We all enjoyed working for her and wished her well. Captain Baimbridge brought in Lieutenant Craig Bellamy to take her place. The day Rachel left, when we were going to throw her a farewell party at the station, I received a phone call from an FBI agent asking for help locating and arresting a bank robbery suspect. The information was that the bad guy was hiding out somewhere on the north side of Houston and was driving a vehicle with a known license plate. Before heading up to the party, I talked to David Smith about the phone call and asked him to run the suspect's license plate in a newly acquired confidential computer program "thingy."

We had just gotten access to the National Vehicle Location System (NVLS) as part of the startup to our commercial business robbery initiative. Actually, none of HPD's DTUs had access to NVLS but Dave had schmoozed or somehow established a personal connection with HPD's NVLS gatekeeper and had been granted access. It might have been that the department's NVLS gatekeeper was a gay man and had a "man crush" of sorts on David. A bit of flirting might have been the way Dave—a happily married heterosexual—was able to first get NVLS access for the NDTU.

NVLS (a motor vehicle license plate recognition system) was an important tool for us and worked just like something out of *1984*, George Orwell's novel of a future totalitarian government. Throughout the country, particularly in the bigger cities, were positioned either in static locations or more importantly on commercial vehicles—like wreckers, taxis, garbage trucks, delivery trucks, or even police cars—cameras that captured the images of passing vehicles and their license plates. The people or companies who drive or maintain these vehicles equipped with these license plate capturing cameras probably made a few cents for each license plate recorded by the system. All the operator of one of these camera-outfitted vehicles had to do was drive. The cameras did the work, automatically grabbing the image of every vehicle it passed by. It was even more efficient if the vehicles were driven through areas of dense concentrations of parked vehicles (like apartment complexes or shopping malls). The cameras mounted unobtrusively on either side of their vehicle automatically captured license plates of all the parked cars as you drove by. The more you drove and/or streets you traveled, the more license plate images were captured by your cameras and therefore the more money you made. So vast was this system that in a city like Houston, many thousands of license plates were captured and recorded daily. These images were then downloaded in a timely fashion into a central informational collecting nexus where the data was archived. Along with each license plate and vehicle image was also included a time and date stamp, as well as the GPS coordinates showing where the image was taken.

NVLS worked to our advantage like this: For example, suppose you have an active commercial business robbery crew. Through whatever means (investigation, snitch, magic phone call, etc.) you're able to identify and figure out the license plate of one of the repeatable support vehicles the crew is using to facilitate robberies. As your investigation was coming together, you were already writing a tracking order, laying out your probable cause, and as soon as the last bit of information is received (the license plate), you immediately have it signed by a state district court judge. As the order is signed or in anticipation of the order being signed, you have to start thinking ahead about locating the target vehicle and then, when it's parked and unoccupied, the NDTU would stage a coordinated team operation to place the tracking device (unbeknownst to the bad guys). But before that all could happen, we had to know where the vehicle "lived." Where was the consistent parking or storage location of our target vehicle? Where could I find it? Where did the bad guys keep it when they were not using it?

To most police administrators, it would seem obvious! Why, just go to the registered address of the license plate as recorded by the state's department of motor vehicles.

Occasionally, this is a good location to find the vehicle but often it is not. In Houston, many of the citizens, particularly in the socioeconomic class of the suspects we were after, lived in apartment complexes. The individual apartment was rented by an unmarried woman with multiple children and whose rent was subsidized by the government. Most of the vehicles, as we found out, that we ended up tracking were actually owned and normally used daily by these same women, who then "borrowed out" their vehicles to their male acquaintances (boyfriends, baby daddy, daughter's boyfriend, son, grandson, etc.)—either wittingly or unwittingly—for the use in facilitating commercial robberies. The women who possessed these vehicles moved often, as they often were behind on their rent or the apartment management evicted them when it was discovered that they were violating the rules (harboring adult males who were not on the lease). The vehicle license plate registration address was often incorrect: the registered owner, having moved several times since the vehicle was first registered and never updated it.

An NVLS inquiry was often the best tool to locate the vehicle of interest, particularly if it had recently been scanned in an apartment complex or at a residence.

And so on the morning of Lieutenant Garza's going-away party, I asked David to check and see whether the vehicle being used by the FBI's wanted bank robbery suspect had recently been scanned by NVLS.

Bingo!

David said that the license plate and vehicle had been scanned by NVLS late the night before in a cheap hotel to our north, just outside of the city, out in the county. David and I conferred and thought it likely that the vehicle was still there because the wanted suspect was probably renting a room for the night. Normal check-out time for this hotel is 11:00 a.m., so we had maybe a short window to get our undercover officers to the hotel to determine whether the vehicle was there and figure which room our suspect was in. Lalo and I launched the NDTU; as fast as we could, we made our way in our respective undercover vehicles to the hotel, which was approximately twenty minutes away. When we arrived, we were rewarded with the sight of the suspect's vehicle still parked, unoccupied, at the hotel.

This tactical problem is easily solved! Maintain eyes on the parked bad guy car and when the suspect enters it, move in with some uniformed units before he could roll out of the parking spot (so as not to have a vehicle pursuit) and arrest him. Or maybe, time permitting, figure out which room he might be renting, confirm that he's inside, surround it, and then call him out using a loudspeaker in a marked patrol unit and then arrest him. If he refuses to come out and "barricades up" in his hotel room, then call the SWAT Detail and let them work the problem, at their leisure, ultimately probably shooting tear gas rounds into the room and forcing him out.

Ben LeBlanc went in to the hotel manager's office. Noting that the employees were of Pakistani origin and thinking they were unlikely to be in cahoots with the suspect (who was black), he identified himself and showed them a picture of the suspect. Immediately, they identified Room #7 as being the room our bad guy had rented.

But was he in the room right now?

Within an hour of setting up our surveillance, we had our answer. Door #7 opened briefly and there was our suspect, in his underwear. Apparently, he had just woken up and was looking outside to see what the weather was going to be like.

Immediately, we surrounded the hotel room and pinned the suspect inside. I didn't want to wait for him to get to his vehicle. Our takedown timing could be off and there might be a high-speed vehicle chase. We then brought up a marked police unit that we had waiting down the street and, using the public address system, "called the suspect out" by his name and the room number he was in, using the stereotypical cop language: "Come out with your hands up", "This is the Houston Police Department. We have you surrounded"—just like in the movies!

Yes! I was so proud! A perfectly executed, impromptu tactical plan.

Or maybe not! The suspects often get the last say in these situations.

Door #7 slowly opened and there the suspect stood, taking stock of the situation. After apparently noting our presence (he was indeed surrounded) and without saying a word, he quickly produced a pistol, put it to the side of his head, and pulled the trigger.

POW!

A stream of blood gushed forth, and he crumpled to the ground. He was very DEAD!

This was Lieutenant Bellamy's first day over the NDTU. While at the farewell party, he got the call from the Command Center that we (his brand-new DTU) were just involved in a "death in custody." He wasn't even able to eat any of Lieutenant Garza's going-away cake.

What a moment! The officers and sergeants of the NDTU met their new lieutenant in front of hotel room #7, with a dead body lying on the ground as a backdrop.

Welcome to the north side!

CHAPTER 9

FIRST STEPS - LEARNING TO DISMANTLE THE ROBBERY CREWS

Lieutenant Craig Bellamy was physically huge. He had attended college at Baylor University on a football scholarship, where he played offensive tackle for the Baylor Bears. After college, he joined HPD and then gravitated to the DWI Task Force. If there was any group of officers and sergeants who saved innocent lives, it was these men and women. Just like robberies, Houston and Harris County led the nation in intoxicated driver-related fatal motor vehicle accidents. The butcher's bill in Houston would have been much higher if not for HPD's DWI Task Force. Their mission was simple: working late in the evening till early in the morning, they patrolled the main thoroughfares of Houston, locating and arresting as many drunk drivers as they could.

Lieutenant Bellamy worked the assignment as an officer, as a sergeant, and ultimately years later when he was promoted to lieutenant. He believed this assignment was important. In a direct way, he knew that his DWI Task Force was saving innocent lives. Lieutenant Bellamy was motivated, personable, and intelligent. Like many other members of the Houston Police Department, had he chose to, he could have been a success in the private sector and multiplied many times his police salary, with a lot less risk to his physical safety and without having to worry about the social justice politics which was now increasingly defining modern policing.

Like some others in HPD, he wanted to do something that made a real, tangible difference.

Because of his size, the guys in the NDTU nicknamed him the "Big LT." A new lieutenant is always an unknown, particularly Lieutenant Bellamy, who didn't have any undercover experience up to that point. Soon we learned, there would not be any issues. He proved to be a fast learner and would listen to what we had to say. But, at the same time, he was not afraid to make decisions. What we all appreciated was that now both our captain and lieutenant were motivated more about doing the right thing rather than the politically correct thing(s) or wanting to ensconce themselves in a safe, cozy assignment with no potential of going afoul of the political wing of the department.

One reason Captain Baimbridge chose Lieutenant Bellamy to head up the North's Tactical Section was his passion for training. Specifically, tactical training as it applied to the real possibility of the NDTU having to take direct direction against armed robbery crews who we might catch in the commission of a takedown-style robbery. The primary emphasis of the training was our firearms proficiency. Fortunately, Lieutenant Bellamy could tap into several of us who were former SWAT and who had also successfully completed the FBI Firearms Instructor School. We also still had connections and/or good relations with other firearms instructors, both within the department and with outside agencies, including the ATF and FBI.

Kelly Huey quickly rose to the top and took the lead on our instruction, bringing all the members of the NDTU to a high level of proficiency with our primary weapon system, the AR15 carbine.

The Houston Police Department does not supply its officers with weapons. It's up to the individual officers to buy their own handguns from an approved list. Of course, every classified officer in the department is required to own and carry a handgun, at all times, while on duty. Then, for the vast majority of the department, the purchase of a department-approved shotgun or carbine is strictly optional.

The only divisions and/or units where the department bought and supplied long guns were: The SWAT Detail (fully automatic, short barrel M4 type carbines for all of its members, along with .308 bolt-action sniper rifles, usually Remington 700s) for those assigned as snipers. Some department guns were bought and issued to the Narcotics Division, Robbery Division, Major Offenders Division, and the department's Downtown Security Detail, which guarded HPD's main administration building. These "city weapons" were a hodgepodge collection of AR-15s and Benelli 12-gauge shotguns that had been purchased over the years.

The only division (other than SWAT) who trained regularly and could be considered proficient with their city-issued long guns were some of the guys in the Narcotics Division who were specifically selected to carry them. The other mentioned divisions hardly, if at all, trained and most of their weapons collected dust in an office closet.

Informally, Lieutenant Bellamy required that all the members of the NDTU purchase an appropriate AR-15 type weapon system. When he first transferred in, maybe only half the guys had a good quality AR-15 with an Aimpoint and a white light system mounted on it. Fewer were qualified to carry one. Fewer still were proficient with it. Before, when the NDTU's primary mission had been "dope and whores," there was little reason to have a long gun. But now that we were going after violent "hijackers," that all changed.

Soon, every member of the NDTU bought his own AR-15, and we trained hard! Shooting on the move, shooting from cover, shooting while dismounting from a motor vehicle, failure drills, and transition to our handguns: Kelly Huey trained us for the gunfight until we all developed a "gross familiarity" with our weapon system.

Firearms training in HPD had always been weak, unless you were assigned to the SWAT Detail or Narcotics Division. The department only required its classified personnel to "qualify" once a year (shoot a minimum score) with whatever handgun you carried. The qualification was not so much training, but demonstrating (for liability reasons) that you could shoot to some minimal standard. The department also didn't normally issue practice ammunition unless you were attending one of its firearms classes.

The problem for the NDTU was that when we started the robbery initiative, between actual field operations, we were now shooting thousands of rounds of ammunition a month, almost all of it .223 caliber. We utilized anyone's firearms range we could get access to. We even squeezed in between the department's daily scheduled handgun qualification lines using a "friendly" firearms instructor at the academy who wanted to help with our new initiative. This unnamed instructor would sneak the entire NDTU into the department's qualification range for an hour or two so Kelly could run us through our firearms drills ad nauseam! Also, because of our "friendly" contacts, we could also use both the FBI and ATF firearms training facilities, which were outside of the city.

Commensurate with all the firearms training, we needed ammunition. The department didn't supply us with any, or at least to the degree that we needed for all the training we were doing. So we bought our own, out of our own pockets, while other well-meaning officers in other divisions who wanted to help us supplied us with some city ammunition (like Narcotics and SWAT) "under the table," as well as our friends in the ATF and FBI. Lieutenant Bellamy and some guys also reached out to private citizens and area businessmen who wanted to do something about the robbery problem. They began donating significant amounts of ammunition. Finally, Captain Baimbridge used some of the North Patrol Division's allocated discretionary monies for ammo purchase.

The Houston Police Department's Command Staff was not helpful. To be fair, about two years later, a newly appointed assistant chief, who we thought highly of and was sympathetic to our needs, facilitated the purchase of training ammunition from the Police Foundation, which is a charitable organization that donates equipment and big-ticket items to the Houston Police Department. Thank you!

About Officer Kelly Huey: Kelly was foremost a "tactical guy." He was always thinking about the best way to handle dangerous situations we might encounter on the streets. This is where he shined. Not so much in the investigative "how do we get there" but was focused instead 100% on what we do when the critical moment arrives. He was always prepared, serious, and not known for having a sense of humor. I know I irritated him sometimes. I was a constant jokester and liked to keep the guys laughing, until our operations moved into a critical phase; then I was all business. Kelly was also SWAT-trained and so he came with many of the training and teaching certifications important for our mission. Kelly had a remarkable resemblance to the character Walter White on the TV show *Breaking Bad*.

Kelly Huey was also a "poop magnet."

Kelly was involved in many shootings, all with different robbery crews. The first three occurred early in the history of our robbery initiative. These first shootings were not as the result of any planned operation; he was just at the wrong place at the wrong time and took the initiative by himself.

Perhaps lacking a sense of humor, it could also be said that Kelly also lacked a sense of fear.

The first incident was when Kelly was attending mandatory in-service training at the Houston Police Academy. On any given day, there are probably several hundred police officers at the academy taking scheduled in-service classes. A certain amount of annual training is required by the State of Texas for every certified law enforcement officer. Almost everyone attends the training day in plain clothes. At about 11:00 a.m., the classes are dismissed for lunch. Most of the officers drive off campus, in their personal vehicles, to grab a bite of lunch at any of the many fast-food restaurants in the area.

Kelly loves to eat Popeye's fried chicken.

So at lunchtime, Kelly drove to the Popeye's just down the road from the police academy. As he pulled into the parking lot, he watched a plain-clothes officer who he had been attending class with—and who evidently beat him to the Popeye's—run out of the restaurant "in much haste." Kelly's "Spidey" sensed something was amiss! Sure enough, a robbery crew had decided that this particular Popeye's would be a great place to rob at the lunch hour, probably not realizing that the Houston Police Academy was but a few miles away. As the crew was inside taking the business down, Kelly's fellow student, who was inside the restaurant, in plain clothes and not carrying a sidearm (even though he was on duty and was required to do so), decided that his best course of action was to run fast—a tactical retreat of sorts? I would like to think maybe he was running for help.

Shortly afterward, the robbery crew exited and moved to their get-away car.

Kelly is always armed, and has a proactive mind-set. In the parking lot, to not endanger innocent civilians, Kelly engaged the crew; he drew his 1911 pistol and ordered the suspects down on the ground. One suspect, brandishing a pistol, made a serious miscalculation and Kelly immediately shot him. Bad guys in Houston are hard to kill! Dropping his pistol and leaving a blood trail, he, along with the other suspects, in all the excitement, made it to their getaway vehicle and escaped.

Fortunately, Kelly was able to get the license plate, and the car turned out to be a rental vehicle. Dave and Justin got involved in the hours after the shooting and put the pieces together and identified the suspect. The "baby momma" who rented the vehicle had a boyfriend who had a long history in Harris County for aggravated robberies and other assorted felonies. Further investigation by David and Justin established sufficient probable cause for a 2B warrant on her boyfriend. In the days following, we hounded the suspect, just missing him at every location we developed. The suspect had received a "through and through" gunshot wound in his arm and, knowing that it would be reported if he turned up at a local hospital, self-treated it. The suspect stayed one step ahead of us and soon he left town. A few months later, he was arrested in South Carolina during a narcotics investigation conducted by the DEA and local police. By the time of his arrest, the wound had fully healed.

When the NDTU moved into the dismantling of robbery crews, the guys started contacting the managers and owners of many area businesses. One of these was the Valero Energy Corporation, which besides being a major petroleum refiner also maintains many retail outlets. These retail outlets sell fuel (gas station) and are also a "corner store" where customers can purchase other items, such as beer, cigarettes, milk, etc. The stations were generally manned by one clerk and in the Houston area were open late into the evening. The Valeros were also consistently being robbed, usually by your less knowledgeable, younger criminals as they began their careers by establishing "street cred" with their peers. They scored a few hundred dollars on each "lick." Of course, in doing so, they might even shoot a few innocent citizens.

These younger suspects were not to be underestimated. We thought they were some of the most dangerous criminals in Houston. They were often armed and consistently demonstrated a certain sociopathic, reckless disregard for human life.

The members of the NDTU were also approached by a supervisor from the Valero corporate office in Houston, who was unhappy with all their stores being robbed and not satisfied with the efforts of the Houston

Police Department in stemming them. He asked, "Would you guys be willing, after your regular duty hours, to drive to and 'check by' on Houston-area Valero corner stores to make sure they were not being robbed, to give the on-duty clerks some sense of protection and security?" Many Houston police officers supplement their income with "extra jobs" and Dave and Kelly took up the offer, working the assignment while off duty and in plain clothes. Both of them needed the extra money, having children in college.

A few weeks later, on a Friday night, Kelly checked by with a clerk (chatting and drinking some coffee) at a Valero in the north side of Houston. Suddenly, a robbery crew, wearing masks and gloves, burst through the door. The first suspect in carried a Remington 870 12-gauge shotgun at port arms. This suspect, not immediately realizing that Kelly was "the Law," began to announce his intentions to rob the store. He never finished his sentence. In one swift motion, Kelly drew his 1911 pistol and shot Mr. Big Mouth with the shotgun right through the chest. Much like the shooting a few months earlier, the suspect dropped his gun and, leaving a blood trail, ran out of the store, escaping into the night.

However, Kelly had shot this one "good!" And even though the bad guy was a tough "street banger," he quickly realized the hole in his chest was causing "some serious discomfort" and a Band-Aid wouldn't cut it.

In the interest of his own self-preservation, the wounded suspect had his buddies drop him off at the nearest hospital emergency room. The on-duty doctors rendered emergency care and probably saved his life. As required, the hospital staff immediately reported a gunshot victim and responding law enforcement quickly put the pieces together. The suspect was arrested and when in stable condition transferred into the custody of the Harris County Sheriff's Office medical facility pending his trial and maybe a long prison sentence—or, more likely (in Harris County, Texas), a plea bargain and a probated sentence.

Wow—the ultimate street cred for a young up-and-coming gang banger/hijacker: getting shot by the police in the middle of committing a lick. I thought getting shot by the law didn't speak well to his proficiency in his chosen profession.

Months later, I received another late-night phone call. Kelly was back working the Valero extra job. Looking forward to an uneventful night, he had parked his SWAT-issued Ford Expedition inconspicuously, watching the front of a "quiet" Valero gas station. He positioned his Expedition about 50 yards out, facing the front door, where he could monitor the customers going in and out and on the older female clerk, who was working the register. Over the previous few weeks, Kelly had become friends with her and saw himself as her guardian. She was apprehensive about working late nights in the robbery capital of the country, but because she was poor and recently divorced, she didn't have many choices.

Kelly was eating his favorite—Popeye's fried chicken.

Kelly hadn't finished his meal when, coming from around the corner, two suspected "hijackers" wearing face masks swiftly entered the store. One acted as a lookout, positioning himself by the front door so he could scan the parking lot. The other, armed with a handgun, threatened the clerk, pointing his weapon at her and yelling for her to hand over all the money.

Kelly was in a bad position: by himself and with no support. He waited for the two suspects to finish robbing the store, intending, maybe, to confront them when they exited and hoping that in the meantime they didn't shoot the clerk.

Kelly could plainly see the robbery going down. The suspect with the gun was becoming aggressive with the clerk. Kelly felt that he had to act; it would be unconscionable if he killed her while he watched. Not to be underestimated, there was also the human element, which sometimes blinds objectivity—Kelly knew the victim personally.

He acted. Armed with a SWAT-issued, fully automatic M4 carbine, Kelly exited his vehicle and moved directly to the front door of the store to intervene. The lookout suspect saw him coming and yelled to his buddy,

"*HEY NIGGA, THERE'S A COP!*", and ran to the back of the store either to hide or try to run out the rear door (there was none).

The armed suspect, hearing his buddy's shouted warning, stopped threatening the clerk and walked to the front door, still with his pistol in his right hand. Then, while peering out through the all-glass door and seeing Kelly approaching, he was heard to say out loud, to himself or to his buddy who was beating a rapid retreat, as recorded on the store's video surveillance system, "*NIGGA, FUCK THEM COPS!*" Then he raised his pistol.

Just as the armed suspect raised his pistol, uttering the last word of his sentence "*...COPS!*" Kelly, seeing an opportunity and acting to protect the life of the clerk as well as his own and while still on the move, fired a burst from his rifle through the glass door and into the torso of the suspect. Mr. Bad Guy was very much incapacitated, immediately dropping his gun and falling to the floor, screaming. Kelly had "center-punched" him with multiple .223 rounds.

But again, Houston bad guys are tough! But this one wasn't able to run away because of all the holes in him. The sixteen-year-old suspect survived.

Many of the officers and sergeants of the NDTU prior to the robbery initiative had already "seen the elephant": they had been involved in previous shootings or shootouts with Houston's north side bad guys. These men would have preferred not having to get into another shooting, but then again they would not shirk their sworn responsibilities, particularly in protecting innocent lives. They were among the "meat eaters" in the department who would run to the sound of the gunfight! They were not filled with false bravado or braggadocio; they were quiet about their experiences and usually only freely and openly discussed them with others in the department who were cut of the same cloth and understood.

The career administrative types, who were only interested in "flying a desk," never understood the men and women in the department who were meat eaters. They were the "grass eaters." So often the grass eaters would talk a big game and the non-initiated might even think they were meat eaters; but all you had to do was observe their actions in a critical incident and then it would be abundantly clear who were the meat eaters and who were the grass eaters. Unfortunately, meat eaters and grass eaters all wore the same uniform; all had supposedly sworn oaths to protect the lives of the innocent, but there was no easy way to ferret them out—until the moment of the critical incident.

I can say confidently that everyone in the NDTU, whether they were ever involved in a shooting or not, were meat eaters.

Even some younger members of the NDTU, still in their twenties, were experienced way beyond their years. John Calhoun was one of our newer members. I had worked with his father, David, back in the 1980s when we were both sergeants assigned to the Homicide Division.

Where I didn't care so much for the assignment (but was grateful for the experience), David thrived and stayed in Homicide for his entire career until the day he retired. David was an excellent investigator and highly respected among his peers. He was an interesting man. Like many investigators, he had an interest in history; David's passion was the American Civil War and he would frequent battle sites where, with his metal detector, he was able to recover many interesting artifacts. Elizabeth "Liz" Calhoun— wife to David and mother to John—was also a member of the Houston Police Department, as an investigator assigned to the Auto Theft Division.

John was dorky funny! Tall and lanky, with a quick wit and quite a sense of humor, he was unmarried, with a reputation as a ladies' man. In our office, John's desk was right next to Kelly Huey's. When days were slow and the NDTU was between operations, Kelly would sit at his desk and read history books, mostly on the Vietnam War, or watch police tactical training type videos, all with a stern, serious, "no nonsense ever tolerated" expression on his face. John, on the other hand, would sit at his desk, right next to Kelly, and read comic books! Batman was his favorite. All the while, John giggled to himself and would make facial expressions, apparently deeply engrossed in his comics. Kelly would note the subject of John's reading and would visibly clench his teeth together in disdain. If I was in the room, he would catch my eye and slowly shake his head back and forth in the negative (*"can you believe this!"*). I would always tell Kelly, "It's okay—it's all good. John just likes looking at pictures of men in tight, form-fitting costumes!" Kelly would then totally disapprove of what I said, clench his teeth again, roll his eyes, and go back to his "serious" reading or video watching.

John was a "perpetual bachelor" and enjoyed life very much! He caused concern for his mother, who I would sometimes run into at the local Walmart, where she would confide in me. At the time that I wrote this book (2019), John was still a bachelor, living in a loft in midtown Houston, pretty much smack-dab in the "significantly" gay community of the city, known as Montrose. Yet hope springs eternal! Liz is carefully optimistic; John has been dating a beautiful young lady—I will call her Denise" (not her real name)—for the past several years. John and "Denise" have been constant companions and Liz hoped that they might someday officially settle down.

In the year before he was assigned to the NDTU, John, while assigned to the North Patrol Division's evening shift, was involved in a shooting with a robbery suspect. The suspect had committed a robbery of a business and area patrol officers spotted him shortly thereafter. The suspect evaded arrest and was hiding somewhere in a wooded area. John and other officers began searching for him. John was the one to find the suspect. As soon as he was discovered, the suspect got off several shots. They all missed. John then finished the gunfight, killing the suspect with more accurate and decisive return gunfire.

A year after this shooting, while again on routine patrol, John was dispatched to investigate a suspicious male, again in the Greenspoint area. He found the suspicious male; while talking to him, the suspect produced a Glock .380 and shot John one time in the torso. John finished the gunfight, hitting the suspect twice "center mass." When the call went out that

John was shot, Lalo and I were close by, running an undercover surveillance operation in the area. We were the first supervisors on the scene. Thankfully, John had worn light body armor under his uniform shirt and the bullet hadn't penetrated his vest. Except for a large nasty-looking bruise to the skin underneath, John was okay. After determining that John was still up and vertical, I checked on the suspect, who was down on the ground and not moving. The suspect was still alive—barely! To my perception, he was already pretty much dead, but his body just didn't know it yet. His eyes were rolled up into his head and his complexion was already taking on a grayish color, although there was yet some infrequent shallow breathing. He was really dead when the paramedics finally arrived and began working on him, but as per some policy, they had to transport him to an emergency room where a doctor could officially declare him "really, really dead."

I would often joke after, in retelling the story, that as soon as we had arrived, Lalo had kissed John's "*ouchy*" (where the suspect's bullet had bruised John's "lower torso") and made it all better. Cop humor!

John had been wearing body armor made by the Safariland Group. In later years, the company touted John around the United States to various police trade shows, where John would talk about his "I am dumb and got shot" experience and how his Safariland vest had saved his life. The marketing folks at Safariland were not stupid. John was personable, reasonably photogenic, and a great salesman for their company.

John was well thought of. Shortly after, we gave him a permanent assignment in the NDTU. He was also selected to be a part-time member of the Houston Police Department's SWAT Detail.

The NDTU began the commercial business robbery initiative. The first few operations were fairly simple and didn't involve cases that a diligent robbery investigator couldn't solve if given enough time. This was the problem for the robbery investigators, who were housed just above our office on the second floor. There were too few investigators being swamped with so many cases. It was much worse for the sheriff's department robbery investigators.

The early vehicle tracking operations I likened to learning to ride the bicycle with training wheels. This was when a vehicle was identified as having been used in one or two robberies. Somehow the license plate, or partial plate, became known to us, often from a witness. Typically, the morning after a robbery, Dave or Justin would read a North Division report called the "Robbery Recap," which was a brief narrative documenting all the robberies from the previous day. This report might "clue us" immediately to any significant investigative leads with what I called actionable intelligence.

The Robbery Recaps we were most interested in were the ones which documented any vehicle(s) that had been used by the suspects in a robbery or relevant suspect vehicle information that had been documented in the initial incident report written by a responding patrol officer. Most important to us was any information in the report regarding the suspect vehicle's license plate. Even if just a partial license plate number was observed by a witness, there were still timely investigative methods to help us figure out the number in its entirety.

This Robbery Recap was produced early in the morning, before we (the NDTU) got to work, and was the product of the Crime Analysis Unit (CAU) of North Patrol Division's Tactical Section, which was staffed by three officers: Blake VanPelt, Amanda Morgan, and Steve Foster. The Robbery Recap was an important tool and instead of Dave or Justin having to read each robbery case that had occurred in our area the day before, we could instead scan the recap for investigative leads, trusting that the folks in the CAU had done their due diligence.

Monday mornings was the big day for me, because the Robbery Recap would contain summaries of robberies (both commercial and individual) from the previous Friday, Saturday, and Sunday. Often there would be well over thirty aggravated robberies, mostly of commercial businesses, in just the two patrol districts that we were responsible for.

The vast majority of the serial robbery crews we dismantled were accomplished in the following fashion.

Let's say, for example, I had thirty-five robberies on the Monday morning recap. The recap might show a high probability that seven of these thirty-five robberies were committed by the same suspect(s). For conversation's sake, the reported description made by the store clerks in these seven crimes was that of an older, heavyset black male with a big afro and armed with a handgun. A witness who was out in the parking lot of one of these businesses reported that just prior to the robbery, he or she had observed a silver Toyota Camry, bearing a Texas license plate, park on the side of the business. They observed a black male, heavyset with an afro, armed with a handgun, exit the vehicle from the rear passenger seat and go into the store and then quickly exit and re-enter the Camry, which then hastily left the scene. The witness stated that besides the armed suspect, there were two other black males inside the Camry, one driving and the other seated in the front passenger seat.

Immediately, I would send some members of the NDTU out to the various robbery scenes and they would canvass the area for any surveillance video taken at the date and time of the robbery and maybe in the hours before the incident. Often, the suspects, before they "hit" a business, scouted and reconnoitered it. Someone's video surveillance system, be it residential or commercial (they are now that common), in the general area of the store might have recorded images of the suspects' vehicle before the robbery. What we needed most was a license plate number, and in this example, we recover video of the vehicle minutes before the robbery as it cruised through the parking lot of the store that was robbed. However, the surveillance camera angle is such that only the first letters of the rear license plate are recorded: "FJH."

We didn't necessarily even need the entire number/letters in the license plate. We could figure it out. With the make and model of the vehicle and with access to certain computer databases, we could then search for all Toyota Camrys, silver in color, registered in Harris County, Texas, with the first letters of the license plate being "FJH." Sure enough, there was one such registered vehicle in Harris County with, not coincidentally, a north side address. The complete license plate number was FJH-1234.

By lunchtime, we had developed a probable license plate number on a robbery vehicle.

My tracking order was already finished and emailed over to the Harris County District Attorney's Office Special Crimes Unit for their review (in an emergency, this step could be omitted) and one of the guys from the NDTU was headed downtown to pick up the completed order to present it to a district court judge for review and approval.

The first step in our example is completed: we have identified the vehicle and have or are obtaining a court order to covertly place a tracking device on it.

Now the next step. Where does this vehicle live? The registered owner in our example is Mary Doe, who according to the vehicle registration lives at 725 Seminar Drive, apartment #12. A quick, confidential phone call to the corporate management of the apartment complex reveals that Ms. Doe was evicted several months previous and left no forwarding address. Fortunately, with our "special access," David could query NVLS and finds that the license plate to our vehicle FJH-1234 has been scanned multiple times in the past few weeks, always parked at night in an apartment complex at 9601 West Montgomery. This location was probably the apartment complex where Ms. Doe moved to after being evicted from 725 Seminar.

Knowing the probable location of the vehicle, I would then coordinate and plan for an immediate middle of the night or early in the morning operation. The objective of the operation was to covertly place at least two ATF mobile tracking devices on the undercarriage of Ms. Doe's Camry, while it was parked, unoccupied, unbeknownst to anyone who might be associated with the vehicle or who might use it.

Windows of opportunity open and shut fast. In my experience, the robbery crews almost always "borrowed" or were somehow only loosely associated with the vehicle they used for commercial business robberies. They almost never used their own "rides."

Often, the vehicle they used belonged to or was somehow facilitated "on its face" by a female associate. She might rent a vehicle in her name for the express purpose of then handing it over to the robbery crew or would just let them, from time to time, "borrow" her own vehicle. The suspects would then use this vehicle for a few "licks" and pay her for its use. The understanding was that if detectives came to her and inquired about who had been using her vehicle, or the vehicle rented in her name (assuming that a witness or security video had captured the license plate of the vehicle) then she was to disavow all knowledge and plead ignorance as to who might have been using it on the day and time in question. If the suspects were really ahead of the game, if detectives approached her, they might even direct her to "plant" information—to have her give a false statement: "Why, yes, Officer, I let Jimmy Jones borrow my car last Thursday night." In actuality, "Jimmy Jones" is a rival gang member to the actual robbery crew and had nothing to do with the robbery. He was not involved and is innocent.

Sometimes, I suspected, that this could lead to wrongful arrests and even convictions! If the detective, in good faith, then showed Jimmy Jones's picture to the victim or witnesses via a photo spread and then Jimmy was somehow picked out, then the overworked Robbery detective might simply supplement the offense report and file a 2B arrest warrant for Aggravated Robbery on poor Jimmy and then move on to the next case. Case cleared! In my mind, the eyewitness identification of suspects, sometime weeks or months after the incident, could be unreliable. I slept better at night knowing that my case had much more additional corroborative evidence than just eyewitness testimony.

As soon as possible, after receiving the magistrate approval for our tracking order for our suspect vehicle, the objective was then to covertly place a tracking device on board. Sometimes, while the order was in the process of getting signed, an NDTU surveillance team was already watching the vehicle, tracking devices in hand, just waiting for the go signal. It made for interesting conversations with the judges, when as soon as he or she signed the order, the involved NDTU affiant would pull out his radio and say, "It's signed—put it on"! Most of the judges were interested in our surveillance operations and many questions would then be forthcoming. Many expressed concern when they realized that often we placed trackers on in the middle of the night, that some of us would be stealthily crawling under the vehicle to do the deed, all the while in plain clothes. Very easily we could be mistaken for an auto thief or car burglar and get shot by the vehicle's owner or a concerned neighbor (particularly in Texas). This is exactly what happened in the summer of 2018, in Chicago, when an ATF agent who was trying to place a tracking device on a suspect's vehicle was shot in the face (he survived).

We elevated the placing of a tracking device to a planned operation and a team event. We would have several surveillance officers watching the parked vehicle that we intended to place the tracker on and when the coast was clear, two other plainclothes officers, who were in the same vehicle, would pull up with the passenger side front door aligned to the target vehicle (so as to shield from view what was about to happen). The passenger side officer would then "roll out" under the target vehicle and place the trackers on the undercarriage of the vehicle.

Also, prior to all of this happening, as part of pre-planning, in the light of day we would locate a similar model and year vehicle, crawl under it, and leisurely figure out beforehand exactly where we would place the devices when it came to the real deal. The trackers had powerful magnets on one side and required a metal surface. You would be surprised how much of the undercarriage of modern vehicles are now covered with plastic. We wanted to have this all figured out beforehand, to minimize our vulnerability, i.e. the amount of time anyone spent under the vehicle.

Often we would go to car dealerships, identify ourselves as police officers, talk to the general manager and politely get permission to look over and inspect vehicles of the same year and model as the one we were targeting, without cuing the employees of the dealership to our use of tracking devices.

We learned several important things about tracker placement and the devices themselves: Always try and place two tracking devices on your vehicle. The batteries in the devices were finite and depending how fast you "pinged it" (sent a computer command to the tracking unit specifying how often it should update its geo coordinates) determined how fast you depleted your battery. Tracking devices were also complicated electronic devices that sometimes inexplicitly "went south." If you placed two devices on, you always had a backup tracker in case of a dying battery or a technical malfunction. If possible, we always tried to build redundancy into our tracking operations to combat Murphy's Law—anything that could go wrong would go wrong.

Another thing we learned by accident proved valuable! We realized that the tracking devices had other status functions, like a tilt warning. If someone found the tracker and pulled it off, they would normally tilt it past 90 degrees from its original mounting position, which would then send us an alert, possibly a sign that the tracker had been discovered. We only had this happen to us once. We were monitoring a vehicle that had been used in several aggravated robberies and had no idea who the suspects were. Suddenly, we received a tilt alert. Even though the vehicle was on a major freeway, it stopped moving. When we physically arrived on scene, our target vehicle was on its side, having been involved in a major accident. We discreetly removed the tracker from the wreck and had to wait several months, until we received information from the FBI on another vehicle that this robbery crew was using, at which time we could put the pieces together and take them down when they were minutes away from committing another bank robbery in a neighboring city. The presence of a tilt alert gave me a certain peace of mind: no tilt alert meant no discovery, so it was one of those unknowns (have we been discovered?) that I could dismiss from my mind and not have to think about.

Another important status function on the tracker came to light when we placed a tracking device on one of the first vehicles we were trying to watch. We placed our device on the vehicle's rear undercarriage, near the exhaust system. We didn't realize it right away but the ATF Sendum mobile tracking devices we were using also measured temperature. This was big for us when we were monitoring our suspect vehicle via computer, when no one in the NDTU had actual physical "eyes" on it.

It worked like this: when the targeted tracked vehicle moves from its home base, it then "breaks" an imaginary geo "fence" that we had previously set around it. The tracker now knows it's moving and immediately sends a message alert (iPhone) to myself, David Smith, or Justin Williams warning us that "our" vehicle was now occupied and being driven by someone! Because the tracker also monitors temperature, as soon as the engine was turned on, the exhaust system near the tracker heated up; it was recorded and the information sent to us. Conversely, if the vehicle was then parked and the engine shut off, the exhaust system would cool down and you would know that, in most likelihood, the vehicle was parked and no one was inside it. Even if we could not physically get eyes on our targeted vehicle, to physically observe it in a timely fashion, we could often tell when the person(s) in the vehicle were likely surveying or reconnoitering a business to rob. If the geo track showed that the vehicle was parked in a business parking lot for an extended period but the exhaust temperature remained hot, that meant that even though the vehicle appeared to be parked, the engine was still running with someone inside it. What were they doing? It could be they were parked and watching a business, planning for a future robbery. Or maybe about to actually commit a robbery?

The trackers that ATF provided us were not purpose built for being placed on bad guy cars. Rather, they were designed to be placed on containers of perishable goods to monitor the shipment's progress and to make sure that these commodities were not subject to any adverse conditions. It just so happened that these design features worked out well for us in tracking vehicles.

Wow, the technology! When I first joined HPD, we still had rotary phones and manual typewriters.

Unless you have done it, putting a tracking device on a suspect's vehicle sounds benign. But this was often done in the darkness, in the worst part of town, and if discovered in the act, it might lead to some extreme unpleasantries. In the beginning, I placed many of the trackers on the vehicles, figuring that because I was smaller and thinner, it would be easiest for me to get under the vehicle and back out. Usually, I would wear dark clothing and a hooded sweatshirt (to hide as much of my "whiteness" as possible), as well as gloves. The only thing I carried was a small penlight to help me find the "pre-figured out" place on the vehicle I would put the trackers on. I left my wallet, ID, and sidearm behind in our surveillance vehicle. From previous experience, when I was assigned to Proactive Internal Affairs, something about crawling under vehicles in the dead of night caused wallets and guns to become dislodged and be left behind under said vehicle. For protection, I would rely on my fellow team members, who were nearby watching, if some intervention became needed.

Sometimes we would have to take a calculated risk of discovery. It might be a now-or-never moment if we didn't make the effort, take the risk, to get the tracker on. Maybe we didn't know where the vehicle was kept, or it was impossible to get access to the vehicle (kept parked at night in a residential garage with the door shut). In these situations, we could only get eyes on the vehicle when it was occupied (rolling) and the entire unit was conducting surveillance on it all day long, waiting for that one opportunity to sneak in and get the trackers onboard. We might lose sight of it and it would disappear into the heavy Houston traffic. When this occurred, when the window of opportunity opened briefly, we were prepared to move fast, to seize the moment. Maybe the driver of the vehicle parked the target vehicle at a convenience store for a few minutes to get a "soda water." In just those few minutes, as the rest of the unit stood watch, one of us would crawl under the vehicle to put trackers on to further enable our surveillance operation.

Often, getting trackers on the target vehicle was the most difficult part of the entire operation.

Two of the biggest men in the unit—Steven Zakharia and Christopher Rozek (Zak and Chris)—became adept at covertly putting trackers on and eventually took over and owned that aspect of our operation. It was always funny to see either of these big men crawling under a small compact vehicle situated low to the ground. But they did it and became very good at it.

Zak and Chris preferred to ride together, and they worked well with the other members of the NDTU. They were also close friends. More importantly, to me, as their sergeant, and the overall mission of the NDTU, Chris and Zak together created a synergy where their riding together created a much greater contribution to the mission than if they were working separately. Some leaders, not recognizing this, might have been tempted to split them up to have them in separate surveillance vehicles (if we had enough) so as to have more "eyes." But I knew better: they were a package deal.

Along with synergy, I also looked for and nurtured another collective intangible "force" with all the members of the NDTU. I defined this as a certain team momentum where everybody was working toward and pushing for the same goal. I wanted all the team members to be mutually supporting each other and "making things happen." I am sure there is some technical term known to the professionals who study group dynamics and leadership. I just knew that with the right combination of people, things "happened"!

CHAPTER 10

THE ALABONSON ROBBERY CREW

The NDTU was now becoming proficient at vehicle tracking and was systematically dismantling and picking apart the north side commercial business robbery crews. As I had already alluded to, most of these tracking operations were to support the Robbery detectives. Once our surveillance had borne fruit and the investigative leads were established, this information was then "back flowed" to the detectives, who could then connect the dots and bring their respective investigations to conclusion by identifying the suspect(s) and filing a 2B warrant.

Once the 2B warrant was filed, we would then pass the information to Heath and his WET, who would then do what they did best: hunt down and arrest the now wanted suspects, while we in the NDTU maintained our focus on other vehicle tracking and surveillance operations.

In the late spring of 2015, the NDTU was contacted by Robbery investigators from the Harris County Sheriff's Office, requesting the tracking services of our unit. The detectives had connected some of the dots and realized that about thirty-plus aggravated robberies of commercial businesses, in their jurisdiction during the past few months, were committed by the same group of suspects, albeit using many vehicles—all of which were stolen. However, in the last few robberies, the suspects had used a white Dodge Charger, which was not reported stolen. By doing their due diligence, the investigators had pulled surveillance video from one of the last robberies and had captured the license plate of the newest vehicle they were using. The Dodge Charger in question was registered to a middle-aged black woman who lived in an apartment complex on Alabonson Street (hence the nickname the Alabonson Robbery Crew).

We agreed to help.

Quickly, we wrote the tracking order and had it signed. That night, we snuck in to the apartment complex and with no fanfare placed two tracking devices on the Charger. We set a geo fence around the apartment complex. The next morning, we were alerted that the Charger was on the move, having broken our imaginary computer-generated fence. Dave Smith then sent, via computer, the command to speed up the tracker so it reported its location to us every two minutes. The entire NDTU then launched out of the office to "get eyes" on the Charger, to see how it was "loaded": did it have several black men in it, who perhaps matched the general description of the county's robbery crew?

It didn't take long.

Most of our robbery crews were centered in the Acres Homes community; this also being where our police command station was located, the NDTU undercover surveillance officers were able to follow the computer-generated track on their laptops and we soon had the Charger in sight. As we followed it, we eventually determined that the vehicle was driven by an older woman. Based on our previous research, it would be the registered owner. Our robbery crew was not in the vehicle.

We followed the woman driving the Charger all that morning and watched as she got her nails done and went grocery shopping and did her errands. Finally, late that morning, she returned to her apartment on Alabonson Street, where we watched as she parked her white Dodge Charger and took her groceries inside her apartment. It was close to noon, so we all broke for lunch at a nearby Mexican restaurant. Dave, not wanting to unduly drain the battery in the primary tracker on the Charger, backed it down, so it reported its location only every fifteen minutes.

We were just sitting down to lunch (fifteen minutes later), when "BING"—Dave and I received alerts on our iPhones, telling us that the Charger was outside of the Alabonson geo fence and on the move. Apparently, as soon as she had parked her car and after we had taken eyes off it, the owner of the Charger must have gotten back in it and left the apartment complex to do some other shopping.

Dave speeded up the primary tracker. The Charger was heading north. It then "landed" at a convenience store several miles away from the Alabonson address. The vehicle was now stationary at this convenience store. The NDTU abandoned its lunch plans and started to head north to intercept the Charger and again to see how it was "loaded." As we were getting close, the tracker showed the Charger leaving the convenience store and making a beeline back to home base on Alabonson Street. Out of an abundance of caution, I wanted to get eyes on it to see who was now in it, expecting it to be the same woman we had followed all morning. Whoever was driving the white Charger made it home to Alabonson before we could intercept it! When we arrived on Alabonson, there it was parked in its usual parking spot, unoccupied, with no one around it.

Then I got a sinking feeling in my stomach.

The Harris County Sheriff's Office was now notifying us that a convenience store in their jurisdiction had just been hit by a robbery crew: multiple black men armed with handguns, wearing masks and driving a white passenger vehicle. Then it hit me—the convenience store that was just robbed was the same one that our tracker had showed that our white Charger had been at while we were trying to get lunch. The suspects, in a short time, launched out of Alabonson, went straight to the store, held a gun to the head of the owner, and by threatening to kill him, forced him to open the safe and then stole all the cash inside it and made it back to Alabonson in record time and "*unassed*" the white Charger.

I didn't see that one coming! Evidently, as soon as the woman had parked our target vehicle and just as soon as we had taken our eyes off it to go to lunch, a robbery crew had immediately loaded up into it and when we should have had eyes on it, they committed a robbery almost right under our nose.

I should have assigned someone to keep eyes on the Charger while the rest of the NDTU ate lunch.

But I didn't.

I had fumbled and had egg on my face and was embarrassed and apologized to the county detectives as well as Lieutenant Bellamy and Captain Baimbridge for "missing the mark." The county detectives, and my supervisors, were all gracious. But now, the NDTU was determined to redeem ourselves and dismantle this robbery crew. To make matters worse, now our own HPD Robbery detectives, in comparing information with the county investigators, were starting also to connect the dots and figured out this same crew was good for twenty robberies within the city limits. To date, this was the most prolific crew that we had tackled and now we would make them "our business."

I don't know how it happened but that afternoon, an FBI agent assigned to Houston's field office got wind of our operation and just how violent and active the robbery crew was that we were now tackling. He came by the office, introduced himself and asked whether there was anything he or his agency could do to help with this surveillance operation. I explained what had happened, and that I expected the robbery crew to use the Charger again, probably in the next few days. I needed a way to physically watch the Charger, while it was parked in the Alabonson parking lot, so I could see when the robbery crew loaded up into it as opposed to when the woman drove it. I was certain that the owner of the vehicle was "renting it out," but to whom? We discussed approaching the owner and interviewing her regarding whom she had let borrow her vehicle, but we both sensed, based on our past experience with Houston-area robbery crews, that this would most likely be a dead end or she would give us misinformation. I couldn't have my guys sitting in one of our surveillance vehicles in the apartment parking lot watching the white Charger for any extended period—they would stand out and the surveillance would be blown. So the nice FBI agent offered up one of the bureau's super-secret "surveillance drop vehicles" for the NDTU's exclusive use in this operation.

The FBI's surveillance drop vehicle was a nondescript, common-looking white work van. On the roof was a rack that contained several large-diameter PVC pipes. For all the world, it looked like a plumber's van. The large PVC piping on top appeared to be storage for long, smaller diameter pipes, to be used at a construction site. Nothing in this van's outward appearance would attract attention. It is what I call in our business a "gray vehicle": it didn't stand out; it was not memorable. It was a similar principle as the "gray man" in that we, as undercover surveillance officers, should not wear clothing or have an outward appearance that was memorable. Sometimes Kelly Huey would have to tell some younger members of the NDTU to stop looking like a walking advertisement for the 5.11 tactical clothing chain. We wanted our personal appearance and the vehicles we used to be average "Joe the plumber" type stuff.

The FBI surveillance vehicle was perfect. It did not require anyone to be physically inside it to do the surveillance. Inside was a large bank of batteries that powered multiple cameras hidden in key places around the outside of the van, and no matter how the van was parked, one or more of these cameras could be remotely controlled to capture the image of whatever you wanted to surveil. The image was a live feed that was transmitted up to the FBI mothership and then back down to Quantico, Virginia, where it was stored. We also could access the live feed on our laptop computers and could monitor the goings-on in and around the white Charger while it was parked in the Alabonson parking lot.

Better yet, if the white Charger broke the Alabonson geo fence and we were not monitoring the live feed of the white Charger, we could simply "rewind" the video recording and view exactly who had entered it: was it Grandma or a multi-member robbery crew?

We immediately appropriated the drop vehicle from the FBI and "dropped" it right into "enemy territory" in the middle of the Alabonson parking lot, where, at my leisure, while drinking my coffee, from our office, I could watch "our vehicle."

The next morning when Dave and I came in (first we got our coffee) and then looked at our video feed from our newly acquired FBI's super-expensive high-tech surveillance vehicle now parked at Alabonson, we noted that the "parking lot" we were viewing was "different" and was now filled with wrecked and damaged vehicles. Another clue that something was amiss was mysteriously, overnight, the pavement in the parking lot had been torn out and was now surfaced in gravel. David and I looked at each other and we realized it at the same time: our borrowed FBI drop vehicle was no longer at Alabonson. Maybe overnight someone had stolen it? We called our FBI friend, who after being informed, told us not to worry—the van had a built-in GPS device for just such eventualities and he would get with his technician to query the GPS device and tell us where the van was. A few minutes later, he called back and sheepishly informed us that the GPS system was not working!

Dave and I spent the next fifteen minutes studying the images from the multiple camera feeds in the van, remotely moving the cameras to every angle to figure out where the van was. Then, clear as day, we found a business sign. The FBI's van was parked up the street close to our station, in a wrecker storage yard. Apparently, the night before, a private wrecker had towed it out of the Alabonson location because it didn't have a proper parking sticker for that apartment complex. Dave and I immediately recovered the FBI's van from the wrecker yard, via our police credentials. Then, we secretly obtained the proper parking permit from the apartment management and had the FBI van back in position at Alabonson, all within the hour. Something else we had not anticipated!

All the traps were set. We just knew that the robbery crew would hit again in but a few days and like before, they would use the white Charger, on which I had two tracking devices on as well as a video live feed of where it was parked. For the NDTU, during the daytime hours (when the crew normally did its robberies), it was an all hands on deck sort of thing. We were loaded and just waiting, knowing "it" would happen at any time. Not only that, but we also had a police helicopter (FOX) standing by, sitting on the launch pad, as well as K-9 and all of WET to support us in their marked units.

We were working closely with both the Robbery detectives from the county and the city. The Alabonson Robbery Crew was now credited with fifty or more armed robberies of commercial businesses. Unlike our other tracking operations, it was looking like we would have to follow this crew into an actual robbery. We would end up catching them in the act—whoever they were.

The days passed. Each day the crew didn't use the white Charger just upped the pressure.

Surely the next day would be "the" day!

The Alabonson Robbery Crew never used the white Charger again.

The crew was still active, hitting a business every few days, only now they had switched vehicles. They were not back to using stolen vehicles, but were still borrowing or "renting" vehicles for their robberies; there was no correlation. They would use a vehicle for two or three robberies. We would then figure out the identity of the vehicle, get a tracking order, locate it, and put a tracker on it, only to have the suspects never use it again. Then, they would use another vehicle for one or two robberies and we would repeat the process. A month later, I had tracking devices on five vehicles that the crew had used for robberies and was hoping that they would eventually recycle and reuse one of the earlier vehicles, one of which I had a tracking device on.

We were one step behind the crew and the number of robberies were still mounting. Fortunately, this crew had not killed anyone yet. But they were becoming more violent and seemed to be emboldened by their success. I was coming under increasing pressure from the supervisors in the Robbery Division to do something! Fortunately, Lieutenant Bellamy and Captain Baimbridge ran interference for us, telling all that the best chance for dismantling this crew laid with the NDTU; we were totally focused on it, but there needed to be patience!

We finally got a break. The Alabonson Robbery Crew switched back to using stolen vehicles, much like they had done when they first started. What had changed? Detective George Grifno from the Harris County Sheriff's Office had a theory. In interviewing some other north side robbery suspects, a name kept popping up: Darius Spears. According to Grifno's source, Darius's specialty was auto theft, and he was stealing and then giving these vehicles to the north side robbery crews for their use. Apparently, Spears was good at his craft and received a finder's fee for each vehicle he stole and then turned over.

Justin and Dave started to research Darius Spears, whose criminal history showed a propensity toward Auto Theft and Burglary of a Motor Vehicle (BMV). More interesting was that the Northwest Tactical Unit, whose specialty was watching parking lots and catching car burglars, had caught Darius red-handed breaking into a Ford truck while it was parked at the Willow Brook Mall. Darius had pled out and then served a few months in jail.

The light bulb moment! When comparing the times the Alabonson Robbery Crew had stopped using stolen vehicles in their robberies and then re-started, we found it exactly coincided with when Darius was arrested for BMV and had been incarcerated.

Maybe Darius Spears was the key to the puzzle?

Did the Alabonson Robbery Crew stop using stolen vehicles because their man—the guy who stole vehicles for them—was "out of pocket" while he served a short sentence for BMV?

Darius lived with his girlfriend in a north side apartment complex. She was gainfully employed in the medical field and had maintained the apartment where they both lived with their young child. A few days spent in surveillance identified two vehicles (both registered in her name); on any given day, Darius would use one or the other.

Another clue was that in one of the latest robberies, the crew, shortly after "hitting the lick," had dumped the stolen vehicle they were using and were picked up by unknown suspects driving a vehicle similar in description to a vehicle owned by Darius's girlfriend.

I wanted to put tracking devices on both vehicles. To convince a judge to sign the orders, I had to write extensively to show the probable (albeit weak) cause. After many questions, the district court judge approved and signed both orders. But, we had run out of tracking devices. So in the middle of the night, we once again sallied forth to covertly retrieve four tracking devices off vehicles that the crew had previously used (I was now taking the risk that they would never be used again by the crew), replace the batteries, and then sneak into the apartment complex where Darius and his girlfriend lived and redeploy the trackers on their two vehicles. Working all night, we were done before dawn.

It was a gamble, a little more than a hunch, pushed forward by George Grifno, Dave Smith, and Justin Williams.

Over the next several days, we tracked both the vehicles connected to Darius and his girlfriend. Soon we knew the work schedule for the woman and she was predictable: drop the kid off at day care, go to work, and late in the afternoon, return home. It got to be as soon as a vehicle broke the geo fence we had set up we could tell almost immediately, based on the track that the particular vehicle was taking, who (Darius or the girlfriend) was in the vehicle. When Darius left the apartment, his route was usually to the Acres Homes community. He would leave the apartment, just after his girlfriend left for work, and then would spend the day with his buddies, smoking marijuana. Predictably, in the midafternoon, he would then hightail it back to the apartment before his girlfriend arrived home from a hard day's work.

Then, one morning after his girlfriend went to work, Darius did something different. After leaving home, he went to another apartment complex at 7313 Northline Drive. There he picked up several other black men. The NDTU "got eyes" and we then spent the next several hours cold trailing Darius and his new friends. All morning and into the afternoon, we conducted rolling surveillance, assisted by our tracking device, and watched as Darius and friends prowled through business parking lots, various parking garages, and most significantly, apartment complexes whose predominant population were Hispanics.

Tensions and expectations within the members of the NDTU started to rise. Our theory about Darius appeared correct and maybe all the man-hours that had gone into the surveillance over the past few months was about to come to fruition. Was Darius and friends looking for a vehicle to steal? Were the other guys in his vehicle our long sought-after Alabonson robbery crew?

Hours later, they still had not stolen a vehicle, and it was getting late in the afternoon. I knew that if Darius held to form, then soon he would have to discontinue whatever he was up to, drop his passengers off at 7313 Northline, and get back to his apartment miles away on Airtex Drive—all before his girlfriend got home. It had become evident to all of us that since he got released after serving his time on the BMV charge that she was keeping him on a short leash (perhaps she knew he had a propensity for getting into trouble). Sure enough, Darius discontinued the search, dropped his friends off at 7313 Northline, and headed back home, fast! I almost felt sorry for him; he was in a race against time. Because we also had a tracker on her vehicle, I knew she had left work and was also headed home. Who would get home first, Darius or his girlfriend? If she got home before him, how much trouble would he be in? Would she revoke his "man card" and/ or driving privileges; maybe even "ground" him? If she did, then maybe we would have to wait several more weeks or even months, until he was "ungrounded." It was a race.

Now we were back at our office and watched on our big-screen computer as the two dots marched slowly across our map of Houston. One dot represented the vehicle Darius was in, while the other his girlfriend's. Who would get home first? We started taking bets. With just moments to spare, Darius came tearing around the corner into the apartment parking lot on Airtex Drive and because we now had the FBI surveillance van with its remote cameras in the same parking lot, we watched as Darius parked "with haste," then sprinted up the stairs to their apartment. Just as he closed the door, in drove his girlfriend, none the wiser.

We all cheered for Darius—he had made it! Our surveillance operation was still viable.

A few days later, in the morning, while again in our office, we watched as Darius's girlfriend left for work. As soon as she was out of the parking lot, we watched as he left the apartment, got into his car, and drove out. Would today be the day, or was it going to be another day of hanging out in the hood, smoking marijuana with his buddies, while the "baby mommas" were at work? We watched our tracking map as Darius drove south from Airtex Drive on Interstate 45. Once he reached Little York Road, if he turned to the right, he would probably spend the day smoking dope. If he turned to the left, then he would be probably heading to 7313 Northline Drive to meet with his "friends" who we suspected might be the Alabonson Robbery Crew.

He turned left and headed to Northline Drive. All the NDTU immediately launched out of the office.

It was on!

Darius drove into the apartments at 7313 Northline. A short time later, out he drove with several other black men now in his car with him. For two hours, they repeated the process of a few days earlier. It appeared they were again looking for a vehicle to steal. We watched as they slowly trolled through a Walmart parking lot in the Greenspoint area, appearing to look over several trucks parked there. Nothing happened. We were doing a loose rolling surveillance and had eyes but were careful not to be spotted. We were letting the trackers on Darius's car do the hard work. Darius and friends then drove east across the North Freeway and they entered an apartment complex. Most of the occupants there were Hispanic and many of them were undocumented. We could not follow them inside the complex   it would be too obvious.

We watched the progress of Darius's vehicle through the apartment complex on our laptop computers or iPhones. All the NDTU surveillance teams were positioned outside of the complex in separate, discreet locations, in public areas, to blend in and not be noticed. The dot representing Darius's vehicle stopped in the middle of the complex for maybe forty seconds.

Then it started to move again. Now the dot headed for the apartment's exit gate. Soon we had eyes again as Darius's car came out of the complex. More importantly, it was right behind a big, older model Ford F-250 truck with an extended bed. Had they just stolen this truck? Could they have done it that fast? We followed both Darius's car and the truck because it was becoming obvious that they were driving in convoy. The tension mounted even more when Ben LeBlanc was able to discreetly get a glimpse of the driver of the truck. It was a black man!

We followed both vehicles, as they traveled together, back to the apartments at 7313 Northline. Both vehicles entered the complex. We could not follow (we would be spotted) and just like at the Hispanic apartment complex earlier, the NDTU covertly positioned their undercover vehicles outside the complex in random, inconspicuous public areas.

About fifteen minutes later, the F-250 and Darius's vehicle exited the apartment complex together, again traveling in convoy. Now I was able to get a good look at the occupants in the truck. Before there had been one, but now there were two black men in it. Both vehicles drove north, out of the city limits, into Harris County. They then drove to a small neighborhood grocery store that was owned and managed by a nice Pakistani family. Darius, in his vehicle, parked across the street from the store. The two unknown black men in the F-250 drove one block north and then backed the F-250 into a private driveway.

I had eyes on the F-250. Were they about to take down the grocery store? Was Darius the "shot caller" and even now calling on his cell phone, telling the robbery crew in the truck when to hit the store? Were the guys in the F-250 the robbery crew? Was the F-250 even stolen?

Minutes went by slowly. I was about a quarter mile away from the F-250. Then, the truck started moving, turning south and headed to the grocery store.

I was following, but not close. The F-250 turned in to the parking lot, where other members of the NDTU had eyes.

Robbery in Progress!

The undercover officer, who had eyes on the front of the store, calmly narrated on the radio as the F-250 came into the parking lot and parked at the gas pumps. Then the doors opened and the two black males who were in it jumped out. But now they had face masks on and were armed with semiautomatic pistols. They ran across the parking lot, headed to the front door of the grocery store.

The oldest son of the Pakistani family who owned the store was working the front register. "Abdul" was not stupid. He looked out the window and saw two black males in the parking lot running to the front door, wearing masks and carrying guns. He thought perhaps that they were up to no good, and it was in his best interest and self-preservation to deny them entry into his family's business. Just as the hijackers were reaching for the door handle, a split second from gaining access and entering, Abdul pushed the button on the hidden electronic door lock next to his register! "Clang!" The door was locked. The two suspects pulled on it for a second and then realized that they had been foiled. Now they were running back to the parked F-250 and soon hightailed it out of the parking lot.

This was just what I didn't want.

Now I knew for certain this was the robbery crew. We had watched them attempt a robbery and because of Abdul's quick thinking (good for him), we had missed the preferred opportunity to confront the bad guys in the parking lot while they were still on foot. Now they were back in their getaway vehicle and it would be a vehicle chase.

I don't like police car chases. They are dangerous to innocent citizens!

But there was still a brief opportunity to stop the F-250 before it turned into a chase. As the suspects drove out of the grocery store parking lot, they "Failed to Yield the Right of Way Exiting a Private Drive" and I plowed into the side of the stolen F-250 with the beat-up old Ford Taurus I was driving.

Yes...I took advantage of the situation, trying to avoid a police pursuit, and with my undercover vehicle I then tried to push the F-250 sideways into a nearby drainage ditch that ran alongside of the road to immobilize them. No luck! The vehicle I was driving was too light and the truck too heavy. The suspect's F-250 regained traction, and they were still moving. Now my piece of junk undercover car was really a piece of junk, because I was immobilized: my engine had stopped running.

The suspects were making their getaway. The NDTU surveillance was following and the uniform police units supporting us were closing in fast.

Then the gunfire erupted.

One suspect reached out the window with his pistol and fired a shot at one of the NDTU surveillance officers. This then elicited a brief barrage of returning gunfire from several of my men as they proceeded to punch numerous holes into the cab where the suspect who fired the shot was seated.

The marked units were closing in from every point of the compass and true to form, the suspects ran—it was a car chase. The worst kind of chase. It was in the middle of the workday, when the roadways were filled with citizens. With speeds up to 100 MPH, the suspects in the F-250 ran from the marked units; then they sideswiped several passenger vehicles, doing minor damage. Still running with a train of patrol cars behind them, they then raced through a school zone. Wisely, a patrol supervisor was on the main radio channel, telling the marked patrol units to back down; the chase was getting out of control. A police helicopter was getting close and would try to call the chase from the air. The suspects were soon headed back to the apartments at 7313 Northline Drive and they kind of, sort of, made it. They were going too fast and couldn't quite navigate the turn in to the complex and plowed into a trash dumpster. They were stopped cold. The suspects were dazed by the collision and were then easily taken into custody by the uniform officers and the members of the NDTU who had followed.

The cab of the truck had a bunch of bullet holes in it, all directed at the idiot suspect who had shot at us. None of the bullets we fired really connected. The bad guy who shot at us only had a minor face wound, which was probably caused by a .223 bullet fragment, from one of the several rounds that Justin Williams had fired with his rifle.

The infamous Alabonson Robbery Crew was in custody. After the shooting and chase, with the suspects in the F-250, Darius Spears tried to slink back home. But because we had a tracker on his car, it was a simple matter to soon locate him. Ben LeBlanc had the privilege of arresting him without any drama.

A few days later, the NDTU had a good laugh! We could access the Harris County Jail's inmate phone recordings. Inmate telephone conversations from within the jail system are recorded, stored, and cataloged per inmate with date and time. It's not a secret and the inmates are made well aware with big signs that as they access the jail phones that their conversations are not private and might be recorded. We listened to the jailhouse phone conversation between Darius and his girlfriend, as he tried to explain to her just how he had been arrested for Aggravated Robbery when, according to her directive, he was supposed to be sitting patiently at their apartment, waiting for her to arrive home from work. I don't remember all of the conversation but do remember it was one-sided. She did all the talking/yelling/shouting/cursing, and it was mostly a whole lot of *"YOU MUTHA FUCKER WHAT SHIT HAVE YOU GOTTEN INTO NOW!"* repeated over and over.

The takedown of the Alabonson Robbery Crew had not gone down as I had hoped. It had turned into a dangerous high-speed police chase, something I wanted to avoid as best as possible in the future.

As the proficiency of the NDTU quickly increased in the identifying and tracking of vehicles the robbery crews were using, it became important to me to better plan for the takedown of these armed suspects, particularly if we caught them in the middle of committing an aggravated robbery.

I wanted an overall strategy that would best protect the lives of innocent citizens.

But if previous history proved correct, the Houston Police Department's Command Staff would be loath to provide any definitive direction to the NDTU, because of the potential of racial unrest.

CHAPTER 11

THE BATTLE WITHIN

A supervisor over a police tactical unit tasked with conducting long-term surveillance on a suspected serial business robbery crew is in a unique situation. During these surveillances, it is possible that a vehicle that has been somehow linked to being used to facilitate these robberies may lead the undercover police surveillance team to a business or area in which a takeover robbery is about to occur, or is occurring.

It should be noted that it is presupposed that there were no, or minimal, chance of significant criminal charges and/or viable investigative leads available to the tactical unit supervisor that would have enabled him to arrest the suspect(s) before being placed in this position—of being physically present, in an undercover/surveillance capacity, when a takeover robbery with multiple armed suspects is occurring.

How does a sergeant over such a tactical/surveillance unit handle this situation: A stolen vehicle has just pulled up to a pawnshop. Five masked, armed suspects are conducting a takeover robbery of the business, holding a gun to the manager's head, trying to get access into the business's safe.

Assuming there is adequate police manpower immediately available on scene, the supervisor can:

- Attempt to arrest the suspects while in the commission of the robbery and still inside the business.

- Attempt to arrest the suspects after they exit and outside of the business and transitioning back to their getaway vehicle.

- Attempt to arrest the suspects after they have re-entered their getaway vehicle.

- Let the suspects go and not attempt to arrest and hope to identify them later based on previous observations.

I believe that all four arrest scenarios are viable. Unfortunately, this entirely new commercial business robbery surveillance paradigm, utilizing mobile tracking devices on vehicles, was something revolutionary for the Houston Police Department and far outside of the experience and understanding of most members of the department's Command Staff. Worse, the implementation and ideas for this new tactic to dismantle the robbery crews had originated from the bottom of the organization (sergeants) and there was no ownership or formal "blessing" from the upper management, much less experienced-based understanding. Other than several assistant chiefs calling a meeting with all the department's tactical unit supervisors and directing that something needed be done about violent crime, in particular aggravated robberies, no specificity or direction was given as to how we were to accomplish this or what tactics we were to use.

So, it was left to individual supervisors, in the absence of any Houston Police Department specific General Order or Standard Operating Procedure or Plan of Action that specifically addressed this issue, to develop a plan of action based on his or her experience and/or common sense—as long as, of course, this plan agrees (doesn't conflict) with any applicable laws or existing departmental General Orders or Standard Operating Procedures, etc.

Many of the tactical sergeants therefore just continued the usual "dope and whores" enforcement operations and gave lip service to the violent crime/aggravated robbery issue, much like I had done initially. But, of course, I was the north side tactical sergeant and the area I covered was "robbery central." And I also worked for a captain who cared and wasn't satisfied with just maintaining the status quo.

Because of recent technical advances and the repetitive criminal activity of these criminal street gangs and the abilities and street savviness of some officers assigned to the NDTU, never in the history of the Houston Police Department was there a chance for this tactical scenario to be played out consistently. Therefore, there was never a compelling reason for the Houston Police Department's Command Staff to develop and/or approve a definitive methodology to handle this situation—until now!

Prior to the drama of the Alabonson Robbery Crew, I had already begun "sounding the alarm" and bringing this issue directly to the attention to the Houston Police Department's Command Staff in official written correspondence, pointing out the need to develop definitive guidance and specific training for these never before repeatable tactical scenarios.

And here was the rub...would the department's Command Staff even provide guidance and place their stamp of approval on a specific course of action? Would they be frozen into inactivity by all the circular reasoning, governed by the what-ifs?

It was not really a hard decision for most of the non-politically motivated officers, sergeants, lieutenants, and captains, with any real tactical background and who wanted to do something about violent crime and robberies.

The course of action to be taken was also a moral decision. Unfortunately, in my experience, morality sometimes now takes a back-seat to the political optics and its considerations. The upper echelon of the department were people who owed their positions to politicians. What would they decide? Would their decisions be tainted by political consider-ations or firmly founded on moral principle?

Regarding the defined courses of action available to the on-scene tac-tical supervisor, all have inherent risk to innocent citizens, involved police officers, and to the suspects. There is no good answer. Again, a Houston Police Department supervisor over a tactical unit now had to choose a course of action in this scenario based on his experience and/or common sense as long as that plan "homogenized" with applicable laws, General Orders and Standard Operating Procedures.

These tactical options included:

Because of insufficient police resources or the number of immedi-ately present innocent citizens, elect to not attempt to arrest the robbery crew and let them go.

Arrest and/or confront the robbery crew immediately after the rob-bery as they exited the business and were attempting to re-enter their get-away vehicle.

Arrest the robbery crew after they re-entered their getaway vehicle and then have to engage in a high-speed vehicle pursuit.

But, beginning in May 2015, when the NDTU first began this initia-tive, absent of any exigent circumstances, my preferred course of action as a supervisor when confronted with an in progress takeover robbery involv-ing multiple suspects would be that the arrest of the robbery crew would occur as the suspects exited the business and were attempting to re-enter their getaway vehicle for the following reason:

The Priority of Life.

ALL HUMAN LIFE IS VALUABLE!

In a police tactical operation, a "priority of life" has to be established for the involved innocent citizens, the involved police officers, and the involved suspects. Therefore, whatever police action is being considered, it must be subject to the prioritization of the three categories: innocent citizen, officer, and then suspect(s).

Fortunately, several years earlier, the Houston Police Department had embraced the Advanced Law Enforcement Rapid Response Training (ALERRT), which had developed a nationally recognized blueprint for first responders in active shooter scenarios. Within ALERRT's written lesson plan and for the first time (that I know of), they provided clear, written guidance on the moral concept of "priority of life." Prior to the reading of ALERRT's lesson plan and the priority of life, this same moral concept was already talked about years earlier and recognized by some police professionals, particularly those in the tactical operations community (i.e., ALERRT wasn't the first). If the priority of life morality model is embraced by either the reader or more importantly by the upper leadership of a law enforcement agency, it provides insight and guidance in prioritizing the risk assignment to "valuable human life" and helps those tasked with such operations in the crafting of police tactical operations.

That priority for valuable human life in descending order is:

Innocent Citizen

Police Officer

Suspect(s)

So my decision-making in choosing a course of action, in conducting a tactical operation, is therefore based on my experience and common sense guided by all applicable laws, Departmental General Order, Standard Operating Procedures, training, etc., within the framework of making the safety of the innocent citizen my top priority, the safety of the involved police officers my second priority, and the safety of the suspects my third priority.

In an ideal world, police operations could be conducted in a manner in which there was no risk to citizens, officers, or suspects. But this is not the case, and a priority has to be established to help guide the course of action to be planned and then taken.

With that in mind, based on my experience, outside of exigent circumstances, the safest course of action—or the least risk to innocent citizens—is to attempt to arrest the suspects in the event of being on scene during a commercial business robbery when the suspects exit the business. I fully understood that this places police officers at some risk and that it places the most risk on the suspects. But it tends (outside exigent circumstances) to be the safest course of police action for the average uninvolved innocent citizen. This course of action (in my view and experience) stays true to the priority of life continuum (citizen; officer; suspect) as laid out in my training, experience, and personal moral code.

My preferred method (outside of exigent circumstances) is arresting the suspects as they exit the business. This still has risk but maintains the priority of valuable human life.

However, later, during the NDTU's commercial business robbery initiative, while in meetings with members of the Houston Police Department's Command Staff, I was "strongly encouraged" and placed under extreme professional duress that if I am put in the position, while conducting such high-risk surveillance, of having a commercial business robbery occur in the presence of the NDTU, that instead of attempting to arrest the suspects at the scene, as they transition back to their getaway vehicle, to instead allow the suspects to drive off and then later attempt a high-risk vehicle stop on the suspects utilizing marked patrol units and hope for voluntary compliance by the suspects.

There is some naive human behavioral theory that suggests that when a criminal suspect is highly excited (a significant amount of adrenaline coursing through his system) like while committing an armed robbery, he (the suspect) has little capacity for logical thought and/or long-term consideration for his imminent actions. However, if the suspect is merely allowed time to "cool off," he will not be in an excitable state and when the nice uniformed police officers initiate a felony vehicle traffic stop, the suspect will pull over and meekly surrender, all without incident.

This is not my experience and to me, it almost always means a vehicle pursuit will ensue—a pursuit involving perhaps several armed suspects during daytime business hours, when the public streets are most filled with innocent citizens. In addition, these suspects are highly motivated to evade arrest, because they not only have just committed an aggravated robbery, are in a stolen vehicle and armed but their identities are obscure. If they can make good their escape, there is little or no evidence that will then link them to the crime.

During my career, I have been witness to and/or have personal knowledge of many incidents in which suspects in motor vehicles who, while fleeing from uniformed police officers, have either killed or injured innocent citizens. On average, there are 1.5 police pursuit-related fatalities daily in the United States.

Simply put, police vehicle pursuits are dangerous to the average innocent citizen(s) driving unaware down the road! Do you want your family driving down the road when one is occurring?

I, as a sergeant, preferred not to be involved or involve my tactical unit or craft a tactical operation whose end would most likely result or even rely on a police vehicle pursuit to arrest the suspects. I believe it's best to attempt other means of arrest if they are available and/or viable. Engaging in high-risk vehicle pursuits with armed robbery suspects, in a stolen vehicle, during daytime business hours skews the priority of life scale and places all of valuable human life on an equal basis, with no priority given to any class.

I would like to think that prior to 2015, the Houston Police Department's Command Staff also recognized the priority of life in conducting police tactical operations. However, things apparently changed.

Although it will never be publicly acknowledged, this reordering of the priority of life is now carefully camouflaged with political rhetoric and talking points (smoke and mirrors).

Some appointed police administrators no longer embrace the moral concept of priority of life and I believe their core values are being skewed by political considerations. Those most susceptible to these political pressures and most likely to minimize or mitigate against their own moral code and subjugate the priority of life to other considerations are those whose careers and positions (particularly appointed police Command Staff members) are reliant on the goodwill of the politicians. Most often politicians of large, left-leaning, Democrat-run urban cities!

I dare say it's a form of police corruption not usually recognized!

I also believe that the core of this priority of life shift or police corruption is because of the #BlackLivesMatter movement.

This is the hard truth, at least in Houston. The vast majority of suspects committing violent crimes, particularly serial commercial business robberies, are black males. If we apply the moral code of priority of life (innocent citizen; police officer; suspect), then we place the onus on the suspects when we arrest them at the scene of the crime. Otherwise, we risk innocent lives by letting them enter their getaway vehicle and having a high-speed vehicle pursuit and the real potential for a catastrophic crash at some intersection, involving perhaps your spouse or child.

If the NDTU embraced the idea that arresting the suspects as they were transitioning from the business they had just robbed to their getaway vehicle as the best tactic to fulfill the priority of life code, then presumably the armed suspects would exit the business with guns in hand! Then, the likelihood is in these circumstances—the involved police officers in close quarters with the suspects, knowing action beats reaction—there is probably not going to be much opportunity (like seen in Hollywood movies) for such verbal discourse as: "Freeze! Police! Drop your gun!" In these fluid, close-range encounters, there is a strong possibility that trained, experienced, street savvy, tactical officers who are well versed in these realities will shoot the armed robbery suspect(s). If on the north side of Houston, this will most likely mean the suspect shot will be a black male!

Going into the commercial business robbery initiative, I suspected that this priority of life issue within the department would be muddled, at least at the highest level. So preparing for this eventuality, I prepared a detailed position paper/plan of action for how the takedowns of these in-progress robbery crews were to take place, putting forth my ideas on priority of life. In emails and formal correspondence to the Command Staff, I laid out the issues and asked, How do you want me to handle it? Do I arrest the suspects at the scene (possibility of shooting a black suspect armed with a weapon) or let suspect(s) re-enter their getaway vehicle, have a high-speed police chase, with a possibility of an innocent citizen being killed or injured in a vehicle crash?

To my immediate supervisors, Lieutenant Bellamy and Captain Baimbridge, the answer was clear: police vehicle pursuits were more dangerous to innocent citizens; arrest the suspects at the scene, and maintain the priority of life!

And the Command Staff's response (2015 through 2017) to our asking for specific direction or validation for our views of the priority of life?

Pretty much a deafening silence!

Our emails went unacknowledged. No written direction was given, and apparently they (the Command Staff) didn't want to acknowledge the priority of life, didn't want to provide leadership or a preferred way of action. If they said it's best to arrest the suspects at the scene, then black men might be shot and there was potential for social upheaval. If the Command Staff embraced the idea of a car chase and gave "license to it" when there had existed the opportunity to arrest the suspects at the scene of the crime before the car chase, and then a car crash occurs with innocent citizens killed or injured, then it would ultimately come out that this reordering of priority of life was their doing.

Failing to get any written response to our requests for direction, Captain Baimbridge, in a face-to-face meeting with his supervisor, purposely sought official direction from Assistant Chief Mark Eisenman how the department wanted us to proceed: vehicle pursuit or arrest at the scene? According to Captain Baimbridge, when asked, Assistant Chief Eisenman remained mute and would not even answer the question.

The prevailing wisdom, perhaps driven by the Houston Department's Office of Legal Services, was that if a suspect(s) kills or injure innocent citizens in a vehicle pursuit that this is unfortunate, but Houston's liability (monetary judgment) is minimized. The position/argument was that it was the suspects who caused the death and/or injury and are therefore responsible. In the case of a heavily armed robbery crew, who are trying to make good their escape, thinking or espousing the theory that the suspects might pull over on their own accord and not evade arrest is a smokescreen and, in my opinion, if stated by an experienced police officer is feigned naivety or blatant dishonesty!

Remember, unlike the normal patrol officer who happens to spot a wanted vehicle and a vehicle pursuit ensues, the supervisor of a tactical unit doing undercover surveillance on a suspected robbery crew had the opportunity to arrest the suspects before they entered their getaway vehicle and before the chase ensued, but made the conscious decision not to and/or is/was directed or "encouraged" by departmental administrators ("We prefer you to have a chase rather than attempt to arrest the suspects at the scene").

It appears that the advantage to Houston (not attempt to arrest at the scene but instead engage in a vehicle pursuit) was so there would be less commercial business robbery suspects (black men) shot by the Houston Police.

Police shootings of citizens (particularly of minorities) are a hot-topic issue in the United States, particularly so for the Houston Police Department, which has faced the real possibility of litigation by the United

States Department of Justice, via a consent decree, under the President Obama-era Justice Department. The fear is (as articulated by former Houston Chief of Police Charles McClelland) that it could be alleged that the Houston Police Department engages in a pattern or practice of using excessive force in violation of the Fourth Amendment to the United States Constitution. In addition, there is also the real possibility of civil unrest/riots as experienced in Baltimore, Maryland, Ferguson, Missouri, etc., as well as local community activist agitation (Black Lives Matter, New Black Panthers, etc.).

The implied subtle position of some in police leadership positions was "better to risk the innocent citizens being killed or injured in a vehicle pursuit than risk having to shoot an armed suspect (particularly a minority) at the scene of the crime!"

Is this police corruption? The reordering of the priority of life principle—innocent citizens first? Is this principle sometimes obscured by a municipality or city government's desire to reduce the amount of monies that may have to be paid out in civil actions and/or limit possible civil unrest? Do police departments develop and implement policies and/or procedures in its desire to limit its exposure to civil liability and/or civil unrest, and either wittingly or unwittingly enact policies or procedures that put the average innocent citizen at greater risk?

Also argued, by the purveyors of those who lobby for the vehicle pursuit instead of arresting the suspects at the scene, is the scenario that if the involved police officers have to shoot the suspects (while in the parking lot), an innocent citizen might be injured or killed. I would agree this is a possibility. However, it is not probable, and I am personally unaware or cannot recall any innocent citizens being accidentally wounded or killed (in the last thirty-nine years) by Houston police gunfire while the involved officer was utilizing deadly force. Further statistics nationwide reflect a much greater likelihood of an innocent citizen being killed or injured in a police vehicle pursuit as compared to an innocent citizen being killed or wounded by errant police gunfire. To further diffuse this argument, the NDTU engaged in much more firearms training than the typical Houston Police Department Tactical Unit and is also one reason in meetings with Houston Police Department's Command Staff, an effort was made to secure funding for practice ammunition and scenario-based training.

What had to be decided—what is the safest course of action in conducting police operations so that these operations (commercial business robbery intervention) place the least risk to innocent citizens, then to police officers, and lastly to suspects, in that order? This priority of life cannot be colored by media interest, increased scrutiny by outside or internal criminal investigative entities, nor can it be reordered by the possibility of potential civil actions or civil unrest.

CHAPTER 12

CHRIS JONES'S ROBBERY CREW

On a fall Friday morning in 2015, I was looking forward to "super date night" with Samantha later that evening. Maybe if all was quiet, we all could go home early, right after lunch, and just "think about police work."

I was in the NDTU office, chatting with the guys and drinking my coffee. We pretty much always had our radios with us and listened to them all the time, monitoring the patrol channels so we could get a head start if the opportunity presented itself to begin immediate operations against a robbery crew. As I have said before, I always preached to the guys that windows of opportunity open and shut fast and when the opportunity presented itself, we needed to act and build that investigative/operational momentum.

Then, like so many times, we heard yet another report of a commercial business robbery. A multi-suspect crew (all black males) wearing masks and armed with handguns and long guns had just taken down a Cash America Pawn. The suspects had gotten away clean after forcing the manager to open the store's safe. The suspected getaway vehicle was a red Chevy Malibu.

We had noticed a recent trend where Cash America Pawn stores had become a favorite target of the robbery crews. We suspected that because Cash America was a large corporation (900 locations in the United States) and they had instituted internal policies forbidding employees from arming themselves that the robbery crews liked to hit them as they didn't have to worry about getting shot by a resisting employee anxious to defend himself. The word was out!

Initially, I didn't think much about another robbery at a Cash America. After all, it would probably be one of several commercial business robberies that would occur this same day.

That all changed thirty minutes later. Sergeant C.W. "CW" Jones, a day shift patrol supervisor, came into our office. We always tried to keep good relations and communication with the uniformed patrol guys. Sometimes in the Houston Police Department, Tactical Units and the SWAT Detail could be perceived as "elitist" and the guys in patrol would not seek out assistance, much less share information, unless it was required by department mandate.

CW said that he had been in the general area at the time of the Cash America robbery and that he spotted what he believed to be the suspects' vehicle traveling at a high rate of speed on Interstate 45 (North Freeway), heading to the Greenspoint area (robbery suspect central). He said that at the time he saw the vehicle, he could not get behind it because he was on a parallel service road and there was no immediate on-ramp. He then gave a heads-up, radioing the patrol units in Greenspoint to intercept the vehicle as it entered or passed through their area. Sure enough, he explained, Albert Pizano, a Greenspoint patrol officer, saw the vehicle exit the North Freeway and then go east on Greens Road. Albert also tried to intercept it, but was unable. But continuing east on Greens Road, Albert "thought" that he found the same vehicle, a few minutes later, parked at a convenience store at the intersection of Greens Road and Imperial Valley Drive. This intersection was the primary hub for street-level drug dealing in the area. Albert Pizano was pretty sharp. As he drove by the now parked, unoccupied vehicle, he pretended to take no notice and rolled off. He then alerted CW to tell us (the NDTU).

A window of opportunity had opened, and the NDTU was out the door.

The guys in Crime Analysis headed to the Cash America to pull surveillance video. The rest of us headed to Greenspoint and got eyes on the parked red Chevy Malibu. When we arrived, we determined, by running it on our laptop computers, that the license plate on the Malibu was that of a rental vehicle. Then, with our contacts in the rental car company, we soon had a scanned copy of the applicable lease contract. The person renting the vehicle was a young black female, which fit the standard operating procedure for some robbery crews. We maintained covert surveillance on the parked Malibu. But, was it really the vehicle used by the robbery crew or a figment of CW and Albert's imaginations?

A short time later, the Crime Analysis officers who had gone to the Cash America sent out screenshots from the security video to our cell phones of the suspects in the robbery, as well as some photos of the vehicle they had used. Yes, it was a newer model red Chevy Malibu, but none of the video recorded the license plate. However, in one image of the robbery vehicle, we noticed a small but discernable scratch on the driver's side door. Did the red Chevy Malibu parked at Greens and Imperial Valley have the same scratch or were we wasting our time?

Ben LeBlanc got out on foot a block away and walked by the Malibu, discreetly taking a picture with his cell phone of the driver's side door. As soon as he was able, Ben sent the photo out to all of us.

Bingo. The door had the same scratch on it as the lick vehicle in the Cash America robbery. We had enough probable cause now for a tracking order and I headed to the office to start writing. We alerted our ATF partners, John and Dom, to what we had and as soon as the judge signed the order, we would get two tracking devices on the Malibu while it was still parked at Greens and Imperial Valley.

An hour later, the tracking order was done and Justin Williams and his "special helper" Steve Kutach headed downtown to get it signed.

Steve "Big Daddy" Kutach was the oldest (besides me) member of the NDTU. Steve had spent most of his career in either the NDTU or the Narcotics Division and was adept at surveillance and at reading the streets. Like me, Steve was soon wanting to retire and was building a barndominium in the boonies out in Washington County.

Recently, the Houston Police Department had completely revamped its entire computerized incident reporting system, from the 1980s OLO system to the brand-new super-duper RMS system. The officers universally hated the RMS system as they viewed it as difficult to navigate and overly complex. It was particularly disliked by us older officers and sergeants, who seemed to have trouble rapidly adapting to new technologies. Some conspiracy theorists, within the department, saw the adaptation to the new convoluted/overly complicated RMS computer system as a nefarious plot by the upper management to force the older officers of the department into retirement. Steve, though, was not ready yet to retire. But how was he going to do his job for the next few months? Because he was really struggling with RMS.

Simple! Steve became "best buddies" with the biggest computer nerd in the NDTU— Justin Williams. And now, with Justin constantly at his side to help him, Steve was back in business. The two of them together would prove to be a good fit!

Before the judge signed the tracking order, the red Chevy Malibu rolled. Because of where it was parked, the guys who were watching for it to move were unable to see who got into it. Now we were doing it old school: rolling surveillance on a suspect vehicle in Houston traffic without a tracking device. We called for help; a police helicopter launched, climbed to altitude, and helped us. Fortunately, the vehicle we were following was bright red and it was daytime, making it easy for everybody involved to keep an "eye."

Who was driving the Malibu? Was there anyone else in the vehicle? After a while, we got a good look. The vehicle was being driven by a young black female and no one else was in the car. She was obviously not a suspect from the earlier robbery. I theorized that she had been directed to pick up the Malibu after the male suspects had parked it. Probably, they had seen either CW or Albert in their marked police units trying to catch up to them and figured that the Malibu was "hot." As soon as they could, they parked it and made some distance from it, blending into the pedestrian traffic in the area. And now, hours later, the woman was retrieving it for them.

The tracking order was signed, and Justin and Steve were soon back with us, along with two mobile tracking devices from ATF. The mission now was to not lose the rolling surveillance and covertly mount the tracking devices on the Chevy as soon as possible. All afternoon, until early in the evening, we followed her, looking for that opportunity. Finally, the woman driving our target vehicle parked, and we watched as she went into an office building off Highway 59 in Northeast Houston. There was no one else in the parking lot and as we covered him, Justin crawled under the target vehicle and mounted our tracking devices.

Justin was safely back with Steve and they were driving out of the parking lot when we spotted the woman coming out of the building and getting back into our target vehicle. But it was all good; we had the tracking devices on. I thanked our air support for their help and we all relaxed.

It was getting late in the day. Super date night with Samantha was still calling my name, and we were all tired from the stress of the all-day rolling surveillance. I thought it was a good idea to call it quits. I didn't really expect the robbery crew (whoever they were) to ever use the Malibu again as it was probably "burned," but by following it over the next few days, we could figure out who she was and then perhaps who the robbery suspects were. I thought it would probably take days or weeks to get to that point. I told the guys over the radio to call it a night and we would pick it up Monday morning and review the historical tracking data we would acquire over the weekend to decide our next course of action.

We were heading home!

Fifteen minutes later, Justin was on the radio, calling for me. Whenever he says, "Hey, boss," I know in his mind it was something significant and I needed to carefully consider what he was about to say.

Steve was driving and Justin was in the passenger seat on his laptop computer, making sure the trackers he had just put on the Malibu were "talking to him," setting how often they pinged and reported their positions. In doing so, Justin noticed something odd. The Malibu was now deep up into George Bush Intercontinental Airport and was headed into one of several car rental companies next to the airport. This probably meant that the woman would turn in the red Chevy Malibu and rent another vehicle for use by the robbery crew in their next lick.

Darn it. No date night tonight. This surveillance was now becoming operationally complicated. We would have to get eyes on that car rental place to see what vehicle she rented. Then try to do another rolling surveillance on it, keeping it in sight, while I wrote another tracking order. Then get the order signed and then try to get tracking devices on this new vehicle. That meant also, that after she left with the new rental vehicle, we would have to pull the trackers off the red Chevy Malibu (I didn't have any others handy at the time) to use on the new one. We would then have the turned-in Malibu processed for physical evidence by one of our Crime Scene Units.

Now the sun was down and it was dark. I doubted that we could hold rolling surveillance on whatever new vehicle she rented while we got the new tracking order signed. The odds were now definitely against us. But the window of opportunity was still partly open, so we would keep trying.

Over the radio, I redirected everyone to the airport and laid out my thoughts. No one complained—the boys were that dedicated to the mission.

I sent all the NDTU to the airport to catch up with Justin and Steve, as I headed to the office to start writing the new tracking order and to plug in the identifiers of the new rental vehicle as soon as the guys figured it out. I guessed that if the guys could hold the rolling surveillance, then ultimately I would be waking up some district court judge in his or her pajamas to sign my tracking order—that was always fun!

I was back at the office, typing the new order in anticipation of having to track a second rental vehicle. Meanwhile, the boys now had the rental car company under surveillance and I was listening to their radio chatter. They had eyes on the woman who was still sitting in the Malibu. She was parked in the front parking lot of the rental car and never went inside. Also of interest, she was now talking to two black males who had pulled up in a truck. It was obvious that they knew each other. So far, there was no effort to turn in the red Chevy Malibu and rent another vehicle.

What was up?

A secret about Ben LeBlanc. We all have "kinks" and unique aspects to our personalities.

Ben's kink was that he loved shoes! Men's shoes! He had a pair for every occasion and somehow his shoes (usually running or athletic type footwear) would always color coordinate with the shirt, pants, and broad-brimmed baseball style hat that he would be wearing that day. I would joke with Ben's wife, Andrea, that her husband had more shoes than she did and he was the Imelda Marcos of the NDTU. Ben had a keen eye for men's fashion, particularly urban, millennial type shoe wear. He was also observant. As they watched the female and two males interact in the parking lot, Ben's brain clicked.

Ben bumped me on the radio. "Sarge, the taller black male is wearing the same type of running shoes that one of the masked-up hijackers was wearing in the Cash America Pawn robbery earlier today."

Okay, I responded (perhaps a bit flippantly)—a happy coincidence. A lot of people wear black or white running shoes. In fact, I had a black pair on at that moment. Ben then explained the taller masked-up suspect in the earlier robbery video was wearing a pair of special edition Air Jordan running shoes and they were somewhat rare. The tall guy he was watching at that moment had on the exact same pair! Not only that, but Ben said this guy was also tall, had the same build, the same color pants, and the kicker, of course, being the Air Jordan special edition shoes. Ben said he was 90% certain that the taller guy they were watching at that moment was a member of the robbery crew from earlier today!

This changed everything. Not only that, but now the girl in the red Chevy Malibu was driving off, as well as the two guys in the truck—all in separate directions. We had trackers on the Malibu but knew she was not one of our suspects. A fast decision was made to reorient the NDTU and follow the men in the truck. Now I was out of the office and headed north to catch up.

We were back to old school rolling surveillance at night, the hardest type of surveillance to do in an urban environment. We followed the truck farther north up into the city of Humble. They drove into an apartment complex, where Justin and Steve watched as the driver of the truck met up with a third guy in the parking lot, where they then did a hand-to-hand. The driver appeared to buy a small amount of marijuana.

The NDTU chatted on the radio and I picked the brains of the collective. Ben LeBlanc had a good feeling that the suspect wearing the Air Jordans was one of our bad guys. So if we developed probable cause for a traffic stop (we already had that), then we stood a good chance of making a reactive robbery case against at least the one suspect based on his clothing. We could presumably seize his cell phone, which might historically show up as being near the Cash America that morning. This would probably be enough to get criminal charges, although the case would be weak and probably dismissed. But if we did a traffic stop, there was also a good likelihood of finding guns or other evidence from the earlier robbery. This would all make a strong prosecutorial case.

Fortunately, in the far "tail" of our surveillance train, out of sight of our suspects and for such an eventuality as this, two members of the NDTU (James Sanders and Travis Curtner) were in uniform and driving a marked police car. They had all the perquisite lights and sirens to conduct a "random traffic stop" or when we needed a uniform police presence.

As we followed the men in the truck to a less occupied roadway, I directed James and Travis to conduct the "routine traffic stop" and under its pretenses to take the person of interest (the tall dude in the truck) into custody, in a low-key manner, assuming they found some contraband (dope, guns, etc.). Or at least until I could call the Robbery detectives, give them the low-down, and see how they wanted to proceed.

James and Travis moved up into position. As a precaution in these types of situations, to reduce the chances of a high-speed vehicle chase, we (the surveillance officers in the undercover vehicles) would in a non-conspicuous way "box in" the suspect vehicle. In this case, the truck with the two suspects was traveling in the number two lane of a two-lane, one-way roadway with a deep ditch running alongside. Steve and Justin maneuvered to the number one lane and ran abreast of the truck, while I positioned my Toyota FJ Cruiser immediately in front. Then the other undercover NDTU officers made a "hole" immediately behind the suspect truck as we all traveled down the roadway at about 60 mph. James and Travis plopped into position behind the truck and turned on their overhead emergency lights. The driver of the truck complied and began slowing down and pulling off to the right, on to the shoulder of the roadway. It all looked good.

Initially, Justin, Steve, and I feigned confusion over who was being pulled over by the marked police unit with all the flashy lights, all for the benefit of blocking the suspects in to make sure they were indeed complying and pulling over. Which they were.

As the driver of the truck pulled over and came to a stop with James and Travis behind them, the rest of the undercover NDTU kept going so as not to alert the occupants in the truck that they were under surveillance and to maintain the charade that this was all a random, routine police traffic stop.

I pulled into a gas station several hundred yards up the road and, with my binoculars, monitored the traffic stop. Already, James and Travis were walking up to the truck. Travis, playing the part of Officer Friendly, was at the driver's window, probably asking, "Please sir, turn off the engine and step out of your vehicle." It didn't work.

As soon as Travis asked the driver to turn off the engine and get out of the vehicle, he put the truck into gear and, with engine racing, pulled onto the road while rapidly accelerating to a high speed. The bad guys left James and Travis in the dust and now they were running back to their patrol car.

It would be a car chase. As the suspects went by my location, I fell in behind them. Fortunately, the patrol car James and Travis were in was new and in excellent condition, and they soon caught up to the truck. As part of our protocol, we all switched from our tactical radio channel to the North Patrol channel and began putting out the chase, requesting uniform back up and a police helicopter (again).

The suspect driver made a bad decision as he came up to Interstate 59. He could go north or south, but chose poorly and turned south. All of our assistance was south of us and headed toward us north on the interstate. As we traveled south on Interstate 59, the suspects, along with James and Travis, were already way ahead; I was just barely keeping the emergency lights on top of James and Travis's patrol car in sight. Our ragtag fleet of undercover junk, of course, couldn't keep up with the bad guys or James and Travis. They were all topping out at well over 100 mph! Not only that, none of our undercover cars had emergency equipment and were rightfully prohibited by policy from participating in vehicle pursuits. But already I could see other emergency lights falling in behind the chase and, better yet, I could see the spotlight of a police helicopter, high in the night sky, charging up from the south.

Sergeant Stewart "Stu" Red, a canine sergeant, broke the air and advised that he was now in the chase. Stu and I had worked together many times in the past. He was someone I trusted.

Immediately, I informed him of the situation: I was in an undercover vehicle and already the lead elements of the chase were out of my sight. "Stu, I am out—can you take over?" "That's clear," he replied.

Now all the NDTU surveillance eased down to the speed limit and followed the chase at a safe distance to see where it would all ultimately land.

The pursuit was now in the domain of the uniformed patrol units, assisted by a police helicopter and an old canine sergeant. During the chase, every time Stu transmitted on his radio, calmly giving orders and direction, his canine partner Bandit—a newly issued, seventy-five pound, male German Shepherd/Belgian Malinois mix, with huge white teeth— could be heard in the background giving his ongoing doggie commentary. Bandit, unlike Stu, was not so calm. He barked furiously. I guess maybe in his doggie mind he was aching to bite a bad guy.

New police patrol dogs, just like many rookie patrol officers, loved the excitement and danger of a nighttime police car chase—Stu and I, not so much.

The high-speed chase lasted for nearly half an hour and eventually ended up in a southeast Houston neighborhood where the driver of the truck started making big, multi-block circles. This we recognized as a common suspect tactic in vehicle pursuits. The bad guys were trying to get far enough ahead, make a corner, to momentarily get out of sight of the pursuing officers, at which time they would bail out. Often this bail-out occurred while their vehicle was still moving. It was a good tactic; under the cover of darkness and while on familiar ground in the hood, they would then try to disappear on foot, jumping fences and trying to put as much distance between them and the police. The NDTU had by then caught up to the chase as it did circles and now we were outside of the neighborhood, waiting for the outcome, letting the uniformed patrol officers do their thing. Because we were all undercover, it would not be a good idea for us to get into the mix at the time.

Sure enough, the passenger in the truck, the guy Ben thought was a robbery suspect from earlier, bailed out of the truck. Too bad for him. The truck was going too fast and when he hit the ground, he lost his footing and tumbled. His special edition Air Jordans failed him! Several of the involved patrol officers peeled off and arrested him, while he was still dazed and trying to recover his wits from his high-speed crash landing.

A few minutes later, the driver of the truck came to a screeching stop in front of a residence. He didn't even have time to make a run for it. Almost instantly, he was surrounded by patrol cars coming in from every point of the compass and the night was turned into day by the spotlight of the police airship just overhead, and all the light from the multitude of emergency vehicles.

So what did the suspect do?

Of course—he held himself hostage. Still sitting in the driver's seat, he put a pistol to his head for everyone to see. No one approached and now it was a standoff.

Stu and I began managing the scene, positioning patrol officers to prevent a cross fire, informing Watch Command to roll the SWAT Detail and HNT, as per protocol for a barricaded suspect. The suspect was parked in front of his home and Mommy was already out in the front yard—frantic, rightfully concerned, that her baby would end up dead either by his own hand or killed by the cops. I felt sympathy for her. After we got Mom calmed down and had an officer escort her inside, we learned her son's name and that he was out on parole from state prison on a gun charge—Felon in Possession of a Firearm.

Over a loudspeaker, while waiting for SWAT and HNT to arrive, I communicated with the suspect, trying to talk him down and reassuring him that life was still worth living. I visualized that he was my son and if the situation was reversed how I would want the police to talk to him. I was playing the nice cop!

Just as the first elements of the SWAT Detail arrived, the suspect put his gun down, fully complied with my instructions, and he was taken into custody. The scene was over.

The passenger suspect, who had tried to run off, was brought to our location, and we identified him as Chris Jones. Chris was far from home; he lived on the north side of Houston, in the infamous Greenspoint area.

Inside the truck were several handguns, including a loaded .45 automatic pistol and several long guns—both rifles and shotguns!

As we were processing the scene and arranging the transportation of the suspects back north, Dave Smith walked up to me, nudged me to get my attention and then stared intently down the street. There, about 100 yards away, was the girl and the red Chevy Malibu. She was watching the police activity intently. Someone must have called her.

Late that evening, Detective Ken Nealy, one of the better north side Robbery investigators, interviewed both of our suspects. Ken's specialty was talking to bad guys and extracting information. Chris Jones confessed to his involvement in the Cash America Pawn robbery earlier that day but wouldn't divulge anything else, like the identities of the other robbery crew members. Ken also determined that the driver suspect who had held himself hostage was most likely not one of the other robbery suspects as his physical description didn't match any of the other suspects in the video. He was charged with Felon in Possession of a Firearm (again) and Evading Arrest in a Motor Vehicle. Chris Jones was charged with Aggravated Robbery (Deadly Weapon). Both men were booked into the Harris County Jail.

Interestingly, none of the guns recovered from the truck that night matched the video image(s) of the ones used by the suspects in the earlier Cash America robbery.

Late the next afternoon, I watched on my computer as the red Chevy Malibu, with our ATF trackers on it and with probably the same girl driving it as the night before, parked at a Greenspoint area bail bond company. Was she going to bail someone out? But who? The driver? Chris Jones? Or both?

About twenty-four hours after committing an armed robbery, during which he had placed a pistol to the head of an innocent citizen and a crime that he had confessed to, Chris Jones was out of jail on a low bond, with not even a GPS ankle monitor. We made a discreet inquiry to the involved bail bond company and we now had the name of the girl driving the red Chevy Malibu. She was the same girl who rented it, and some fast analysis on her social media revealed that she was Chris Jones's girlfriend, Teneka.

And now, Chris Jones would need money to pay back his girlfriend for his bond and any other costs associated (like a good lawyer) because of his arrest.

How was Chris going to get the money? In my mind, he would probably resort to committing more robberies of commercial businesses, looking for a "big lick."

Lalo and I had a meeting with all the NDTU, along with our ATF partners. We lined out our theory about Chris Jones and another robbery. Chris was our link. We had no idea who the other members of the crew were. Most importantly, we knew about the red Chevy Malibu and we had tracking devices on it. Maybe it was still "cool," since the chase and Chris's arrest had all occurred in connection with another vehicle.

Would Chris use the Malibu again to facilitate another robbery? Would he enlist the other members of the crew? Chris Jones didn't know that the NDTU knew about the Malibu and we still had two tracking devices on it.

Over the next few days, it became obvious that our theory was correct. We never saw Chris Jones's girlfriend Teneka drive the Malibu again. We realized that as soon as she bonded him out of jail, she turned the rental vehicle back over to him and now we were spending our days watching him as he drove around the Greenspoint area, hanging out with his friends and smoking marijuana. Just like Darius Spears, while Chris goofed off all day, his girlfriend worked a legitimate 9-5 job.

It also became our observation that Chris Jones had some following or notoriety among the street thugs in Greenspoint. Whenever he pulled into a parking lot, instantly he was swarmed by the other "hanger outers" and Chris would then have animated conversations with them. Not sure what was said, but when Chris talked, he did a lot of gesturing with his hands. It also appeared that there was some connection between Chris Jones and the guys who were "slinging" small amounts of marijuana, most often at the corner of Imperial Valley and Greens Road. We surmised that, in addition to Aggravated Robbery, Chris was also making money somehow in the street-level marijuana selling business, although he was not selling it himself. As best we could tell, he was not a mule bringing the product to the street-level sellers for distribution. Our pet theory was that he was some overseer or enforcer, employed by someone above the street-level dealers to keep the marijuana-selling minions in line. We just didn't know.

More information started to come in. Dave and Justin dug into the city-wide crime reports and talked to outlaying law enforcement agencies, reviewing videos and connecting the dots. Chris Jones and his robbery crew were more prolific than we suspected. There were many commercial business robberies with one of the crew members being rather tall, as well as a red, four-door sedan being used for a getaway vehicle. It looked like over the past few weeks, this crew had been on quite a spree. We were looking now at previous robberies from as far south as Galveston to northern Montgomery County in the city of Porter. All the information was passed off to the respective Robbery detectives, but there was nothing really else to go on. In Chris Jones's arrest for the Cash America robbery, we could not recover his cell phone, so any historical information linking his phone to the time and date of the other robberies would not be a possibility.

Most of the Robbery detectives cleared their cases by insufficient evidence or arrests made in other cases (our Cash America store). We (the NDTU) knew that for the time being we had shut Chris Jones down, but eventually he would activate his robbery crew and would be back in the game, looking for easy "big money."

Most of the robbery crews in Houston don't like hitting banks. There is a lot more investigative law enforcement attention and effort in bank robbery investigations, mostly because it brought in the FBI and all the federal government's resources. Not only that, but banks had secure vaults, alarm systems, sophisticated surveillance systems, as well as dye packs and GPS tracking devices disguised as money packs, which could be slipped into the outgoing pile of cash by the bank employees. This was all common knowledge. In the mind of the robbery crews, the better places to hit, to avoid all the FBI entanglements involved in bank robbery, was to target softer, easier locations like cash stores (check cashing—high-interest loan type businesses) or pawnshops. Cash stores and pawnshops had (if you hit them at the right time) large amounts of cash on hand and were a prime target, particularly if you could force an employee to open the store safe. Local police departments and not the FBI investigated robberies of these softer targets.

About two weeks after the Cash America robbery, we began watching Chris Jones in his red Chevy Malibu as he started to scout or reconnoiter both cash stores and pawnshops. We clandestinely followed him as he would drive from cash store to cash store or pawnshop to pawnshop, looking over the parking lot, maybe checking to see where the surveillance cameras were situated. Sometimes, he would go inside a business, spend a short time inside, and soon walk back out. Occasionally, he would do this scouting with another unknown male. We knew that eventually something would happen.

Chris seemed to have a great interest in the north side Houston Cash America stores. If I had to guess, at that time, I would say that he would hit one soon. But which one? On what day? How were we to discern the difference between a day of scouting and the day that a robbery would go down? Out of an abundance of caution and to have a clear conscience, we contacted the corporate security of Cash America and told them of our concerns. They were quick to act; they hired and placed armed security guards in all the Houston north side Cash Americas that Chris was scouting. Sure enough, as soon as this happened, when Chris saw the armed security, he never went back to that location. I guessed that because of the presence of a security guard, he mentally crossed that store(s) off his list.

The problem was that there were so many other pawnshops and cash stores he could choose from. Sometimes, we would watch as Chris would drive up to a pawnshop, retrieve a ratty-looking pair of sneakers or an old broken-down gas-powered weed eater from the trunk of his car, as a ruse to get buzzed in and get past the electronically locked doors of a pawnshop: "Sir, can I pawn these sneakers or this weed eater?" To which the employees would inspect the "merchandise" and politely decline—it was worthless junk. It was all a ruse. Chris, while inside, was looking over the interior of the pawnshop, making his plans. We also realized that Chris was more than a member of a robbery crew; he would be the leader of a crew that home-based out of Greenspoint. He was a "shot caller."

We also observed something that initially was only mildly interesting during our surveillance of Chris and the Malibu. Frequently, while in Greenspoint, we observed Chris meeting with two guys driving around in a beat-up white Buick four-door, with paper (temporary) license plates. The Buick had assorted dings and dents, as well as a missing driver's side mirror. Otherwise, it was pretty unremarkable and non-memorable.

We had a strong feeling that eventually Chris would orchestrate a robbery. As the days and then weeks went by, I decided to hasten the inevitable and take out one of his "income streams" and create an acute cash flow crisis for him. Namely, I would shut down the nickel-and-dime marijuana street corner dope dealing he was involved in. So we switched tactics. Every time we observed Chris moving to a Greenspoint street corner to facilitate/supervise his minions and their weed dealing, I would alert a patrol unit and have them park in proximity to the area, which immediately suppressed any customers trying to buy weed. Chris and his minions would then move a few blocks over and try to move their business to another corner. Immediately, I would then bring in another patrol unit and have it park there, and so on.

After a few days, at least for the time being, all the marijuana street dealing in Greenspoint came to a screeching halt. Fortunately, the undercover officers in the NDTU had good working relations with the area patrol officers and we were transparent about what we were trying to do. The uniformed officers were eager to help. From a distance, one evening, I watched as Chris had a meltdown in a city park on Greens Road. He was surrounded by his worker bees, and by his highly animated hand gestures and agitated state, I could just imagine him cursing out the uniformed cops making life difficult for him.

Our tactic worked.

The next day, something interesting happened. Chris, alone in the red Chevy Malibu, followed by the beat-up white Buick four-door with paper plates—which was now loaded down with several males—left Greenspoint in convoy. We clandestinely followed. We all traveled west on the Sam Houston Tollway, many miles out of their home turf, deep into the west part of Houston. There we landed at a Cash America Pawn, one that didn't have a security guard inside.

Chris, in his Malibu, posted up in the parking lot, positioning his vehicle where he could watch the front door of the pawnshop. We had observed him do this several times before, but never so far away from the north side and never in coordination with another vehicle. As Chris sat in the parking lot watching, the guys in the beat-up Buick drove off and disappeared into a nearby white, middle-class residential neighborhood. We tried to hold a rolling surveillance on it, but because we were in a residential area and could be easily spotted, our surveillance had to be loose and sure enough, we soon lost it. We then regrouped and instead focused on watching Chris, who was still stationary in the parking lot, watching the Cash America.

About half an hour later, the guys in the beat-up Buick reemerged out of the neighborhood. They and Chris Jones briefly met and talked in the parking lot, then they left the area. They got back on the beltway and traveled straight back to Greenspoint, with all the NDTU surveillance in tow.

What was that all about?

Justin, Dave, and Ben surmised—and I agreed—that what we witnessed was most likely an attempted robbery of this west side Cash America. Chris Jones, in the Malibu, was keeping an eye on the Cash America (shot caller) while the unknowns in the beat-up Buick searched for a vehicle to steal (probably a truck). Immediately after stealing the truck, the guys in the Buick would park their vehicle a short distance from the Cash America, then load up into the stolen vehicle. When Chris called the robbery crew on his cell phone, telling them that the coast was clear, they would roll in and hit the Cash America. After robbing the business, the crew would escape in the stolen vehicle, drive a short distance to where the Buick was parked, dump the stolen vehicle, and transition back into their beat-up Buick. Then they'd make their getaway back to Greenspoint. At least, that was our theory. We alerted Cash America corporate security, who that same day placed an armed security guard at the location.

Justin convinced me to write a vehicle tracking order for the beat-up white Buick with paper plates, which I did that evening. The problem was we didn't know where this vehicle lived and because it had paper plates, we could not acquire any NVLS clues about where we might find it parked and unoccupied to get our ATF trackers on it. After I wrote the order and got it signed, I sort of put the Buick in the back of my mind. I really wrote the tracking order to appease Justin; he felt so strongly about it and kept pestering me: "Sarge, I really think…." I strongly doubted that we would ever get any of our tracking devices on it. We didn't know where to find it, parked and unoccupied. But Justin felt differently.

Two days later, Justin woke up early and headed into work before dawn. He had a hunch and randomly drove through some Acres Homes apartment complexes to the south of Greenspoint. I don't know what the little gremlins that lived inside his head were telling him, but he found the beat-up white Buick, parked and unoccupied, in an apartment complex. It was like finding a needle in a haystack! We were all flabbergasted—how did he think to look for it there? Not only that, Justin carried one or two ATF tracking devices with him at all times and since no citizenry was around, he slapped the trackers on the Buick by himself and quickly hightailed it out of the parking lot.

The window opens and soon shuts: Justin seized the opportunity— good for him. Mostly, I always wanted the placing of trackers on suspects' vehicles to be a carefully choreographed team event (for safety), but I understood. Besides, I couldn't say much because I had done what Justin did on other occasions, when I felt it important enough and the one-time opportunity justified the risk.

Just as I arrived to work the next morning and settled down with my coffee, I received a text alert on my iPhone. Chris Jones and the Chevy Malibu were on the move and out of the Greenspoint geo fence. A quick inquiry on the tracking app showed he was headed south.

All the NDTU launched out of the office, trying to catch up with Chris, who was already on Interstate 45 and way ahead of us. It was a long time before we could catch up. Finally, he exited south of Houston and was now in Pasadena. We found him and watched as he sat in the Malibu, parked in a parking lot, watching a bank. We could also tell there was at least one, maybe two, other passengers in the car with him.

We spent the entire morning in Pasadena, clandestinely watching as Chris and his friend(s) drove from bank to bank, looking each one over carefully. What was he up to now? Was he planning a bank robbery? Was this another day of scouting and planning or was this the day to pull the trigger and do a robbery? I surmised that it was probably another day of scouting and planning. We had never followed him this far south, and this was the first time that he was showing an interest in banks.

Unexpectedly, close to noon, Chris and friend(s) abandoned their efforts in Pasadena. They entered back onto Interstate 45 and started driving north. We followed a few miles behind, letting the trackers on his car do the hard work for us.

We were getting hungry as it was lunchtime, and fortunately so were Chris and his friend(s). They exited off the freeway in south Houston, pulled up to a fast-food drive-through and ordered some hamburgers. We gave them a little space as they ordered their food, careful to place a car or two between us in line, to not arouse suspicion. We all then lined up at the same drive-through and ordered.

Soon we were all back rolling, northbound on Interstate 45. Then, in the middle of Houston, they converged on to Interstate 59, heading northeast. We kept heading north, eventually passing George Bush Intercontinental Airport, then back out of Houston, past Humble and deep into rural Montgomery County. Suddenly, Chris exited the interstate, made a U-turn at an underpass, and headed back south on Interstate 59. We kept a loose tail and followed him as he drove all the way back into the middle of Houston and exited downtown into the business district. Then, for the next few hours, Chris and whoever was in the car with him drove to and looked over different cash stores, no longer interested in banks.

I forget how many cash stores they went to that afternoon, but it was many. There are that many of these types of cash store businesses in Houston! We followed them as they slowly worked their way back to the north side of Houston. We leapfrogged from cash store to cash store.

Sometimes they would linger at a cash store and would sit and watch for a while. So we would, unnoticed, sit also and watch them watch! Then, we would be off to the next one.

Midafternoon, we were at yet another cash store in northwest Houston. Again, Chris and his friend(s), all in the Malibu, were posted up, watching. Yawn! We were all tired from doing this surveillance all day, just like the previous days. More scouting?

But today was the day!

One passenger, wearing a yellow work vest, casually exited the Chevy Malibu, walked to the front door of the cash store, and patiently waited as the employees buzzed him in. I guess to the employees, Mr. Yellow Vest appeared to be a legitimate customer, and he was given access.

Mr. Yellow Vest swung the front door open and stepped across the threshold, into the interior. Then, quick as a flash, two other suspects from inside the red Chevy Malibu were out of the vehicle, running through the open door of the business just behind Mr. Yellow Vest. Only now these two guys wore face masks and gloves, and had semiautomatic pistols in their hands.

ROBBERY IN PROGRESS!

All the NDTU undercover officers watched patiently as Chris Jones and his robbery crew took down the cash store. We gritted our teeth as we watched as the robbery crew jumped the counters and put guns to the heads of the employees. We watched as Mr. Yellow Vest collected the cash and stuffed it into a bag. We watched as they ran out the front door, heading back to the Chevy Malibu—their getaway vehicle.

Unfortunately for the armed suspects, they ran out into the parking lot, right into our arms. Also, bad for them they chose poorly that when they came out running, they still had their guns in hand, all in plain sight. There was a brief fury of NDTU gunfire and both of the armed suspects were down and severely incapacitated.

Mr. Yellow Vest, who was not armed, and was therefore not shot, got confused and kept running in the opposite direction of where the Chevy Malibu was parked. Fortunately, our ATF agents Dom and Big John had just caught up with our surveillance train, having been in federal court all day. Big John and Dom then got to play police officer as they chased Mr. Yellow Vest into a nearby computer store where, as the panicked employees ran out, he barricaded himself somewhere deep within the store.

I stayed at the scene of the shooting. Two of the suspects were lying face-down. The first one I checked was dead! He had caught multiple .223 rounds as well as several 12-gauge, 00 buckshot loads in his chest cavity.

The other downed suspect I recognized as Chris Jones. Like the dead guy, he also had been hit by multiple .223 rounds from our rifles. Unlike the dead guy, Chris had not been hit by any close-range 12-gauge buckshot loads and was still alive. But, maybe not for long. Chris was bleeding out; there was a large pool of bright-red arterial blood on the sidewalk that you couldn't help but walk in. I wasn't carrying a tourniquet on my heavy body armor, but arriving on the scene was David Enlow, one of the uniformed guys assigned to Heath's WET.

Dave was always prepared and never got excited—I guess because he had been a long-serving United States Marine (David Enlow was no "crayon eater" either; he had a master's degree in public information). I asked David to use his tourniquet on Chris's arm, which was spurting blood out. David looked at me and sort of shrugged, as if to say, "Why bother?"

I understood. Chris's blood was everywhere. Not only that, but a bunch of his teeth (molars mostly) lay out on the sidewalk, mingled in among the spreading pool of blood. Either one or more .223 rounds had entered the side of his face and knocked a bunch of his teeth out like they were lined-up dominos. I figured Chris only had a short time to live. Even though we had shot him, now that he was down and no longer a threat, it was our responsibility to save him.

I reaffirmed my request for a tourniquet. "Dave, let's try anyway!"

Dave Enlow replied, "Sure thing!" and as if it were something he did every day, threw his cigarette down on the ground, extinguishing it with the toe of his combat boot, then bent over and cinched his tourniquet around Chris Jones's upper arm and stemmed the flow of blood (at least, out of that hole).

There were so many other holes in Chris's torso that I didn't know where to put direct pressure. Or, was that what I was supposed to do? I could hear the wail of the paramedics approaching, so the best thing I could think of was to talk to Chris as he slipped off into eternity. After all, who wants to die alone on a Houston sidewalk?

I bent over and tried to talk to him. "Chris, I don't think you're going to make it! Is there anything that you want me to say to Teneka?" Chris tried to respond but because of the gunshot to his face, he wasn't able to form words. I felt empathy for Chris! But the moment soon passed and now the paramedics were working on him, cutting off his clothing, sticking needles in, trying to stop the blood loss—doing things that paramedics are trained to do!

David Enlow might have saved Chris Jones's life, all because he was prepared and carried a tourniquet. The paramedics were able to keep Chris alive until he reached a medical trauma center, where the surgeons cracked him open and fixed the critical damage.

Jonas Tizzano aka Mr. Yellow Vest was eventually fished out of his hiding place in the attic of the computer store by the Houston Police Department's SWAT Detail. That evening, he was charged with Aggravated Robbery. He was back out on the streets, on bond, the next day.

The dead guy had a long criminal history and was also the lead suspect in a recent Houston murder case; he just had not yet been charged and a 2B arrest warrant issued.

A few days after the shooting, the NDTU and ATF were back on surveillance. We were all still curious about the beat-up white Buick, the one with temporary paper license plates on it and the guys driving it. The same vehicle that Justin Williams had convinced me earlier to write a tracking order for. The vehicle Justin had found, on a hunch, parked and unoccupied and put tracking devices on. So with nothing else on our plate and waiting for the administrative dust to settle from our last shooting, we began casually watching as the guys in the white Buick rolled around and hung out at the usual locations in Greenspoint, smoking weed.

Then Dom called me one day. He was out in the field, watching. "Sarge, guess who the guys in the white Buick are hanging out with? Even as we speak?" I didn't know.

Dom replied, "Jonas Tizzano!"

Very interesting I thought!

Fortunately, John and Dom, working with Richard Hanes and Heather Winter in the United States Attorney's Office, took over the investigation and prosecution of the "Chris Jones Robbery Crew" case. Eventually, a physically diminished Chris Jones was transferred from the Harris County Sheriff's Office prisoner hospital ward into the loving arms of the United States Marshals and remanded into the custody of the federal government. Word from our Marshal friends was that when Chris heard that he was being charged in federal court, he physically broke down and cried, "WHY ME!"

Jonas Tizzano probably thought as a consequence for his part in the cash store robbery, he would take a plea bargain and get a Harris County probated sentence—until we snagged him "sashaying" down a sidewalk in Greenspoint and turned him over to the United States Marshals. Both Chris and Jonas are in federal prison, where they will be for a long time.

The other member of the Chris Jones Robbery Crew was buried in an Acres Homes cemetery.

CHAPTER 13

VALU PAWN

A few days after the shooting at the cash store, the NDTU was back on the trail. We had tracking devices on the beat-up old white Buick, which displayed various temporary paper license plates. This vehicle and its occupants had been hanging around with Chris Jones and we had followed them to a Cash America Pawn store in far west Houston. Were they getting ready to hit that Cash America? Were the guys in the Buick part of Chris Jones's robbery crew or was the happenings at the west side Cash America the portents of a future collaboration between two different Greenspoint robbery crews? My interest was further piqued when, after the cash store shooting, and while still out on bond, ATF Agent Dominic Rosamilia, clandestinely watched as Jonas Tizzano met up and "interacted" with the guys in the white Buick. Another happy coincidence….I can almost imagine Tizzano telling them, "*Whatever you guys do, don't do a cash store—they have police stakeout teams watching them!*" And so it began all over again.

We began following the white Buick—all day, every day. We really had not definitively linked them to any known commercial business robberies, although there were enough red flags to convince a state district court judge that there was sufficient probable cause to place tracking devices on this vehicle. The foundational basis was our observations at the west side Cash America. At the end of the day, though, it was more of a hunch—a "cop instinct."

As the days went by, we saw a similar pattern. There would be several unknowns in the white Buick and they would spend the day going from pawnshop to pawnshop, going inside to browse. Or, they would hang out in Greenspoint, smoking weed and visiting with the usual crowd that congregated in the parking lots and street corners. The guys in the NDTU were divided over whether we were on to a real robbery crew or were wasting our time. Even one of my most experienced guys, Steve Kutach, who was the best in reading the streets and who could usually discern the intentions of those who we had under our surveillance, was convinced the guys we were watching were petty street criminals, hustling to make a buck. They were not hijackers.

As a supervisor, it's hard to keep a team focused for hours a day, seven days a week, on surveillance if your people think it's a wasted effort. Lalo and I had been pushing the team hard and after so many weeks, starting with the Chris Jones Robbery Crew, we were all tired. We all could use a break and maybe a slower tempo was in order; besides, it was almost Friday and everybody knew Friday night was Sergeant Andersen's date night!

Friday, October 30, we all came into work that morning a bit late. We were all dragging.

Lalo and I had already decided to make it an easy day; perhaps we could go home early and "think about police work." That morning, I just wanted to unplug, wind down, drink my coffee, and watch the morning local news with the guys.

The NDTU office is a large, open work space. Each member has a desk and computer. There are no cubicles per se, so it's easy to communicate or talk to someone else across the room. Also, there are several big-screen television sets mounted on one wall, where we could watch TV programs or DVDs. The big screens are also wired to project the vehicle tracking map, so everyone can see, as well as other operational displays as needed, such as live pole camera videos. My favorite thing to do in the morning, on slow days, was to sit at the big table in the middle of the room, drink my coffee quietly, and listen to the friendly banter and good-natured ribbing between the members of the NDTU. To my sergeant "ears" it was the sign of a healthy unit, with good morale and all was well.

I don't know why, but James Sanders liked to watch *The View* and because he was closest to the big screens, he usually controlled what was on. I think maybe James had a thing for Whoopi Goldberg. Steve Kutach, on the other hand, strongly disliked *The View* and was verbally berating James, intermixed with a lot of "James, turn that shit off!" It was all in good fun, though; we were all laughing, enjoying Steve's discomfort.

Justin came into the office, got his cup of coffee, rolled his eyes at James, sat down at his desk, and turned on his computer. A few minutes later, he looked up from his computer and looked at me. "Hmm…Boss, did you notice that the white Buick is rolling and is outside of its geo fence?" Justin was checking the computer-generated track on his computer and it initially looked as though we had missed the alert when it left its home base. Later we determined that the vehicle had spent the night down near Pasadena, where we had not set a geo fence. Now, whoever was in it had been driving around in the early morning hours and we had not taken notice. We had gotten complacent; we didn't know how it was loaded, nor what the occupants had been up to. I was not too worried, though. It was still early and most Houston-area businesses where just now opening.

Apparently Justin didn't care so much for *The View* either and he unceremoniously turned it off, over James's objections, and put the tracking map up instead, which showed the current position of our white Buick. It was now north of us, outside the city limits in Harris County, east of Stuebner Airline Drive at a location I didn't recognize.

Justin sent a command to the computer to translate the geo coordinates of the white Buick's location to a Google Street View and then panned the view around 360 degrees to give us a clue about what type of location the vehicle was at. As Justin panned around, all we could discern was a parking lot with a large office building in the background: a white-collar type of workplace. Unless we missed something, the guys who drove the white Buick were decidedly not office worker types.

Justin switched the tracking map to satellite view, which gave us an overhead view of the vehicle's location superimposed over a satellite photo of the area. It was maybe 400 to 500 yards east of Stuebner Airline Drive, in the middle of a parking lot. It was not moving, although the temperature of the trackers indicated the engine was still running.

Then Justin's brain clicked. "Boss, the white Buick is parked behind the Valu Pawn!"

The Valu Pawn was on Stuebner Airline Drive. Behind it was an alleyway and then behind this alleyway was the parking lot for an office building, this being where the Buick was now parked. The parking lot was big and encompassed several acres. A small tree-lined or wooded area also separated the two locations (the alleyway for the Valu Pawn and the office building parking lot).

There was a momentary silence in the room as the significance of the Buick's location sank in. We had watched several days before as the guys in it had visited the same pawnshop. Maybe they were not "shopping" that day, but maybe they were indeed scouting a pawnshop to take down. Now the Buick appeared to be parked behind the Valu Pawn, albeit several hundred yards away.

A coincidence? I didn't think so!

We were out of our office as fast as we could, running to our respective undercover vehicles, which were always preloaded with our tactical gear. Justin stayed behind to monitor the tracking because the rest of us would be driving fast. The Valu Pawn was maybe a ten or fifteen minute drive away, and there were still the remnants of the morning rush-hour commute to contend with. I drove as fast as I could, pushing the envelope. My drive to the Valu Pawn, although it only took minutes, seemed to me like a long time. I arrived first. As I slowed down and pulled into the parking lot, I scanned the area. Everything seemed quiet; nothing was amiss. The Valu Pawn was in a strip center with several other businesses and the front customer parking lot was already crowded with parked vehicles.

I parked my Ford Escape to the northwest of the front door of the Valu Pawn about 50 yards out so I had a clear view. Then, as the other members of the NDTU arrived, I assigned them, over the radio, other positions, all in the front parking lot, placing the bulk of my manpower to cover the pawnshop's front door from several angles. If this place was going to be robbed, the bad guys would hit the front. I breathed a little easier. Within a relatively short time, we had the front parking lot locked down, and I had upward of five undercover officers in the parking lot with me, all unnoticed.

Other members of the NDTU were still arriving. The next place to lock down was the rear door of the pawnshop—just in case. The next two NDTU undercovers arriving also happened to be some of the "shooters" from two weeks previous, who had decimated Chris Jones's robbery crew. *Perfect*, I thought; *I will keep these guys out of any potential impending drama (another shooting) and place them in the rear of the store, in the alleyway, which we had seen on the Google satellite view.*

The Valu Pawn was now covered from all angles.

Next arriving was Ben LeBlanc. Over the radio, I told Ben that we had the Valu Pawn covered. I next needed to see what the guys in the Buick were doing. I was back on the radio: "Ben, I need you to go into the parking lot of the office building, behind the Valu Pawn, get eyes on the white

Buick, and tell me how it's loaded. How many people are in it and what are they doing?"

Ben acknowledged and drove off to locate the Buick. It would take a few minutes; the office building parking lot had maybe a hundred or more vehicles parked in it.

Ben had spotted the Buick and reported back. "It's parked. NO ONE IS IN IT!"

My heart sank. Instantly, I grasped the significance. An armed robbery crew was about to roll in and hit the Valu Pawn; they would now be in an unknown stolen vehicle. The bad guys would do a takeover robbery and probably try to get into the business's safe. After which they would use this unknown stolen vehicle to make their escape, drive a short distance to where the Buick was parked, and then transition to it, dumping the stolen vehicle.

Commercial Business Robbery Crew 101: they would probably use a freshly stolen pickup truck that had not yet been reported to the authorities.

The NDTU was about to be in another gunfight!

Just in case it wasn't apparent to the rest of the NDTU, I told them over the radio what I thought would happen. "Look for a stolen truck coming in to the parking lot—they're about to hit the pawnshop!"

I kept scanning the parking lot, looking for the robbery crew that I knew would hit the pawnshop any minute. I tightened the surveillance perimeter around the pawnshop by placing one or two more of my undercover officers in other key locations as they arrived. Yet, at that moment, I only had a handful of officers to deal with what was coming.

Back at the office, the members of the North Division's Crime Analysis Section were acting as an ad hoc command post and alerted the Harris County Sheriff's Office about what we thought was about to occur.

The front parking lot of the Valu Pawn was full of parked, unoccupied vehicles. We concentrated on the vehicles driving into the pawnshop's front parking lot, trying to pick out the one containing the robbery crew.

The minutes ticked by.

Suddenly, a movement caught my eye.

I WAS WRONG!

The robbery crew was already here and had been with us sitting in the same front parking lot the whole time!

I followed the movement and watched as the doors on a large crew cab pickup truck, which was parked near the front door of the Valu Pawn, exploded open. I counted as four suspects—all wearing masks and gloves, and armed with handguns—ran into the pawnshop.

I advised over the radio: "Too late—ROBBERY IN PROGRESS!"

Uniformed police units were being summoned, but by the time the word got out, the dispatcher typed up the call slip, made the necessary notifications, and before the uniforms could arrive, it would all be over. In my mind's eye, I pictured the crew forcing the manager to open the safe. It wouldn't take long; soon the crew would come back out the front door, headed back to their stolen getaway truck.

I propped the driver's side door open of my undercover vehicle, got my short barrel rifle ready, and waited.

Sure enough, one suspect was coming out. Or was he a lookout? The front door of the pawnshop opened and I could see a masked, hooded face scanning the parking lot. I settled the dot of my Aimpoint on the side of his head, pushed off the safety, took a deep breath, exhaled about halfway, and got ready to take the shot. But fortunately for him, I couldn't see his hands. I didn't see a gun; he was not threatening anyone at the moment, so I didn't perceive him as an imminent threat.

So I didn't kill him.

The lookout suspect eased back into the pawnshop and the front door closed.

We waited patiently for him, along with the rest of the robbery crew, to make their run from the front door to their vehicle. The seconds went by and even now in the far-off distance, I could hear the wail of police sirens as the uniformed units received the word and rushed to back us up.

These suspects were smart. They had a Plan B, just in case they couldn't use the stolen truck as their initial getaway vehicle. If need be, they could escape out the back door of the Valu Pawn and make their way on foot, across the alleyway, through the wood line, through the office building parking lot to the white Buick and get away that way. They must have realized that there was a police stakeout team in the front parking lot waiting for them and so they quickly transitioned to Plan B.

They chose poorly!

Two members of the NDTU were still posted up in the alleyway—the same two guys I was trying to keep out of any drama, because they were some of the shooters of the Chris Jones Robbery Crew two weeks previous. The Houston Police Department's Command Staff takes a dim view of its officers being involved in multiple shootings, no matter how righteous—political optics and all.

But which rear door would they come out of? This was in the back of a strip center, with multiple businesses; each business had a rear door, and none of these doors were marked. Which rear door belonged to which business? The guys in the alleyway had it narrowed down to three doors.

Was it going to be door number one, door number two, or door number three?

It turned out to be door number two!

Out came the robbery crew with guns in hand!

From my position in the front of the Valu Pawn, I heard a brief volley of gunfire. Then, over the radio: "Three suspects down!"

The suspects had run out, almost on top of the NDTU guys in the back alley. The police gunfire was short and decisive. Each of the suspects caught two or three .223 rounds, center mass.

I also noted several handguns lying impotent interspersed among the bodies.

Quickly, as trained, we secured the suspects, handcuffing them, even though I was certain one was already dead. But you never know.

Soon the uniformed police first responders were with us, as well as the Cypress Creek paramedics. These guys were good—at least, to my untrained emergency medicine eye—and they started immediate triage on the living suspects. Eventually, multiple Life Flight helicopters landed on Stuebner Airline Drive to transport the wounded suspects; the sheriff's department had blocked all the vehicle traffic. One suspect died on the operating table. The third survived— barely.

At the time that the shooting broke out, the getaway driver in the stolen truck parked at the front of the Valu Pawn decided that it was time to leave. With tires squealing, the truck pulled out of the parking lot. Fortunately, both Ben and Lalo picked up on it and followed it out. The driver of the truck was driving fast even though, at that moment, there were no uniformed units behind it. Ben and Lalo were calling for help and the men and women in our command post were on several patrol radio channels, alerting area patrol officers as to the direction and speed of the stolen truck. A marked sheriff's unit with lights and sirens got into the chase and took the pressure off Ben and Lalo. Then the driver chose poorly and headed into the Houston city limits, right into the HPD units coming out of Greenspoint to help. Someone threw out road spikes, and the chase was over. The female driver was in custody.

The parking lot of the Valu Pawn was now flooded with first responders as well as lieutenants and captains from several police agencies, all of who asked whether we were okay and told us what a great job we did.

264

Even an assistant chief from the Houston Police Department arrived. He did not appear happy about having to leave the safe confines and air-conditioning of his ivory tower downtown.

I say this because I still remember him getting out of his car with a scowl on his face and with his nose up in the air. He didn't even have the decency to check on us, unlike the upper supervision of the other agencies. The mannerisms and perceived arrogant elitist attitude of this assistant chief didn't go unnoticed by the other members of the NDTU, who made the quick determination that our assistant chief was, in their exact words, "A *Real Fucking Asshole!*"

Arithmetic is not one of my strong suits, but I was sure I counted four armed suspects jump out of the pickup truck and run into the pawn-shop. The driver didn't count; she never got out of the vehicle. In the back alley, there had been three bodies. I checked with my shooters in the back: *How many bad guys came out the back door?*

"Sarge, only three for sure; we shot everyone who came out!"

One suspect was missing. Was he still inside the pawnshop? We called for a police K-9 Unit, who made a thorough search of the interior. It was reported all clear; no one was inside. We were still not convinced! The Valu Pawn was outside of the city limits, so the crime scene belonged to the Harris County Sheriff's Office, who now had control over it. After the K-9 searched and found nothing, we convinced the sheriff's department supervisors to search again.

Several patrol deputies entered and searched; still nothing.

Okay...maybe I added wrong.

Two hours later, we were still in the parking lot of the Valu Pawn, waiting patiently as the sheriff's office evidence technicians processed the scene and we did a walkthrough with the Homicide and Internal Affairs investigators, our personal lawyers, and the Harris County District Attorney's Civil Rights attorneys to explain to all what had happened.

After we were finished, Big John and Dom from ATF approached me and said something was strange. They had noted "a lot" of the "thugs" from Greenspoint had somehow, mysteriously, gotten wind that several of their friends had been shot and had made the several- mile trip to the Valu Pawn shortly after the shooting and were now circling the area like a bunch of vultures. There were many. And because they were also making veiled verbal threats against law enforcement, the sheriff's office thought it prudent to bring in more uniformed personnel to keep them at bay and from interfering with the investigation at the pawnshop.

Then there was a commotion at the front door of the Valu Pawn. Out walked a Harris County Sheriff's Office evidence technician. In one hand, he had his camera (he had been taking pictures, documenting the crime scene); in his other hand was his pistol, which was leveled at the back of a black male, who had his hands up and he was leading out.

Yes…I could count: there was a fourth suspect. He had been hiding in a back room, inside a stack of tires. The police dog missed him, the deputies missed him, but the guy taking pictures found him.

Later, we determined, in reviewing the Valu Pawn's video, that the fourth suspect was the last in line to run out the back door and upon seeing his buddies all ahead of him getting shot, never made it fully out the door into the back parking lot of death. He reversed course, deciding instead it was much wiser to stay inside the pawnshop and hide in a stack of tires. In the hours he was hiding, he sent a flurry of messages out on his cell phone to the other members of his street gang: *"they ain't found me yet"*; *"I am hiding in the back of the pawnshop"*; *"The laws shot everyone else—but not me"*; *"COME GET ME!"*

The thugs Big John and Dom noticed circling the area were the recipients of these messages and they were collectively trying to figure out how, or looking for an opportunity, to extract their gang banger buddy, who they knew was still alive and hiding in the pawnshop. But when they saw

him being walked out at gunpoint by the "switched on" picture-taking officer, they dissipated from the area, heading back to Greenspoint to regroup.

CHAPTER 14

DIRECT CONFRONTATION WITH THE COMMAND STAFF

Shortly after the NDTU shootings of the five suspects at both the Cash Store and the Valu Pawn, Assistant Chief Eisenman and Assistant Chief McKinney ordered the supervisors of the NDTU to attend a meeting at Houston Police Headquarters. Both assistant chiefs had been the same ones who had previously directed the departments DTUs to do something about the scourge of Houston-area commercial business robberies. Captain Baimbridge, Lieutenant Bellamy, Sergeant Torres, Harris County District Attorney (ADA) Nathan Moss (Special Crimes Unit), and I attended this meeting.

The meeting topic seemed to be "Was there something that we could do prior to the robbery to arrest the suspects? Can't we arrest them for conspiracy to commit a robbery?" Captain Baimbridge, Lieutenant Bellamy, Sergeant Torres, and I explained that as per our written Plan of Action if, during the surveillance, we saw a strong indication that the suspects were about to commit a robbery—putting on masks, possessing firearms— we would initiate a takedown as soon as possible, assuming that adequate police resources were available. ADA Moss then "schooled" the two assistant chiefs on how charging a robbery crew under surveillance with the offense of Criminal Conspiracy prior to a robbery being committed was difficult and would require a "discoverable" criminal informant with knowledge about the planned robbery, besides some sort of overt act by the suspect(s).

The meeting also discussed the Plan of Action that I had written for Commercial Business Robbery Surveillance and Intervention. Captain Baimbridge, Lieutenant Bellamy, Sergeant Torres, and I explained why we were attempting to arrest the suspects at the scene and not allow them access to their getaway vehicle—to not have a police high-speed vehicle pursuit like the one we had with the Alabonson Robbery Crew. I pointedly asked Assistant Chief Eisenman, who seemed to be ramrodding the meeting and who had, in my opinion, an established departmental reputation for timidity and indecision: would he rather I have a vehicle pursuit with the suspects as opposed to attempting to arrest the suspects at the scene? I needed to know whether he wanted me to amend the Plan of Action for Business Robbery Surveillance and Intervention. To which Chief Eisenman responded, in a low voice, "I don't want any chases." I pressed and asked specifically whether he wanted me to change the plan. He only said that he didn't like the word "proactive" because it sounded too aggressive and wanted it taken out of the title.

So I did.

Later, after the meeting, ADA Moss, who had been working with us to make sure that the wording I was using in my tracking order affidavits was sound, shook his head and said he actually felt sorry for us (Captain Baimbridge, Lieutenant Bellamy, Sergeant Torres, and me) because of Chief Eisenman's objection to the "too aggressive" word "proactive." He thought this member of the Houston Police Department's Command Staff was, in his words, "weak-kneed."

It was never said openly but the tenor of the meeting was that the NDTU should go back to Narcotics and Vice enforcement (dope and whores) rather than continue with the Robbery initiative. The original direction to us to do something about violent crime, which might cause the shooting of armed criminals, was only made for appearance's sake—maybe for a press release to make the citizenry feel good that the police department was doing something.

It was, however, Captain Baimbridge and Lieutenant Bellamy's intent for us to keep dismantling the robbery crews, particularly considering there wasn't any direct order to the contrary from above. The NDTU continued its anti-robbery mission, much to the Command Staff's chagrin.

There was other tension and drama behind the scenes. Captain Baimbridge was now in trouble with Executive Assistant Chief Michael Dirden and was on the verge of being transferred out of the North Patrol Division and sent to "Police Commander Siberia"—to the Jail Division.

Part of the responsibilities of the North Patrol Division is in the Houston area known as Acres Homes. Acres Homes is almost exclusively a well-established, black, lower income neighborhood, with a somewhat semi-rural, country flair. Within this area were many small lots where the locals kept, of all things, horses (after all, isn't this Texas!). Unfortunately, some owners of these horses were not diligent in the care and feeding of their animals, and starving or malnourished horses were not an uncommon sight in the community. Captain Baimbridge was an animal lover and couldn't stand going to work and having to drive past these pitiful creatures with their ribs showing and all. So because he was the commander of a large patrol division with many resources, he ordered his Differential Response Team (DRT) to do something about the animal cruelty in the area. The DRT officers began their enforcement. Working with the Houston Humane Society (HHS), DRT began to rescue abused animals and hold their owners criminally accountable. The DRT and HHS started making headway and the life for the average horse living in Acres Homes was significantly improved. Word had gotten out in the community that if you owned a horse, you had better take good care of it, or the DRT/HHS were coming after you.

This new paradigm of having to take care of your animals didn't go well with some politically connected residents who lived in Acres Homes and complaints were voiced and lodged with Houston City Hall. These complaints soon rolled downhill to Executive Assistant Chief Michael Dirden, who then verbally directed Captain Baimbridge to stop enforcing the animal cruelty laws! Captain Baimbridge refused and tactfully requested that Chief Dirden provide him with a written order directing him to not enforce established criminal law. Of course, this didn't go well with Dirden and as a result, he was actively pushing the chief of police and the rest of the Command Staff for their support in removing Baimbridge from his command over the North Patrol Division and send him to the Jail Division. Fortunately, there were other Command Staff members who came to Baimbridge's defense, and he survived Dirden's attempted purge. But just barely.

Executive Assistant Chief Dirden probably had his eyes set on becoming the next chief of the Houston Police Department. Maybe this was why he was willing to subvert the enforcement of the animal cruelty laws, to appease those who might be able to influence those who would be on any future search committee making recommendations for the next chief of police. He probably didn't know this at the time, but because of this incident and several similar ones, he probably lost the confidence of the leadership of the Houston Police Officers' Union and they quietly nixed their support for him in becoming the next chief of the Houston Police Department.

After our meeting with the assistant chiefs and Captain Baimbridge's near involuntary transfer, we began to look around the country for other tactics for our use in taking down the robbery crews, perhaps a way less likely to result in us shooting more bad guys. We found that the Los Angeles Police Department Special Investigations Squad (LAPD SIS) had been the forerunners of high-risk surveillance and were now allowed by their administration to use a method called the Vehicle Containment Technique (VCT) in the takedown of armed robbery crews while they were in their getaway vehicles.

The LAPD SIS had been doing for many years what the NDTU had been doing for just a relatively short time. They enjoyed support by their Command Staff, a large budget, excellent undercover vehicles, as well as dedicated air support. The SIS had also, when conducting surveillance on commercial business robbery suspects, had faced the same dilemma—a desire to do what was safest for the public when making the arrest. Much like the NDTU, they first attempted to arrest the suspects as they exited the business and in such a manner as not to let the suspects go mobile and then have a vehicle pursuit. Much like the NDTU, they were involved in many shootings and killed several armed suspects.

Desiring to reduce the number of officer-involved shootings and at the same time not have vehicle pursuits, the LAPD SIS was allowed to "pin" the suspect vehicle in place with their undercover vehicles after the suspects left the scene of the robbery. It was known as the Vehicle Containment Tactic.

Intrigued with this tactic and thinking perhaps it could be used by the NDTU, both Captain Baimbridge and Lieutenant Bellamy went out of state to a school hosted by members of the LAPD SIS and were thoroughly trained in their technique.

Upon returning, they both expressed some confidence in the SIS method and that it might be an answer to the NDTU's problem with the Houston Police Department's Command Staff's evident objection with our doctrine of the priority of human life. The adoption of the LAPD SIS VCT would provide another option. Rather than trying to arrest the suspects at the scene or engaging them in a high-speed vehicle pursuit, it was now Baimbridge and Bellamy's hope that the Houston Police Department's Command Staff would allow this tactic.

Personally, the VCT appeared to me to be a win-win solution for the Command Staff as it might reduce the number of police officer-involved shootings and also the number of police high-speed vehicle pursuits. It would maintain the safety of innocent citizens. But, it was also my opinion that this tactic placed more risk on the involved undercover officers who were executing the VCT as opposed to arresting the suspects at the scene as they transitioned from the business they had just robbed to their getaway vehicle. Correctly performing the VCT would require the NDTU to be in very close proximity of armed robbery suspects desperate to escape.

Captain Baimbridge and Lieutenant Bellamy tried to push this new tactic forward for incorporation by the NDTU, making several written requests for its implementation to the Houston Police Department's Command Staff. But to my knowledge, neither received any response from the Command Staff regarding this new tactic. The allowance of the NDTU's use of the VCT would also require modification to the written rules of the Houston Police Department because under the then-present policy, this tactic—which amounted to ramming a suspect vehicle with several undercover vehicles—was explicitly prohibited.

As like in so many things, ideas generated from below, even in this case captains and lieutenants, were not looked on in favor by the upper echelon of the department. The processing of new ideas requires work and decisions and there was still the unspoken rule in bringing out-of-the-box thinking forward; to the upper reaches of the Houston police administration, "it's not a good idea until it's our idea"!

Letting the Houston Police Department's NDTU incorporate the LAPD SIS's VCT was decidedly not the Command Staff's idea, so it did not receive serious consideration! Even when others in the department—namely the Tactical Training Unit at the Police Training Academy— approved it, still the Command Staff would not make a decision and eventually Baimbridge's and Bellamy's proposal died a slow death—all but forgotten until 2018, when there was a new police administration in place.

The NDTU continued dismantling robbery crews. Because we were still guided by the original plan of action of trying to avoid car chases, this inevitably led to more shootings involving armed serial business robbery crews. In the next few months, the NDTU shot five more black males, all who were in the actual commission of armed robberies. Like in our other cases, Big John, Dom, Rick, and Heather ramrodded the follow-up federal government's prosecution of the survivors, many of whom received long sentences in prison with little possibility of parole.

The NDTU's commercial business robbery initiative was an unqualified success.

According to the Houston Police Department Crime Analysis data, the rate of commercial business robberies (on the north side of Houston) involving two or more suspects (crews) had been reduced 80% since the start of our initiative and the murder rate 58%. The north side criminal street gangs had realized just how dangerous and unprofitable it now was for them to victimize innocent citizens at gunpoint. If they didn't get killed by undercover police officers, then they would languish away for many years in some federal prison. More telling, the rate of commercial business robberies and murders for the rest of the city had risen during the same time the North Patrol Division's had dramatically fallen.

But at what cost? The NDTU was challenging the established order of the city's politics. Wasn't it better that the police merely report crime or help manage the citizenry's fear of crime by driving around in marked police vehicles, smiling and waving? By being so "proactive" or "aggressive," the NDTU was threatening the positions of the politicians and/or appointed Command Staff members who wanted to pander to the Black Lives Matter activists.

The actual proactive police protection of innocent citizens had now become secondary to the appeasement of political activists in the "modern era" of American policing.

On March 23, 2016, Lieutenant Bellamy, Sergeant Torres, and I (Captain Baimbridge was out of town) were ordered to attend yet another meeting, this time held by Executive Assistant Chief Dirden and Assistant Chief Eisenman. Acting Chief of Police Martha Montalvo was concerned about the amount of robbery suspects being shot by the NDTU. Supposedly, Chief Montalvo was now mandating (but not in writing) that the arrests of these in-progress robbery crews should not be attempted at the scene but rather later with an attempted high-risk vehicle stop utilizing marked patrol units—which would undoubtedly result in a police high-speed vehicle chase. Dirden and Eisenman implied that I should rewrite my Plan of Action to include another option other than attempting to arrest the suspects at the scene. I argued other options were already written into the plan, but maintained that all things being equal, it was safer for the uninvolved innocent citizen that the arrest/confrontation be at the scene of the crime rather than having a car chase!

Our "discussion" became heated! With no written correspondence to leave a trail of accountability, I was being leveraged in having to engage in exclusively police vehicle pursuits—all because the political optics were better.

I wasn't having it and definitely stepped way out of my lane as a sergeant by arguing with both an executive assistant chief and assistant chief. I kept pressing the issue.

Finally, Assistant Chief Eisenman cut me off, having lost his temper: "SERGEANT, WE ARE NOT GOING TO TELL YOU WHAT TO DO! BUT AFTER YOU DO IT, THEN WE WILL TELL YOU IF YOU DID THE RIGHT THING!"

The meeting was now over—and I had knowingly put one foot into the grave of my career.

The next morning, I was summarily ordered to Assistant Chief Eisenman's office. After waiting a half hour, I was told that for the time being I was being restricted to only administrative duties. I am sure this was intended as an unspoken message: I had better read between the lines and do what they were not actually willing to tell me to do.

Ultimately, I barely survived the fallout from the meeting held by Assistant Chief Eisenman and Executive Assistant Chief Dirden, but only because of some counter political brinksmanship. The Chief of Police Charles McClelland was retiring. Martha Montalvo was appointed the Acting Chief of Police, until the mayor, city council, etc., decided on a new one. Many of the members of the Command Staff, including Michael Dirden and Martha Montalvo, were throwing their hats in the ring and vying with each other to be the next chief of police. Presumably, anyone who wanted to have a chance for the position needed to project the image of the highest integrity, with no internal intrigue or hint of malfeasance that might impede their consideration. That was the advantage I had at that moment.

Through ranking members of Houston Police Officer Union who acted as my intermediary, I made it known that I was going to the sixteen members of the Houston City Council and frame the whole priority of life issue (innocent citizen first; arrest at the scene or police chase) to them. I would also lay out the actions (or inaction) of the Command Staff regarding the matter. Maybe I would even have some protected "whistleblower" status. In fact, I already had a prepared written statement for the city council's consumption. I am not sure what happened behind the scenes but the entire matter was later dropped, with little fanfare. I am sure that those who were vying to be the new chief of the Houston Police Department were eager to avoid any controversy that might have adversely affected their chances.

I was still the senior sergeant over the NDTU, for the time being. But in threatening the "nuclear option," I had made several powerful enemies. It would not be forgotten.

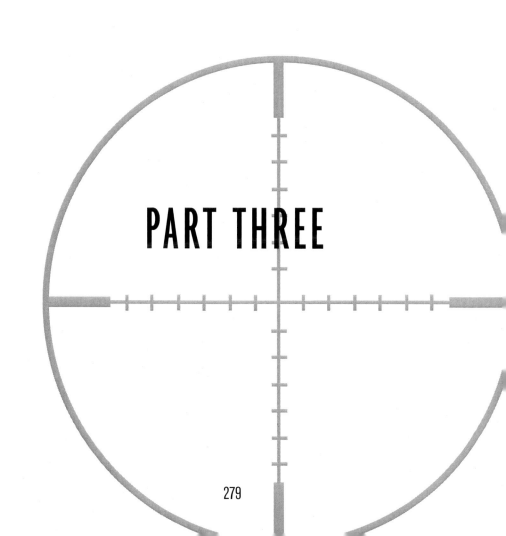

PART THREE

CHAPTER 15

A SNIPER?

The Houston Police Department is a bit of a closed society and there is an acknowledged, active rumor mill. It's like a small town, in that there are not that many secrets. Some investigators in the Homicide Division were sitting on a big one and the detectives "in the know" were trying to keep a lid on the information to not panic the public.

Captain Baimbridge and I, having been former homicide investigators with more established contacts into that "circle" of the departmental rumor mill, had gotten wind that something big was up.

One of the Houston robbery crews was conducting complex operations using a sniper. The sniper was concealed in an unknown location and made precision shots from a distance to kill armored truck guards. The primary objective in killing the guards was to steal the money bags/canisters that the guard was carrying to either service automated teller machines in the bank's parking lot or to carry inside the bank. The sniper only had a narrow window of opportunity to make the shot, this being the minute or seconds when the guard was exposed and was placing the monies into the ATM or carrying it into the bank.

After the sniper shot and presumably killed the guard, then the sniper would serve in an "overwatch" type function, remaining within his concealed position. Other members of the robbery crew would then immediately move in after the "execution" and retrieve the money bags from the dead or dying guard. The "pick-up" crew, after retrieving the money bags or canisters (monies destined for ATM are preloaded in canisters), would then make good their escape. All the while the sniper, who never revealed himself, would then "melt away" from the area of the shooting, "invisible" and not attracting any attention from witnesses.

Besides the sniper and the pick-up crew, there were also an unknown number of other suspects conducting counter surveillance in the area, alerting the sniper or pick-up crew if law enforcement was nearby or to actually trail the armored truck while it was on its route to advise when it was nearing the ambush site.

There was also evidence that this robbery crew had first started its operations by ambushing armored truck guards at close or point-blank range, when he or she stepped outside the safety of the armored truck. The plan of action was that one of the crew was the designated "shooter" whose assigned task was to immediately, with no warning or provocation, shoot and kill the guard. Once the guard was down, just like when the sniper was used, other members of the crew close by would rapidly move in and grab the bags or canisters. As soon as the money was recovered from the dead or dying guard, then the crew collectively would make good their escape, using a stolen vehicle.

One of the first times (as postulated) that this robbery crew conducted a known operation was when a white Ford F-150 was used in a February 20, 2014 attempted robbery of a Brink's armored truck, at a Wells Fargo Bank on Almeda Genoa Road. In this incident, the guard was exiting the truck while carrying money bags into the bank. He was then shot twice by a masked black gunman in a sudden, close-range ambush. However, the robbery was thwarted when another guard intervened and shot at the gunman with her pistol from within the armored truck through one of its purpose-built gun ports. The wounded guard survived. The suspects in the white Ford F-150 escaped.

Nearly a year later, on February 15, 2015, Alvin Kinney, a Brink's security guard, was ambushed and killed on Westheimer Road in the parking lot of a Capital One Bank. The investigating Homicide investigators noted that Mr. Kinney was shot at close range in the head by a masked gunman. Other suspects then backed up a white Ford F-150 truck to the open door of the armored truck and off-loaded approximately one million dollars in cash. It was also reported that the suspects may have been wearing ballistic helmets and body armor. The Ford F150 the suspects used was stolen and was later found abandoned a few miles away. Presumably, the crew transitioned into another unknown vehicle and then disappeared into the heavy Houston traffic. This was a good strategy, divesting themselves as soon as possible of the lick vehicle, which might have been seen by witnesses. The vehicle description would be reported to the police, who would then look for that vehicle. During the time the crew was in the lick vehicle immediately after the robbery, they were vulnerable to being spotted by uniformed police units. Strangely, much out of the usual, the white Ford F-150 used in this million-dollar robbery/killing had been stolen over a year before.

Could the white Ford F-150 truck used in the Almeda Genoa Road, Wells Fargo attempted bank robbery have been the same white Ford F-150 used in the Westheimer Road, Capital One Bank robbery and murder? If it were the same vehicle, then it would mean that both crimes were committed by the same robbery crew.

The next time this crew reemerged (again, presupposed) was nine months later, on November 6, 2015. In a similar operation, a gunman armed with a short-barreled .223 rifle tried, with no provocation, at a close distance, to kill the guard of a Loomis armored truck who was carrying money bags into a Bank of America on North Shepherd Drive. The guard was severely wounded in the barrage of close-range gunfire but was able to return fire on his assailant and put the suspect on the defensive. Fortunately, the wounded guard was close enough to the armored truck that his partner, who was inside the truck, was able to drag him into the safety of its interior and slam the hatchway shut, thus thwarting the robbery and saving the life of his coworker. The suspect's .223 caliber short-barreled rifle, based on witness statements, may have been a fully automatic weapon (a machine gun). Upon seeing that the wounded guard and the money were now out of reach, the gunman was picked up by other suspects in a dark-colored vehicle and they all escaped. The getaway vehicle was presumed to also be stolen, although never recovered.

In the February 20, 2014, February 15, 2015, and November 6, 2015 robbery/shootings, surveillance video in the area showed indications that the unidentified members of the crew had reconnoitered these bank locations for several days prior to the attacks. Presumably, to time the ambush to coincide with the schedule of the respective servicing armored trucks.

Five months later, on March 18, 2016, the crew hit again. A Loomis armored truck guard, who was not driving the truck but was just outside of it servicing an ATM, was fatally shot during an attempted robbery in a Chase Bank parking lot on Airline Drive.

Initially, what was reported or thought was that several masked men had ambushed the guard at close range and shot him several times (just like in the previous cases). The Loomis guard was mortally wounded but exchanged gunfire with the masked suspects who were approaching him. The guard, Melvin Moore, was a brave man. Even though he was dying, having been shot several times in the chest, he was still able to thwart the robbery. The suspects fled the scene without getting any of the monies. Witnesses at the scene believed that Mr. Moore was able to shoot and wound at least one of his assailants in the gunfight.

Homicide investigators reviewed the bank's parking lot surveillance video, which showed that the suspects had been waiting in the parking lot before the arrival of the armored truck. At first it was presupposed that the method of operation for this robbery was the same as the February 15, 2015 killing of Brink's guard Alvin Kinney and the November 6, 2015 shooting and attempted robbery of the Loomis armored truck guard in the Bank of America parking lot: well-planned military type operations using a short-range ambush-type assault, with the objective to take out the guard.

But the capital murder at the Chase Bank on Airline Drive was not a close-range ambush! Slowly, as the evidence came in, a new theory began forming; something was not adding up. A careful review of the bank's parking lot surveillance video revealed that the masked suspects who had approached Melvin Moore that day on Airline Drive were all armed with handguns. The surveillance video(s) also showed that the masked suspects approached Mr. Moore *after* he had already been shot, wounded, and was lying on the ground. To the surprise of these approaching suspects, Melvin Moore was not dead; he got back on his feet, full of fight, drawing his pistol and shooting one armed suspect approaching him before collapsing for a final time. The suspects fled without getting the money.

Then the autopsy results came in; Melvin Moore had been killed by a .223 rifle.

The Loomis armored truck guard in the Chase Bank parking lot, Melvin Moore, had been fatally wounded by another gunman not seen on the Chase Bank surveillance videos. The suspects visible on the videos were all armed with handguns; Melvin had been shot by someone else, who was shooting a .223 rifle.

Carefully, the eyewitnesses were queried again. "Did you see anyone with a rifle?" No one saw a rifle. The investigators painstakingly went through all the surveillance video from the surrounding businesses; again, no gunman in view with a rifle. Maybe it was that the witnesses and surveillance cameras just didn't "see" or "record" the gunman with the rifle.

*March 18, 2016 - Murder scene investigation of Loomis Guard
Melvin Moore at the Airline Drive Chase Bank.*

I don't know who first had the light bulb moment. Maybe it was one of the Houston Homicide detectives or an FBI agent or one of the Houston Robbery investigators who work with the FBI as TFOs. Someone started thinking out of the box. Someone said maybe they used a sniper! The sniper theory was way out there. Whoever first introduced the theory probably had it discounted immediately; it had never been seen before, even in the most sophisticated of robbery crews. It was the stuff of elite military units, political assassinations, or Hollywood movies. It was not real life Houston, Texas, violent crime. Many of the investigators didn't even want to entertain the idea; it was an even lower level of sociopathic criminality. Cold-blooded murder first, then rob!

The only real evidence that kept the sniper theory alive was a distant surveillance video recording of a blue van seen across the street, on the east side of Airline Drive, a considerable distance away from the bank. The blue van pulled into the stall of a self-serve car wash with its rear end facing to the west, in the approximate direction of the bank. No one was seen to get out and after the shooting, it left the area. Was there a sniper in the rear of the van, shooting out the rear window? The video was so poor it could not be discerned. Also detracting from the sniper theory was that the attack had occurred on a weekday at noon. The shot had to cross over the 5200 block of Airline Drive, from east to west. Airline Drive at midday is a busy divided four-lane roadway. A sniper would have to take the shot and time it to not hit any of the passing vehicles during the brief window of time when the guard was exposed. The level of marksmanship required was far beyond the abilities of the typical inner city street thug we dealt with on a day-to-day basis. The sniper theory did not seem likely, but it was possible.

The Homicide investigators investigating the scene did not release to the news media any of their suspicions or crazy theories about a sniper.

Melvin Moore, on the day he was murdered, wore a body armor carrier on the outside of his uniform. Inexplicitly, the pockets of the carrier, which are designed to hold actual armor panels in place, did not contain bullet-resistant type material such as Kevlar. Instead, his body armor carrier contained cardboard inserts. The fatal rifle round easily penetrated the cardboard and went into his chest cavity, ultimately killing him; it would probably not have made a difference, though, even if there were "real" ballistic panels in them. Normally the armor that is worn by uniformed police officers and armored truck couriers is light body armor. This armor is designed and rated to defeat projectiles fired by handguns, which, compared to rifle rounds, have considerably less penetrative capability as well as terminal effect. As noted, it was determined in the postmortem investigation that Melvin Moore had been killed by .223 or 5.56mm rifle fire.

These caliber designations are nearly identical and are almost synonymous; they can be normally chambered and fired in the same weapon system. By far the most common weapon system for this caliber is the AR-15 or M16, M4, etc. family of weapons common to the United States military, as well as being popular with civilian shooters. To defeat .223 or 5.56mm projectiles, the body armor carrier would have had to contain "rifle plates," which are much heavier (made of steel, ceramic, or other composite materials) and are not normally worn because of their weight and bulk. Also, the normally expected threat (common criminals/urban centers in the United States) was primarily projectiles fired by handguns.

Captain Baimbridge and I heard the rumors of "maybe a sniper" from our contacts in the Homicide Division, but discounted it as just an interesting theory. There was no other information forthcoming on the March 18, 2016 Capital Murder of Melvin Moore and the investigation went cold. We didn't have time to sit around and ponder on murder investigations that were no longer our responsibility (we were former Homicide detectives). We had our hands full, and the NDTU continued working long hours dismantling other serial business robbery crews. Because of the support of the ATF, we started branching out into dismantling other types of serial criminal activity, all by tracking vehicles.

Word was getting out to other divisions in the Houston Police Department and other area law enforcement agencies that "we" (the NDTU) were becoming adept at tracking bad guy vehicles and excelled at undercover high-risk surveillance operations. More importantly, as best we could, we would help other divisions and agencies in their investigations if our skill sets would be of benefit, but, we also had to be selective because we were getting so many requests for assistance.

We also started tracking the vehicles being used by serial criminals who committed a Burglary of Motor Vehicles (BMV); these suspects often committed several burglaries a day. We only became involved in this type of surveillance because we recognized that often the suspects committing these crimes were "fishing" for guns. The more BMVs you committed, the greater the chance of finding a gun, unsecured, in a vehicle. These guns were a hot commodity to be sold to criminal gang members, who then used these weapons to commit robberies. We even took out a large-scale crime ring that was stealing hundreds of vehicles, mostly Jeeps and trucks— smuggling them across the southern border where they were then being bought up by the Mexican drug cartels for use in their criminal operations within Mexico.

Or we conducted combined operations with ATF agents, arresting suspects who were buying up Barrett semi-automatic .50 caliber (12.7 x 99mm NATO) heavy sniping rifles in the United States and then smuggling them into Mexico—again, for use by the Mexican drug cartels in their frequent gunfights with each other, the Mexican military, or federal police.

All the operations and resulting successes of the NDTU were really only made possible because of the goodwill and assistance of the ATF (Big John and Dom), who orchestrated the use of so many mobile tracking devices for the NDTU's exclusive use and as well as helping to facilitate federal prosecution.

The Houston Police Department's Command Staff, though, remained mute, either unwilling or unable to comprehend the reasons for our success and were still "paralyzed by analysis," which tended to breed inaction. They still were not willing to sanction any course of action as to when and how we should arrest these suspects (at the crime scene, at the end of a vehicle chase, or let us "pin" the suspect vehicle like the LAPD SIS). Our emails were still unanswered. Even the vehicle pinning tactic, the lesson plan of which had been forwarded to Houston Police Academy's Tactical Training Unit had received their endorsement. But, when it all went up the chain of command for final approval, to the top decision makers, the

Houston Police Department's Command Staff, there was only silence: no direction, no leadership, no decision—continued paralysis!

I honestly believe that the involved members of the Command Staff were hoping the whole NDTU vehicle tracking initiative targeting primarily commercial business robbery crews would just go away so they would not have to make a decision. They were more comfortable with the status quo as opposed to having to make a difficult decision, which—good or bad— would ultimately have their "fingerprints" on it. Better to let the rank-and-file (the expendables) make the hard decisions.

We didn't know it but the trajectory of the NDTU was about to change dramatically.

On August 29, 2016 (Monday), after another long day in which the NDTU had facilitated the arrest of a "solo" robbery suspect in a "short and tight" surveillance operation, I was driving home in the early evening. As usual, I was listening to the local radio channel 740 AM's *Michael Berry Show*. At the top and bottom of every hour, there is a short local news broadcast. This was when I heard the first reports of another murder of an armored truck guard. The reports indicated that the killing had occurred during a robbery and that the suspect was a black male, who had left the scene in a blue Toyota Camry.

I wondered whether it was the workings of the same robbery crew I had heard about five months previous, when Melvin Moore was killed on Airline Drive and who might be responsible for the other killings of Houston-area armored truck guards stretching back to February 2015, when Alvin Kinney was ambushed and killed, one million dollars stolen and never recovered.

The next morning, I started making some discreet phone calls to my contacts in the Homicide Division. My curiosity was piqued. But I didn't have any ownership or really any business sticking my nose into the investigation, so I was careful not to bother the actual assigned investigators of the most recent murder/robbery (they had their hands full). Rather, I talked to others with a firm second-hand knowledge of the previous day's events.

The murder occurred in the parking lot of the Wells Fargo Bank on Hollister Road near Highway 290. Just like in the murder of Melvin Moore in the Chase Bank parking lot on Airline Drive, the Brink's armored truck guard, identified as twenty-five-year-old David Guzman, had been loading money into the ATMs in the parking lot. Word of mouth was that the parking lot surveillance video showed Mr. Guzman working on the ATM when he suddenly collapsed (there was no audio) and then a blue, four-door sedan (a Toyota Camry) pulled up next to the nearly motionless guard, who lay on the ground dying. A black male is then seen to jump out of the backseat (there was someone else driving) and swiftly grab the loaded canister of money from out of the still open ATM and jump back into the backseat of the getaway car. The vehicle then speeds off, out of camera view. No license plate number was recorded. There was also no sign that the suspect(s) in the getaway vehicle had done the actual shooting.

Witnesses outside in the general area reported hearing several gunshots, perhaps five.

No witnesses reported seeing a gunman.

No one knew who killed the guard other than he had been shot several times; some rounds struck his torso, defeating his light body armor and penetrating deep into his chest cavity.

New life was given to the sniper theory by the on-scene Houston Homicide detectives, but not all the initial scene information was yet in; the investigation had just started.

Later that morning when I reached the office, I grabbed a cup of coffee and went upstairs to Captain Baimbridge's office. Captain Baimbridge and I talked. As was our custom, before we talked current business, we reminisced about unsolved murders that we or people we knew had investigated years ago. This morning's topic: the 1990 Lover's Lane Murder case that my former Proactive IAD partner, Billy Belk, had investigated sixteen years before. The murder involved a boyfriend and girlfriend who were found murdered in a wooded area that was often used as a make-out spot, hence the nickname Lover's Lane. The female victim had her throat slit, but before dying she had been sexually assaulted. Her boyfriend was tied to a nearby tree and was nearly decapitated in a knife attack. Evidence at the scene suggested that the girl was raped and killed first, while the boy was forced to watch and listen, before he was also killed. Billy, for years after the murders, even when we were assigned to Proactive IAD, wanted so much to solve the crime to give the victims' families some closure, maybe some measure of comfort knowing that the killer(s) of their children had been brought to justice.

This near obsession was not uncommon in former Houston Homicide detectives who had investigated unspeakable murders. When investigators got to know the victims' families, it sometimes became personal. My Proactive IAD Lieutenant Dennis Gafford had been fixated on the 1991 unsolved murder of Roxyann Allee. She was an off-duty Harris County Sheriff's Office deputy who was abducted from the Greenspoint Mall and whose body was found the following day. Lieutenant Gafford, years later in the downtime between our doing police corruption cases, still had Billy and me running down possible clues on Roxyann's murder, even though we were no longer assigned to the Homicide Division.

Captain Baimbridge and I also had our unsolved murder cases. At the end of the day, though, we decided that we would have to be content with the idea that "vengeance" belongs to God and that He is the ultimate "detective" and "judge." Still, we wanted to see these cases solved, for the family's sake.

Then our conversation shifted. I told him what I knew about yesterday's murder of yet another armored truck guard. That I had made discreet inquiries, and more and more it looked like the work of a serial robbery crew who had "grown" from killing the guards in close-range, premeditated "assassinations" to using a hidden sniper.

It was unprecedented! At least in the world of commercial business robberies.

Captain Baimbridge reflected that if there was ever a "clue" or if the "window of opportunity" ever opened—some way we could dismantle this sniper/robbery crew—he wanted his DTU to drop everything and put all their effort into it, before the window could shut.

We both never imagined that this window of opportunity would ever open.

Two days later, I received a phone call from Sergeant Jason Robles in the Homicide Division. "Can you come to a meeting; it's important. We need to talk to you."

CHAPTER 16

THE INFORMANT

Lalo and I met with HPD Homicide investigators Sergeant Jason Robles and his partner Officer Eric Wohlgemuth, as well as FBI Special Agent Jeffery Coughlin and FBI Task Force Officers Sergeant David Helms and Officer Jessica Bruzas. David and Jessica were actually HPD Robbery investigators, but wore "two hats" and were assigned to work directly with the FBI. They all had ownership in the most recent murder of an armored truck guard: the Homicide investigators because of the Capital Murder that occurred within the Houston city limits and the FBI because it involved a robbery of an armored truck.

Jason and Eric were capable, motivated, and well experienced. They were good at what they did: reactive homicide investigations; putting the pieces together, after the fact. But unlike what is portrayed on television, Homicide detectives are not proactive, nor do they do undercover surveillance or tactical operations. They are foremost investigators; they wear suits and ties and carry note pads. This is also true of most FBI agents and their TFOs, particularly those who were assigned to investigate bank robberies or, in this case, armored truck robberies.

Jason and Eric had been "first out" and had "caught" the August 29, 2016 murder scene at the Wells Fargo Bank ATM at Hollister Road near Highway 290, where David Guzman had been shot and killed. Jason and Eric had quickly figured out that this murder was like the murder of Melvin Moore on Airline Drive several months previous. They, too, were now thinking that a sniper had been used in "their" robbery/murder. As usual, after getting the first facts of the murder, it was up to them to either brief the news media or provide a tight written summary with limited information about the incident for dissemination to the local news outlets. Jason and Eric, in dealing with the news media, were careful to not mention or allude to a sniper theory, only that the suspect was possibly a black male and seen leaving the scene in a blue Toyota Camry.

At that time, only Jason and Eric knew that the suspect(s) in the blue Toyota Camry was not the shooter(s) but part of a bigger robbery crew. The suspects in the blue Camry were there to retrieve the ATM money canister(s) immediately after the guard was killed. In this case, the pick-up guy could only grab one money canister, which contained $120,000.

Lalo and I closely watched the surveillance video from the Wells Fargo Bank. I could see David Guzman unlocking and opening the ATM. He then pulled the empty money canister out. Shortly after, he began to load the fully loaded canister with the $120,000 into the machine. While the front of the ATM is still unlocked and open and before Guzman can close and secure it, he suddenly collapses to the ground, having been shot. At the same moment, a blue Toyota Camry pulls up; the rear passenger side door opens and a masked black male jumps out and begins reaching for the loaded canister within the ATM. But David Guzman is not yet dead and makes a slight movement; he is immediately shot once or twice again. In the video, you can see the rounds impacting his body. As these additional shots are being fired into Guzman, the masked black male abandons his initial effort to grab the money canister and starts to re-enter the Camry, perhaps because there was still ongoing gunfire, or maybe because the guard was still alive. But he quickly reconsiders and returns; he successfully retrieves the loaded money canister, jumps into the backseat of the Camry and the vehicle speeds off out of camera view. All of this transpires in a few seconds.

Immediately, I thought of the shooting on Airline, where Melvin Moore, although mortally wounded, was able to foil the pick-up crew. But now, in the latest operation, the bad guys had learned. There would not be a repeat, no possibility of just wounding the guard and not getting the money. This time, the sniper would make sure the guard was dead and as added insurance, he pumps several extra bullets into David Guzman's body, just to be sure!

Then Jason and Eric showed us a surveillance video from a hotel across the street from the Wells Fargo Bank. The video was taken on the same day and approximately at the same time of Guzman's killing. It was of poor quality, grainy, taken from a long distance, but showed the image of a white SUV-type vehicle, parked in the back parking lot of the hotel. The white SUV is parked alone, away from any other vehicles and is backed up to a row of bushes that line the right of way that runs between the hotel parking lot and Hollister Road. The clincher: where the white SUV was parked, its rear end was perfectly aligned to the Wells Fargo ATM, which was across the street (four lanes of traffic) and in the middle of the bank parking lot, a good distance away.

Jason and Eric thought perhaps (like the Airline Drive sniper theory), a sniper was used.

If the hidden sniper theory was correct, the only logical place, based on the trajectory of the fired shots relative to David Guzman's positioning at the time he was first hit, had to be in the general area of the hotel across the street from the bank. Maybe the sniper had used a hotel room, but the windows in this particular hotel do not open. In a process of elimination, they had had surmised that maybe the white SUV had been used as a hidden sniper platform.

David Guzman

But, the two Homicide detectives and the FBI investigators had not called the sergeants of a DTU to brief them about a murder/robbery for no reason. They needed our help.

Sergeant Jason Robles had been contacted by an investigator in the Harris County District Attorney's Office. The investigator relayed to him that an informant who had provided reliable information to him in the past (related to a large shipment of narcotics) contacted him and said that he had seen the previous evening news story about the murder of the Brink's guard and thought he might know who was behind the shooting.

The informant didn't know the correct name of the individual he was referring to, but knew him as "Red" and thought his last name was "Batistey."

Jason then talked with the informant. He explained to Jason that he and "Red" had been "acquaintances" years before and:

- Red followed armored trucks every day to learn their routes and schedules.

- He shoots the guards from a distance with an assault rifle that has a telescopic sight on it.

- He practices with the rifle in a bayou in the Acres Homes community.

- He owns many vehicles—a black Jeep and a black Cadillac—and uses these vehicles to scout the armored trucks.

- To maintain his lifestyle, "Red" needed to commit 3-4 armored truck robberies each year.

- "Red" kept other vehicles that he used to facilitate these robberies hidden away in an unknown north side apartment complex.

It's not unusual as a Homicide investigator to have citizens with varying motives (almost always reward money) contact you with "information" about their pet theory or what they believe is relevant information about a "whodunit" sort of murder they saw on the evening news. As a Homicide investigator, you have to be able to discern this incoming "helpful citizen" intelligence: from the nuts, the wild guesses, to the legitimate. But the information from this "spy" was red hot.

Only a small circle of Houston-area law enforcement (a few Homicide and FBI investigators) even suspected a sniper. The person providing this information on "Red" nailed it, maybe not specifically saying sniper, but the "shooting from a distance" and then describing a sniper-type rifle had gotten everybody's full attention.

This, in the technical language of homicide investigators everywhere, was known as "a clue!"

The window of opportunity had just cracked open.

The Houston Homicide investigators and the FBI wanted to bring the NDTU into the investigation, to run surveillance on "Red" and help connect the dots. If the informant's information was correct, the clock was running. The next sniper killing of an armored truck guard and robbery would happen three or four months later, in or around November/ December 2016.

I told everyone at the meeting about my discussion just days before with my boss, Captain Baimbridge. Yes, the NDTU was fully in and would drop everything to help stop the killings.

The first problem: who was "Red Batistey"? What was his real name? Where did he live?

What vehicles did he drive? Who were the other members of the crew?

FBI SPECIAL AGENT JEFFERY COUGHLIN—**"FBI Jeff"**

My previous career experiences with the FBI had not always been "overwhelming wonderful." Some in the Houston Police Department, maybe out of jealousy, envy, or more likely because of the competitive nature of cops, denigrated FBI agents as mere "accountants with guns" or that the acronym FBI stood for "Famous But Incompetent." Over time, I realized that the FBI was like my organization: there were many competent, dedicated agents. But just like HPD, they also had their fair share of "squirrels" and like HPD, some in the FBI's upper management seemed more concerned about political considerations, rather than the law enforcement mission.

Captain Baimbridge had a bad habit of surprising me and catching me off guard. One morning in early 2016, I was drinking coffee with the rest of the squad in our common room, as usual. Suddenly, the door opened and in walked my captain. We always tried to look busy when the boss came in, but here we were, looking not so busy. It was worse. Behind our captain marched several somber-looking men, all with correctly fitting suits and ties. They looked professional. The older man leading the pack, I discerned, was some supervisor. He carried an air of authority and deference was given to him by the rest of the suits. Ominously, he was carrying a black binder in one hand and a pen in the other, ready to write and document.

I "smelled" FBI.

Oh no, I thought; *had we done something wrong?*

Captain Baimbridge introduced the older FBI guy—Supervisory Special Agent Mark Telle (*Mr. Telle*), the head of the Houston FBI Division's Violent Crime Squad. Mr. Telle was about my age (56+) and to my eye, he looked "old school," whereas the other agents all looked pretty fresh, maybe just out of the FBI Academy. These guys were not kids, but they all had that fresh, bright-eyed and bushy-tailed, ready to go look to them.

I was a little relieved when Mr. Telle told us that "they" (the FBI) wanted to help us with our commercial business robbery initiative and perhaps he could assign an agent to work with the NDTU?

Perhaps? I think it was a little more than "perhaps"! Captain Baimbridge immediately responded out loud to Mr. Telle's query, "Absolutely!" It was a little awkward. Big John from ATF was in the room and there was a professional rivalry between the two federal law enforcement agencies. Already I could see Big John's big forehead wrinkle and his eyes narrow.

But what my captain wants, he gets.

I quickly drank the Kool-Aid. I then addressed everybody in the room—my troops, the FBI dudes, my ATF special friend, as well as my boss—in a loud, somewhat sincere, clear voice: "Of course, we would all welcome the assistance of the FBI!" So as to kiss up to my captain.

I was being facetious (at least inside my head). The last thing I want to do is babysit some young FBI agent.

Mr. Telle then appointed one of his new agents to work with us. "This is Special Agent Jeffery Coughlin. I am assigning him to work with your unit!"

I looked over Special Agent Coughlin: about 5'10" or 5'11", stocky, powerful build, fair complexion, good-looking guy, with reddish hair slicked back with some hair goop in an urban, professional "metrosexual" style foreign to my generation. Maybe of Irish or Scottish heritage? Again, Coughlin was impeccably dressed in a suit and tie, with fancy shoes that had little dangly decorative things where boot laces ought to be.

There was an awkward silence and an air of expectation hung in the room. Everybody looked my way, as if I were to make a further decision to affirm Mr. Telle's "gift to us." Was I to also reciprocate? Maybe make a grand gesture?

Have you ever seen the movie *The Heat* starring Sandra Bullock as an uptight, proper, attractive, educated professional, yet somewhat naive FBI agent, who teams up with a local law enforcement officer played by Melissa McCarthy? Melissa McCarthy's character is crass, profane, a sloppy dresser, but street savvy. The two come together in the movie and despite being different, from dissimilar backgrounds, resolve their "issues" and together solve some "big crime" (I forgot what).

The walls of the NDTU office are decorated with several movie posters. One of which is a poster advertising *The Heat* with images of the two actors posed in law enforcement regalia. At the moment that I was "thinking fast" and taking in the movie's premise, sitting right under the poster, at his desk, looking bored was Mark "Muscles" Smith. Mark had his feet up, chewing tobacco and spitting it into a cup, wearing a gold chain, some old blue jeans, cowboy boots, his whole ensemble topped off with a T-shirt with some inappropriate comment printed on the front.

Mark Smith was "my" Melissa McCarthy and Special Agent Jeffery Coughlin was Mr. Telle's Sandra Bullock.

Yes! I thought. *Just like in the movie, I will "appoint" someone from my NDTU to work with Special Agent Coughlin.* This way, I could keep this FBI guy out of my hair and instead "bless" one of my subordinates with this "great privilege."

It's good to be the sergeant!

"Why, yes!" I announced. "We all look forward to working with Agent Coughlin and…I will have Officer Mark Smith partner with him." I didn't mention anything about the movie and how it inspired my decision-making.

This all came as a rude awakening to Mark, who suddenly became alert and was now upright in his chair, almost choking on his tobacco chew. He looked like an alerted meerkat who just spotted a pack of prowling hyenas. Mark caught my eye and gave me his "*WTF?*" look. "Yes…" I continued, "I think it will be a great match!" Some other guys in the NDTU softly chuckled. Mr. Telle, having no pre-knowledge about Mark Smith, seemed pleased and then, with the other agents except Coughlin, left the room, escorted by Captain Baimbridge.

In fairness to Mark Smith, the FBI was getting an experienced undercover officer who had well proved himself and was invaluable to our mission.

"FBI Jeff" stayed behind and made small talk and further introduced himself. As we talked, he asked pointedly "what can we, the FBI, do to help." I laid out my ongoing problems with getting undercover vehicles. Jeff responded with, "I will see what I can do." But I didn't expect much. Later, after some small chitchat and after Mark admonished Jeff to "stop wearing that shit!" (suit, tie, pretty shoes, etc.), Jeff left the office. As soon as he left, I asked Big John about Agent Coughlin (figuring that because Big John was

ATF, maybe he had crossed paths with FBI Jeff). Big John said he "knew him" and that he was "okay" for an FBI guy. Coming from an ATF agent, that was actually a good endorsement.

A few hours later, Jeff called me. Unexpectedly, he went right to the subject of undercover vehicles. The FBI could help, but could only supply vehicles to FBI TFOs. They had two TFO positions open; they would give Mark Smith one position and if I could name another qualified member of the NDTU, they would then make him a TFO also and give them both vehicles. It was an easy decision: Ben "White Chocolate" LeBlanc would be the other FBI TFO!

Having four members of the NDTU as either ATF or FBI TFOs went a long way to ease our undercover vehicle problem.

During the months since Ben and Mark became FBI TFOs, I had seen little of FBI Jeff. We talked occasionally and the NDTU helped the FBI with some of their operations, but nothing high speed or significant. I was content with the arrangement (my guys had "take-home Fed rides") and the FBI seem happy with our occasional help.

But now, on the morning of September 1, 2016, a few days after the murder of David Guzman, the Houston Homicide detectives were outlining the information from an informant regarding a "Red Batistey." I realized that if anything was going to happen, to keep the window of opportunity open, the NDTU's relationship with the FBI (specifically with Special Agent Coughlin) would have to rise to an entirely different level.

I want to be careful to not disparage Sergeant Jason Robles or Officer Eric Wohlgemuth. They are top-notch Homicide investigators. But they are not "crafters" of proactive police sting operations, surveillance operations, or experienced in the long-term management of criminal informants. Even if they were, their assignments would not allow them to devote the time necessary to what lay ahead. In but a few days, they would be back to being "first up" and would catch another homicide scene, and a few days after that yet another, etc. Just like me, twenty-five years before, they were part of the Homicide Division's assembly line of death investigation. Presumably the murders in Houston would not stop and the killing of David Guzman would soon be one of many Eric and Jason investigated during their careers, only remembered by them because Guzman was maybe killed by a one-of-a-kind sniper.

As soon as the meeting was over, I called FBI Jeff. I laid out the issue with the informant. I explained to him that somehow, without offending Jason or Eric, he would have to get control of the informant. This investigation is going to go on for a long time and you're FBI; you have the credibility, you have the time, and your agency has deep pockets. The informant had told Jason and Eric that he had come forward only because he "didn't want to see anyone else get killed." I told Jeff I didn't believe that. It was possible, but in my experience the informant was looking to make "big money" off his "snitching." I explained to him, you have to be the one to manage the informant—be his handler—establish contact with him, start giving him some FBI money and gain his confidence; in short, get him on the "hook!"

My confidence in Jeff Coughlin was not blind or misplaced. Even though Jeff had only been with the FBI for two years (when we first met), he was not without some significant life experience. A graduate of the United States Military Academy at West Point, he had served several combat tours in both Afghanistan and Iraq, rising to the rank of captain in the United States Army's 75th Ranger Regiment. While serving in Afghanistan, he had gotten to know an FBI agent who was assigned to his unit and whose job was intelligence gathering relative to terror threats on the United States mainland. Jeff had a wife and two small children, and for the sake of his family, a career in the FBI offered more "be at home" time and stability for his young family than a career in the military.

FBI Jeff was not an accountant with a gun!

Sometimes I joked with him that my experience in the 1970s-era NJROTC program was somehow co-equal with his military combat experience.

That same afternoon, without offending anyone, the informant was "attached" to FBI Jeff. Later the same day, Jeff and Sergeant David Helms met with the informant. They had done some quick computer research, looking for similar names to "Red Batistey," in particular anyone with a similar name who had a prison record and resided in the Houston area. They were trying to figure out "Red's" real name. FBI Jeff and Dave narrowed their search to a former prisoner who had been sentenced to five years in federal prison, for Making False or Factitious Statements in the Acquisition of Firearms.

This person of interest's name was Redrick Javon Batiste.

David and Jeff then showed a photo spread to the informant: "Do any of these guys look familiar?" The informant recognized the photo of Redrick Batiste as the man he knew as "Red Batistey" and who he believed was behind the recent armored truck guard killings.

The informant made some FBI money that afternoon and now the hook was in his mouth.

As soon as FBI Jeff and Dave Helms were clear from meeting the informant in southwest Houston, Jeff called me. The subject for our surveillance was Redrick Batiste.

We were up and running.

I messaged Captain Baimbridge and Lieutenant Bellamy. The NDTU was green-lighted to pour all of its time and resources into this case by doing what we did best: high-risk surveillance.

As soon as we had the name, Dave Smith and Justin Williams were already digging in and researching. I wanted an overview/summary of Redrick Batiste. But most importantly, I needed to know what vehicles he drove and where he lived.

Redrick Batiste was in his late thirties, with an arrest record for Unlawfully Carrying a Weapon, several assault charges, Possession of Marijuana, Driving While Intoxicated, Evading Arrest in a Motor Vehicle, Evading Detention, etc. But more significant was the five years from 2000 to 2005 that he had spent in federal prison for what the ATF called a "straw buy." Because of his criminal convictions, he was precluded from buying or possessing firearms, so instead he was having a girlfriend buy guns (she was not excluded and could pass the federal firearms background check). These guns were then delivered into his possession. After serving his time in federal prison, Batiste was then arrested and convicted for several charges of Credit Card Abuse and was incarcerated again for a total of 21 months. But since then, there had been no significant interactions with law enforcement since 2009, nearly seven years previous—with one exception. During a recent routine police vehicle traffic stop, Batiste was found to be in possession of a small amount of marijuana and arrested. The misdemeanor charge of Possession of Marijuana had not yet been adjudicated and was still working its way through the Harris County judicial system.

Dave and Justin pulled up the Harris County Sheriff's Office report and noted that in Batiste's most recent arrest, the deputy had documented that he had been driving a black Jeep Wrangler. The deputy had also noted its Texas license plate number. This was significant as it dovetailed nicely with the information the informant had provided. Now I thought I had enough probable cause for a tracking order and started writing.

Also, David after checking the Harris County Tax records, discovered something interesting. In 2015, Batiste started buying many residential properties in the north and northeast parts of Houston—maybe $150,000.00 worth, all modest homes. But where did he get the money to buy real estate? He didn't seem to have any employment. It was a big red flag and in my mind correlated with the February 15, 2015 murder of Alvin Kinney, the Brink's security guard and the million-dollar heist on Westheimer.

Going through social media, Justin found Batiste's current girl-friend. Her name was Buchi Okoh. We all had trouble rolling her name off our tongues, so we started referring to her as the "Nigerian girl." Buchi Okoh was tall and had been a bit of an athlete, playing volleyball at Lamar University in her earlier years. In March 2015, she had given birth to a daughter, the father being Redrick Batiste. Buchi was living in a house Batiste had purchased in northeast Houston. Unlike Batiste, Buchi was gainfully employed at the Sterling McCall Cadillac dealership on the Southwest Freeway in south Houston. On her personal Facebook page was a picture of her brand-new vehicle, a black Cadillac CTS, and fortunately the license plate numbers were in clear view.

More probable cause for my tracking order. The informant also said that Batiste used a black Cadillac (along with a black Jeep). It looked as if we had found and identified both vehicles, just as the informant described.

This informant was gaining some credibility in my book.

Friday morning, I was down in Texas District Court, presenting the applications for my tracking orders, to a judge, in private, in her chambers. She slowly read each order, pausing from time to time to glance at me over her reading glasses. When she was finished, she signed the orders and looked at me. "This is incredible, Sergeant. Please be careful!"

"Yes, ma'am," I replied.

CHAPTER 17

OPENING MOVES

After the meeting with Homicide and the FBI and after obtaining the tracking orders, the NDTU had a group meeting. Usually I don't use or like emotional pep talks, but this was the time for one. Lalo and I laid out all we knew about Batiste. We suspected that Batiste and the other unknown members of this crew where a highly organized, serial, business-type robbery crew, that were also serial killers and the clock was now ticking down for their next planned robbery/murder in three to four months. We, the NDTU, would give this investigation 100%. To inspire and appeal to a deeper emotional commitment that is sometimes difficult to find in violence-hardened, cynical street cops, Lalo and I pulled on heartstrings to have our team identify with the victims and their families at a more personal level. On our operations board in the office, we posted family pictures (taken from social media) of David Guzman and Melvin Moore, the last two guards who had been murdered, and the heartfelt, emotional comments posted by their loved ones after their deaths. These pictures

308

remained on the board for nearly the next four months as a constant motivator to all of us.

We also showed the team the parking lot surveillance video of Guzman being gunned down. Lalo and I reiterated that it would be primarily up to the NDTU to prevent the next killing(s).

That weekend there was a rain front moving in, due to arrive late Saturday evening or early Sunday morning. The NDTU would mount an operation under the cover of the early Sunday morning darkness and rain to locate Redrick Batiste's black Jeep Wrangler and Buchi Okoh's black Cadillac CTS. Hopefully, both vehicles would be parked in the open and not in an enclosed garage. David and Justin were not sure where the vehicles would be found or even where Batiste "laid his head" at night, but thought Okoh's known residence would be a good place to start. There was a list of other properties that Batiste either owned or was associated with and were also potential possibilities. Lastly, there were also recent NVLS scans of Batiste's Jeep Wrangler, which were recorded at night. Scans showed the Jeep parked and unoccupied in an apartment complex in Humble, to our north. This Humble location also looked like a good location to search and I was hoping to find the Jeep there. It's infinitely easier and much safer to covertly sneak tracking devices on a suspect's vehicle(s) while parked at night in an apartment complex than at a private residence. Particularly if your suspect is a serial killer and not one of your typical north side, run-of-the-mill, "highjackers". I was hoping this was the apartment complex the informant was referencing when he said Red kept other vehicles that he used to facilitate robberies, which were supposedly hidden away in an unknown north side apartment complex.

Sunday morning, starting at three a.m., while most of Houston and Humble slept, the NDTU scoured the areas where our intelligence had led us to believe the Jeep Wrangler and the Cadillac CTS might be located. Our priority was Batiste's Jeep Wrangler, this being his primary everyday vehicle. Okoh's Cadillac we viewed as being of secondary importance. We first headed to Humble to the apartment complex where the Jeep Wrangler had been scanned by NVLS. It was not there. As the time ticked away, we carefully scrutinized all the white SUVs parked in the complex, looking for one that somehow "wasn't right": maybe it was stolen, maybe it had paper temporary license plates—something that would clue our cop instincts to the stashed white SUV that Eric and Jason (the Homicide investigators) thought might have been used as a hidden sniper platform.

Of course, in this apartment complex, there were a bunch of white SUVs, which are so common. Each one had to be carefully looked over and the license plate registration researched on our portable laptop computers, looking for some clue that this was "the" white SUV. We had to remain covert and could only examine the vehicles in question from a distance through binoculars, in case it was the vehicle—to not tip off the robbery crew or any sympathetic corroborators who might send out the alarm that the lick vehicle had been discovered. After an hour in the apartment complex, it was a washout. No Jeep Wrangler and nothing to show that any of the white SUVs parked there were at all suspicious.

Lalo and most of the NDTU stayed in Humble and started checking the adjoining apartment complexes to look for the mystery SUV. We realized in our experiences with other robbery crews that they sometimes parked and stashed the vehicles they used for their robberies at locations other than where they lived. If Batiste (maybe he wasn't home; maybe he had been out partying Saturday night and was laid up somewhere else) or another member of the crew lived in the Humble apartment complex, maybe the white SUV was stashed close by.

It was looking bad, like a needle in a haystack scenario.

David Smith, Steve Zakharia, and I were together in one vehicle and Ben LeBlanc, who was in his FBI ride, split off and headed to Buchi Okoh's residence in northeast Houston. She lived in a house that Batiste had bought for her on Flossie Mae Street. When we got there, we were relieved to find her black Cadillac CTS parked in the driveway. The problem was that it was backed up to the house; we wanted to place the trackers underneath the rear of the vehicle, near the exhaust systems, so we would have to squeeze between the Cadillac and the house while sliding under beneath the car. It was doable, even in the dark and rain, but it was tight.

Zak got out of our vehicle, about a block away, with two trackers hidden in his sweatshirt, and walked down the street. He had his black hoodie on, and the only thing that really stood out on him, out of the ordinary, was the big, white Middle Eastern heritage nose that poked out from under the hood. Zak moved up out of the street and was making his way up the driveway. He was at the front of the Cadillac when some dog inside Okoh's house started to bark. Somehow its doggie senses became alerted that an undercover police officer was trying to put tracking devices on her master's car. I don't know how the dog figured it out. Zak made no noises (that I could hear) and the shades were all drawn on the house. It was uncanny.

Zak backed off and came back to our Ford Expedition. "Damn, I don't know how that dog knew I was there."

We waited half an hour, to let things settle down, and then Zak would try again. At the appointed time, Zak was again moving, extra stealthy, not breathing (much), careful that the legs on his blue jeans didn't "swish" together as he walked, careful that each footstep was deliberate and soundless as it made contact with the ground. Zak was almost at the back of the Cadillac.

Then: "*Yap, Yap, Yap, Yap!*"

Zak retreated again and was soon back with us. "Sarge, we're not going to be able to get any trackers on the Cadillac here. I don't know what it is, but that dog has some super powers we don't know about!"

I don't know what kind of dog Buchi Okoh kept, but I want one for my house.

At least we had found the Cadillac. Then word came back from the rest of the team: no luck finding the mystery SUV up in Humble. Since it was only an hour or two from sunup, everybody headed home. Dave Smith had a few other locations he wanted to check. These were other properties that Batiste owned, all in Acres Homes. We headed that way, methodically checking them, but still not finding the black Jeep Wrangler.

There was one location left, 1351 Tarberry, which was in a residential neighborhood just to the east of our police station. It was a location that we had assumed Batiste rented out as part of his newly acquired real estate empire. As we turned the corner on Tarberry Street, there it was: parked in the front yard, right under our noses, was Redrick Batiste's black Jeep Wrangler. Thankfully, it was not in the garage, but parked on the grass of the front lawn, right next to the front door of the house.

Soon it would be sunup and it had already stopped raining. Our window of opportunity was closing. Was Batiste an earlier riser? We still had to wait: one of the neighborhood crack heads, who was an early riser, was already rolling around the neighborhood on his bicycle. We waited patiently for him to clear the area—soundless, hidden, "buttoned up" in our blacked-out Ford Expedition. As the crack head's random meanderings brought him close to our position and before he rolled past us, Dave shut the engine off, to not alert him. As soon as he was past us and around the corner, Zak was out and moving. Dave lowered the rear passenger side window on the Expedition so I could cover him with my rifle, in case he was spotted by our supposed serial killer. I buried myself deep into the backseat so the telltale sign of the muzzle of my rifle didn't protrude out of the vehicle.

Zak was almost to the Jeep.

My point of aim was on the front door of Batiste's house.

Now Zak was under the Jeep.

Dave, in the driver's seat, put fingers in each of his ears, in case I fired that short barrel rifle from inside our Expedition.

Zak was now flat on his back under the Jeep, using a small flashlight to help him position the first tracker. Dave and I held our breath as the seconds agonizingly ticked by. The first tracker was going on, but Zak was a little fast and the powerful magnet on the tracker pulled it out of his hands an inch from the metal frame under the Jeep. There was a reverberating "clang" as the tracker "self-attached." It sounded loud, but fortunately nothing stirred in Batiste's house (no hyper-vigilant yappy dog lived here). Zak placed two more backup trackers on the Jeep; this time he was much quieter and as soon as he was done and satisfied with the positioning of his handiwork, quickly rolled out from under the Jeep and moved back to Dave and me.

As soon as Zak was back in the Expedition, we were out of there. We didn't fit into this neighborhood and couldn't afford to jeopardize the mission by being spotted by any of Batiste's neighbors.

Later that Sunday morning, we programmed the primary tracker on Batiste's Jeep Wrangler to report its position every five minutes. We also programed an electronic geo fence around his residence at 1351 Tarberry. Every five minutes when the primary tracker reported its position and if the reported position was outside of the Tarberry geo fence, a text message would be immediately sent to my iPhone, alerting me that the Jeep was on the move. I could then access the tracking map on either my laptop computer or iPhone to determine the location and direction of the Jeep. When the Jeep was moving, I would remotely manipulate the tracker and tell it to report its location, for example, every fifteen seconds to give us a better idea where the Jeep/Batiste was going, to not miss any locations he might stop along the way.

Pinging it faster also drained the battery faster, so it was a bit of a balancing act. If we deemed it important and were available, we could also then physically intercept the Jeep in our undercover vehicles and place it and Batiste under actual physical surveillance, "getting eyes" to get better insight as to what was occurring or what he was up to. The tracking devices also gave the NDTU the opportunity to document Batiste's activities, the locations he traveled to, and maybe most important, the people he met. One of our goals was to figure out who the other members of the robbery crew might be. All of this information would then be recorded into a master surveillance file that FBI Jeff could also access.

On Monday morning, presumably Buchi Okoh would go to her job at the Sterling McCall Cadillac dealership on Southwest Freeway. We were certain that she would drive the black Cadillac CTS, and we figured while she was at work and inside the dealership, there would be an opportunity to sneak a team of NDTU undercover officers into the employee parking lot and place the tracking devices on her car there. All because she had an effective security system (her dog) inside her residence on Flossie Mae Street. About half the NDTU, the first thing that Monday morning, were off headed to the dealership to await Okoh's arrival. In the meantime, the rest of the NDTU would stand by to get eyes on Batiste and his Wrangler if he left his house on Tarberry.

FBI Jeff, Sergeant David Helms, and Officer Jessica Bruzas drove over from their office so we could brief them on what we did Sunday morning as well as drink coffee and talk shop. As we were chatting, telling them that some of the guys were set up at the Sterling McCall Cadillac dealership waiting on Batiste's girlfriend and her black Cadillac CTS to arrive, Justin Williams, who, as usual, was on his computer, searching various social media accounts, spoke up and added to our conversation.

"Hey, Boss, this is interesting! Did you know that before she (Buchi Okoh) worked at Sterling McCall Cadillac, she worked at the Joe Stewart Cadillac dealership?"

There was a stunned silence in the room.

I don't know if Justin knew it when he said it, but FBI Jeff, Dave Helms, Jessica Bruzas, and I did. The owner of the Stewart Cadillac dealership, Joseph Stewart, a multi-millionaire, had been murdered in a home invasion by unknown gunmen. The killing occurred at his Montrose area residence in Houston on May 8, 2015 during an ambush-type robbery, just as he had arrived at his house. His body was found in the garage. The motive for the robbery was thought to be related to large amounts of cash and/or other valuables Stewart might have kept inside.

Looking at her employment timeline and digging deeper, Justin determined that after his death, the Cadillac dealership that bore Joe Stewart's name had gone out of business. Buchi Okoh then moved on and was hired by the Sterling McCall Cadillac dealership.

Joseph Stewart's murder was still unsolved, with no viable leads.

Did Redrick Batiste's robbery crew target and kill Joseph Stewart to steal money and other valuables he might have kept in his residence?

Did Buchi Okoh, either knowingly or unknowingly, provide intelligence about her employer to her boyfriend, Redrick Batiste, and his crew to help them facilitate the robbery and murder of her employer?

Or was it all a happy coincidence?

We didn't think so.

But could we prove it?

Later that Monday morning, I was monitoring the NDTU radio traffic and listening as several of the guys located Buchi Okoh's car at her job site and as they waited for the coast to be clear so they could crawl under her Cadillac and put the trackers on.

Bink! "Exit Tarberry Geo Fence—Jeep Wrangler," my iPhone announced. Batiste's Wrangler was moving. The primary tracker recognized and now reported that "it" was outside of its designated geo fence.

The available NDTU members quickly followed and we soon had rolling surveillance on the Jeep. This would be our first time to place Batiste directly under our observation. Something that would become nearly a daily occurrence in the months to come.

Redrick Batiste drove around in the southeast part of Houston for several hours. I was again hoping that he would lead us to the mystery SUV. Maybe Batiste had misled the informant about stashing vehicles on the north side; maybe the key to the puzzle hid in some other part of the city.

As we followed him, I reflected on the 2015 million-dollar armored truck robbery and killing of Brink's guard Alvin Kinney and how the Ford truck used in that crime had been stolen nearly a year before it had been used in that particular murder/robbery. Where had that stolen truck been hidden for all that time? Maybe it had been secreted away all that time somewhere in southeast Houston?

As we were tailing Batiste on Lockwood Drive and because of the flow of traffic, he ended up right next to me, stopped, at a red light. I took a quick glance out of the corner of my eye, careful to not draw his attention by looking directly at him. Both of our vehicles had a heavy window tint, but because of the way the sun was positioned he was back lighted and I had a view of his side profile or silhouette. Redrick Batiste, from the side, somewhat resembled Abraham Lincoln, the sixteenth president of the United States. He had a beard without a mustache, long, thin neck, prominent Adam's apple, and similar facial bone structure. It was uncanny. It eventually got to be that I could recognize his unique profile from quite a distance.

That first day Batiste drove around, he didn't go to a job site (he was unemployed), never visited anyone, never stopped anywhere other than to stop and get gas, nothing out of the ordinary. It appeared to me as random driving around on the other side of town from where he lived, which was maybe unusual.

What was out of the ordinary was that Batiste, although appearing relaxed, was alert. He was always constantly checking his "six o'clock" and his head was always "on a swivel." He studied the traffic and vehicles around him. When he got out to gas up his Jeep, he carefully watched the vehicles passing by as well as the cars parked around him. I was impressed and also alarmed. This potential adversary was a totally different class of bad guy. He was methodical, attuned to his environment, slow, deliberate, deep thinking. This would be something that the NDTU would have to carefully heed and factor into our future surveillance of him.

When it came to criminals, this man was on the top of the food chain!

Thankfully, the guys back at the Sterling McCall Cadillac dealership reported that they could get the trackers on Okoh's Cadillac and were headed back to our office.

Eventually Batiste also headed back north, back to Acres Homes and home to 1351 Tarberry. How convenient is that—running a high-risk surveillance operation, where your target lives so close to your workplace, almost in our backyard! I joked with the guys about having them take shifts and climbing to the top of the ridiculously high radio communication tower near our station and monitor his house with a set of binoculars. John Calhoun retorted back to me that sitting on the top of the radio tower sounded more like a sergeant's job. Ha! I didn't tell him I did not enjoy heights or swimming in cold water.

The following day was like the previous. Batiste would leave his house late in the morning and drive around southeast Houston with no apparent agenda. The only difference was when Okoh came home from work, late that afternoon, Batiste drove over to Flossie Mae Street and visited for a few hours, before driving back home to 1351 Tarberry.

I knew it had only been a few days, but I was having problems foreseeing how we would find the mystery white SUV. Batiste was driving all around the city and there were literally thousands and thousands of white SUVs in Harris County. How were we going to find it? I couldn't see a light at the end of the tunnel and started having my doubts, but was careful to keep my thoughts to myself to not demoralize the team.

Maybe the SUV had been dumped and was no longer in play? Justin was going through all the reports of recovered stolen vehicles in the region, since the time of the August 29 murder of David Gonzales, looking for a recovered white SUV that somehow stood out. We were not sure how to find the white SUV, only that if we kept trying or, as I called it, "keep getting up to bat" maybe eventually the god of surveillance operations would smile upon us and we would get a hit. Justin found one or two stolen and recovered white SUVs that fit the time frame but with further digging, he could eliminate them from consideration. They were not going to be "our" white SUV.

The mystery SUV still had to be out there—somewhere.

We retraced our steps. We got a copy of the surveillance video taken from the hotel across the street from the Wells Fargo Bank on the day of Guzman's murder that showed the indistinct image of the white SUV, parked in the back parking lot, lined up with the Wells Fargo ATM across the street. Justin and Dave Helms studied the image, trying to decipher what model and make vehicle it was, trying to narrow it down. Dave Helms thought perhaps it was a Nissan Pathfinder, Justin thought maybe a Toyota 4Runner. No one was sure.

Lalo and I went out to the murder scene, to the hotel parking lot where the white SUV had been recorded, double-checking for clues, looking for something, anything.

Lalo found something! Going to the spot in the hotel parking lot where the SUV had been parked, he found that the hedges/ornamental bushes between the spot where it had been parked and the ATM off in the distance had been carefully trimmed. Someone had manicured the hedges to facilitate an unobstructed view from where the white SUV had been parked to the ATM—or, more probable, to make sure that any shots fired from the SUV didn't strike or deflect off any intervening vegetation. A precaution I also took years before in New York when I was a deer hunter.

I called FBI Jeff. He took the hedge trimming thing seriously and made sure that someone from his office went out and recovered samples of the vegetation in case, someday, we could recover the hedge trimmer that had been used. If so, then maybe the FBI lab could compare the known vegetation to whatever was smeared or left on the blades of the trimmer; maybe the plant material(s) would match. Good potential circumstantial evidence—thinking ahead!

CHAPTER 18

THE WHITE TOYOTA 4RUNNER

Early Wednesday morning, September 7, 2016, 0130 hours

Bink! I had been sound asleep and my iPhone on my night-stand announced an incoming message alert. I groped for it in the dark. Apparently, the *bink* woke Samantha up too; she said something uncomplimentary about my phone, rolled over and went back to sleep. Not only did I have to find my phone in the dark, but because of middle-age far-sightedness, I also had to reach around and feel for my reading glasses. Otherwise, anything I tried to read would be a big, indistinguishable blur. Finally I located everything, got it all correctly situated, and could read the instant message.

"Exit Tarberry Geo Fence—Jeep Wrangler." Presumably, Batiste was in his Jeep and on the move—in the middle of the night.

We had only been tracking and surveilling Redrick Batiste for a few days, so I didn't yet have a good handle on his usual schedule and/or habit patterns. So I was curious.

It's easier to view and manipulate the Sendum Vehicle Tracking Application Program on a big-screen computer rather than on my little iPhone. Also, I didn't want to wake my wife up again. So there I was, 1:30 in the morning, in my underwear, in the office of our house, logging on to our home computer.

Batiste's Wrangler was on the move and heading north out of Acres Homes. I sent a command to the tracker, to speed up its reporting and watched as the dots on the map, representing the track of his Jeep, marched across the Houston north side. In less than ten minutes, the Jeep was on Blue Bell Road just outside the city limits and was soon stationary in the 1400 block. I switched to a satellite view of the area and it appeared that the Jeep was inside an apartment complex. There are so many apartment complexes in the north side of Houston and Harris County (hundreds) and I knew nothing about one in the 1400 block of Bluebell. I was thinking maybe it was actually an industrial park but clearly, according to the overhead view, it was an apartment complex.

The Wrangler was now parked in the apartment complex and the temperature of the tracking device started dropping. The Jeep's engine was turned off and the exhaust system, near where the primary tracker was mounted, was starting to cool.

I thought to myself that maybe it was a late-night "booty call" with a secret girlfriend, unbeknownst to Okoh, or most probably a personal use, marijuana resupply run.

Minutes later, Batiste's Jeep moved again, and I watched as it left the apartment complex and traveled straight back home. My iPhone announced its arrival: *Bink!* "Entry Tarberry Geo Fence—Jeep Wrangler." As soon as the Jeep arrived home, its engine was turned off and the exhaust system started cooling. Apparently Batiste then went back to bed and so did I. Maybe soon after, he was fast asleep, but I wasn't. Just like when I was a Homicide investigator, my mind started processing all the what-ifs and "what was he doing" scenarios. I like having answers.

In the morning, I arrived at the office, but soon had to leave to go downtown. FBI Jeff and I were meeting with the Assistant United States Attorneys Richard Hanes and Heather Winter to brief them on the case, what the informant had said, and the NDTU's progress in the surveillance.

I was still thinking about Batiste's early morning venture to the apartments at the 1400 block of Blue Bell Street.

Maybe the mystery white SUV was stashed there? But it didn't seem likely. Batiste was only there for a short time, definitely, maybe, meeting someone or to pick something up. I almost dismissed it from my mind, convincing myself that he had made a quick run to Blue Bell to re-up his personal supply of marijuana. But the uncertainty kept nagging; the little voice in my head kept bringing it up and wouldn't let it go.

Before I left for my meeting downtown, I asked two members of the NDTU (they will forever remain nameless) to backtrack the early morning path of the Jeep Wrangler, which I had watched hours earlier, to see whether they could locate the mystery white SUV. As soon as the words were out of my mouth, I could sense they were smelling "bullshit!" "Sarge, how are we going to find it? What will make it stand out from all the other bazillion white SUVs in the city?" I told them I understood, but held my ground and gave the "let's try anyway" pep talk, and added (perhaps a little sarcastically?), "You guys can watch TV another morning."

I don't like meetings, but it was always good to visit with Rick and Heather. Although, it was quite a hassle to park downtown, to find a parking spot, get through security at the federal courthouse, lock up your side arm, and jump an elevator to the seventh floor where "our" AUSAs worked. FBI Jeff and I filled Rick and Heather in: the evolution of the crew, the shootings of armored truck guards, Joe Stewart, the informant, Redrick Batiste, Batiste's recently acquired real estate, Buchi Okoh, the sniper theory, tracking devices on the Jeep and Cadillac, and the hunt for the mystery SUV. Rick was especially intrigued and remarked how his boss kept asking about the 2015 million-dollar armored truck heist/murder.

It was important that Jeff and I start "spinning up" the AUSAs. If this case ever got wings, we wanted the federal government to prosecute it. It would be big.

After the meeting and because I was downtown, I went to Houston Police Headquarters (I hated going there—that's where all the police/politicians lived and I was bound to run into one or two of them) to the Homicide Division, to make sure that our relationship with Jason Robles and Eric Wohlgemuth was still good. I figured I might have to do some "fence mending" as there might be some hard feelings after I helped orchestrate FBI Jeff's takeover of "their" informant. As I was driving from the federal courthouse to police headquarters, I "bumped" the two guys I had earlier assigned to backtrack Batiste's early morning excursion to Blue Bell Street to look for the mystery white SUV. On the NDTU's secure radio channel, I asked, "Any luck?"

There was an awkward silence. Then one responded. "No, we haven't gotten to it yet. We went to Top Brass instead."

Now there was another long awkward silence—on my part. Instead of what I asked, they had decided it was more important to go shopping (Top Brass is a military/police surplus store). I don't normally get irritated but when I do, I like to cool down before I say anything that I might regret. So I said nothing for a while and I guess my silence then said it all. After all, I had been up much of the night tracking Batiste and now my morning was filled with detested meetings. I was not a happy sergeant!

Zak then broke the air on the radio, ending the impasse. Both Zak and Chris Rozek were still at the station, watching and waiting in case Batiste rolled out of 1351 Tarberry. But it appeared that Batiste was sleeping in.

Zak said, "Hey Sarge, Chris and I are not doing anything. It's all quiet right now. We can do it!"

I thanked Zak and Chris, as I headed to the Homicide Division.

Up in Homicide, I was relieved to find that Jason and Eric were not offended about the informant "stealing" and being the professionals they were, totally understood. I also filled them in on Batiste's girlfriend, Buchi Okoh—that she had been employed at the Joseph Stewart Cadillac dealership at the time Joseph Stewart had been murdered. Jason and Eric found that tidbit of information interesting and, like me, suspected that it was not coincidental. They also filled me in on some of the backstory on Joe Stewart's murder investigation. In particular, how he had been killed with a .40 caliber pistol. I then brought them up to date on our tracking of Okoh and Batiste's personal vehicles and promised to keep them in the loop as things developed.

At last, all my morning meetings were finished, and I was headed back to my office.

Bink! I had a message on my iPhone. Even though I was driving on the main lanes of the North Freeway, I took a quick glance. Chris Rozek sent me a picture. I didn't have my reading glasses on, but I could tell the image was of a white SUV.

I pulled over to the shoulder. My reading glasses had slipped under the seat of the car and I had to grope around for a while, with one hand, to find them, as I tried to study the blurred image of the white SUV. I finally found my glasses and could now really see the picture Chris had sent. The image was clear; it was the side view of a white Toyota 4Runner.

Bink! Another picture arrived: the same white Toyota 4Runner, this time from the rear. But something was odd about the rear tailgate, in the area next to the license plate. I enlarged the picture. Clear as day, there was a clean hole, cut in the tailgate, immediately next to the license plate. The hole appeared to go all the way through and inside the vehicle; something white, of an unknown material, blocked or covered the hole. The "porthole" was large enough for someone lying down in the rear of the 4Runner to sight and shoot a rifle from inside, without having to extend the muzzle of the rifle out.

From my experience in SWAT and reading on the subject, I recognized the porthole in the tailgate as a sniper's loophole.

Chris Rozek and Steve Zakharia had, against all odds, found the mystery white SUV and broken the investigation wide open!

I immediately called Chris, and he gave me the details of what had just transpired.

Chris and Zak had driven straight to the 1400 block of Blue Bell Street, a nice apartment complex known as the Meadows on Blue Bell. It's a gated complex, but a gate was open for contractors who were doing construction on an apartment unit. They easily accessed the property, then drove through the entire complex, writing down license plates of any white SUV-type vehicles parked within. There were several, including two Toyota 4Runners, as well as a Nissan Pathfinder. After jotting down the license plate numbers, they quickly exited the complex to not arouse suspicion from any observant eyes. They then drove down the road and conducted computer inquiries on their laptop computers, reviewing each vehicle's registration.

One of the license plates they reviewed came back registered to a green Toyota 4Runner.

Strange! They had only recorded the license plates of white SUVs.

They drove back into the apartment complex and located the vehicle in question. It was undoubtedly white (not green) and it was a Toyota 4Runner. The year model on the registration also appeared incorrect for the model, and out of the ordinary (for north side Houston) was the Vietnamese-sounding owner's name, and a south side address listed on the registration.

Chris, who was in plain clothes, had Zak drop him off about 50 yards away and then he casually walked up on the vehicle so he could quickly check the rear license plate. The white Toyota 4Runner was backed deep into a parking spot, with its rear end (the tailgate area) nestled between some ornamental shrubbery. Not wanting to attract any attention, Chris quickly walked to the rear of the 4Runner and, keeping his iPhone at waist level, took a quick picture of the back license plate and then, without lingering, returned to Zak and they drove back out of the complex. Chris, when he took the picture, realized that something was amiss with the tailgate, but didn't want to loiter and risk "burning" the 4Runner (be spotted by bad guys taking his undue notice in the vehicle). He waited until he was back with Zak to closely examine the picture he had taken. Chris realized what the hole in the tailgate meant and immediately sent the pictures to me. They then ran the rear license plate number after noting it differed from the number on the front plate. The registration on the rear plate correctly belonged to a white Toyota 4Runner of the same approximate model year. But again, suspiciously, it was registered to an owner with yet another Vietnamese-sounding name with an address in Stafford, Texas—a small city well to the south of Houston.

Now the rest of the NDTU were headed to the apartment complex. Covert physical surveillance was set up around the white Toyota 4Runner, until we could get a court order so we could then put our tracking devices on it.

I went directly to the office to write the application for the court order to track the "sniper vehicle." I suspected that the vehicle would be stolen. I could have pushed the envelope, in that during a police investigation, we could put tracking devices on a vehicle, only it might be ruled later on in court that the documented historical data which the tracker recorded prior to a judge's approval might be found to be inadmissible. I wasn't going to take any chances. We were going to physically watch this Toyota 4Runner like a hawk, until the order was signed, and then we would covertly mount our tracking devices on it.

The bad guys screwed up! If they had put a license plate belonging to a *white* Toyota 4Runner on the front of the vehicle, Chris and Zak would have never checked the rear license plate.

But they didn't.

September 7, 2016 - Against all odds, the Houston Police Departments NDTU discovers the "mystery white SUV" with its purpose built sniper loop hole cut into the rear tailgate, immediately to the right of the rear license plate.

I called FBI Jeff. Sounding casual, I complimented him on the way he had been dressed earlier, noting the fancy suit and tie, all with matching loafers with silly little dingle ball thingies on their tongues. Jeff had been all official-looking and gussied up for his visit to the federal courthouse to meet with Rick and Heather. I (because I am undercover and hate suits and ties), wore my red *Star Wars* Millennium Falcon T-shirt (purchased from Target), old blue jeans, and a pair of well-worn Marine Corps-issued combat boots. After Jeff and I bantered a bit about the earlier meeting and I told him how Jason and Eric were good with the hand-off of the informant, I then, just before ending our conversation, acting as it were almost an afterthought, nonchalantly, told him!

"Oh, by the way, Jeff, we found the sniper vehicle!"

Probably for the first time in my career, I had made an FBI agent happy!

The court order for tracking the white Toyota 4Runner was signed and approved several hours later. I immediately headed to the Blue Bell Street apartment location to hook up with the rest of the NDTU as well as Big John and Dom from ATF, who had come out to assist in the surveillance and who were bringing out several more tracking devices, which they then passed off to Chris and Zak to mount when the order was signed and the opportunity presented itself.

Chris Rozek asked me over the radio, "Sarge, how many tracking devices do you want to put on it?" I asked how many they had. "John and Dom just gave us three, all ready to go, fully charged!" I had them all put on—I wanted a backup to the backup. I knew we would have to ping this vehicle hard, so if needed we could get eyes on it fast, as soon as possible, if it ever rolled.

As soon as Chris and Zak mounted the trackers, Dave then immediately set up the geo fence around the 4Runner. Now we all could relax a bit.

I can't understate how important the discovery of the sniper vehicle was. Without finding it, it is doubtful that the unit motivation for a surveillance operation of such long duration and high intensity could have been maintained for the months to come. The operation would have eventually bogged down and we would have missed significant surveillance intelligence acquisition opportunities.

I also thought the 4Runner would serve as a "trip wire" for any proactive direct-action type tactical operation against this robbery crew. Undoubtedly, because it appeared they had not discarded it after the last murder/robbery and were taking pains to keep it under wraps, they intended to use it in their next operation. As far as the bad guys were concerned, no one knew about the 4Runner.

But now we had three hidden tracking devices on the sniper vehicle, surrounded by an invisible geo fence, to alert us within thirty seconds if the bad guys ever drove it out of the apartment complex.

As we relaxed, my mind raced. Why did Batiste go to the Meadows on Blue Bell apartment complex in the middle of the night? Why did he only stay for such a short time? A safe assumption for us was that another member of the robbery crew lived in the complex and the 4Runner was kept there so this person could keep a close eye on it. Maybe Batiste had been also visiting this person? How were we going to identify him or her? Maybe we would be able to somehow observe them interacting with the 4Runner, which would then tip us off to their identity?

We couldn't stay long in the apartment complex; there was too much of a risk of our undercover vehicles being spotted by a bad guy, if they lived there.

We needed to get a pole camera up in the area, one with a bird's-eye view of the 4Runner. But would we be able to get one with a view inside the apartment complex where it was parked? Maybe there were some nearby utility poles, just outside the perimeter, running along Blue Bell Street, that would work? I didn't know.

Fortunately, Big John and Dom had several ATF pole cameras available, and they placed a rush order with the Houston Police Department's CID to survey the Blue Bell Street address to see whether it was feasible to get a view on the parked 4Runner. They also placed orders for pole cameras at Batiste's Tarberry and Okoh's Flossie Mae residences. We also had a good relationship with one of the CID officers responsible for pole camera installation, Mark Chapnik (he used to be an NDTU member) and we wouldn't have to wait till CID "got around to it." A quick phone call alerted Mark about what we had and after swearing him to secrecy, we got his complete cooperation and a promise to survey the sites that afternoon.

As usual, Justin was observant and was studying the passenger side of the 4Runner through his binoculars, when he broke the air on the radio. "Boss, it looks like there are two bullet strikes on the passenger side of the 4Runner."

I had not noticed. Getting out the spotting scope that I kept in my car, I turned off the vehicle's engine to stop the vibration. By bracing the scope against my side window for a clear view, to minimize any movement because of its high magnification, I looked at the area Justin was talking about. He was right; it looked like two bullet holes. The projectiles had not entered the 4Runner at a 90-degree angle to make nice clean round holes, but they had penetrated at an angle, making long, oblong holes. I filed Justin's observation away for future reference.

We noticed several other things about the 4Runner. The window tinting was dark, not standard factory issue. The license plate bracket surrounding the rear license plate also advertised a car dealership's name: Sterling McCall—where Okoh now worked.

That afternoon, Dave Helms and Jessica Bruzas drove to Stafford, Texas to check the registered owner's address listed for the rear license plate number found on the white Toyota 4Runner parked at Blue Bell. Sitting at the registered Stafford address was another white Toyota 4Runner, with a rear plate identical to the one we found at Blue Bell. Carefully, Dave and Jessica maneuvered through the residential neighborhood to get a front view of this same white Toyota 4Runner. When they did, they saw the front license plate was missing.

It was probable the bad guys had gone many miles away to another city and stolen the front license plate from the Stafford white Toyota 4Runner, to then use on the rear of their white Toyota 4Runner to obscure that the 4Runner at Blue Bell was stolen. The bad guys needed "clean" license plates to put on their vehicle. If the original stolen plates were left on, then there was a good chance that their 4Runner would be discovered and recovered by the police.

Dave and Jessica didn't approach the registered owners in case they were somehow connected to the bad guys. More likely, the owners hadn't noticed that their front plate was even missing or if they did, never reported it to the police.

Late that evening, "my guy" in CID called with good news and bad news. Yes, they could get pole cameras up to view both Batiste's Tarberry and Okoh's Flossie Mae residences.

The Blue Bell location and getting a camera view on the 4Runner would be a problem. None of the utility poles were of the correct type and even if they were, a camera would not be high enough to get the unobstructed view we needed.

Early that next morning, HPD CID, with their aerial bucket truck, looking for all the world like a common electric utility company truck and work crew, mounted camouflaged cameras on street utility poles near the two residences.

What about Blue Bell Street? A quick call to FBI Jeff, and the NDTU was given the use of the same drop surveillance van disguised as a plumber's work truck that we had used in the Alabonson Robbery Crew investigation. FBI Jeff brought it over the next morning and immediately we took it to the apartments on Blue Bell, parked it directly across from the 4Runner—maybe about 10 yards away. Back at the NDTU office, Justin remotely sent several commands and positioned the cameras on the FBI's surveillance platform for an optimum view of the 4Runner.

Soon we had a live feed of Okoh's house, Batiste's house, and one of the sniper vehicle all being "piped" to the big-screen monitors mounted on our office wall. All these cameras were recording; the images could be retrieved and reviewed later.

Just like in our other surveillance operations, slowly the traps were being set and now we would have to be patient and process the intelligence as it came in.

But it would be a slow process. Nearly a week later, nothing of significance had happened. Like clockwork, in the morning, Okoh took her children to day care and then went to work at the Cadillac dealership, and then went home that evening after picking the kids back up. Batiste usually got up late in the morning and if he left the house, would go shopping or eat lunch at one of several nicer restaurants in Houston. In the evening, he would drive to the Flossie Mae address and visit Okoh, returning late in the evenings, or sometimes spending the night and then returning to Tarberry Street the next morning, after Okoh left for work. Very boring, very routine! Nothing out of the ordinary: just like in many of our other robbery crews, the male (Batiste) was unemployed, while the female in the relationship (Okoh) worked a full-time job.

The 4Runner was still parked at the same spot at Blue Bell. As best we could tell from our constant monitoring of the cameras in the FBI surveillance van, no one approached the 4Runner or interacted with it. Nothing! No clues confirming the presence of an unidentified member of the crew who might live at the complex and who was to watch over it. We thought about approaching the apartment manager, who we had identified as an elderly white woman who, from her office, was always scrutinizing the vehicles coming and going through the apartment's entry and exit gates. From our perspective, she seemed to be a bit of a busybody. Maybe she would have some relevant information, but we couldn't be sure that she would keep our inquiry confidential and "back-feed" information to her tenants, maybe in some innocent gossip: "Very exciting! The police and FBI are asking questions about a white Toyota 4Runner parked at our complex!" And thereby our bad guys would be alerted that law enforcement had discovered their sniper platform.

We still wanted to know more about the 4Runner. Was it stolen? We needed to see the factory vehicle identification number (VIN). This number could normally be seen through the front windshield and was permanently mounted on the top of the dash on the driver's side. So one afternoon, in the heat, when no one was around, while we watched covertly, Lalo Torres, dressed as a Mexican yard worker, walked up to the 4Runner, leaned over its front hood and snapped a quick photo of the VIN plate with his iPhone.

Like we suspected, the white Toyota 4Runner was indeed stolen. We knew the license plates on it didn't belong to it, but now we knew for sure. The 4Runner had been reported stolen on June 14, 2015, well over a year before, to the Pearland Police Department (another small city to the south of Houston). The person reporting the theft was an out-of-town business-man from Missouri who had flown into George Bush Intercontinental Airport—on the north side of Houston—and who had then rented the 4Runner from Budget Rent a Car. That same day, he had driven to and then stayed the night at a hotel in Pearland. The next morning when he went to get into his rental vehicle, to drive to his meeting, it was gone! The investigating patrol officer noted that there was no broken glass on the ground where the 4Runner had been parked (the presence of broken glass is an indication that the thieves had broken a window to gain access into the vehicle, to hot-wire the ignition and drive it off). The officer also documented that the victim still had in his possession *both* keys issued to him by Budget Rent a Car.

The bad guys had stashed and kept the stolen Toyota 4Runner hid-den in plain view for well over a year! Presumably they waited to use it in the August 29, 2016 armored truck robbery and sniper killing of David Guzman. This hiding out of vehicles for such an extended period was a new tactic. Maybe the bad guys thought the police were no longer looking for vehicles stolen over a year. Maybe they thought the police report was inactive (they were right). All of this was like the armored truck robbery and ambush killing on February 12, 2015 of Brink's guard Alvin Kinney at the Capital One Bank in Houston's "ritzy" Galleria area. The robbery crew had used a Ford F-150 truck that had been reported stolen a year previous. Then, seemingly after its initial theft, this truck had dropped off the face of the planet, only to re-emerge a year later in a million-dollar heist.

What about the armored truck robbery and sniper killing on March 18, 2016 of Melvin Moore? The homicide investigators who worked that scene suspected that a minivan had been used as a sniper platform in this case. Maybe they were wrong? Or maybe, even though this robbery crew had possession of the Toyota 4Runner, they didn't use it for this operation? Or did they use it, but in another capacity that we didn't know of? Maybe it was used by the crew for surveillance?

What about the November 6, 2015 armored truck guard ambush and attempted robbery at the Bank of America on North Shepherd Drive where the guard was critically wounded by a gunman armed with a .223 rifle? Where was the 4Runner then?

Often informants exaggerate and "over spin" the information they provide to police. This raw information needs to be heavily vetted to be taken seriously. But, the informant in this case had alluded to "vehicles" (plural, not singular) which "Red" (Batiste) kept hidden away to facilitate robberies. Maybe the informant (now known as the "Original Informant") wasn't exaggerating?

Could it really be that Batiste and his robbery crew kept a fleet of stolen vehicles, hidden away, ready to use in criminal operations?

This was truly shaping out to be a "tier one" robbery crew! Never seen before: the use of a sniper, concealed mobile sniper hides, several coconspirators performing different roles to ensure mission success, all with access to multiple stolen vehicles. It all was making sense.

What also made sense (if true) was the bad guys were probably using the vehicles once or maybe twice for their planned criminal operation(s) and then discarding them. The stolen vehicle, after accomplishing its intended purpose, was then abandoned on some side street or other out-of-the-way location. The eventual recovery would be of little significance to the responding patrol officer. It was just another routine police report call, among the many other thousands of similar stolen vehicles recovered each year in Texas. The involved police agency recovering the stolen vehicle, because of the dearth of evidence, never realized the part it had played in some heinous crime.

Maybe we were too late! FBI Jeff was digging in on his end of the investigation and had now connected Batiste to the apartment complex at Blue Bell. One of Redrick Batiste's former girlfriends still lived there. Maybe his early morning visit on September 7 had been to see her?

Maybe the Toyota 4Runner had already been abandoned by the crew, conveniently at a location Batiste was familiar with, but not directly associated with? Coincidently, dumped inside a big apartment complex of an ex-girlfriend, but who he sometimes still visited? Maybe the Toyota 4Runner was never to be used again? We had seen no human activity around it on our secret FBI cameras. No one approached it; no one took an interest in it. Maybe it would be a dead end? Or maybe the ex-girlfriend was the designated guardian of the 4Runner?

Those thoughts ran through my head, particularly late at night when I was trying to sleep.

Over the next week, the NDTU began searching the locations Batiste had been to, looking for any of the other vehicles identified as having been used in the crew's previous armored truck robberies. Of particular interest was a nondescript blue Toyota Camry used by the crew to retrieve the ATM money canister next to a dying David Guzman in the last sniper-initiated attack. The obvious location to check was the apartments on Blue Bell. Carefully, every blue sedan-looking vehicle parked there was carefully scrutinized, the license plates painstakingly researched and then, when able, a clandestine physical confirmation of the VIN. We didn't find it at Blue Bell Street. Everywhere Batiste traveled, we backtracked and looked for the mystery blue Toyota Camry, not exactly sure what to look for because we didn't know the license plate number. Much like we had searched for the white Toyota 4Runner, we carefully looked over every blue Camry we saw in proximity to where Batiste was or had been. Nothing!

It was boring, mind-numbing, and tedious work.

We even believed it possible that the Camry might be hidden under a tarp, inside the fenced-in backyard of Okoh's Flossie Mae residence. We couldn't quite discern what was under the tarp from our pole camera, so Ben LeBlanc caught a ride with one of our police helicopters and did a fast flyover of her neighborhood, to get a quick overhead look at her backyard, just to rule out the possibility. It was not there. We never found the blue Toyota Camry or any other vehicles previously used by the Batiste Robbery Crew. I am confident all of them, the ones they used to support their other operations, were all stolen and then later abandoned after their perceived usefulness was over, to not leave any tangible links back to the crew. Then, after being discarded, these vehicles were eventually recovered and then returned to their rightful owners by unknowing law enforcement agencies.

Thankfully, the god of police high-risk police surveillance operations smiled on the NDTU yet again.

The Batiste Robbery Crew should have abandoned the white Toyota 4Runner, with all our hidden tracking devices plastered underneath it after using it in the murder of David Guzman. They should have replaced it in their lineup with the "next up" stolen vehicle. Instead, they decided to use it just one more time!

As events would show, the 4Runner wouldn't sit forlorn, abandoned, in the parking lot of an obscure apartment complex in north Harris County.

CHAPTER 19

WHERE DID HE GET THAT?

Late Wednesday evening, September 14, 2016, 2115 hours I had just fallen asleep.

Bink! My iPhone sounded an incoming message. Samantha woke up, grumbled something, rolled over, pulled the sheets over her head, and went back to sleep. I hadn't been in a deep sleep this time, so it was much easier to locate both my reading glasses and iPhone, all atop my nightstand.

"Exit Tarberry Geo Fence—Jeep Wrangler."

Batiste was leaving the house and on the move. I headed for my home computer.

He was headed north out of Acres Homes, following the same track from exactly a week earlier when he went to Blue Bell Street in the middle of the night. I sent a command to the tracker to speed up its reporting and watched again as the dots on the map representing the track of his Jeep marched across the Houston north side. Sure enough, he was back at the apartments and now the Jeep was stationary inside the complex.

Ideally, if the strength or accuracy of the tracking device's GPS signal is optimum, you might pinpoint exactly where in the apartments the Jeep was parked. But, the conditions in the 1400 block of Blue Bell were not all that conducive for GPS signals. The tracker's "cone" of uncertainty as to its exact location was nearly 100 yards in diameter. I was not exactly sure where Batiste's Jeep Wrangler was in the parking lot. But, by switching to the tracking map that showed the location of the primary tracker on the 4Runner, I noted that the two dots representing each vehicle now overlaid each other. This told me that both vehicles where in the same general area, or at least within 100 yards of each other.

I switched back and forth, carefully watching the trackers on each vehicle. Both vehicles appeared to be motionless. Then the temperature on the Wrangler tracker dropped. Its engine had been turned off. More interesting, at about the same time, the temperature on the Toyota 4Runner's primary tracker began to rise.

The nagging doubts about the sniper vehicle having been abandoned by the crew were gone. Presumably, Batiste had parked his Jeep, turned off the engine, then gotten into the 4Runner and turned on its engine.

Where was Batiste about to go with the 4Runner, assuming it was actually him?

I sent out a message to all the members of the NDTU, alerting them to what was happening and that we might have a callout to get eyes on the 4Runner when it moved out of Blue Bell.

But it was a false alarm!

Within a few minutes, the temperature of the tracker on the 4Runner began to cool. It also didn't initially appear to have moved, although I thought I detected a slight "warble" or a small shift in its reported GPS location. A "warble" or small shift was not unusual. Also, Batiste's Wrangler was now back on the move, out of the apartment complex and heading back home to 1351 Tarberry. The Jeep was at Blue Bell for just a few minutes.

What was that all about, I wondered.

I went back to bed, but really didn't sleep.

At 0500, I was up and out of the house, headed into the office, to beat the rush-hour traffic. When I got close, I swung down Blue Bell Street and made a quick drive-by through the apartments to check on the 4Runner.

The sniper vehicle had been moved!

It was now parked, backed up again, in a different parking spot, approximately 50 yards from where we had first found it. But who had moved it? Logically, because of the timing, it appeared to have been Redrick Batiste, but we couldn't be sure until we accessed and reviewed the FBI's video recording from the super-duper, uber-expensive, taxpayer-funded, drop surveillance van with all its high-tech, remote-controlled camera system thingies inside.

Really, without seeing and/or videoing Batiste in the 4Runner, we hadn't definitively connected him to the sniper vehicle. We really had nothing connecting the 4Runner to the August 29 murder/robbery. The whole thing was still little more than a hunch or a theory.

First thing in the morning, back at the office, we went to "roll back the tape" on the FBI surveillance video back to 2110 hours the evening before. Ominously, when I walked in the office, the big screen showing the live video feed from the FBI's drop surveillance van was blank. The pole camera live videos from both Tarberry and Flossie Mae were up and running on their respective screens, but on the designated Blue Bell Street/ sniper vehicle screen, nothing! We then accessed the historical recording from the FBI's drop van and found that the system had crashed and went off the grid shortly after we had left the office the previous afternoon. We didn't have a video to identify the individual who moved the 4Runner. A quick check on the recording of the pole camera at Tarberry showed the

Wrangler being driven out of the garage at 2107 hours, but you couldn't even see who was driving it.

We had nothing!

Only a warm feeling brought on by the reassurance that the sniper vehicle was still in play.

So why was the sniper vehicle moved?

The 4Runner was probably being safeguarded and maintained for a future criminal operation. It had likely been stored at the apartment complex for over a year (in plain sight) and it seemed safe to assume that one or more of the conspirators moved it periodically to a different parking spot within the complex. This was done so "Ms. Busy Body," the ever-vigilant apartment manager we had watched from afar, didn't take undue notice of the 4Runner parked all the time in the same spot and then think it was abandoned. Thinking it abandoned and not being claimed by any of her tenants, she might then have it towed off her property. She could easily come to that conclusion. We observed her once or twice on an apparent daily basis patrolling "her" complex. Her diligence and "nosiness" when it came to maintaining order in "her" complex was somehow probably known to the bad guys.

Also, the 4Runner's engine was probably being run periodically to ensure the battery was kept fully charged. After all, you have to do equipment maintenance!

Ms. Busy Body appeared to be a good apartment manager and without knowing it was keeping the robbery crew on their toes.

Redrick Batiste should have probably chosen an apartment complex to stash the sniper platform where the apartment manager didn't take her job so seriously.

But he didn't!

We pulled the FBI surveillance van out of Blue Bell and drove it over to the FBI's office for their technicians to look over. I called FBI Jeff and gave him the rundown and how their surveillance platform *"was ate up!"* I also explained how just a few hours before, someone moved the sniper vehicle and "his" cameras had stopped working. We did not have a video recording of whoever had moved it.

Later, FBI Jeff called back and gave me the news that "his" technicians had found that the batteries that ran the camera systems in the surveillance were bad and had to be replaced. I joked with him how it would be nice if the FBI was as diligent as the Batiste Robbery Crew in keeping their batteries charged. It was all good-natured fun—sort of.

So maybe, approximately, every week or so the bad guys were moving the 4Runner to a different location to keep it "cool." A video recording of the individual(s) moving it from location to location was important from an evidentiary standpoint. This could end up being a key piece of evidence for the federal attorneys (Rick and Heather) to use later in their prosecution, if we could bring this operation to fruition.

I saw a big problem. As the crew moved the 4Runner from parking spot to parking spot, we couldn't keep having the same ginormous white van with all the pipes on it (the FBI's drop surveillance van) follow it around, coincidentally always parked nearby. This would be suspicious and we didn't want to take the risk of being discovered. Redrick Batiste was too sharp, too observant, too alert. We would have to find other long-term remote surveillance platforms or drop vehicles to park near the sniper vehicle as it was shuffled around to different parking spots.

We were on the phone calling other agencies, asking to borrow their drop surveillance vehicle(s). Several offered theirs up, but they were all white vans and looked similar to the FBI's.

Big John from ATF, though, had a good idea. The ATF had plenty of pole cameras; maybe we could take the internals of a pole camera thingy, power it with multiple, heavy-duty car batteries and hide the whole contraption in any one of the NDTU's many nondescript undercover vehicles. If the sniper vehicle was moved again and we wanted to give a different look to the vehicles parked around it (to not arouse any suspicion), we could then move the camera and batteries into another undercover vehicle and so on.

In a day or so, the ATF technicians had concocted a portable "Rube Goldberg" surveillance system. Justin and I hid it in the Silver Bullet (the NDTU's infamous silver Toyota Corolla). Then, as I followed, Justin drove it into the Blue Bell Street apartment complex, following a tenant who lived there and who had pressed the correct code to open the entry gate. Ms. Busy Body spotted our vehicles and, not recognizing us, tried in vain to frantically flag us down, each in succession, as we passed her. We both politely ignored her and drove on. Around the corner, Justin parked the Silver Bullet across from the 4Runner, confirmed the camera system was working, and checked over the radio to make sure there was a perfect video feed back at our office. He then jumped into my vehicle and we were out of there. As we drove out of the apartments, the now irate Ms. Busy Body tried again to flag us down and we again politely ignored her, being able to outrun her in my Toyota FJ Cruiser, since she was handicapped with a walking cane and all.

During the next few weeks, every time Batiste left the house, the NDTU conducted its rolling surveillance, careful to not be spotted, documenting the places he went and, as best we could, the people he met. There was nothing of significance. Although, one day, he met a Hispanic male in a parking lot of a north side business where they both talked for a few minutes. As usual, we photographed the meeting and recorded the license plate of the vehicle driven by this Hispanic male. Later, we could research the plate and identify him by name. Interestingly, he was a full-time paid firefighter for a local city.

September 28, 2016 - Redrick Batiste beside his black Jeep Wrangler.

Everything we observed and documented was immediately forwarded to FBI Jeff for his consumption. All members of the NDTU were now working seven days a week, either physically surveilling Batiste or Okoh or monitoring the various cameras at four different locations (we had now placed a pole camera outside Batiste's parents' home in Acres Homes because he visited there frequently) or the tracking devices on three different vehicles. We were gathering and compiling a lot of intelligence information, with really nothing substantial to show for it. Early, Thursday morning, September, 22, 2016, 0111 hours I was sound asleep.

Bink! My iPhone sounded an incoming message. Samantha didn't wake up this time. I guess she was getting used to all the *bink-binks* of incoming message alerts.

"Exit Tarberry Geo Fence—Jeep Wrangler." Batiste was leaving the house and on the move. I was out of bed, headed for my home computer.

Batiste's Wrangler was headed north out of Acres Homes, following again the same track from over a week previous when he went to Blue Bell Street late in the evening. I sent a command to the tracker to speed up its reporting and watched as the dots on the map again made a beeline to Blue

WHERE DID HE GET THAT?

Bell Street. Sure enough, he was back in the apartments and soon the Jeep was stationary inside the complex.

The tracker on Batiste's Wrangler showed that it was again in the same approximate area as the 4Runner. Again, I switched back and forth, carefully watching the trackers on each vehicle. Both vehicles appeared to be motionless. Then the tracker's temperature on the Wrangler dropped. I knew its engine had been turned off. Right on cue, the temperature on the primary tracker on the Toyota 4Runner began to rise. Then, unlike last time, I could tell it was moving. The 4Runner was then driven and parked on the other side of the apartment complex. Soon its engine temperature dropped; shortly afterward, Batiste's Jeep Wrangler was moving and soon was back at Tarberry, inside the garage, its engine turned off.

Finally, after weeks of hard work, it looked as though we had recorded the sniper vehicle being moved and logically it had to be Redrick Batiste who had done so. Hopefully, in the morning, we could review the video from our ATF surveillance platform (good thinking, Big John!) and positively identify the person who did it.

I started thinking ahead. If we had the video, then maybe Rick and Heather would want to "throw the dice"? Maybe they felt there was enough evidence to convince a federal judge to authorize a search warrant on Batiste's residence? Maybe inside his house we find the sniper rifle or other evidence? Maybe we could then get Batiste's cell phone with all the historical, possible incriminating evidentiary "goodness" within it? Maybe Batiste would confess? Maybe we would then have enough to identify and implicate the other members of the robbery crew? Unfortunately, that was a lot of maybes.

I didn't sleep well. So early in the morning, I was up and out of the house, headed into the office, again to beat the rush-hour traffic. When I got close, I swung down Blue Bell Street, but this time in case Ms. Busy Body was up early watching, I didn't go inside the apartment complex, being able to get a long-range visual peek from the outer perimeter and thereby

343

a confirmation that the 4Runner had been moved again. Like before, it was backed up deep into a parking spot, this time close to a wooden privacy fence that surrounded the patio of a ground-floor apartment. Someone was taking pains to make sure the tailgate area was not readily seen. I doubted there was enough room to even walk between the fence and the rear of the 4Runner.

I headed to the office and made the coffee. Glancing at the big bank of big screens on the wall, I noted with satisfaction that all the cameras at the various locations were functioning properly. The only difference from yesterday was that the ATF camera hidden in our Silver Bullet parked at Blue Bell Street now only showed an empty parking spot where the sniper vehicle had been.

I waited for the guys to arrive and someone with more geek knowledge than myself to fire up the applicable program on the computer that could retrieve the historical video from the Silver Bullet, with its high-tech ATF camera inside, which should have recorded the scene from a few hours earlier, when the 4Runner was moved.

An hour later, when David Smith tried to access the much anticipated recorded video, I almost spit out my coffee! Although the ATF camera at Blue Bell was working (I was watching it), it was not recording!

We again didn't have the much sought-after evidence. We didn't have a video of Batiste moving the sniper vehicle.

I was not a happy sergeant!

As soon as we realized something was amiss with the ATF camera system, we were out of the office and back at the apartments on Blue Bell Street. Now we had to orchestrate an operation to retrieve the Silver Bullet with its non-recording camera from the complex, without alerting the ever-vigilant Ms. Busy Body.

Some of the guys were able to get eyes on her and when she was preoccupied with something else and not looking, I jumped the apartment's fence and drove the Silver Bullet out of the complex and straight back to our office. From there, Big John retrieved the camera system and took it straight away to "his" technicians. Later that morning, he brought it back and sheepishly told us that the involved ATF technician had "forgot" to push the record button on the system. But not to worry; now the button had been pushed and the system was definitely guaranteed maybe to work.

We all had to laugh it off. What a comedy of errors. I joked with Big John and FBI Jeff how it was nice to know that the federal government's surveillance equipment was just as messed up as the Houston Police Department's.

The next time the bad guys moved the white 4Runner, I was determined that we were not going to miss out. As soon as the record button had been "pushed" in the ATF camera, we placed the whole system into a different NDTU undercover vehicle: an old pickup truck, which had no air-conditioning and was never driven in hot weather. We also had the FBI's drop surveillance van back with a bank of brand-new batteries inside to run its cameras.

I should have done it before: build redundancy in the operation—one is none, two is one!

But I didn't!

This time, I put two surveillance platforms on the sniper vehicle. I figured one or the other was bound to work—if there was a next time.

Again we had to get eyes on Ms. Busy Body and waited patiently for lunchtime. Then, as she drove out of the complex, some of the guys kept her under surveillance as she went to a fast-food restaurant a few miles away, where she got into line at the drive-through window. As soon as the coast was clear, the rest of us drove a convoy of vehicles into the apartment complex. We set up temporary, discreet physical surveillance around the 4Runner and when we were sure no one was watching, carefully parked and positioned both the FBI's drop surveillance van and our old pickup truck (with the ATF surveillance system inside). We confirmed over the radio that we had a good view of the 4Runner back at our office, for each of the systems, taking our time, double-checking and making sure all the buttons were pushed, wires connected, batteries charged, etc.

As an added precaution, Justin came by my house and installed a computer that was linked to all the surveillance cameras we were running. If needed, I could view the 4Runner parked at Blue Bell, Batiste's house on Tarberry, Okoh's house on Flossie Mae, or Batiste's parents' house. At the same time, with my personal computer, I could also watch and manipulate the trackers on any of the three vehicles we were monitoring.

Early, Saturday morning, October 8, 2016, 0155 hours

Over two weeks had gone by and the sniper vehicle had not been moved. I had expected the bad guys to move it by now. They were overdue. The nagging uncertainty of whether the 4Runner was still in play was creeping back into my mind. Every night I slept fitfully, waiting.

Bink! My iPhone had an incoming message alert.

"Exit Tarberry Geo Fence—Jeep Wrangler." Batiste was leaving his house and moving. Seconds later, I was at my computers, speeding up the tracker on his Jeep, double-checking that both cameras recording the 4Runner were up and running. They were!

Batiste's Wrangler followed the same track as all the other nighttime visits to Blue Bell Street. Soon he was inside the apartments and now I watched as his Jeep drove across the camera view in front of the sniper vehicle and then back out. Seconds later, I saw the unmistakable image of Redrick Batiste walk up, get into the 4Runner, start the engine, and drive it out of the parking spot and out of camera view.

Finally, after all that work, we had our first real tangible evidence that linked Batiste to the sniper vehicle.

The tracker showed the 4Runner now parked in yet another part of the apartment complex and Batiste was headed back home to Tarberry. Minutes later, he was home and parked his Jeep in the garage. Shortly, the lights were off in his house and I suppose he went back to sleep.

Just to be sure, I checked, to make certain, for my peace of mind, that the cameras recorded everything. They had!

I went back to bed and fell fast asleep. It was the first good sleep I had in weeks.

First thing in the morning, I called FBI Jeff. This time, I didn't mess with his head (as much). I complimented him on trying, oh so hard, to wear the appropriate undercover clothing so he could blend in with my undercover officers. Jeff was getting better! But, his blue jeans were starched and pressed with creases down the front and his polo shirt, broad-brimmed baseball hat and running shoes all looked "shiny and new." His pristine clothing was not the only issue. It was also the way Jeff carried himself, something about his overall bearing; he still retained the intangible, yet unmistakable look of a federal agent or military officer. I gave him some more advice: "Jeff, take some cues from Mark Smith or Ben LeBlanc. Try slouching, scratch your butt, or pick your nose." He laughed. Then I nonchalantly told him, "Jeff, he moved it last night, and we got it all on video!"

Later in the morning, we were all at the office to watch the video of the 4Runner being moved. I hadn't noticed it at first. But, in the video, Batiste was clearly seen unlocking the doors to the 4Runner with a remote electronic key fob.

Where did he get that?

The 4Runner was stolen. The Pearland police officer who had investigated the theft wrote in his report that the victim (the out-of-town businessman) who had rented it was still in possession of both the ignition keys. He also noted that there was no broken glass at the parking spot where it had been parked overnight.

How did Batiste come into possession of a remote electronic key fob programmed to unlock the stolen 4Runner? Maybe by providing the VIN of the 4Runner to an insider at some Toyota car dealership or similar privileged person and had one fabricated? Maybe Buchi Okoh, who worked at a car dealership, had the connection? Or maybe Batiste had an inside person who worked at Budget Rent a Car who had then provided him with the key? But if the insider at Budget Rent a Car was true, which seemed the most likely scenario, how did the bad guys then later locate the 4Runner, to steal it, after it was rented out and parked, many miles away at a hotel parking lot in Pearland?

We just didn't know.

Later, FBI Jeff and I were downtown to brief Rick and Heather and let them see the long-awaited video. As we walked into the US Attorney's office, Heather took one look at Jeff's "undercover clothing ensemble" and gave me a knowing smile. Rick, on the other hand, seemed oblivious of Jeff's new look.

After reviewing the video, Rick sat back in his chair and paused for a few seconds to think. "Chris, the video is good stuff, but we still really don't have anything!" He explained we still couldn't positively link the white Toyota 4Runner as having been used in the last murder. At best, we had (because the 4Runner was stolen) a weak case for Unauthorized Use of a Motor Vehicle (UUMV). Because it had been stolen for over a year and we knew Batiste had keys to it, it would be a difficult case to prosecute (how do you prove that Batiste knew the 4Runner was stolen?). Further, this criminal charge would have to be prosecuted by the Harris County District Attorney and even if convicted, it was a minor felony. Batiste would most likely receive a slap on the wrist—a short, probated sentence via plea bargaining.

Did we really want to settle with charging a serial capital murderer with UUMV?

All four of us discussed the merits of keeping the surveillance operation going indefinitely. We were going to hope to gleam more intelligence "fruit," which would then ultimately "prove up" the murder/robbery allegations against both Batiste and all the other conspirators. Heather reminded me that the federal government had a death penalty statue for murder committed during robbery and it was a possibility in this instance that the Justice Department would authorize Rick and Heather to pursue this punishment. We all decided we also wanted to provide some measure of closure for the families of the murder victims. Most importantly, we all wanted to ensure no other innocent citizens were killed or wounded.

We all agreed, however, that if the NDTU, in its surveillance of Batiste, observed him in possession of a firearm (hopefully "the" .223 caliber sniper rifle), during our day-to-day surveillance, we would initiate his arrest. At the least, the federal charges for firearms possession, related to Batiste's prohibited person status, would put him back in prison for several years, even if nothing else came to fruition in "proving up" the multiple murders.

We still had a long way to go. If the Original Informant was right, we had maybe only two months before the sniper's next killing.

CHAPTER 20

URBAN SNIPING

I don't pretend to be an expert on this matter with all the technical knowledge and requisite skill sets contained within the broad subject of "sniping." But I am not ignorant on the subject either.

A sniper is a marksman who shoots and kills human beings from a concealed position.

Often the sniper is deployed in a surprise ambush scenario and the intended victim(s) are caught unaware.

The shot(s) the sniper fires from this hidden position are normally also undertaken from a great distance, with great accuracy. The distance and concealment aspects are utilized to exceed the intended victim's ability to detect the sniper.

The sniper is also afforded some measure of protection because of this distance and concealment from commensurate retaliation (accurate return gunfire on his position), after he fires, from a now alerted enemy.

It might be that trained military forces on the receiving end quickly realize that their personnel attrition is being caused by sniper fire, but cannot pinpoint the sniper's exact location, because of the sniper's disposition using both concealment and distance.

However, the Achilles' heel from the sniper's perspective is when he "takes the shot," because of the loud noise, the report.

The opposing forces, upon hearing the shot fired by the sniper, can then approximate and maybe locate the sniper's exact position. The more shots the sniper fires, from the same position, the more the likelihood his adversaries, instead of just approximately affixing his position, can then pinpoint it. If they can pinpoint the sniper's position and have the means, then they can "neutralize" the sniper himself with extensive counter small arms gunfire or if in a military engagement, if available, with artillery or an air strike, or with armored vehicles.

In World War II, if say the approximate location of the sniper was thought to be in a building, then the most risk adverse (for your personnel) might be to call in an artillery barrage or have a couple of Sherman tanks go level the entire building and, just to be sure, raze the adjacent areas as well, handily solving your tactical problem.

The reliance on the detection of the sniper by the gunshot report can be complicated or minimized if the sniper uses a suppressor mounted on his weapon.

Contrary to movies and popular culture, a rifle suppressor (silencer) does not make the gunshot report of the sniper's weapon silent ("without sound"). It instead moderates it, much like a muffler on an internal combustion engine. The degree of suppression and moderation of the gunshot (measured in decibels) depends on a host of variables outside the scope of this book. But even though the use of a suppressor does not, per se, silence the weapon, it makes finding the approximate location of the sniper more difficult. The noise generated by a bullet traveling above the speed of sound (supersonic) can mask the suppressed gunshot report at the origin, from where the bullet was fired (the sniper's concealed position).

Human beings on the receiving end of suppressed sniper fire look more in the direction to where they first heard the supersonic "crack" of the bullet. Which is not necessarily in the same location or direction from where the shot originated from—the sniper's concealed location.

The recipients of gunfire from concealed, long-range gunfire, fired by a suppressed weapon, look in the wrong direction! Fully explained: The recipient(s) of gunfire, fired by a sniper using a suppressed weapon, will tend to look in the wrong direction. They will look in the general location to where their ears or brain perceive this "sonic crack" and not so much in the location of the muffled, subdued "bang" originating from the sniper's position, maybe hundreds of yards away. This is a great advantage to the concealed sniper and increases his chances of surviving a military engagement, because along with distance and concealment, he remains undiscovered.

The loud sonic crack of the bullet "whizzing" nearby serves to mask the subdued gunshot report from its origin, which arrives before the gunshot report from the concealed location, since the bullet is traveling several times the speed of sound.

Overall, a suppressor will distort the sound of the gunshot in such a way that it is also not immediately recognizable to people in the area as an actual gunshot. For example, the suppressor I run on my 300 Blackout (7.62X35mm) AR-15 type rifle sounds to my ear more like a pneumatic nail gun that carpenters use rather than a firearm.

A much quieter gunshot report can be realized by using a suppressor and subsonic ammunition. A subsonic bullet travels below the speed of sound and does not have the loud "sonic crack" as supersonic ammunition. But because of the reduced velocity, the range and lethality of the weapon system, using subsonic ammunition is not as efficient. The use of subsonic rifle ammunition, with suppressors, is also somewhat uncommon because it is not nearly as proficient in "killing stuff." This is true with a .223 caliber weapon system, which uses a small caliber, lightweight bullet, dependent on its hyper-velocity (several times the speed of sound) for some efficiency in its ability to "kill stuff."

The rifle(s) being used by the armored truck sniper robbery crew were .223s.

Some of us thought it possible that the armored truck sniper crew was using suppressors on their sniper rifle(s). This was because of the divergent and confusing statements of some civilian witnesses who were in the general area of the time of the two previous armored truck robbery/murders. The witnesses said they heard gunfire and thought they knew the approximate direction from where the killing shots of David Guzman and Melvin Moore originated from, but in reality didn't.

Was it possible, given the sophistication of this robbery crew, that their designated sniper was using a rifle with a suppressor?

If I were a sniper, besides using distance and concealment to ensure my survival in some sort of armed engagement, I would want to also use a suppressor on my weapon.

The possession of a legally manufactured suppressor in the United States is becoming more common. But the legal acquisition of a suppressor takes much time, is expensive, and also requires a lot of government paperwork. It also requires a background check and fingerprint submission of the applicant before they can take possession of a suppressor. What is also possible are unscrupulous individuals who possess some machining skills and have access to the right equipment can manufacture suppressors and sell them on the black market to individuals who, because of their criminal history, could not pass the required federal government background check. The manufacture and/or possession of these black market suppressors is highly illegal.

Within the overall subject and skill sets of sniping, there is a subset known as "urban sniping." This includes all the above, but set in more densely populated areas. The way the United States military deploys its snipers in Afghanistan might be the more traditional view of the role of a sniper. Operating in a rural environment, the sniper laying in the prone position, armed with a precision bolt-action rifle equipped with high-powered telescopic sight with an observer (using a spotting scope) at his side, both carefully camouflaged in ghillie suits, nearly invisible among the ground cover, placing shots on an unsuspecting enemy combatant, many hundreds of yards (perhaps well over a thousand) away. The sniper and his observer, because of the long ranges involved in their shooting, have to make numerous calculations (wind, distance, air density, and other factors) to successfully aim and launch the projectile for that sought-after "one shot—one kill."

Urban sniping is different. Maybe more like in the insurgency conflicts after the United States invasion of Iraq and the overthrowing of Saddam Hussein and his military forces. The sniping that occurred in the cities of Iraq were often of shorter engagement distances and the concealment locations positioned within normal, mundane, manmade structures.

In the modern era, somewhere, somehow (maybe in operations conducted earlier by the Irish Republican Army or maybe in Bosnia during the "ethnic cleansing" campaign), military, paramilitary personnel, and/or terrorists came up with the idea, in conducting of urban sniping operations, to conceal their sniper in a motor vehicle. This was true particularly if they happened to be the "insurgents" fighting against a larger, superior force. Using a motor vehicle as a sniper "hide" was smart. Civilian vehicles are common in many urban areas and can be easily positioned on streets or parking lots near the location of the expected ambush area (within several hundred yards with an unobstructed view). Unmoving civilian vehicles, parked where they are supposed to be, particularly if they are "vanilla-looking" are not normally objects of suspicion. The "not being suspicious-looking" and "easily overlooked" aspect is true in areas or conflicts where the use of civilian vehicles as mobile sniper hides had not been previously experienced. The targeted forces are caught unaware and eventually (perhaps after taking many casualties) figure it out, becoming wise to the tactic, and then take effective countermeasures.

We were fortunate that some Houston Police Department Homicide detectives could figure out so soon what was happening. Particularly fortunate were those men and women employed as couriers/guards in the armored truck industry.

One thing FBI Jeff and I talked about was the possibility of other criminals in the country using a sniper in coordinated ambush attacks against armored truck personnel, with the motive being financial gain. Jeff made inquiries with the FBI Field Offices around the country. No one had heard of such a thing.

There were historically in the United States several sniper-type mass killings of civilians, but the motive for these attacks had nothing to do with money.

The one previous case which was brought to my mind was the DC Sniper of 2002. Two suspects, over a course of several weeks, ambushed and either killed or wounded many innocent citizens. The sniper team in this case used a .223 rifle with a telescopic sight. They also used a nondescript four-door sedan as a mobile, concealed, sniper platform, in which they had crudely cut out a hole through the vehicle, a sniper porthole, located near the rear license plate, to be able to shoot from within, while hidden in the vehicle. This was the same fundamental method of operation being used by the robbery crew we were now surveilling. The DC Sniper(s) were black men who were motivated by racial hatred and their sniping/murders were a convoluted plan to redress wrongs, allegedly perpetrated by "white America."

The robbery crew we were working appeared to be much more operationally sophisticated, with other conspirators fulfilling different roles for operational success. The overall motivation appeared to be money.

But, where did Redrick Batiste and his cronies come up with the idea of using a sniper, maybe with a suppressor-equipped rifle? Where did they get the knowledge of urban sniping methods, using a civilian vehicle to hide in and shoot from? Maybe they came up with the idea on their own? Maybe they learned it from an extensive internet search? Maybe Batiste had previous military/sniper training? We checked—he didn't.

I believe that Redrick Batiste was inspired by the DC Sniper and incorporated their basic method of operation into a grand scheme to rob armored trucks. Later, with the uncovering of other intelligence information, another side of Redrick Batiste came to light.

Like the leader of the infamous DC Sniper team, Redrick Batiste hated white people. But maybe even more than his hatred of white people was his hatred for the police. Redrick Batiste also identified strongly with black supremacy and black nationalism ideology.

Redrick Batiste was a cop-hating racist.

CHAPTER 21

WE NEED A SAFETY NET

The Original Informant told us it was approximately every three or four months that the armored truck sniper crew planned to conduct an operation so its core members could maintain a steady, dependable cash flow to support their "lifestyle(s)". Since their last operation was on August 29, this would indicate the next sniper-initiated armored truck robbery could be "on the schedule" for November or December 2016. It was now early October, so we still had some time before the next sniper/robbery to focus on the surveillance and continue intelligence gathering, striving to find enough evidence to dismantle the crew before then.

But what if the Original Informant was wrong?

What if the crew decided to do a "hit" earlier than we anticipated?

Maybe someone in the crew had immediate financial needs and didn't want to wait a few months?

Heck, maybe one coconspirator wanted to buy a new car for his mommy, to present it to her on her birthday? We had seen that before in other serial robbery crew investigations.

We could not presume that we had such a large window of several months before the planned next murder. We would have to be prepared to take direct action against Batiste and his crew immediately if they started to deploy, setting up to do another sniper ambush. For all we knew, that deployment could happen tomorrow.

Even though we had Batiste under surveillance and we had not seen him do any scouting or reconnoitering of banks, maybe this pre-scouting was actually the assigned responsibility of other unknown crew members.

It could be they were doing the scouting even as we watched Batiste or had even already completed this preparatory part of their operation.

Maybe they had already chosen a bank?

Maybe they had already been watching this bank long enough, to have a good idea of the days and approximate times the armored truck came to service it?

If all of this was true, then all that was necessary for the bad guys to complete their operation would be to move the Toyota 4Runner (their mobile sniper platform) from the apartments on Blue Bell to the vicinity of the chosen bank, where they would then set up, ready to shoot the armored truck courier when he arrived.

Although the NDTU was working seven days a week and maintaining twenty-four-hour surveillance on Batiste and the 4Runner, now we would also have to plan for and be ready to switch gears, to be prepared to take immediate direct action against the crew, to prevent another innocent citizen from being killed.

It was a heavy responsibility. If we were caught flat-footed and didn't correctly read the signs, the sniper would strike again—maybe right under our noses. In some sense, we would have the blood of an innocent citizen on our hands.

Again, we knew the Toyota 4Runner was our "trip wire." As long as it sat unused, safely ensconced within the apartments on Blue Bell Street, yet still periodically moved to different parking spots, we felt safe to assume it was still destined to be used in their next sniper/robbery operation. As long as it was parked in the parking lot, the NDTU could relax a bit, knowing that another murder was not imminent. We could then focus on maintaining the around-the-clock surveillance on Batiste and keep gathering intelligence.

But when the 4Runner broke its Blue Bell Street geo fence and rolled out of the apartments, then we could probably expect a sniper attack soon thereafter.

We had to expect the unexpected. We couldn't become complacent, thinking we had weeks or months before the next shooting. We had to be prepared.

We needed a safety net!

We would be dealing with a sniper shooting from within a concealed position (a motor vehicle). We were not in a war and the NDTU was not a military unit, so we didn't have the luxury of neutralizing the sniper threat with an artillery barrage or air strike.

We had access to two civilian law enforcement tactical remedies for dealing with a sniper in a concealed position: neutralize him using a counter sniper or use an armored vehicle to assault the sniper's position.

The Houston Police Department Tactical Operations Division SWAT Detail has several of these armored vehicles, any of which was covered in sufficient armor to defeat incoming rifle fire (particularly the .223 flavor). Maybe we could call the SWAT Detail and "borrow" one, for a few months, just in case? After thinking about it, I didn't even bother asking. The SWAT Detail needed their armored vehicles and the drivers who went along with them for their operations and couldn't just lend them out to a DTU, particularly for such an extended length of time.

More importantly, any of these law enforcement armored vehicles were large military-looking things, painted flat black with large, bold lettering "HOUSTON POLICE" printed everywhere. This was so even the most ignorant, unaware citizen could readily recognize them from a mile off. The whole world instantly knew what they were: a police armored vehicle. Whenever one of these things was driven on Houston roadways, they instantly became objects of great interest. Sometimes traffic would come to a standstill as people watched it drive by. They attracted a lot of attention—there was nothing stealthy about them.

If Batiste's sniper crew was set up at a bank, waiting to take a shot, with the other crew members in attendance to do counter surveillance ("lookouts") and if we were to use one of SWAT's armored vehicles, we would soon be spotted. Maybe initially not by the sniper and his observer (if he operated with one), but surely by the other members of the crew, who would then sound the alert via whatever communication they used (commercial two-way radios/cell phones, burner phones).

We wanted to have a great advantage; in any direct operation we undertook, we wanted to maintain Surprise, Speed, and Violence of Action for greater assurance of operational success (so we didn't get hurt and got to go home to our families). If we relied upon using big, military-grade, plainly marked police armored vehicles, we would surely lose the element of surprise!

What the NDTU needed was a Trojan horse or an "undercover" armored vehicle.

I talked with FBI Jeff. Jeff had the contacts to the upper management of the armored truck companies in the Houston area. I told him of our need for an armored vehicle in our operation, if we had to engage the sniper while he was in the Toyota 4Runner. I explained how any of the law enforcement armored vehicles we had easy access to (Houston SWAT or even one of the FBI's) would not work out. If we used one of these vehicles, we would be at a disadvantage, because we would be spotted a long ways off.

"Jeff, the bad guys would see us coming a mile away."

"Jeff, what we need is an armored vehicle that will not arouse suspicion or much interest, something that is common to the streets of Houston."

"Jeff, we need an armored vehicle from one of the armored truck companies!"

I also knew that any of the upper management for these armored truck companies would be likely to help, considering it was their guards being killed.

Jeff thought it was a good idea and was soon on the phone.

Two days later, a supervisor from Brink's regional corporate security delivered to the NDTU the largest, heaviest, and most heavily armored truck in their fleet. It weighed 12.5 tons (as opposed to the average weight of a passenger car, which is 1.4 tons). The windshield and side windows had bulletproof glass several inches thick! It was a behemoth, a veritable rolling bank vault on wheels. It was "lent" to us for our exclusive use in this operation and we could have it for as long as it took. The security guy drove it in from Dallas, Texas, to not alert any of the Houston-based Brink's employees. The knowledge that the Houston Police Department's NDTU was using a Brink's armored truck to support their surveillance operation was a closely kept secret, just in case Batiste or his crew had a Brink's employee as "an insider" within their Houston operation back-feeding them armored truck routes and/or schedules.

How were we going to use this Brink's armored truck?

Simple: if we had to take down the sniper, we would use it to ram the 4Runner.

This "direct intervention" would occur while the 4Runner was parked and in position, with the sniper inside, presumably laying down in the back, waiting on the real armored truck to service the bank.

If we hit the 4Runner hard enough with our undercover, diesel-powered, multi-ton, rifle fire-proof armored "tank," we might even overturn the sniper vehicle. At the least, this ramming or "hard contact" would sufficiently rattle or distract the sniper, impeding his ability to shoot, giving us a great tactical advantage.

As soon as the 4Runner was rammed, in the shortest amount of time possible, heavily armed members from the NDTU, ATF, or FBI would rapidly egress our Brink's armored "tank" and the support vehicles escorting it, and engage the thoroughly distracted and rattled sniper, killing him if necessary (Surprise, Speed, and Violence of Action).

Maybe the sniper would be so disoriented and overwhelmed by all that happened that we could just "call him out" from behind cover and he would surrender?

We didn't pre-position our newly acquired Brink's armored truck at the North Police Station. It was too close to Batiste's house, and he drove by our station every day. If he glimpsed it in our back parking lot, he would probably think it strange. It would look suspicious. It was also too big and tall to fit in our garage at the station.

Instead, we parked the Brink's armored truck in a large truck bay at a Houston Fire Department station, which was a few miles south of the apartments on Blue Bell Street. At this fire station, it would remain out of view (with the bay door closed) and if needed, there was also diesel to refuel it.

During the daylight hours, when the banks were open and the real armored truck crews were running their routes, several members of either the NDTU or WET were assigned to stay at the fire station and be prepared to roll out in the Brink's armored truck if we needed them. I asked them to "play fireman": hang out at the station all day, eat, take naps, work out, and watch TV unless we needed them.

Easier said than done!

Over the weeks and months, it fell mostly on the guys from WET to stand by with our special Brink's armored truck at the fire station and play fireman. Whereas real firemen (or women) might be good at this, the guys in North WET were best characterized as having short attention spans and/or attention deficit. They craved action! The WET guys would get bored sitting at the fire station, picking their noses, and after an hour or so, would sneak off to go run warrants and arrest bad guys. A few times while we were out following Batiste, I would hear chatter on back radio channels used by other tactical units, emanating from North WET members. Their chatter indicated they were not where they were supposed to be (at the fire station, waiting) but in some other part of the city, running warrants. They were way out of position, and if we needed them on short notice to man our undercover armored vehicle, they wouldn't be able to.

It became a constant battle to keep WET focused on the mission. They surely didn't have any patience for surveillance, much less sitting around a fire station for days at a time with nothing to do. Lalo tried hard to keep them physically on task, to stay at the station, ready to go!

He even jokingly brought them some little kid coloring books, to help them pass the time. As Lalo put it, he was trying to keep their "cave-man simple," single-focus, one-dimensional brains occupied *("ME WET! ME RUN WARRANT! ME PUT BAD GUY IN JAIL!")*. They didn't appreciate Lalo's humor, but I thought it was funny!

I finally had to snitch on WET and their apparent lack of focus to Lieutenant Bellamy, who then ordered them, as well as their sergeant (Heath Bounds), to stay put at the fire station and focus on the sniper mission only.

You have to love the WET guys! They were a dedicated bunch and provided a great service to the citizens in the community. But, not so good when it came to long-term surveillance operations that required a lot of patience.

Besides our Brink's armored truck, the NDTU also quickly developed a limited counter sniper capability if needed to take out the sniper. By department policy, personnel within tactical units are precluded from using "traditional" long guns more suitable for counter sniping operations, such as a Remington 700, chambered in .308 Winchester (7.62X51 NATO) equipped with a powerful telescopic sight. Not only would this type of weapon system afford us with more precision than our .223 carbines with Aimpoints, but the .308 Winchester would be much more capable if it became necessary to penetrate (shoot through) the Toyota 4Runner and "incapacitate" the sniper inside. From our experience, a .223, 55 grain soft tip bullet was unreliable in penetrating or defeating intermediate barriers. A Houston Police Department Tactical Unit is also only trained in close quarter battle type tactics, not long-range precision shooting or sniping. However, since several of us in the North Division Tactical Unit were present or former members of the SWAT Detail, there was some knowledge of sniper tactics, not present in any of the other department's tactical units.

We needed our own "counter sniping" team. Just like the WET team standing by, ready to man our undercover armored vehicle at a moment's notice, we needed our own snipers, just in case. It was an added precaution, a safety net, if we read the "tea leaves wrong." We wanted to add insurance to make sure we could handle any situation Batiste's sniper robbery crew threw at us. No innocent citizens would die on our watch!

I called a sergeant friend, Tommy Colabro, over at the Houston Police Department's SWAT Detail and, after asking him to keep it confidential, laid out what we had. *"Tommy, we're really not expecting another sniper-initiated robbery for maybe a month or two, but just in case, can I borrow a couple of your snipers for the duration—please?"* Tommy laughed, just as I thought, but it didn't hurt to ask. SWAT had their own mission and responsibilities and couldn't just assign a few of their trained snipers to sit at a fire station, playing "coloring book" with the guys from WET on the off chance Batiste's crew jumped ahead of schedule. But Tommy assured me, that if need be, if it "started looking good," he could assign some of their snipers and even an assault team to help.

After a quick meeting and discussion with the other members of the NDTU, we added an ad hoc counter sniper capability to our unit for this operation only. We would have to "bend" the rules slightly regarding our weapon systems as it would be futile in the time we had to get permission from our Command Staff. There would have to be countless committee meetings and much waffling before anyone would make a decision. It would probably take a year (I am not exaggerating!).

We obtained bonded ammunition (the lead core of the bullet is molecularly bonded to the outer copper jacket) for our rifles. A bonded .223 round is less likely to fragment when striking an intermediate barrier—in our case, the sheet metal body of the Toyota 4Runner—and there was nothing in our department's policy that precluded our using this ammunition.

We also got low-power telescopic magnifiers that were quickly detachable and fit behind our electronic red dot sights. By using these magnifiers, we could increase the accuracy and range of our gunfire, giving us a limited counter sniper capability. Our use of magnifiers was definitely in the department's "gray area" and would probably send our assistant chief into conniptions...if he knew. In just a few days, either out of our own pockets, or with the assistance of area businessmen, several members of the NDTU had their rifle magazines loaded with bonded ammunition and rifles with magnifiers on them. A quick trip to the rifle range, and our rifles were zeroed for 100 yards.

We were still concerned, though, about having to shoot and penetrate the body of the Toyota 4Runner to incapacitate the sniper. Taking nothing for granted, we went by a Toyota dealership outside of the city and, not explaining why, asked whether we could closely examine and/or borrow a Toyota 4Runner of the same year as the one parked at Blue Bell Street. The general manager of the dealership was happy to oblige.

We noted several things. By folding down the back seats of a 4Runner, there was room for a shooter to lay in the back, in the prone position, to shoot out of a sniper port hole cut in the tailgate. We also knew that most people are right-handed. Assuming that our sniper was also right-handed, we could calculate which side of the porthole his body would favor, or the greater portion of his "center mass" would be, or even where his head would be if he were laying down in the back and ready to shoot out of the porthole. We took careful measurements, all to visualize the various angles we would have to shoot into the 4Runner to incapacitate a sniper.

A potential problem arose. Several of these angles would require the penetration of multiple layers of sheet metal and other heavy parts of the vehicle's frame, particularly at the door posts. Just to be sure, we went to the SWAT firearms range, where several old "sacrificial" undercover vehicles where set aside for just such training purposes. Sure enough, depending on the angle and location, even our "super-duper" bonded .223 ammunition was not guaranteed to penetrate the interior of the vehicle.

Our bonded .223 ammunition, although better than the standard ammunition, was still "iffy." We really needed a larger caliber weapon, firing a much more powerful projectile with a heavier penetrating mass.

It was far from optimum, but we again improvised. We dusted off our 12-gauge shotguns and with the quick permission from Captain Baimbridge, sent two of the NDTU's fun-loving, young Millennials (Nick Mihalco and John Calhoun) on a two-hundred-mile road trip to Austin, Texas. There in Austin was a police supply company, which stocked special 12 Gauge, "Deep Penetrating" rifled slugs. The "kids" were given to what amounted to as the North Patrol Division's "credit card" to buy 250 of these rounds. They were also admonished to buy nothing else and to bring back the receipt! We (Lalo and I) told them (some employees you have to micromanage) to go straight to Austin and back; no "dillydallying around" (we know our Millennials)!

Nick and John were excited to go, probably wanting a break from all the tedious surveillance we were doing, and now "Mom and Dad" were trusting them with a special assignment. Lalo and I got a bad feeling when one of them shouted "Road trip!" as they jumped into one of our undercover vehicles, which was guaranteed to "definitely maybe" make the trip to Austin and back. As we watched the "kids" roar out of the station parking lot, at what we sergeants considered an excessive amount of speed, Lalo and I looked at each other and shook our heads. What had we done!

I guess that since Batiste was not really doing anything, our Millennials perhaps felt empowered to ignore Mom and Dad's instructions. Over the course of the day, we had to endure an endless parade of selfies taken by our two heroes, as they posted an assortment of photos to Snapchat documenting their "big adventure." Included on social media were all sorts of cheesy poses taken of each other as they went sightseeing around the Texas capital, flouting their nice sergeant's instructions. They even posted a video as they drove back. There for everybody in the unit to watch, the two sang along in unison to Cyndi Lauper's iconic 80s song "Girls Just Want to Have Fun," which happened to be playing on their car radio at the time. It was all in good fun and was good for unit morale. Everybody had a laugh, and it eased the stress and tension we were all feeling.

It's important the members of a small unit can laugh, even if it's at their supervisor's expense. Besides, it was a slow day, and no harm was done. Even old police sergeants like Lalo and I had a sense of humor.

The NDTU now had a safety net in place for that "just in case" event: a specific tactical operation plan; our own undercover armored truck, along with the added personnel to man it; bonded ammunition for our rifles; and magnifiers for our Aimpoints.

Then, as an added precaution (redundancy in the system), if you had to absolutely, positively, make big holes in a motor vehicle, a supply of one-ounce, copper-covered, hardened lead, 12-gauge "deep penetration" rifled slugs. Although they were low in velocity (1350 feet per second), they were of sufficient mass to punch holes all the way through a Toyota 4Runner (except the engine block), to kill any sniper shooting at us from within. Using shotguns and slugs was more of a throwback to another era in police weapon technology, but it was the best we had at that moment.

CHAPTER 22

HAVING LUNCH WITH REDRICK

Other than the linking Redrick Batiste to the Toyota 4Runner, our everyday surveillance on him had produced nothing suspicious. Batiste was a loner. He didn't really hang out with anyone else, appeared to have no close friends, except for occasional visits with Buchi Okoh and their baby. He also didn't go partying or out to clubs. He led a quiet life. He was an introvert.

One late morning, in October, we were following Batiste as he drove his Jeep Wrangler out of Acres Homes and around the north side of the city. At first, he seemed to meander with no apparent destination in mind. That all changed when he drove into the parking lot of the Wells Fargo Bank where David Guzman had been killed. Batiste didn't stay there long, just lingered in the parking lot for a few minutes, never getting out of his vehicle. Soon he was back on the move. I thought that was interesting or maybe just a coincidence.

We continued our rolling surveillance. Fifteen minutes later, Batiste was headed south on North Shepherd Drive and then pulled into the parking lot of the same Bank of America where the Loomis armored truck guard had been severely wounded in a close-range assassination and robbery attempt nearly a year earlier. Batiste again only stayed a short time, never got out of the Jeep, and was soon back on the road.

Twenty minutes later, Batiste was in the parking lot of the Chase Bank on Airline Drive, where Melvin Moore was killed, again lingering for a few minutes like at the other bank locations.

We followed him as he headed south toward downtown Houston, where eventually he stopped for lunch at Torchy's Tacos on West Nineteenth Street.

Torchy's Tacos is a popular Houston eatery. It was also one of Heather Winter's favorite places to eat. Heather, our AUSA, at that same moment that Batiste was ordering his food, had just sat down in Torchy's with several other attorneys to eat their lunch.

One way I kept everybody in the loop about what was happening in the NDTU's surveillance of Batiste was via a dedicated group messaging system on my iPhone. If anything of interest was happening, I would send out periodic updates. Watching Batiste "visiting" three out of the five bank locations where armored truck couriers had either been shot or killed certainly arose to that notification level and Heather was monitoring my messaging.

She was especially interested when I put out "he is stopping for lunch at Torchy's." Soon, Heather got an unintended, personal, and close-up view of our serial killer ("in the wild") who was the object of a criminal investigation that she was a part of. How often does that happen in the career of a federal prosecutor? Heather watched discreetly as Redrick Batiste came in and ordered his food, sitting down alone just a few tables from hers to eat. All during lunch, munching on her tacos and jibber-jabbing with her other lawyer friends, she sent out regular updates, as to Batiste being alone, what he ordered, when he was leaving, etc.

Heather also took notice of something else. Redrick Batiste, like a "switched on" off-duty cop, was careful to sit at a table and to position himself with his back to a wall, at a location inside the restaurant where he had a clear view of both the entrance and exits to the restaurant. While eating, Batiste often looked up from his food to glance and check over each customer as they came in and ordered their food. Heather, like I had observed earlier, saw Batiste as being alert, always evaluating and assessing his environment. He was a different type of criminal.

After lunch with Heather, Redrick Batiste was back on the road, headed south. And, not to be left out, he eventually drove down Westheimer Road to the Capital One Bank where Alvin Kinney had been murdered.

I think it was Nick Mihalco who said over the radio what many of the guys were thinking at that moment: "This guy is a sicko! He is getting his jollies by going to all the places where they killed people. He's reliving it all."

I wasn't thinking so much that Batiste was being titillated or getting some perverse gratification by visiting the scenes of these crimes (although this was a distinct possibility). I suspected something else. He was going to the locations where he had previously participated in armored truck robberies, mentally reviewing what had gone right or wrong in each operation. He was mentally critiquing each one of them.

If you will, Batiste was "polishing the cannon ball"!

This was a harbinger of things yet to come. We didn't know it yet, but Batiste was entering into the planning stage for his next sniper-initiated armored truck robbery.

A day or two later, we followed and watched Batiste when he drove to and entered the Gander Mountain Sporting Goods Store on North Freeway. Ben LeBlanc followed him into the store a few minutes later and discreetly monitored from within. Thirty minutes later, Batiste made a purchase, left the store, and drove back to his house. After he was gone from the store, Ben felt it was safe to identify himself and then interviewed the employee at the gun counter who Batiste had talked to and whom he had asked to handle and examine several of the handguns on display. The employee was cooperative and told Ben in their conversation that Batiste claimed he was "looking for a gun for his girlfriend," that he "really liked Glock pistols" and alluded to owning several.

More interesting was that Batiste had purchased a single Magpul 40-round capacity (not 10, 20, or 30, but 40) .223/5.56mm rifle magazine, designed to fit AR-15-type rifles. Batiste was a convicted felon and was prohibited from owning or possessing firearms. However, the law did not prohibit him from owning a high-capacity magazine that was used in a firearm. What it meant to us was that Batiste or one of his minions was likely in possession of an AR-15-type rifle, a weapon the caliber of which was the same as used in the last murders.

This tidbit of information went a long way to further our probable cause in obtaining a search warrant for Batiste's Tarberry Street residence. If we could recover an AR-15 rifle at Tarberry and later ballistic testing showed it to be the same gun used in the previous murders, we might have what we needed. Just for such a possibility, we acquired a copy of the receipt from Gander Mountain of Batiste's purchase and also a copy of the store video showing him buying and in possession of the rifle magazine.

FBI Jeff and I were back on the phone with Rick and Heather. We discussed the pros and cons of maybe now "rolling the dice" and pushing to obtain a search warrant for 1451 Tarberry. Because if we could recover the AR-15 used in the murders inside Batiste's home, we might get a conviction in state or federal court for murder. Or, if we recovered any firearm, we could at least get some state or federal felon in possession of a firearm charge.

If we hadn't had so much insight into Batiste and how canny and calculating he was, we might have taken the chance with a search warrant then. But, we all had a nagging doubt that he kept any guns, much less any ones he used in robberies and murders, inside his house. We thought it more likely he kept them at another location. A location that we didn't know about, all for just such an eventuality (the police running an evidentiary search warrant "where he laid his head").

Besides, even if we recovered the murder weapon, it still wouldn't lead us to the other coconspirators who were as equally culpable as Batiste, or even prove that Batiste was the actual trigger man or sniper. Even if we took Batiste out, it didn't mean the killings and shootings of armored truck couriers would stop. The core group of conspirators would still be intact and they could replace Batiste with someone else in whichever role he had filled.

We still wanted to make all the coconspirators accountable for their crimes and bring closure to the victims' families.

In our ongoing surveillance of Redrick Batiste, we now had another looming problem. The batteries in the trackers Zak had put on Batiste's Jeep Wrangler, back on September 4, were dead or dying. Because our surveillance of Batiste had been so intense and we were so reliant on the tracking devices, we had run them hard. The primary tracker's battery had died weeks before and now we were using the backup trackers and were rapidly draining them. Tracker maintenance on Batiste's Jeep Wrangler would be a bigger problem than I first realized.

We had been fortunate to have found his Wrangler parked in his front yard that morning. Because now, over a month later, we observed that he rarely—if ever—parked it there and almost always kept it overnight, safely ensconced, locked up in his garage where we could not access it.

We had missed the opportunity to change out the trackers when Batiste went to the Gander Mountain store a few days before and now we were querying the remaining backup tracker, sparingly, if at all, not knowing when we could replace it.

It was another thing to worry about.

Fortunately, Redrick Batiste still had the pending Possession of Marijuana criminal case that sometimes required his presence in state court, in downtown Houston. Providentially, we were coming up on one of those court dates and because getting fresh tracking devices on his Jeep had become a major priority, we planned several operations, in concert with each other, hoping that Batiste would be in court that day and away from his Jeep in an area we could access it. Sure enough, on the morning of his scheduled court appearance, we watched on our Tarberry pole camera as he left the house in his Jeep. I waited ten minutes and pinged the working tracker just one time to make sure he was headed in the direction of the courthouse. He was! Most of the NDTU, along with FBI Jeff, Dave Helms, and Jessica Bruzas headed in the same direction. Once we were all down in the vicinity of the courthouse, we pinged the almost dead tracker and located Batiste's Wrangler parked, unoccupied, in a "Pay to Park" parking lot near the courthouse. Unfortunately, there was a lot of foot traffic in the immediate area, with many individuals coming and going from the courthouse itself. We couldn't take a chance of changing out the trackers in view of any random citizen, so we had to wait patiently. It was taking longer than we thought it would.

As a precaution, FBI Jeff, Dave Helms, and Jessica Bruzas went into the courthouse, to the same courtroom where Redrick Batiste was waiting for the judge to decide on a motion for continuance that his lawyer was filing. The three of them individually infiltrated the crowded courtroom, blending in with everyone else seated inside. From within the courtroom, they could then instant message and warn us immediately when Batiste left, so he didn't catch us putting tracking devices on his Jeep. Interestingly, FBI Jeff noted, that while in court, Batiste, while waiting for his case to be heard, spent his time reading some book on self-improvement and the secrets of success.

Meanwhile, there was finally a gap in the foot traffic in the parking lot and we quickly pulled off the dead and dying trackers from underneath the Jeep Wrangler, replaced the batteries with fresh ones, and then waited again for a gap in the foot traffic. We then put the trackers back on. It sounds simple and easy, but it wasn't. Other members of the NDTU, knowing that Batiste was downtown in court, were sneaking into the apartments on Blue Bell Street, past Ms. Busy Body, and covertly performing the same tracker maintenance on the Toyota 4Runner.

This was the first time I was in close proximity to Batiste's Jeep. Often, while trying to pick out his Jeep from a distance, one of the markers I looked for to differentiate his black Jeep from any other black Jeep that was in the area was a round yellow sticker on the bumper. I could never make out what the sticker or decal said because it was pretty small. But now I had the opportunity. The sticker had the image of a honey badger with the wording "Honey Badger Takes What It Wants!"

For those readers unfamiliar with a honey badger, it is a small carnivore and a member of the weasel family. It's known for its ferocity and courage. The honey badger is also mean, ill-tempered, smart, and solitary. It eats anything it wants. It's widely reputed to be, pound for pound, the most aggressive and fearless of all of God's creatures.

We thought it telling that Redrick Batiste would have such a sticker on his vehicle.

Kelly Huey also noticed something else about Batiste's Jeep Wrangler, which gave us cause for concern. Something we had never seen before. Inside the Jeep, mounted on the front windshield, looking forward, was a GoPro-type video camera. If the camera was on and recording while Batiste was in court and if he then reviewed it later, there was a possibility we would be discovered. Normally I would think such an eventuality was unlikely—it was way out there. But Redrick Batiste was cautious, almost to the point of paranoia, so it was possible. All we could do was hope that the camera wasn't on and our surveillance hadn't been compromised.

Later that day, after Batiste's court appearance was over and he was back at Tarberry Street, I met with FBI Jeff and his supervisor Mr. Telle, filling them in on the GoPro camera and the status of our vehicle tracking operation. Mr. Telle, after hearing about the discovery of the GoPro, remarked regarding safeguarding the integrity of the surveillance operation: "In the old days, we (the FBI) would have broken out the windshield and taken the camera!" I thought he was joking. But maybe years earlier, in the J. Edgar Hoover days, the FBI did such things.

The GoPro must have been turned off and not recording. In the days following, there was no indication our surveillance of Batiste had been uncovered.

Redrick Batiste should have had his surveillance camera recording while he was in court.

But he didn't.

CHAPTER 23

FIRST SIGNS

Our daily surveillance of Batiste was boring! The only things of note were the approximately weekly late-night visits to move the Toyota 4Runner around at the Blue Bell Street apartment complex, the purchase of an AR-15 rifle magazine, and his trip down memory lane, visiting the locations where armored truck robberies and/or attempted robberies had occurred, where guards had either been killed or wounded.

But by late October, we observed two changes in Batiste's weekly habit patterns. The first one was that besides his visits with Buchi Okoh, Batiste now had a side girlfriend. Several times we had observed him, usually in the afternoons, leave his house, drive down to Martin Street, and pick up a young woman, who would wait for him in front of a trailer park. They would go back to Batiste's house, where she would spend the night and then early the next morning, he would drive back to Martin Street and drop her off. We didn't know her name (then) but came to call her the "Martin Street Girl."

Their time together became so predictable that by noting the time and the initial route Batiste took when he left the house, we knew instantly that it was a booty call. At about the same time, since we were constantly monitoring Buchi Okoh's social media accounts, we discerned that there was "trouble in paradise." Even though she and Redrick were still regularly spending time together, Buchi was posting comments for all the world to read, voicing her dissatisfaction with her relationship with Batiste and that he had little interest in being a father figure to their child.

The status of their deteriorating relationship was made clear when we followed Redrick Batiste and Buchi Okoh to George Bush Intercontinental Airport and watched as they boarded a commercial airline flight bound for Las Vegas, Nevada. They were traveling with another couple and they all went together for a long weekend, partying and gambling before returning early the next week. FBI Jeff was able to determine their return flight and several of us were in position inside the terminal to get eyes on the four of them as they exited the airplane and walked through the terminal building. Mostly, we were trying to identify the other couple traveling with them, thinking perhaps they were other members of his robbery crew. We later determined that this other couple were not part of the criminal conspiracy. More significantly, when Buchi and Redrick exited the airplane, they were not walking together. It was plain to see that they were now estranged. Buchi appeared to be the stereotypical "angry woman." I am not sure what happened in Las Vegas, but apparently the adage "whatever happens in Las Vegas, stays in Las Vegas" is not true.

After seeing this, we briefly entertained the idea of trying to turn Buchi Okoh into our informant, to quietly approach her about what we suspected—that her "baby daddy" was part of a serial killing robbery crew, relying on the evident dissatisfaction in their relationship, something we knew because she was voicing it on social media and also revealing (we had video) that he was cheating on her with another woman (the Martin Street Girl). Maybe the "scorned/jealous woman" emotional factor plus generous FBI informant money would flip her to our side.

Approaching Buchi was not as farfetched as it seemed, if we had decided on this option. After all, it was a scorned/angry woman who many years earlier enabled Billy Belk and me to undo Officer Donald Sutton and his dope ripping/home invasion operation.

But as we considered this, there were some obstacles. First, we couldn't be sure how Buchi Okoh would react and she might back-feed information to Batiste, alerting him to our operation. Maybe she wouldn't be upset? Maybe they had an "understanding" or some open relationship.

The other factor was we didn't know whether Buchi Okoh was involved or somewhat culpable in the murder of her former employer, Joe Stewart. It might be when this whole operation was over and settled, Buchi Okoh would be on trial in federal court for her role in facilitating the murder of Stewart. Rick and Heather didn't want to make any deals with her because of this possibility.

This surveillance operation had so many twists and turns. We were endeavoring to keep the operation quiet and it was not general knowledge, even within the Houston Police Department. The whole thing was on a need-to-know basis only. I don't know at that time whether Captain Baimbridge had even told the Command Staff about it, given their past propensity for screwing these types of sensitive operations up, mostly because of their lack of operational experience.

But our surveillance operation was nearly undone in October 2016, in a way we never saw coming. The Houston metro population area is home to nearly seven million people. Houston itself is the fourth most populous city in the United States. These figures don't even take into account the significant numbers of people who live in other outlying counties and commute into Houston each day for work and/or business.

What are the odds that someone close to the NDTU, who had a general knowledge about what we were doing, would also have a relationship with one of our suspects?

But at the time we didn't even realize it.

Officer Elizabeth Calhoun was an investigator in the Houston Police Department's Auto Theft Division. She had a "thing" for Cadillacs. In 2014, she bought her first one. She went to the Joe Stewart Cadillac dealership to "gawk" several times, because it was conveniently located near her office. Eventually, she considered buying one and test drove several models. The salesperson and her point of contact at Joe Stewart Cadillac was none other than Buchi Okoh.

During this time, the two women connected. One topic and commonality they shared was that Buchi had been a college volleyball player, much like Liz's son, John Calhoun, who had also played volleyball (or maybe it was basketball—I don't remember) while he was in college. Eventually, Buchi was able to "seal the deal" with Liz and sold her a Cadillac CTS, just like the one Redrick had bought her.

Over the next two years, the women kept in touch and in 2016, while the NDTU was running surveillance on both Buchi Okoh and Redrick Batiste, Liz Calhoun decided she wanted to trade in her Cadillac CTS for a different model. Liz now wanted a Cadillac XTS. So she looked up her old friend Buchi Okoh at her new place of employment, at the Sterling McCall Cadillac dealership, to help her facilitate a trade-in and a new purchase. The two women reconnected and had lunch, catching up on life, in particular what Liz's son John was up to and whether he would finally settle down and get married. Buchi lamented to Liz about her boyfriend problems and whether he would ever settle down, marry her and be a good father to their child.

Within this conversation, Liz told Buchi that John was now a member of an HPD Tactical Unit. And as she was about to divulge more information about our current operation, she stopped herself. As the first words were on the tip of her tongue, a red warning light flashed in her brain and Liz held her words. Instead, she only said that John and his unit were following around some "crazy guy" and left it at that.

380

Liz held her tongue, not because at the time she knew anything about Buchi's relationship with Redrick Batiste or even knowing that Buchi was a suspect in a serial murder investigation. It was because Liz Calhoun, as an experienced police detective, knew not to talk about ongoing investigations with others (outside the circle of trust)—in particular, with a citizen.

It was only days later, when John was admiring his mom's new Cadillac XTS, that the subject came up and he filled her in more on Redrick Batiste and that Buchi Okoh was a "person of interest" in the murder of Joe Stewart, who had been the owner of Stewart Cadillac. It was then that Liz connected all the dots and got a sick feeling in her stomach, realizing how close she had come to compromising our entire surveillance operation.

If Liz Calhoun had less discretion, if she was a person prone to gossiping, everything the involved Homicide investigators, ATF agents, FBI agents, federal prosecutors, and the NDTU had worked for would have been in vain.

But she didn't!

Oh, to have an insider, a snitch, in the midst of a gang of criminals you're trying to undo! A "spy" working for you, who is reporting to you every move the bad guys make. A "spy" makes police high-risk surveillance operations so much simpler. It's such a force multiplier. Many times, having a well-placed informant makes all the difference between your operation's success or failure.

What we needed in this case was a well-placed spy!

Thinking about and then rejecting the idea about trying to flip Buchi Okoh to our side brought FBI Jeff and me back full circle. We began to think back to the Original Informant, who FBI Jeff had "hooked" on FBI money. Maybe he was willing to become more involved? Could he be an actual insider for us? Was he trusted enough by Batiste and the others to assist them in the next armored truck sniper robbery? If we could place "our man" inside the crew, it would be an intelligence bonanza and probably through recorded conversations (wearing a wire), we would have enough evidence to achieve our objectives and arrest Batiste and his coconspirators well before they were actually set up to "take the shot" and kill another armored truck guard.

A meeting was arranged with the Original Informant. Would he or could he be our inside man?

The short answer: No!

Let's just say the Original Informant was an acquaintance of Batiste. Because his identity is still protected, it's important while writing this book to not include any specific information that could lead others to connect the dots and identify him. His life was and is still in danger.

It's also not to say that our Original Informant was a saint! In talking to him, another picture emerged. Our Original Informant's specialty was (or is) home invasion robberies! Preferably these robberies were orchestrated against drug dealers believed to have large amounts of drug money secreted in their residences. Our Original Informant had heard through "street talk" that Redrick Batiste was sitting on one million dollars he had gotten in a lick. Which, if the street talk was true, most probably, had to have come from the February 15, 2015 murder of Alvin Kinney, the Brink's security guard who was ambushed and killed on Westheimer Road in the parking lot of a Capital One Bank.

So, the Original Informant, being a man of opportunity, reconnected with Redrick Batiste, his old buddy, maybe with the ulterior motive of trying to figure out exactly where Redrick lived. Because presumably, in this house, secreted somewhere within, was a million dollars cash.

It might have been that the Original Informant, along with his crew, were planning on conducting a robbery/home invasion on Batiste wherever he lived, to steal the million dollars that Batiste had gotten in the Westheimer Road armored truck robbery. The problem for the Original Informant was that Batiste was "too cagy" or "too secretive" and he could never figure out where Batiste lived, to actually carry out his robbery home invasion plans.

So our Original Informant did the next best thing and cut his losses (like he had done in the past). He "snitched out" what he knew about Batiste to law enforcement so he could make some money that way.

The Original Informant also explained that Batiste and his crew were a "closed operation" and that for a person to be included, he would have to be "heavily vetted" with the requisite "street creds"(violent criminal record). The Original Informant had the street creds, but said that Batiste didn't trust him enough. Besides, the Original Informant explained even if Batiste trusted him enough and included him in the next armored truck robbery, if he became further involved, if he undid Batiste in an actual "first person" betrayal, it would not go well for him. Because, as he explained, "Red's people will kill me!"

FBI Jeff had an answer to all of this: the federal government's Witness Relocation Program.

But the Original Informant was a man of unusual vigor and had many children (born to different women) who he said he loved dearly and didn't want to leave behind. All of his children lived in the Houston area and it would be financially difficult for the FBI to justify the expense of relocating him, all of his children, and their respective mothers to somewhere else in the United States, even if all the parties involved were willing to go.

Even though the FBI's pockets are deep, they weren't that deep.

There were other "minor" informants, who knew of Batiste, with some "crumbs" of information. But these other informants had zero potential of being invited to participate in the next planned armored truck robbery (they were all recently incarcerated, for one thing). All of them had come forth earlier to other investigators, and, although their information amounted to little more than "jailhouse snitch stuff," it had been documented. Their relevant, although unsubstantiated information, however, had never reached the people who needed to know about it, in a timely fashion, until now. But now these tidbits of information, put in the proper context, were making some sense.

Batiste, in a conversation with an unnamed informant, had allegedly stated that he shot and killed an "old white man, in his garage, with a .40 cal," which correlated with the murder of Buchi Okoh's employer, Joseph Stewart on May 7, 2015.

Another unnamed informant alleged that Batiste had murdered a man in Louisiana. According to the informant, the victim was part of the crew in one of Batiste's armored truck robbery schemes, but who had been wounded in a shootout with the police but was able to escape. Shortly after being shot, he was then taken by Batiste to an unknown "crooked" veterinarian for emergency treatment of his gunshot wound. Then, sometime later, Batiste became concerned that the wounded man, who was not part of Batiste's "trusted" core group and who was considered an "expendable crash dummy," might talk. So Batiste then traveled to Louisiana, where the "crash dummy" was hiding out, recuperating from his wound. Batiste shot and killed him and then dumped the body in a rural swamp area, to be disposed of by hungry alligators. This informant's tidbit (if true) correlated with the March 18, 2016, Loomis armored truck robbery at the Chase Bank on Airline Drive where it was reported that Melvin Moore shot and wounded one member of the robbery crew's pick-up team before Melvin died of his wounds.

What was interesting about the whole Louisiana angle was that weeks earlier, when we had first gotten tracking devices on Batiste's Jeep Wrangler, we tracked him one weekend deep into Louisiana, where he stayed overnight. We were not sure what he was up to as the NDTU could not keep eyes on him and physically watch him during the time he was over there. Because of the distance and logistics involved, we would have needed permission from our Command Staff to cross state lines, so the NDTU stopped following him in Beaumont, just before he crossed out of Texas. While Batiste was in Louisiana, FBI Jeff reached out to the New

Orleans FBI Field Office for help in the surveillance but none was forthcoming. I understand it was on the weekend, short notice, and we had no reason to suspect that Batiste was up to anything nefarious while over there.

It might have been that Batiste, while on this trip, was "tying up some loose ends" and eliminating a potential security leak, which threatened to undo his operation. Or maybe, he was visiting friends. To this day, we still don't know what he was up to on that weekend trip.

Months later, both FBI Jeff and I, regarding our surveillance operation, were severely criticized by a "very senior" law enforcement administrator that we should have somehow facilitated the infiltration and/or "in placement" of a "black undercover officer or agent" within the armored truck sniper crew. Then, after the infiltration or "in placement" and then after this black undercover officer/agent became a trusted member of Batiste's crew, he could "wear a wire" and be our inside man, feeding us all kinds of good information, etc.

Really!

A man unknown to Batiste and his trusted coconspirators, could (unsolicited) somehow ask, *"Hey guys, can I help out in your next sniper-initiated armored truck robbery?"*

That might happen in Hollywood movies, but not in real life. This thinking was naive, in my opinion. But it was disturbing, as it showed (again) a basic lack of real-life, operational experience by some law enforcement higher-ups. They should have known better but they couldn't (or wouldn't) grasp the nuances and complexities, as well as the operational risk(s) associated with trying to "magically parachute" an undercover law enforcement operative into the passenger seat of Redrick Batiste's Jeep Wrangler.

Unfortunately, there would never be an "insider" for us in our surveillance operation.

After the Las Vegas trip and estrangement from Buchi Okoh, the second change we saw in Batiste's weekly habit patterns was that he began to scout banks and ATMs on nearly a daily basis. The exception were the days and nights he was "servicing" the Martin Street Girl. Maybe Batiste had lost big gambling in Las Vegas and because he had no job, now needed more money to, like the Original Informant told us, "maintain his lifestyle." Maybe this was why he now had a sudden interest in banks and ATMs right after returning from Las Vegas.

The first time we saw this shift in habit patterns was when we were following Batiste in his Jeep Wrangler on West Little York Road just outside the Acres Homes community. At the intersection of West Little York Road and North Houston Rosslyn Road, on the north side is a Chase Bank with several drive-up ATMs in the middle of its parking lot. As we were following Batiste past the bank, it just so happened that the ATMs there were being serviced by a Brink's armored truck. As per protocol, one guard sat in the driver's seat, watching for any potential threats while a second guard was outside, working on the ATMs. As soon as Batiste saw the Brink's armored truck and what was occurring, he whipped his Jeep into the parking lot and took up a position unnoticed by either guard, where he could watch or study what was going on.

Unnoticed by either Batiste or the Brink's guards, the NDTU then also slid into the same parking lot and took up positions to carefully monitor him as he watched what the Brink's guards were doing. We were not expecting him to commit a robbery (he was alone and the sniper vehicle was still parked at Blue Bell Street), but we had to be careful just the same. While still in our undercover vehicles, we slipped on our plate carriers (heavy body armor) and made our rifles ready. Lalo and I began coordinating and positioning our people to avoid a cross fire if we had to engage Batiste. At the same time, the WET guys back at the fire station, who were monitoring our radio traffic, without being told, put down their coloring books, loaded up into our Brink's armored truck and began rolling to the scene.

Soon, the real Brink's armored truck crew were done and drove out of the bank parking lot. After they left, Batiste lingered. Maybe he was in deep thought, evaluating, planning? But now that the danger had passed, we all relaxed a bit and the WET guys turned around, headed back to the fire station and their coloring books.

Was it just "professional curiosity" that had caused Batiste to pull into the parking lot to watch the guards servicing the ATMs at the Chase Bank?

But what I knew was if Redrick Batiste was inclined to rob a Brink's armored truck at the Chase Bank on West Little York Road, he now had the first "piece of the puzzle." He had an inkling to the approximate time and day the ATMs at this bank might be serviced. As these pieces started coming together, he and his crew could then coordinate to successfully commit another murder/robbery.

Later that night, after we saw Batiste watching the servicing of the ATMs at the Chase Bank, it became abundantly clear that the long-anticipated scouting and reconnoitering had begun!

CHAPTER 24

SCOUTING THE BANKS

Late that evening, after another day of following Batiste and after watching him take a strong interest in watching the armored truck servicing the ATMs in the parking lot of the Chase Bank on West Little York Road, I was at home, sound asleep. *Bink!* "Exit Tarberry Geo Fence—Jeep Wrangler." Batiste was leaving the house and on the move.

Man, I thought, *doesn't this guy ever sleep!*

I was out of bed, headed for my home computer.

It wasn't time yet for the weekly "move the 4Runner to a different parking spot" routine. So what was he up to now? Maybe heading to Martin Street to pick up the girl?

I fired up my computer and logged on. By the time I sent out a command to speed up the tracker on Batiste's Jeep Wrangler, he was already out of Acres Homes and headed west on West Little York Road. I became fully awake and interested when his Jeep reached the intersection of North

Houston Rosslyn Road, where he then drove back into the parking lot of the Chase Bank. What was he doing? All the businesses were closed this time of the night and the parking lot must be empty.

Carefully I watched as the dots representing Batiste's Jeep slowly circled the approximate area where the bank's ATMs were located. Then he crossed over to the south side of West Little York Road and into the parking lot of an Auto Zone. There he remained stationary. He had parked close to West Little York Road, directly across from the ATMs.

Soon, Batiste was on the move again. This time to North Houston Rosslyn Road, to the northeast side of the intersection and into the parking lot of a large supermarket. After circling around again for a while, he stopped. There he parked, (according to Google Street View) next to a large Food Town billboard.

After approximately a half hour, Batiste left the area of the Chase Bank and headed back home for the rest of the night.

The next morning, as soon as I got to work, while Batiste was still at his house, Dave Smith and I drove out to the Chase Bank. Using the historical tracking data from the night before as our frame of reference, we parked in the same spots that Batiste had parked hours before in both parking lots. We calculated the distances from both locations where Batiste's Jeep had been stationary to the ATMs across the street. The distance from the Auto Zone parking lot was just over a hundred yards, while the distance from the Food Town parking lot, near the sign, was well over 150 yards.

It was obvious what Batiste was doing. He was carefully analyzing the lay of the land, figuring out where to position the sniper and the Toyota 4Runner. He was factoring in all the variables, making a careful analysis, all for that successful shot, when an armored truck and its guards were replenishing the money at the Chase ATMs.

We also noticed, that just like in the previous sniper attacks, both of the locations where Batiste was considering placing his sniper team were places they would have to shoot across busy four-lane roadways into an equally busy bank parking lot. Shooting across a busy roadway added to the concealment of the sniper team, further obscuring, to witnesses, where the gunfire originated from.

To some readers, a 100-yard or 150-yard shot doesn't sound so difficult. I disagree. If you factored in all the other issues, all germane to an urban environment, it would be a difficult shot and would require some skill as well as careful planning and timing.

Dave and I could see why Batiste didn't long consider placing the sniper in the Auto Zone parking lot. Even though this location was closer to the ATMs than Food Town's, the Auto Zone parking lot was much smaller. The sniper team would have to be parked close to the front door of the business, where there was customer foot traffic in and out. Not good! If I were a sniper considering all the variables and locations around the Chase Bank ATMs with a desire to remain hidden and undiscovered, I would choose the same spot that Batiste apparently had. I would place my sniper platform right next to the Food Town sign. Even though the distance was farther, it was tactically sounder—it was more "doable."

While Dave and I were still at the Chase Bank, one of the guys back at the office gave us a heads-up on the radio. "Sarge, he's rolling out of the house!" Batiste was on the move and headed our way.

We waited and watched on our computers as he drove into the area. First, he drove through the Chase Bank parking lot, where David was able to get some good video; then he drove across the street and parked near the Food Town sign, facing toward the ATMs—the same spot he had parked in the night before. There he sat and waited. In the same spot I would have chosen if I were in his shoes.

The rest of the NDTU was soon out of the office and for the next few hours we carefully monitored and watched Redrick Batiste as he carefully monitored and watched the ATMs.

No armored trucks came by that day.

But, seeing Batiste back again at the Chase Bank location, I thought this would be the place for the next sniper-initiated armored truck robbery.

I called FBI Jeff and told him what I thought.

On a side note: I also congratulated Jeff for "going feral." Special Agent Jeff Coughlin no longer looked like an FBI agent or a West Point-educated former United States Army officer. He now looked disheveled; his clothes were well worn and his beard and hair were scruffy. He also looked older—or maybe, like me, he was tired from lack of sleep. When we first met, he looked like a well-bred, well-kept, pampered, show-quality poodle. But after months of grinding around-the-clock surveillance and investigative effort, FBI Jeff now looked more like a stray, mangy dog of undetermined lineage.

I then laid out to Jeff why I thought maybe the Chase Bank would be the location. We also talked about how Batiste was the only member of the robbery crew we had identified for certain. We knew, based on our previous experience in dealing with other Houston north side robbery crews, that there would be several other core members.

There would be a leader (Batiste?), someone who was in charge and made the decisions. There would be the actual sniper. Maybe working with the sniper would also be an observer/spotter to assist him. Maybe this designated observer/spotter would also be driving the Toyota 4Runner. There would also be at least two suspects in the pick-up car: one to drive, the other to jump out and retrieve the money after the guard was killed. Most likely, there would be an unknown number of other bad guys doing counter surveillance in the immediate area of the bank while the sniper and pick-up team waited for the armored truck. Lastly, it was also possible that Batiste would have some guys trailing the targeted armored truck, doing rolling surveillance, as the guards did their rounds, prior to their arrival at the Chase Bank, to give the rest of the crew some preparatory warning (this is what I would do).

Regarding the actual identity of the sniper, we were not sure Batiste was the sniper (despite what the Original Informant had told us). We thought whoever Batiste and his crew were using as a sniper, it would be someone who had prior military/sniper training. We knew that Batiste had never served in the military and as best as we could determine had no formal sniper training. We saw Batiste as more of the "shot caller" or the crew leader, and whenever the Original Informant had referred to "he," he was referring to both Batiste and "his" crew collectively. But now, here at the Chase Bank, seeing Batiste himself carefully determining the locations from where the sniper shots might be taken from, we reconsidered.

Maybe Batiste wore two hats? Maybe he was both the leader of the crew, as well as the sniper?

Or maybe Batiste was thorough, a hands-on type of operational commander and he was the one to decide where to position the sniper team?

I was concerned that any day now the crew would be ready to go, ready to take the shot at the Chase Bank when the next armored truck showed up. I didn't feel we were ready to do a takedown. There were still way too many unknowns in my book and I was not confident.

FBI Jeff, though, wasn't so worried. He now had good reason to think we were still some weeks away from the next sniper attack, even if the Chase Bank would indeed be the place.

Jeff and the FBI had just finished analyzing and researching a mountain of historical cell phone data and had come to some significant conclusions. His analysis would give us great predictive insight as to how Batiste and his crew operated, particularly in their scouting and preplanning phase.

Jeff scheduled an intelligence briefing at the FBI office to better explain (he had a thorough presentation with a lot of complicated-looking graphs, charts, and diagrams). The next day, leaving a skeleton crew to watch Batiste as he again watched the Chase Bank, the key stakeholders of our ad hoc task force were seated in the FBI's conference room for Jeff's briefing.

Before Jeff started, I gave the audience an overview of the NDTU's surveillance operation and focused on the events of the previous days (Batiste's preoccupation with the Chase Bank on West Little York Road). After I did my part, David Smith narrated his surveillance video of Batiste scouting the same bank. Then Jeff began. What he and the FBI analysts uncovered was informative, and I came out of the meeting feeling much better about the operation.

During the previous weeks, FBI Jeff hadn't just been standing in front of a mirror perfecting his undercover look. While the NDTU and ATF were doing the surveillance thing,

Jeff and his side were doing their thing. The FBI had been carefully pulling apart the August 29, 2016 sniper attack and now felt confident about how the next one would go down. FBI Jeff and friends had unleashed all the "techno goodness" that they had available to them, carefully studying the cell phone traffic patterns in the immediate area of Wells Fargo Bank on Hollister where David Guzman was killed. In particular, they were looking at the cell phone traffic around the bank during the weeks prior to as well as on the day of Guzman's murder.

It's complicated, but it boiled down to this:

We had Redrick Batiste's known cell phone number, at least the cell phone number he was using and presumably had been using during the previous year or more. FBI Jeff had obtained a search warrant for the historical records of this cell phone. These records showed that in the weeks prior to August 29 (David Guzman's murder), Batiste's cell phone, when in actual use, was frequently (not on every day) pinging off of cell phone towers that placed his cell phone near the Wells Fargo Bank on Hollister Road and Highway 290.

Cell phone towers have an antenna array on the top that is three-sided and the historical records can show which side of the tower received the strongest signal from the cell phone in question. Through triangulation from multiple cell phone towers, an approximate historical location for that phone when it was in use can then be established. It was reasonable to believe that because Batiste's phone was shown in the area of the Wells Fargo Bank frequently prior to August 29, he was scouting it, just like we were now seeing him do at the Chase Bank on West Little York Road.

The FBI determined that Batiste's scouting of the Wells Fargo Bank had gone on for several weeks prior to the August 29 shooting. Jeff surmised he was probably reconnoitering the area, figuring out exactly where to place the sniper and, just as important, ascertaining the approximate day(s) and time(s) during the work week that the armored truck guards serviced these ATMs. This was exactly the summation I had come to regarding Batiste and the West Little York Road Chase Bank. Jeff also added that he thought Batiste was probably checking to see how the guards positioned the armored truck as well as themselves while doing their ATM servicing, which would also help fine-tune the exact location to place the sniper.

Then the FBI also looked at the many cell phone numbers that Batiste's cell phone had been "talking to" during those weeks. After obtaining the appropriate judicial approval, they scrutinized the historical records for these other cell phones. Jeff found two cell phone numbers that also in the weeks prior to August 29 had been found to be frequently pinging off of the same cell phone towers near the Wells Fargo Bank. That placed these other cell phones in and around the Wells Fargo Bank. Coincidence? Jeff didn't think so.

As best as Jeff could determine, one or more of the involved cell phones (either Batiste's or the others'), appeared to have been always in the area of the Wells Fargo Bank during business hours, in the weeks prior to August 29. Again, the approximate historical location of a cell phone could only be determined if it was being used—sending or receiving calls and/or messages.

Whoever was in possession of these other cell phones relative to the Wells Fargo murder/robbery might be some other core members of the now infamous armored truck sniper crew! Some unknown core members of Batiste's robbery crew were in the area, doing their part to help in the surveillance of the bank and/or familiarize themselves with the area prior to the next sniper-initiated armored truck robbery. Interestingly, not only were these two cell phones "talking" to Batiste's cell phone, but they also "talked" to each other.

But, who was using these phones at those times? Jeff had the cell phone subscription/contract information with names to go along for each of these cell phones. It was possible that the subscribed owners for each respective phone were the actual names of the other crew members. But maybe not. We didn't know for sure. We knew from previous experience, it was often not that simple.

There was also a big fly in the ointment. Jeff carefully explained that during the actual time of the murder and robbery at the Wells Fargo Bank, Batiste's cell phone was not pinging in the area of the bank; his cell phone pinged at his home on Tarberry Street, in Acres Homes, miles away. A closer analysis showed that Batiste's phone, while at his house, received several incoming calls, but none of these calls connected (no one answered).

This was not unexpected and our assumption all along was that Batiste was savvy and so, as to thwart just what the FBI was now doing, had switched to a burner phone shortly before implementing his operation.

Now the FBI's cell phone analysis had in some ways provided a readymade defense for Batiste and/or his crew in any future criminal prosecution. "*Isn't it true, Agent Coughlin, that the FBI's own scientific analysis shows that my client's cell phone was not in the area at the time of the murder?*"

We were certain that although Batiste's personal cell phone may have been at his house on Tarberry Street at the time of David Guzman's murder, he wasn't.

Though it appeared that Batiste had left his phone at home, the phone records of the other known cell phones connected to the other members of the robbery crew showed to be in the general vicinity of the Wells Fargo

Bank during the time that David Guzman was murdered. More importantly, the known phones of the other members of the crew were also in contact with a new number. This previously unknown cell phone that had never showed up before in the historical record, which was now also in the area of the Wells Fargo Bank. FBI Jeff strongly suspected that this new phone, this never before seen phone, was Redrick Batiste's burner phone—only used for a short time and then disposed of immediately after the murder/robbery.

Jeff and the FBI had also gone back and gotten more of the security video taken from the hotel across the street from the Wells Fargo Bank. The video we had previously reviewed, the one which HPD Homicide had gotten, was from the same day and around the same time of Guzman's killing. This video showed the grainy image of what we now believed to be the white Toyota 4Runner parked in the hotel's back parking lot with its rear facing the Wells Fargo ATMs across the street. Although it took a while, FBI Jeff was able to get the video from this same camera in the same hotel parking lot, but on the days prior to the August 29 murder. This newly secured video showed the white 4Runner, parked in the same spot in the hotel parking lot days before David Guzman's murder. Not only that, but when the Toyota 4Runner drives into the parking lot in the mornings, no one ever gets out of it. Then, at the end of the business day, it simply drives off, out of camera view.

Jeff then summarized his findings, putting it all together for us.

The armored truck sniper crew had spent weeks watching the Wells Fargo Bank prior to taking the shot.

Different members of the crew took turns or shifts to watch the bank during this extended time period.

When the bad guys were confident and ready for their sniper to squeeze the trigger, they did two things: they brought out the 4Runner and placed it into position, and Batiste went "black," switching to an untraceable burner phone.

The days Batiste's alleged burner phone and his friends' phones pinged in and around the Wells Fargo Bank were also the same days the 4Runner was positioned in the hotel parking lot across the street. Presumably, on these same days, the sniper was inside the 4Runner, ready to take the shot, while the rest of the moving parts—the other crew members—were all in the area to perform their respective assignments.

Jeff also surmised that when the crew was ready to take the shot, when the burner phone was being used and the 4Runner was in position, even the immediate presence of an armored truck crew servicing the Wells Fargo ATMs didn't automatically mean that the sniper could or would shoot. There were many unpredictable variables: civilian motor vehicle traffic in the intervening roadway, as well as random vagaries as to where exactly the armored truck would park on any particular day and/or where the guard would position himself, etc. If all the stars didn't line up and if the sniper didn't have a clear shot, he was probably disciplined enough to not rush; the crew was content to simply wait several more days for a better opportunity during the next servicing of the ATM by the armored truck guards.

Whereas I had been concerned that another attack was imminent at the West Little York Road Chase Bank, I now knew it wasn't.

The bad guy's surveillance had maybe just started.

Only Batiste had showed up at the Chase Bank.

We had seen no other members of the crew doing surveillance.

The 4Runner was still safely parked at the apartments on Blue Bell Street.

Best of all, because of Jeff and the FBI, we now had a starting place, a good clue, as to the identities of the other core members of Batiste's crew.

FBI Jeff had most likely identified the other core members of Batiste's crew via their personal, everyday cell phones usage in and around the Wells

Fargo Bank. They had been using these phones prior to August 29 and were probably still using them to this day routinely!

There was still work to be done. Even though the core crew members who we were looking to identify might be using these phones, it didn't mean they were the actual subscriber or owner of the phone. But it was a good starting place.

In our experience, for a variety of reasons, the personal cell phones of these types of bad guys were often in the name of a female relative or other women in their sphere of influence. It would be a bad idea for us as law enforcement investigators to then approach these women and inquire who was using the phone. The whole surveillance operation would then be compromised.

After the meeting, we pumped all the FBI's cell phone intelligence over to our Crime Analysis Section, where Blake VanPelt, Amanda Morgan, and Steve Foster began pulling apart the data and accessing numerous intelligence sources (particularly social media). They followed a winding trail to identify the likely actual users of these phones. A few days later, they had two names for us of likely coconspirators with links to both each other and also Redrick Batiste. They were also able to provide a list of possible vehicles these individuals were likely driving. In the weeks ahead, their work would prove to be remarkably accurate.

The two cell phones that Jeff had identified as working in concert with Batiste in the August 29 sniper attack were linked to Marc Anthony Hill and his nephew Nelson Alexander Polk. Jeff also identified another cell phone of interest. Even though he had not identified this cell phone as being in the area of the Wells Fargo Bank during the August 29 time frame, through the historical records, he found it interesting that this phone was often "talking" to either Redrick Batiste's presumed burner phone or to Marc Hill's or Nelson Polk's personal cell phones. This cell phone was identified as probably being used by John Edward Scott. All of these men were black males, with criminal records, all with links to the north side of Houston.

We still watched Batiste almost every day and sometimes even at night as he kept scouting the Chase Bank on West Little York Road. Every time he was there, the NDTU was watching him. Even on the days he wasn't at the Chase Bank, we were still there, checking to see whether Hill, Polk, or Scott were there instead, taking their shift, as FBI Jeff predicted would eventually happen. But as best we could tell, only Batiste looked at this Chase Bank; none of the others showed up. But even though we never saw any of the other members of Batiste's crew there watching, we were confident they would eventually show up, as soon as Batiste activated them for their additional help in the surveillance of this bank. Batiste would mostly likely need the others to assist him in better establishing the approximate schedule of the armored truck that serviced the West Little York Road, Chase Bank ATMs.

As we patiently waited for the other members of the crew to show their hand, the NDTU began making detailed tactical plans. We had many discussions as to where to place our resources and what was needed for a successful intervention. Again, fortunately, because of FBI Jeff's work, we knew the sniper attack/robbery was still probably at least a few weeks away and we had an abundance of time to prepare.

I was in a good place.

Then, unexpectedly, Redrick Batiste stopped going to the West Little York Road Chase Bank. He lost all interest in it and apparently crossed it off his list. To us, it appeared that Batiste had concluded via his initial surveillance that this bank was not a good location to conduct another sniper-initiated robbery.

Because I had spent so much time out there on West Little York watching Batiste while he watched the Chase Bank, I think I know why.

At first, I also thought it was a good location (if I were going to be the sniper). But after being out there for several days, I realized there was too much vehicle traffic on both West Little York and North Houston Rosslyn, especially at the controlled intersection where these roads crossed each other. The traffic tended to "stack up" in a long line at the intersection. During business hours, the line of vehicles waiting for the traffic light to cycle was often so long it would block the view between the Food Town parking lot and the Chase Bank ATMs. From this position, too frequently— in my opinion—the sniper would not have a clear line of sight and thus a clear shot to the ATMs across the street. At least, this was my assessment and apparently it was Batiste's also.

Redrick Batiste then began scouting other bank locations, and he never looked back at the West Little York Road, Chase Bank.

The scouting of these other bank locations became both a daily and nightly occurrence and followed the same pattern we saw earlier. During the day, Batiste would leave his house, with the NDTU trailing him, and we would follow him as he went from bank to bank, looking at the ATMs. Often the ATMs that seemed to interest him the most were ones that stood alone in the front of the bank, often in the middle of the parking lot. Sometimes he also showed interest in ATMs in a bank's vehicle drive-up line.

It seemed like Batiste drove to all the banks on the north side of Houston and to many outside the city limits in Harris County. He spent hours looking for an ATM setup that suited him. I imagined he was factor- ing in all the nuances in the area surrounding each bank, looking for one that was just right. Then, in the middle of the night, he would again leave his house and would drive to maybe one or two of the banks he had looked at during the daylight hours. There, just like at the West Little York Road Chase Bank, we would watch as he drove to different positions around these banks that apparently had made his initial cut, looking for the ideal spot to shoot from.

Then, soon after Batiste left the area around a bank, I or someone from the NDTU would go park in the same spot where he had parked, using the historical GPS coordinates from the tracking devices we had on his Jeep Wrangler to ensure we were as close to the spot he had just been in and facing in the same direction as he had. These locations faced an ATM but were always a significant distance away, often across a well-used roadway. Redrick Batiste did this for weeks as we waited patiently for him to find a bank location that better suited him.

Batiste's seemingly never-ending scouting both night and day was fast wearing our small unit down. We resorted to taking naps in our undercover vehicles or, if he was at home on Tarberry Street, we would try to catch some sleep on the office floor.

During this time, Batiste showed strong interest in two banks that warranted several additional nighttime and daytime visits. After he made a nighttime visit to one of these banks, we found that some intervening ornamental hedges had been cut down. These hedges had partly obscured the view of the ATM he was considering. We didn't actually see him do this but noticed the mysterious hedge trimming the next day when we were following him to that same bank yet again. But for whatever reason, he decided against this bank and never went back, even after trimming the bushes. He was smart to have picked a location to do his gardening work where there was no surveillance camera to record his handiwork.

The second bank Batiste showed a strong interest in was a BBVA Compass Bank on the North Freeway just outside of the Houston city limits. Batiste's interest in this bank as a location for a sniper-initiated robbery caused me some heartburn. One thing I was counting on as the sign of when the robbery crew was ready to implement another attack so we would be geared up and ready with our intervention, was when the bad guys moved their sniper platform (the 4Runner) from Blue Bell Street to the pre-spotted location at whichever bank they finally choose.

But at this BBVA Compass Bank, Batiste had something else in mind. As we observed him in and around the area surrounding this bank, it became evident that he was considering placing his sniper team in a wood line approximately 175 yards to the northwest of the bank. The access to this wooded area would require the sniper and observer to either park their vehicle or to be dropped off in a nearby apartment complex, where they would then have immediate access to this same heavily wooded area. From there, they could then make their way through the woods to the wood line that faced the bank and then set up a sniper hide. From this hide, they could wait for the armored truck—well hidden—and take the shot from this same position. The setup of the apartment and the wooded area was such that there was a minimal chance that either the sniper or the observer would ever be noticed by any random person who might live in the complex.

If Batiste decided that this secluded BBVA Compass Bank would be the place, then his crew wouldn't have to use the 4Runner to shoot from. If they didn't use the 4Runner, then we lost our "early warning system" and we could possibly be caught out of position and ill-equipped or prepared for the takedown and intervention.

Shortly after one of Batiste's visits to the BBVA Compass Bank during the day, he then went to a nearby military surplus on the other side of North Freeway called the Command Post. As he went inside, via the radio, Big John reminded me that some of these surplus stores sold body armor to civilians, but because of Batiste's prior criminal convictions it would be a federal violation for him to actually purchase and possess such a ballistic vest. There was no background check for the purchasing of body armor, to weed out prohibited persons, and Batiste could easily buy one and walk out the door with no one the wiser. If he bought body armor, it would be much like catching Batiste in possession of a firearm and Big John was confident that with vigorous federal prosecution, he would be incarcerated for many years. As soon as Batiste entered the store, I sent Chris "Kut" Cutshall to follow him in and while acting as a customer, monitor what Batiste purchased. If he bought a bulletproof vest, we would then let him take it back to his house on Tarberry Street and immediately obtain a search warrant and call HPD SWAT to have them "knock him down." This is one of the tactical operations that our SWAT Detail trained for all the time and they were proficient at it.

Alas, Batiste didn't buy any prohibited body armor. Instead, Kut watched him buy two earth tone-colored coveralls (green and brown) and most ominously a camouflaged face veil, which is often worn by both turkey and deer hunters for use in wooded areas to cover their faces and to break up the outline of their silhouettes while they sit motionless in a blind, to not be seen by their prey. Batiste's purchase of this camouflaged face veil was a sign to us he was not going to deploy the 4Runner, but instead would conceal his sniper in and among natural cover.

While in the store, Kut noticed that when Batiste was checking out at the register, he took a liking to a patch displayed on a nearby rack. Batiste didn't buy the patch, but contented himself by taking a picture of it with his cell phone. He noted that the patch had the printed word "SNIPER" on it, with the depiction of a sniper in a prone position, preparing to fire his rifle.

But that night, Batiste must have had another change of heart about the location and even though he had just bought the camouflaged face veil, he must have decided against the BBVA Compass Bank and crossed it off his list of locations.

We knew this because the next morning he was back at it—looking at other banks. Redrick Batiste never went back to the BBVA Compass Bank.

I don't remember how many banks Batiste drove to and looked over, but the entire NDTU was getting antsy as we trailed and tracked Batiste in his Wrangler all over the city, day and night. It became a joke among the guys as we tried to guess and/or took bets as to which bank location would be "just right."

CHAPTER 25

THE T3

Friday Night—post-date night.

Bink! "Exit Tarberry Geo Fence—Jeep Wrangler."

Batiste was leaving the house and on the move—yet again!

I had been expecting this. He was right on schedule. It was about time to move the 4Runner to another parking spot within the apartments at Blue Bell Street. It was the same routine.

Still, just in case, I was out of bed, headed for my home computer. I fired up the tracking program and switched on the monitor for all the surveillance cameras. The monitor had a split screen view, showing all the video feeds; most important for me right now were the ones showing Batiste's house and the parked 4Runner at Blue Bell Street.

Soon enough, Batiste and his Wrangler were inside the apartments at Blue Bell Street. I watched as he walked to the 4Runner and used his key fob to remotely unlock the doors. He got in, started it up, and drove out of camera view. I assumed he was moving it to another parking spot a short distance away, just like all the other times.

Bink! "Exit Blue Bell Geo Fence—Toyota 4Runner."

After two months of surveillance, Redrick Batiste was driving the sniper vehicle out of its hiding place and was now on the move, out into the streets of Houston.

I sped up the tracking device on the 4Runner and instant-messaged everyone in our task force, sounding the alarm. For us, this was a big deal.

What was Batiste up to? The banks were all closed and none of the armored truck companies were running at this time (armored trucks didn't "roll" when the sun was down).

Fortunately, even though it was late and on a Friday night, Ben LeBlanc was still near the North Police Station. He jumped into his undercover vehicle and headed toward the track of the 4Runner to do an intercept. Other members of the NDTU were getting ready to leave their residences and head in to support Ben.

Over the radio, I narrated my tracking of the 4Runner so everyone could listen. But mostly, it was to help guide Ben in his attempt at the intercept, allowing him to just concentrate on driving. Batiste and the 4Runner were moving east toward the North Freeway; Ben was a few miles behind but was closing rapidly. Batiste pulled the 4Runner into a gas station. Finally, Ben was able to catch up, stealthily pulling into a parking lot across the street. Ben parked and killed his headlights, then watched as Batiste pumped gas into the tank of the sniper vehicle.

Okay, I thought to myself; *not a big deal.* So the 4Runner needed gas. I told everybody listening: "Hold up—don't launch just yet…stay at home. He's just putting gas in the sniper vehicle."

Ben watched as Batiste finished gassing up the 4Runner and drove off. I told Ben I would track Batiste, no worries; just tail him from a long distance. I didn't want Ben to get too close to our target, on a one-man, nighttime, rolling surveillance. He could easily be spotted, particularly by someone as situationally aware as Batiste.

Batiste didn't take the 4Runner straight back to the apartments on Blue Bell Street. He instead drove deep into Acres Homes. I then watched as he pulled into his driveway on Tarberry Street. His garage door automatically opened; he drove the 4Runner inside, and then the garage door closed shut. Soon Ben was in the neighborhood, parked just down the street, watching.

In the next half hour, I talked to both FBI Jeff and Big John as we all discussed options. Maybe this was when we pulled the trigger to obtain a search warrant for Batiste's Tarberry residence and execute it as soon as possible, while the 4Runner was still parked inside.

Maybe this was the moment we throw the dice?

Maybe we search his house and get lucky and we come up with the murder weapon?

Jeff called AUSA Rick Hanes, waking him up, and explained the immediate situation to him. Rick was supportive in whatever we decided. There was no right or wrong answer at this moment. It was a gamble. But, just in case we decided to roll the dice and in the morning went with the search warrant option, FBI Jeff headed in to his office to write the search warrant affidavit. I then had several members of the NDTU head in to help Ben with the physical surveillance of Batiste's home—just in case. I also made a call to one of my contacts within Houston SWAT, giving them a heads-up—again, just in case.

It was all for nothing.

Less than thirty minutes after he arrived home, I watched as the garage door at 1341 Tarberry went back up. The 4Runner pulled out and Batiste drove it straight back to the apartments on Blue Bell Street, where he parked it. After that, he drove his Jeep Wrangler back home.

We all went back to bed. I barely slept.

What was Batiste up to now? I understood having to gas up the Toyota 4Runner, but why did he take it back to his house? Why was he there for such a short time? I thought he might be getting it stocked and ready for the next sniper attack. Maybe he was putting equipment that would be needed for their surveillance—food, water, a chemical toilet? But that didn't make sense, because as best we could tell Batiste still hadn't decided on the bank.

As I drove to the station early the next morning, just as the sun was coming up, I snuck inside the apartments on Blue Bell Street. Ms. Busy Body must have still been asleep. I located the 4Runner, parked in its new location. Making sure no one was around, I walked up to it and tried to look inside the back windows, to try to confirm my theory about needed equipment prepositioning. But I couldn't see a thing inside; the window tint was too dark.

Then I walked around the rear of the vehicle.

Bingo!

Before, the sniper porthole in the tailgate had been obvious to us and this was probably the reason Batiste always parked the rear of the 4Runner tight up against some hedges or a fence to better conceal its existence. No casual observer could easily see the hole. But now the sniper porthole in the tailgate was completely covered up. A large piece of magnetic tape, cut square and painted white, covered the entire porthole. The porthole was now all but invisible from the outside, but I could also see that if the sniper inside the vehicle wanted to shoot, it would be an easy thing to move the magnetic covering aside.

Very clever!

I discreetly took a picture of the "new and improved" sniper porthole and left the area, headed to our office.

Even though it was early Saturday morning, I thought I might be the first to arrive at work and only expected a handful of other members of the NDTU to arrive later, who were scheduled to help on the surveillance of

Batiste over the weekend. I thought I would be the only one in the office, where I could drink my coffee in solitude and think.

I was wrong.

The office was packed with people, including all the members of the NDTU and the Crime Analysis Section. Big John, Dom, Captain Baimbridge, Lieutenant Bellamy, and FBI Jeff were there too. No one else had slept well and though the vast majority of these supervisors, officers, or agents had not been scheduled to come in, they came anyway. Every one of them thought maybe today would be the day, and they were all ready to go!

But we were in for a disappointment. After the initial excitement of the sniper vehicle's late Friday night excursion out into the nighttime streets of Houston and then Batiste's subsequent modification of the sniper porthole in the 4Runner, nothing else happened.

Later that same Saturday afternoon, Batiste was back at it, methodically looking over different banks, apparently still looking for that perfect setup. Again, just like every day for the past two months, we continued our surveillance on him. The initial Friday night excitement faded and morale slumped. We were back at it, the same old grind as we covertly trailed Batiste and continued watching and waiting for his next move.

Later that week, Heather Winter and Rick Hanes invited FBI Jeff and me down to the United States Attorney's Office for some discussion and brainstorming about the investigation.

Rick and Heather had been carefully monitoring the progress of our investigation and received daily updates. They also recognized that time was running out and soon Batiste might finally settle on a bank. They surmised that in the days or weeks to come, unless there was a significant investigative breakthrough, we would have to entertain the idea of taking down the entire sniper crew when they were all set up to take the shot at some yet unknown bank. We would have to do a tactical intervention when all the coconspirators were in place.

Again, the successful culmination of such a complicated tactical operation would permanently dismantle this serial murdering robbery crew, hold them all accountable for their past crimes, and ensure no other innocent lives were lost. Not to mention bring closure and some solace to the family members of the victims.

Rick was pretty pumped about Batiste modifying the sniper porthole in the 4Runner. According to Rick, this now showed that he had "foreknowledge." If we arrested Batiste at a future date, he couldn't effectively deny any knowledge of a "sniper porthole" cut into the back of a stolen 4Runner, which we could show that he had "care, custody, and control of" on many occasions. In Rick's prosecutorial mind, this was big stuff.

The responsibility for a future takedown of this sniper crew rested heavily on both Jeff and me. Rick and Heather wanted to know how we felt about it—were we comfortable going all the way through with it; to orchestrate such a sting/tactical operation on the day the armored truck sniper crew were all in position and prepared to take the shot? I reassured both Rick and Heather and explained that I felt better about taking down this robbery crew, while in the act, as compared to all the other robbery crews the NDTU had done to date. I mostly felt this way because even though all the dots had not yet been connected, Jeff had now figured out who some likely crew members were and also had developed a fairly clear picture of how we could expect it all to go down, or at least I thought so.

Again, we talked about how the white Toyota 4Runner was the key. We hoped it would still be our early warning system. When the bad guys moved it out from the apartments on Blue Bell Street, we needed to be on high alert and ready to go.

Jeff also explained that he had an excellent relationship with the upper management of all the Houston-area armored truck companies and talked of the coming time when Batiste and his guys finally settled on the bank, how we (the good guys) would be one step ahead of them.

This was because whenever we could discern, through our around-the-clock surveillance, that Batiste had finally chosen the bank, we would be ahead of the game. Jeff would be able to figure out in just one phone call to the concerned armored truck company that serviced that bank, the daily or approximate time schedule of the targeted armored truck. We would then be ready for our tactical intervention before the bank was next serviced. We would have this critical bit of information days or weeks before the bad guys could definitively figure it out by their own surveillance.

Jeff could make a call and have any or all the Houston region armored truck companies immediately cancel any pending money deliveries. He had the power to immediately shut down all the armored truck money deliveries across the entire city at the same time and direct the respective guards of these armored trucks to not get out of their vehicles until further notice.

This communication would be imperative, particularly if we were not ready for the takedown of the sniper and his observer. By having FBI Jeff in control of the delivery schedule, the innocent guards of the targeted armored truck would never be in any danger.

Jeff reiterated that all the armored truck companies in Houston were on board to assist us in whatever we needed. They might not have known about a sniper, but through Jeff they sensed that something big was in the works. They all wanted to help.

At this meeting, I began thinking outside the box, looking forward to a future tactical operation. I began thinking about using a decoy armored truck to help facilitate the eventual takedown of this sniper robbery crew.

We still kept a "borrowed" Brink's armored truck for use as our own undercover armored personnel carrier, which was all good. But I now began visualizing ahead to our end game—the day when Batiste and his sniper crew were at the bank and were set up to take the shot. How were we going to take them down? What could we do to better facilitate a successful tactical operation, so no innocent persons were injured or killed?

We still wanted three things for any upcoming takedown: Surprise, Speed, and Violence of Action.

If we borrowed yet another armored truck, one from whichever company turned out to be the target for the next sniper attack, we could, on the day of our operation, drive this decoy armored truck up to the ATM or bank and pretend to be about ready to service it. To the bad guys, it would look like the guards inside were about to get out and deliver the monies.

This decoy armored truck could be driven by one of my undercover NDTU officers while wearing a guard's uniform. As long as he stayed inside the decoy (assuming it was rated to defeat rifle fire), he would be safe.

As the armored truck sat there, parked right next to the ATM or bank, the bad guy sniper team—the sniper and the observer—would wait with high expectation for the guard to soon exit with the money bags. They would be totally focused and would have tunnel vision, as they waited to squeeze the trigger and kill the guard, thus initiating the robbery. The rest of the bad guys would be in a similar state of mind: waiting, holding their collective breaths and similarly entrenched with the view and with what was about to happen. At this moment, all the bad guys would not be cognizant as to what was going on around them, particularly behind them.

We would have the element of surprise.

My undercover officer would never exit the decoy armored truck to ever be endangered. But in these few minutes of "target fixation" by the bad guys, our tactical elements, which we would have covertly put in place prior, could then move into action and make their respective approach(s) unnoticed and unobserved.

Then, in a well-timed, coordinated assault, the takedown of the sniper team, the pick-up team, and the shot caller, as well as any suspects who might be doing counter surveillance, would commence. It would also be most important in any future coordinated operation that the bad guy sniper team be neutralized first or at the same time as the others.

By far, the bad guy sniper team was our greatest threat.

It would be the most complicated tactical operation I had ever ran or planned for. It would require careful coordination and synchronization of our various team members. But with the level of operational sophistication the NDTU possessed and along with our ATF and FBI partners, it was feasible.

I was optimistic.

Rick and Heather liked what they heard, that Jeff and I both felt good about what we were going into.

Then Rick threw FBI Jeff a curveball!

"Jeffery, it's not usually done in these types of cases."

"In my experience, I have only done it in big narcotics trafficking/ conspiracy investigations."

"Jeff, I want to go up on Batiste's phone."

"I want a T3!"

Richard Hanes, the lead United States Attorney, was telling FBI Jeff to write out an application for a federal warrant for the electronic surveillance of Redrick Batiste's cell phone. Rick wanted us to listen in on Batiste's phone calls in real time. He thought it was possible that we might uncover some "golden nuggets" in the short time we had left. He also thought if Jeff could do it soon enough, it also might be a big help to us in any future tactical operation or later in the federal prosecution.

Richard Hanes was so right!

I am not sure whether Jeff had ever had to write up a Title III Affidavit (T3) before, but he was up for it. It would be a lot of work on his part (his affidavit ultimately ended up being 100 pages long). Getting a T3 up and running wouldn't happen overnight, or even in a week or two. After Jeff finished writing the affidavit, he would then have to send it to FBI lawyers for their review, back in Washington DC. Then, if it was "blessed" by the FBI higher-ups, it would come back down to Houston, where it would be reviewed by a federal judge for ultimate approval. As soon as a federal judge signed the warrant, then the "switch could be flipped" and a twenty-four-hour surveillance of Batiste's cell phone could commence.

Just listening in on Batiste's personal cell phone would be a manpower-intensive operation. Although the calls were recorded, someone had to be physically present in the FBI's dedicated Listening Room, which was located deep within the bowels of the FBI Houston Field Office, monitoring any potential communication(s) 24/7.

Whoever was in the FBI's super-secret Listening Room monitoring Batiste's phone calls would have to have the commensurate security clearance (FBI agents or FBI TFOs). But whoever was listening also had to be street savvy enough to correctly understand, and then translate to others, the unique blend of Houston north side, street thug, Ebonics slang these bad guys used. This translation could be subjective.

You couldn't take an inexperienced FBI agent, with a degree in accounting, who graduated from some Ivy League university in the Northeast part of the United States and expect he or she would be able to correctly discern what the bad guys were actually talking about.

To fully exploit the T3, assuming FBI Jeff could get it up in time, the people doing the listening would have to quickly figure out what the bad guys were actually saying to each other. The correct and timely interpretation of this unique "thug code" would prove important. The information would be needed to be passed on immediately, in seconds, of its interception to the NDTU, who would be out in the field watching Batiste and who were "cocked and locked" to be able to take whatever action was immediately necessary to protect innocent life.

Running a "wire" or a T3 electronic intercept is a much more complicated process than what is portrayed in the movies.

Potentially, to get the right people listening to Jeff's T3, I might also lose the field surveillance services of some of my best team members, in particular Mark Smith or Ben LeBlanc, who were already FBI TFOs and were probably the best "translators" to listen in on Batiste's thug code conversations. They, along with David Helms and Jessica Bruzas (who were not tactical officers), would also be good fits for the FBI's T3 listening assignment. Not to mention FBI Jeff, who would be "ramrodding" this new dimension to our investigation.

There was another important reason FBI Jeff getting the T3 "off the ground" might be critical.

At this time in history, there were several Black Lives Matter-type protests and subsequent marches in the Houston area (as well as across the country). Many of these Houston-area protests occurred in the southeast part of the city.

One of the primary leaders and facilitators of these protests was Quanell X (Quanell Ralph Evans), a Houston-area black activist, the leader of the area's New Black Panther Party and who was also associated with the Nation of Islam.

Both of these organizations could be termed both "anti-police" and "anti-white." Yet even with his sometimes public anti-police and racism rhetoric, Quanell X enjoyed ready access and communication with members of the Houston Police Department's Command Staff.

Allegedly, in times previous, the Houston Police Department's rank-and-file were appalled, when HPD higher-ups decreed that Quanell X and his entourage (bodyguards) were not required to pass through the metal detectors and submit to other security protocols while entering the main police administration building on Travis Street, when and if Quanell desired to access the Command Staff.

In July 2016 (approximately four months previously), a man by the name of Micah Xavier Johnson killed five law enforcement officers during a Black Lives Matter-type protest march in Dallas, Texas—just a few hours' drive to the north of Houston.

What is not so commonly known was that Micah Xavier Johnson had been a former member of the New Black Panthers (according to Quanell X himself), but had been asked to leave the Houston chapter because he violated the Black Panther's "chain of command" and supposedly wanted the organization to purchase even more weapons and ammunition than they already possessed. Johnson allegedly also wanted to attack black church leaders who he believed were more interested in lining their pockets with money, than serving God.

The added importance of obtaining a T3 in the Batiste investigation came to light when I had received a discreet inquiry from my contacts within HPD's SWAT Detail. As I previously noted, in our earlier surveillance of Batiste, I had given a SWAT supervisor a confidential courtesy call to tell him we were working a crew that might be using a sniper to initiate armored truck robberies and it might be possible that we would need SWAT's assistance.

Weeks after I had made this call, the HPD SWAT Detail had then received a discreet, confidential call from an investigator in HPD's Criminal Intelligence Division. CID had some "soft" intelligence they wanted to share with SWAT: the more radical members from within the Houston-area Black Lives Matter-type movement were planning to kill a law enforcement officer at an upcoming march or protest. Their plan was to kill this unknown law enforcement officer with a sniper firing from a hidden position somewhere along the route of an upcoming protest march in southeast Houston!

In Houston, whenever there is a large protest (no matter the cause), there is a significant contingent of uniformed and plainclothes Houston police officers to monitor the event, to keep the peace and to ensure that the demonstrators can exercise their constitutional rights to free speech. Elements of the SWAT Detail are also sometimes present behind the scene, out of sight, in a "just in case" capacity.

When HPD SWAT heard what HPD CID had to say about a possible sniper attack on law enforcement, someone in SWAT remembered my phone call about the NDTU's surveillance of a robbery crew using a sniper. They then put two and two together. After all, bad guy snipers in the

United States are not that common. The "switched on" SWAT guy rightly believed it possible that they might be related.

Could it be that the Batiste sniper team, which as far as we knew had only been used in armored truck robberies, could also be "hired out" to kill a police officer on behalf of the Houston-area black radicals?

We thought it was possible.

The only thing I could tell the inquirer from SWAT was when the NDTU first started tracking and following Batiste in early September, he had spent a fair amount of time down in the southeast part of the city, driving around aimlessly. It was possible that maybe he was scouting a place for a sniper attack during an upcoming Black Lives Matter protest. But that's all I knew, and it was speculation on my part. But I did add, from what we could discern from social media and other classified information sources, that Redrick Batiste fit the profile, given his anti-police, anti-white, and anti-government ideology.

Batiste and his sniper crew could certainly pull off this type of attack on law enforcement and even get away with it. Just like they had gotten away with the other armored truck robberies and murders.

Now hearing of the street rumors CID had picked up on, of a planned sniper attack on a police officer, the NDTU felt even more the pressure and it heightened the importance and intensity of our surveillance of Batiste, to be able to undo his sniper operation.

Everybody in the task force was feeling the stress. Now we had to consider that Redrick Batiste might be part of a domestic terrorist team intent on "sniping" and killing a police officer. If Jeff could get the T3 up, it was possible we might hear a conversation between Batiste and others, planning the assassination of a police officer.

CHAPTER 26

LITTLE VOICES IN YOUR HEAD

Redrick Batiste was still on the move—still traveling daily to banks all over the Houston area, always shadowed by the NDTU, as we continued to monitor the financial institutions he was scouting.

Sometimes, though, Batiste and his Wrangler traveled into areas of the city where it would be unwise for our surveillance team to follow—particularly, into well-established black neighborhoods in the heart of Acres Homes. Our unfamiliar vehicles would immediately arouse community suspicion and we would be "burned" (identified as undercover police officers)

Our tracking of Batiste saw him sometimes visiting and spending time in and around an abandoned house on Willow Street. These visits were usually in the evening, just before sunset. The area around Willow Street is rural, with large, isolated wooded lots, small pastures for horses, and older, somewhat dilapidated houses. Although we could track Batiste in his Wrangler down into Willow Street, we couldn't get physical eyes on whatever he was doing there. The risk of being spotted was too great and we would jeopardize the operation. Lalo and I theorized that if Batiste himself was the actual sniper, then perhaps he was conducting target practice.

It was an ideal location, even if it was inside the city limits of Houston. Batiste and his crew could shoot their rifle(s) from deep within an abandoned house and out the back door; using a suppressor would mitigate any gunfire sounds and noise complaints to the police by residents in the immediate area. By shooting out through the back door of the abandoned house and out into the adjacent horse pasture, they could have access to nearly a 100-yard firing range and could practice shooting to their heart's content.

As Batiste kept traveling down into this area, Lalo wanted to risk it all and follow him; maybe we could see him in possession of "the" rifle. I wanted no part of it and strongly felt it was too much of a gamble. We tried to get a pole camera up in the area but as it turned out, we couldn't. Lalo still pushed for physical surveillance and I was adamant not to. It was probably the only time that Lalo and I, in the years we worked together, argued. What ultimately swayed him was the other members of our task force. They also opposed the idea, thinking we would get burned.

The abandoned house on Willow Street was one location we never tried to get eyes on Batiste, to not compromise our overall surveillance operation.

There were other locations we didn't follow Batiste into. Again, mostly because we didn't want our undercover surveillance compromised. But sometimes, because of our familiarity with the north side of Houston, we could figure out he was doing mundane, ordinary things, like grocery shopping, getting a haircut, or visiting his mom and dad, etc.

We also knew that Batiste was a "connoisseur of marijuana" and sometimes went to locations, particularly in the Greenspoint area, to buy weed (or so we thought).

Lalo and I, along with the rest of the NDTU, had spent years working undercover in the Greenspoint area of Houston, knocking down street-level dope dealers. We knew of all the nooks and crannies where the dealers liked to sell weed or other drugs.

Sometimes, late in the evening or at night, Batiste and his Wrangler would foray up into a Greenspoint traditional dope hole meeting-type place. There he would stay for a short time and quickly return home, probably to smoke his weed.

I was confident these late evening/nighttime Greenspoint excursions were all about small amounts of marijuana. This activity was not even a blip on our radar, particularly since the decriminalization of marijuana.

But then I began to notice Batiste more frequently visiting a specific Greenspoint location, which was behind a business strip center at the southeast corner of Imperial Valley Drive and the Sam Houston Tollway. Over the years, the NDTU had made several minor drug arrests behind this same strip center. There was actually a fairly large parking lot there, but it was isolated and off the Greenspoint "beaten path." Every time I tracked Batiste, at night, in his Wrangler going to this same parking lot, I mentally crossed this isolated parking lot off my list of suspicious things Batiste was doing. After all, I was confident that I was so familiar with the area and just knew there was nothing there but an isolated parking lot where small-time drug dealers liked to meet their customers.

But…

I hated not knowing for sure. I also reminded myself that I had been wrong the first time I tracked Batiste to the apartments on Blue Bell Street. When I first tracked him there, again late at night, I thought maybe it was to buy some marijuana or for a booty call. I didn't like leaving things to chance. When Chris Rozek and Steve Zakharia backtracked Batiste's path hours later, in the vain hope to find a suspicious white SUV, they had hit pay dirt with the discovery of the 4Runner, with its custom sniper porthole cut into the tailgate.

What if I was wrong about this isolated parking lot behind a Greenspoint strip center?

We had to be right and just couldn't assume anything, particularly if we had the means to easily double-check. I didn't want to get lazy or complacent, thinking we might start cutting corners where it didn't appear to be that important. I suppose, in my mind, I was waiting on FBI Jeff to finish his T3 Affidavit and get it approved by a federal judge, so then we could listen in on Batiste's communication. I anticipated that getting the T3 up would prove to be the next big breaking moment in this case.

Late at night, early November, 2016.

Bink! "Exit Tarberry Geo Fence—Jeep Wrangler." Batiste was leaving the house and on the move.

I was out of bed, headed for my home computer.

I tracked Batiste in his Wrangler as he left the house and traveled north to Greenspoint to that familiar parking lot behind the strip center. There he parked and sat for maybe eight to ten minutes, and then traveled straight back to his home on Tarberry Street, where he stayed for the rest of the night.

I had trouble sleeping again that night. What was Batiste doing there? It just had to be a dope deal!

But a little voice in my head kept saying: "Don't assume anything."

Early that next morning, before the sun was up, I was out of the house and drove to the parking lot Batiste had just visited hours before. By consulting the historical tracking of Batiste's Jeep on my iPhone, I positioned my vehicle at the same location and in the same direction Batiste had been in earlier.

Looking about 100 yards out in front of the nose of my vehicle, just under a parking garage, was an ATM!

I thought I knew the Greenspoint area so well and was so sure there was nothing in this parking lot of interest to Batiste other than purchasing some marijuana.

All of Batiste's nocturnal visits behind this strip center on the North Sam Houston Parkway, which I had previously discarded as irrelevant to our investigation, were trips to survey yet another place to conduct a sniper-initiated robbery of an armored truck.

I had almost missed it.

We quickly determined that the ATM Batiste was looking at was part of a bank that fronted the Sam Houston Parkway Service Road. The bank building itself was large, with multiple stories and with what appeared to be several floors for both administrative and/or business offices above its main business lobby.

Immediately behind the bank was a large five-story parking garage. At first glance, looking from the back parking lot from behind the strip center, it was not immediately apparent to the casual observer that there, at the ground floor of this nondescript parking garage, was one solitary ATM. Also underneath this same parking garage was the bank's customer service driveup window, with one or two tellers behind bulletproof glass, at the same level as the ATM, situated deep underneath the parking garage.

It would be accurate to say that of all the banks and ATMs Batiste had scouted and/or reconnoitered, this one was the most isolated and "out of the way" of all.

So much for my "expert knowledge" of Greenspoint!

The bank that was now becoming the center of Batiste's universe was the Amegy Bank.

A closer review of the historical nighttime tracking of Batiste's Wrangler the week previous had also shown him parking for a short time—again, all late at night—in an apartment complex on Imperial Valley Drive near Benmar Drive. This apartment complex happened to be to the south or rear of the bank's parking garage complex. Running between this apartment complex and the rear of the Amegy Bank was a large, deep, and wide bayou that at this juncture ran from east to west. Besides this natural barrier separating the rear of the strip center parking lot and the Amegy Bank's parking garage from the apartment complex, there was also a six-foot chain link fence that ran along the bayou between the apartment complex and the bank rear parking lot.

By positioning myself in the same place and in the same direction that Batiste's Jeep Wrangler had previously parked in this same apartment complex, I noted that it also afforded a good view of the bank's ATM; the distance between the two points was well over 150 yards away, way across a bayou.

I didn't think the apartment complex location would be a good place for Batiste to place his sniper. For one, the distance (150+ yards) was a lot farther than the other sniper shootings that we knew about. More importantly, there was also that chain link fence between the two locations. If the sniper fired from this spot, his bullet(s) might inadvertently strike the fence during their flight, which would cause the projectile to destabilize and/or ricochet, missing the targeted armored truck guard. If the sniper fired numerous rounds in rapid succession, it would be reasonable to assume that one or more of the bullets would pass unscathed through the fence without striking it. Batiste, to me, seemed to be too calculating for such a chance, and unless we saw that after one of these late-night visits that the fence had been cut, similar to seeing hedges clandestinely trimmed at the other bank location, I believed that the apartment complex was not where the sniper would shoot from.

However, the apartment complex location was an ideal place to monitor the ATM as well as having a commanding view of the rear of the strip center's back parking lot. It was the perfect location to sit and conduct surveillance, particularly if you wanted to lock down the weekly schedule of any armored truck that delivered to the Amegy Bank and its ATM.

I also thought on the day when Batiste and his crew were in position and ready to take the shot, this apartment complex location would be where Batiste himself would be positioned. I still viewed Batiste as probably the operational commander or shot caller for this robbery crew and the apartments would be an ideal location to get an overview of the entire operation. If I were heading up and coordinating this sniper/robbery crew and calling the shots, this is where I would position myself.

If Batiste brought out his sniper crew to the Amegy Bank, I was sure that the sniper and observer/spotter would be hidden within the 4Runner, which would then be pre-positioned in the 400 North Sam Houston Parkway strip center rear parking lot, approximately 100 yards to the east of the Amegy Bank's ATM.

In this rear parking lot, there was a perfect location to take the shot: a parking spot next to a utility pole, between a trash dumpster and small fenced-in area, all in the middle of the parking lot. The bad guys could back the Toyota 4Runner into this parking spot and the sniper team would then have an unobstructed view or shot at the ATM. This "perfect" location was not so much conjecture on my part as it was actually the same parking spot that I had tracked Batiste's Wrangler to, in the middle of the night.

We almost missed it, but now we could add the Amegy Bank to the long list of banks that Batiste was surveying or had surveyed.

CHAPTER 27

TRACKING DEVICES DISCOVERED?

In mid-November, everything changed.

A new pattern emerged.

Redrick Batiste stopped looking at any other banks and now the only one he clandestinely visited was the Amegy Bank, but still only at night.

Then, a few days later, he started visiting the same location during daylight hours.

Maybe the Amegy Bank was slated to be the one? The Original Informant had told us that Batiste and his crew planned on doing a sniper-initiated armored truck robbery every three or four months and now we were deep into November, getting closer to the three months' mark since the August 29 murder of David Guzman at the Wells Fargo Bank. Was the Original Informant's information accurate?

I felt we were getting warm!

As soon as Batiste shifted his sole attention to the Amegy Bank, I felt great confidence in my assessment. This would be the place! I was soon on the phone with FBI Jeff, who I hadn't wanted to bother with irrelevant minutia. Jeff was still buried deep inside the FBI Houston Field Office, working daily on finishing his hundred-page T3 Affidavit. He was getting ready to send it off to Washington DC for review.

"Jeff, I think it's going to be the Amegy Bank!"

I then laid out to my FBI friend what the NDTU had now discovered—Batiste's initial interest in the Amegy Bank and now his single-minded, day and night preoccupation with it. I also carefully explained to him, that if it was going to be the Amegy Bank, then I suspected that Batiste would be parked in the apartment complex to the south, across the bayou, acting as the shot caller, while the 4Runner with the sniper and observer/spotter would be in the parking lot to the east of the Amegy's ATM. Of course, at this point, we both really had no idea where the pick-up team or other members of the crew (counter surveillance) would be situated on the day or what vehicles they would be driving. But now some pieces were really starting to fall into place.

FBI Jeff and I talked strategy.

We decided that we would now, on that day, immediately begin a continuous daytime covert surveillance of the Amegy Bank. The hope was that over the days or weeks ahead we would be able to spot and iden-tify other members of the sniper/robbery crew, doing their part, helping Batiste with the surveillance of the bank. This was so the bad guys could nail down the all-so-important regular scheduled deliveries of the armored truck that serviced it.

We knew that until the bad guys had a firm grasp of the approximate schedule of the armored truck and had a good idea about what day it would show up to service the bank, not until they had taken into account all fore-seen eventualities, were they going to roll out the Toyota 4Runner with its sniper, along with all the rest of the crew. When all of this was done, when all the mission preparation was completed, then that would be the day they were coming out in force with their guns, ready to commit another murder/robbery. We also believed that during the process of mission prep, the bad guys wanted to limit their potential exposure to any random discovery by a suspicious citizen or a curious patrol officer.

After calling Jeff, I went up to Captain Baimbridge's office and let him know what I was thinking. As I filled him in, his big question was, "WHEN?" When would Redrick Batiste bring out his sniper and the rest of the robbery crew and try to take down another armored truck? I really didn't know. The only firm clue was the statement made by the Original Informant (every three to four months).

But, because I took whatever informants said with a grain of salt, I hedged my bets, took a deep breath, and looked my captain in the eye. "Boss, my best scientific wild ass guess is that they will try to pull the trigger in December, probably before January."

So began our continuous daylight watch of the Amegy Bank, whether or not Redrick Batiste was present. Fortunately, the parking garage itself was a perfect place to set up our surveillance. Through a discreet contact with a trusted person within the Amegy Bank corporate office, we could acquire remote access cards that would let us drive to the upper levels of the parking garage. Then, by carefully positioning two of our undercover vehicles on the fourth floor, the plain clothes officers within them were all but invisible to anyone down in the parking lot below, or even in the apartment complex to the south across the bayou. Two or more mobile undercover officers were always positioned down in the parking lot or the apartment complex so if needed, they could stealthily position themselves to look over any suspicious vehicles that were brought to the attention of the guys in their perch way up in the fixed position of the garage's fourth floor.

The rest of us kept a sharp eye on Batiste wherever he was, looking to see whether he shifted his interest away from the Amegy to yet another bank. Fortunately, he never did. Every day that we watched Batiste, as he continued to watch the Amegy Bank exclusively, we grew more and more confident that this would be the place.

As we grew in our assurance that the Amegy Bank was going to be it, the NDTU officers and ATF and FBI agents began to "grossly familiarize" themselves with the area around the bank as well as that part of the Greenspoint area. We were looking forward and planning for the day when we would do the takedown.

Jeff, who was also a member of the Houston's FBI's Office regional SWAT Team, brought over eight other agents who were also FBI SWAT team members. Several of these men, I noted, had impressive military pedigrees.

The FBI SWAT members would be the rough equivalent of Houston's SWAT Detail.

The FBI guys were familiar with the Batiste investigation and would be of great help.

Between all the members of NDTU, Big John and Dom from ATF, and a bunch of SWAT-trained FBI agents, we had enough personnel—or more precisely, tactically skilled operators—to do the takedown of the entire armored truck sniper crew, with all of its moving parts, on the day.

These newly added FBI agents worked to intimately familiarize themselves with the area around the Amegy Bank, as well as Redrick Batiste and his other possible coconspirators. Better yet, everybody involved was totally focused on the mission at hand and we all enjoyed an unprecedented level of cooperation between members of different agencies.

It was all good!

FBI Jeff found out Loomis serviced that Amegy Bank and confirmed its schedule. We now knew the day of the week and approximate time frame the armored truck would deliver money to the Amegy Bank, something Batiste and his crew still had yet to figure out.

Also, with the total cooperation of their corporate security office, I soon had my own

Loomis armored truck, hidden out of sight, parked inside an enclosed vehicle bay at the North Police Station right next to our office. All in case we used it as bait on the day. This armored truck was smaller than the Brink's that we already possessed. Fortunately, it, too, was rated to defeat rifle fire.

The guards who worked and who were assigned to ride in Houston-area armored trucks were nervous. They all knew about a violent robbery crew that was intent in gunning them down. None of them knew about a sniper and all assumed the previous attacks had been close-range assassination-type "hits." In late 2016, whether it was real or imagined, some Houston-area armored car guards began to believe that suspects were following them in vehicles as they made their cash deliveries. This paranoia was understandable.

We took this information seriously and couldn't discount the possibility of this type of bad guy rolling surveillance on armored trucks. We figured it probable that other members of Batiste's crew would be assigned to get eyes on the Loomis armored truck, prior to its arrival at the Amegy Bank. The best place for them to do this (if they hadn't already figured it out) would be to have one of the other members of the crew "posted up" at these other banks. Then, when the Loomis armored truck showed up there, they could follow it as it headed up to Greenspoint and the Amegy Bank. This way, Batiste and the other members who were set up at the Amegy Bank could be forewarned and ready to spring the sniper-initiated robbery.

Because of FBI Jeff's contact within Loomis, we had the complete route for the Loomis armored truck that serviced the Amegy Bank. Of particular interest to us was the bank that was normally serviced immediately before the Amegy Bank. Maybe Batiste and his crew had someone watching this bank.

As a safeguard, the NDTU began carefully watching this other bank. But we could never figure out in the time remaining and with our available undercover manpower whether the bad guys were watching it.

As it turned out, they were!

Despite our attempt at secrecy, the patrol officers at the North Police Station had eventually figured out that "their" DTU was working on something big, something involving armored truck robberies. The rumors about our operation also started leaking out well beyond our patrol station. It had recently come to our attention that it had become a pastime for detectives in some investigative divisions, as well as patrol officers at other stations, to secretly "listen in" on the NDTU's secure radio channel, out of professional curiosity, as we ran our Batiste surveillance operation from day to day.

One Saturday, one of the "in the know" patrol officers called me on his cell phone. "Sarge, can you come talk to this guy?" The uniformed patrol officer had been dispatched to meet an armored truck crew in the Greenspoint area. The involved guard was sure that he was being watched by a black male driving a Chrysler 300 with paper license plates. The suspicious vehicle was no longer trailing or watching the armored truck, but the patrol officer now on the scene with the armored truck guards wanted very much to make sure that the information was heard by the "right ears" (mine).

I perked up when the officer told me it was a Loomis armored truck!

When I arrived on the scene, I introduced myself to the guard, but only told him I was a "detective" who investigated robberies. The poor kid was a nervous wreck. He reminded me a bit of a young Justin Williams, because of his red hair and matching beard, and just like Justin, he talked fast. I slowed him down, got him to relax a bit, got him talking about his wife and young children, his job, etc. Then I slowly walked him through, question by question, as to what he had observed. After we were finished, I was certain that the Chrysler 300 had not been following his armored truck.

The Loomis guard and I continued to talk for quite a while. Like I said, he was a young man and just like David Guzman, he was just starting out in life and wanted one day to become a police officer. I gave him some career advice and then we started talking about the handgun he had been issued, as well as the body armor he wore. He was pretty proud of his ballistic vest and said his company had just bought it for him. It was brand-new, the best on the market! He was glad to have it, because of all the armored car guard shootings and killings. I asked him whether I could examine his new body armor and then noted it was only rated to defeat handgun ammunition, not rifle. Tactfully, without giving any confidential information away about what I knew, I casually remarked to him it might be good if he could get a vest that was rifle rated. He sort of looked at me quizzically, wanting more information, but I couldn't say more.

We had to be careful not to let any knowledge about a sniper, or Batiste and/or our surveillance, leak into the Houston armored truck guard community, particularly within Loomis. There was always the possibility that, unknown to us, there might be an insider within, back-feeding information about armored truck routes and schedules to Batiste and his men.

I identified with this young man on a real and personal level. It made succeeding in our operation even more urgent. The responsibility was sobering. I later shared the conversation and my observations about this young "Justin" with the other members of our task force. If possible, it increased everyone's resolve to successfully complete the operation all the more.

Batiste was getting ready and so were we!

Then—a near disaster! One morning, Batiste and his Wrangler was back up at the Amegy Bank; he sat in the apartment complex, studying the area, waiting to observe an armored truck delivery. By afternoon, nothing of interest had occurred and Batiste left the area and appeared to be driving back home. As he left, we tracked him and presumed he was "heading to the barn." But unexpectedly, his Jeep suddenly detoured, and it was stationary at an unknown business along the North Freeway in the southern part of Greenspoint.

What was he up to now?

A few of us broke off to see what was happening.

It was one of our worst fears.

The "business" was actually a car dealership. Batiste's Wrangler was parked inside the Vehicle Service area.

Redrick Batiste was getting the oil changed in his Jeep and there were three ATF tracking devices in Pelican boxes, all stuck to the bottom of its undercarriage.

We knew if that Jeep went up on a car lift for servicing, the tracking devices would be easily visible to the mechanics. If they were to check the fluid level of the rear wheel differential, it was almost a certainty our tracking devices would be discovered because that was the same area where we had mounted them. If the mechanics discovered our tracking devices, they might alert the owner/customer to the "strange black boxes" with magnet thingies all stuck to the bottom of his vehicle.

As other members of the NDTU kept watch from outside, I parked my vehicle and walked into the Service Area, straight to the customer waiting room. As I walked in, there was Redrick Batiste, waiting for the work on his Jeep to be completed. Fortunately, just like when he had lunch with Heather Winter, our AUSA, he sat with his back to the bay window that looked out into the Service Area where his Jeep was being serviced and was seated where he could face and monitor the doorway into and out of the waiting room.

I hadn't expected having to be up-close and personal with a serial killer ("in the wild") and wasn't dressed for such an occasion. I was wearing my ever-present *Star Wars* T-shirt and old, well-worn blue jeans. As I walked in, Batiste gave me a careful look-over, as he lifted his head up from some book he was reading with a blue and white cover. I met his gaze and gave him a polite smile, appropriate for the situation—two customers waiting for their vehicles to be serviced.

I guess Batiste passed me off as a harmless old white guy who was really into the original 1970s *Star Wars* movie, because with a nod of his head and a grunt of acknowledgment, he went back to reading his book.

I sat across from him. The waiting room was small and from my position, I could look over Batiste's shoulder out the bay window and into the service area, where I could then see his Wrangler already being elevated on the lift for servicing.

I pulled out my reading glasses and pretended to be engrossed in my iPhone, as I sent messages and gave updates as to what was happening to my guys outside.

Out of the corner of my eye, I was looking for any clues in the body movements of the mechanics who were working on Batiste's Jeep—movements that might indicate they had noticed something unusual, like tracking devices.

The minutes ticked by slowly.

Then I saw it.

One mechanic stiffened slightly, altered his position, and looked directly up at one of our trackers just above his head. Heck, even from my position, I could just make out the tracker myself. This mechanic called over his buddy and now they were both looking at the same tracker, probably saying, "*What's that?*"

Batiste had his back to the entire scene unfolding directly behind him, still unaware.

Something had to be done to forestall the mechanics from alerting Batiste.

I walked out of the customer waiting room, directly into the service area. There I quickly identified the service manager and approached him, while discreetly holding out my police identification and telling him who I was.

I am not sure the FBI would have approved, but in a few short sentences I told him what was happening.

"We were following the ringleader of a robbery crew who we suspected had orchestrated the killings of several armored truck guards. We had tracking devices on the ringleader's Jeep, of which your mechanics were now servicing up on the vehicle lift. I believe that your mechanics had just taken notice of our tracking devices and I was afraid they would spill the beans and tell my 'bad guy' about them. The ringleader is at this very moment sitting in the customer waiting room with his back toward us."

God bless Mr. Service Manager. He believed me and didn't ask questions. He just said, "No problem. I will take care of it!" And he did!

As I walked back to the waiting area to "hang out" with Redrick, the service manager gathered his mechanics in a huddle. I watched as they talked for a few seconds. Then the huddle broke up, and the mechanics went back to Batiste's Jeep and finished the job, never again looking at the trackers above their heads.

Soon the work was done. The Jeep Wrangler was down off the lift. Batiste paid the cashier, got into his vehicle with all of its still yet undiscovered secret ATF-issued trackers on it and drove off. Soon the guys outside picked up the surveillance, and they tracked Batiste as he headed back to his house on Tarberry Street.

After Batiste left, I felt I owed Mr. Service Manager and his mechanics a word of thanks and some closure for their "instant" cooperation. After talking to them briefly, I then swore all of them to silence on the matter. The last thing Mr. Service Manager said to me as I walked out was, "Hope you guys get that asshole!"

Maybe Redrick Batiste should have sat on the other side of the customer waiting room, where he could have watched the work being done on his Jeep Wrangler.

But he didn't!

Maybe Redrick Batiste should have taken more notice of the harmless-looking old white guy with the *Star Wars* T-shirt. Who, upon closer scrutiny, was also wearing United States Marine Corps-issued combat boots and that the bulge on his right side, under his shirt, was a cocked and locked 1911 automatic pistol, stuck deep in his waistband.

But he didn't!

A few days after the near discovery of our trackers, our static surveillance of the Amegy Bank began to pay off. That morning, while Batiste was still at home on Tarberry Street, Justin Williams and Big John, up on the fourth floor of the parking garage, spotted a suspicious vehicle parked in the apartment complex to the south of the bank and across the bayou. What made this Toyota Camry interesting (it was not the blue Toyota Camry used as the pick-up vehicle in David Guzman's murder) was that the driver seated in it (a large black male) was positioned in such a way to watch the Amegy Bank's ATM several floors beneath them. They could see the Camry's license plate number and ran the registration on their laptop computer to see who owned it.

Just like FBI Jeff had predicted, other members of Batiste's robbery crew had been "activated"! The suspicious vehicle belonged to none other than Marc Hill. Presumably he was also the guy in it, watching the ATM and waiting for an armored truck to service it, so he could report back to Batiste.

FBI Jeff's earlier cell phone analysis had showed Marc Hill's personal cell phone in and around Wells Fargo Bank when David Guzman was killed. Jeff had theorized that Hill would be a core member of the robbery crew and that he might show up at the Amegy Bank to help Batiste in the surveillance.

Special Agent Coughlin was right.

At first, Batiste's and Hill's presence at the Amegy Bank, during the day, was a bit hit or miss. But then, over the next few days, they settled in. Hill and Batiste took turns, from morning till late afternoon, as they kept a constant watch over the Amegy Bank. Sometimes their surveillance would overlap and they both would be at the bank.

It was obvious they were trying hard to nail down the delivery schedule of the armored truck.

434

We were confident that Batiste and Hill were still only scouting because they were the only ones from the robbery crew (that we knew of) who were out at the bank and we had the reassurance that the Toyota 4Runner was still parked at the apartments on Blue Bell Street.

On the day before Thanksgiving, Marc Hill and Rodrick Batiste's efforts were finally rewarded.

On this day, both Batiste, who was driving his Wrangler, and Hill, who was now driving his black Infiniti QX56 (normally Marc Hill's wife drove their Toyota Camry), were in position, conducting surveillance at the Amegy Bank.

Finally, after so many days, a Loomis armored truck had arrived and we all carefully watched both Hill and Batiste as they watched the guards making a money delivery to the Amegy Bank.

The entire time the guard was outside the armored truck, doing his job delivering the bags of money, was a bit surreal. There was total radio silence. We were all on a razor's edge.

Out of an abundance of caution, just in case Batiste or Hill had something immediately nefarious on their minds, something we hadn't envisioned, out of sight and unknown to either of them, several undercover NDTU officers and ATF agents had them both in the gunsights of their rifles and were prepared to neutralize either one or both at a moment's notice—if we needed to protect the guards.

The Loomis guard was blissfully unaware of the two predators watching him.

As soon as the Loomis armored truck crew finished their work at the bank, they prepared to leave and were about to make off to their next delivery.

But these guards were having a bad day!

As they tried to pull off, their armored truck broke down right next to the ATM. From what we could tell, it appeared that the driver could not shift the truck into drive and it was stuck in park.

They were stranded!

Now the armored truck was stuck and for the next hour, everybody sat tight. The guards inside the armored truck waited for help to arrive, while Hill and Batiste continued to watch, while all the undercover officers carefully monitored everybody!

I am sure this entire scene was all so stimulating to Hill and Batiste! To see all of that money (it must have been several millions of dollars) stranded, so close and yet so far. It must have been so exciting that one of them called another member of the robbery crew to come see what was happening!

Eventually, Loomis dispatched another armored truck to the Amegy Bank scene. Batiste and Hill must have been salivating as they then watched the guards form a line, swing open the rear door of the broken-down truck, and then pass all the money bags inside it into the newly arrived one.

While this was all transpiring and as we waited and watched as the money was being transferred between the two armored trucks, Ben LeBlanc spotted another suspicious vehicle, speeding into the area. This vehicle, a Chevy van with Ohio license plates, also took up a position to watch the Amegy Bank and the transfer of money between the armored trucks.

A computer inquiry on the Chevy van's license plate revealed it to be registered to Nelson Polk.

Nelson Polk's name had popped up in FBI Jeff's analysis of the cell phone traffic in the area of the August 29 Wells Fargo murder of David Guzman.

Now here, on the day before Thanksgiving, we had three of the presumed core members of the armored truck sniper crew at the Amegy Bank watching a money delivery.

After the functioning armored truck with all the money had driven off and left the area, Batiste, Hill, and Polk then drove to the north side of the Greenspoint Mall parking lot on the other side of the Sam Houston Parkway to the north. There, in the middle of the mall's parking lot, Polk stood outside of his Chevy van (we began calling it the Scooby-Doo van), talking to Batiste, who sat in his Wrangler, and with Hill, who sat in his black Infiniti. As I watched them from a distance through my binoculars, it appeared to me that Polk was pretty excited about seeing all that money, given his highly animated hand gestures and mannerisms.

Mark Smith and Ben LeBlanc thought fast. Ben jumped into the back of Mark's car and they drove by the three suspects while they were all talking in the parking lot. Ben was then able to take several pictures of the meeting.

After the meeting, Batiste, Hill, and Polk broke off and went their separate ways. We then tracked Batiste to his home on Tarberry Street, where he stayed for the rest of the day.

I guess that on November 23, Redrick Batiste, Marc Hill, and Nelson Polk felt good about their day's work. They probably thought they had their first clue regarding the regular delivery schedule of monies to the Amegy Bank.

Maybe every Wednesday was one of the days?

If they thought that—they were right!

Time was running out. It could very well be that the next Wednesday would be the day for the unveiling of the sniper and the shooting of the guard servicing the Amegy Bank.

Still, who was the sniper? Who was the actual trigger man?

If I had to guess at that moment in time, I leaned toward Nelson Polk. Marc Hill was big and fat. It would be hard for him to lay down in the back of the Toyota 4Runner, even with the rear seats down. I still figured that Redrick Batiste was the shot caller or the leader.

But Nelson Polk was more of an unknown. FBI Jeff thought Polk's build and mannerisms somewhat matched the depiction in the bank surveillance video of the shooter in the November 6, 2015 armored truck robbery. It was at this bank where a gunman, armed with a short-barreled .223 rifle, in a close-range assassination attempt, had tried to kill the guard of yet another Loomis armored truck that was delivering money bags to a Bank of America on North Shepherd Drive.

The guard in this case was wounded, and the shooter escaped.

But we still didn't know; it was all conjecture. We felt that there would still be other members of Batiste's robbery crew yet to emerge.

Also, to help in our surveillance of the Amegy Bank, we decided to put up pole cameras in the back parking lot. One would have a view to the east to capture and record the parking spot where we were certain the Toyota 4Runner would be parked and from where the sniper would shoot from. The other camera was to be positioned to look south across the bayou into the apartment complex where we assumed Batiste would be parked on the day. The placing of these cameras would also lessen the chance of our fourth-floor parking garage surveillance being spotted, as well as ensuring the historical video recording of any events that might be of value to Rick and Heather in their later prosecution of Batiste and his crew.

The only problem was that we had no more pole cameras; both HPD and ATF were out.

All the cameras were spoken for. The only ones immediately readily available were the FBI's. Because it was secret FBI "techie, techie" surveillance equipment, it was required that FBI agents and technicians themselves physically install them.

Very early in the morning of the FBI's scheduled pole camera install, well before dawn, FBI Jeff, along with his other agent/technician buddies, were up in a generic bucket truck, setting up the cameras in Amegy's back parking lot. Of course, it was raining, and the installation was delayed.

Then, for whatever reason, Batiste thought he would get an early start on his watch at the Amegy. I watched with growing alarm as we tracked his Wrangler as it moved out of Acres Homes and began heading north to Greenspoint.

I immediately called Jeff.

"Hey, dude, Redrick is heading your way. He's maybe ten minutes out!

But it was all good. Jeff and his guys were just then finishing up their camera install and as Redrick Batiste pulled into the Amegy Bank parking lot, they were pulling out. Perfect timing!

Soon I had another laptop computer issued by the FBI, back at my house, so I could monitor 24/7 the FBI's pole cameras at the Amegy Bank.

On Saturday, November 26, 2016, Redrick Batiste's Amegy Bank surveillance continued to pay off—or so he thought.

We tracked Batiste's Wrangler to the rear parking lot. As soon as it arrived, the undercover officers hidden on the fourth floor of the parking garage spotted him. Again, we were still confident that Batiste was still scouting the bank, considering he was the only one of his robbery crew who was actually out at the Amegy Bank this day. We knew that a sniper-initiated robbery was not about to go down. Especially since the Toyota 4Runner was still at the apartments on Blue Bell Street, and Nelson Polk or Marc Hill were nowhere to be seen.

When the Loomis armored truck arrived, Chris and Zak carefully moved in behind the parked black Jeep Wrangler, with Batiste in it, and clandestinely took several photos, all capturing an interesting scene: Batiste watching the armored truck guards delivering money to the Amegy Bank.

November 26, 2016 - Redrick Batiste in his black Jeep Wrangler, watching a money delivery by a Loomis Armored Truck (far left) to the Amegy Bank.

While this was happening, there was total radio silence. We were all on a razor's edge.

As before, out of his sight and unknown to him, at the exact moment his picture was being taken, undercover NDTU and ATF agents had Redrick in their gunsights—just in case.

As soon as the Loomis armored truck guards finished their work at the Amegy Bank, they left (their truck didn't break down this time) and were off to the next delivery. Batiste left the area and went back home. We all breathed a sigh of relief.

I guess that on November 26, 2016 Redrick Batiste again felt good about his day's work. He probably thought he had another clue regarding the regular delivery schedule of monies to the bank.

Maybe every Saturday was also one of the days?

Fortunately, I knew something that Batiste didn't. Through FBI Jeff's contacts, we knew that the Saturday's money delivery was an anomaly and not part of the bank's regular delivery schedule. Thanksgiving (November 24) had been on the Thursday previous and banks as well as their ATMs normally experience a run on cash during these types of holidays. Bank customers also need money for Black Friday, the day after Thanksgiving, which is a big retail shopping day. Like other financial institutions, the Amegy Bank anticipated being low on cash immediately after the Thanksgiving holiday and Black Friday, and had requested Loomis make a special delivery. If Batiste thought a Saturday was a day to bring out his sniper team and the rest of his crew, he was wrong.

Batiste didn't realize it but he really had only one solid lead about the Loomis armored truck's actual regular delivery schedule to the Amegy Bank. Indeed, Wednesday was the day.

But if the next Wednesday would be the day when the bad guys were set up to shoot, then FBI Jeff could easily call Loomis's head of security and cancel the delivery, no questions asked, to protect the guards.

We were still ahead of Batiste and still had time to carefully plan our operation. We had everybody who was to be involved in the upcoming tactical operation (NDTU, FBI, ATF) carefully go out to the Amegy Bank and memorize the area so they would know the area intimately: the bank, the ATM, the parking garage, the nearby apartment complex, the roads, the parking lot, entrances, exits—everything!

I can't stress enough, how in these types of planned tactical-type undercover sting scenarios, the importance that everyone involved have a good working knowledge of the area of operation!

Don't assume that your people are familiar with the area. If given enough time, make them go physically to the location and rehearse well before the day of operation, to the exact location and "live it"! Looking at an overhead map or pictures is not the same thing and not nearly as beneficial.

Do everything to help ensure that your team(s) keep and maintain Surprise, Speed and Violence of Action! Minimize the chance for mistakes.

I began writing and formatting a Tactical Action Plan for a take-down of the entire sniper-initiated armored truck robbery crew, to occur at the Amegy Bank. Tracking orders were obtained for the three vehicles that Marc Hill was known to possess, as well as Nelson Polk's Scooby-Doo van. We could only sneak in and put a tracker on one of Hill's vehicles (the Toyota Camry) while it was parked in his driveway. The one tracking device we placed on Hill's Camry eventually malfunctioned and went dead. But it didn't matter, because it was almost exclusively driven by Varfeeta Sirleaf, Marc Hill's wife. We were never able to get tracking devices on any of Hill's other vehicles or Polk's Scooby-Doo van. It was too risky given where they kept them parked.

CHAPTER 28

A 3/32 INCH STAINLESS-STEEL PIPE AND STINGRAY

Sunday morning, November 27, we were all at the office. Moments earlier, we had watched our pole camera as Batiste left his home on Tarberry Street home and headed north. It was a Sunday, so we weren't expecting him to go to the Amegy Bank; he probably knew the bank was closed and there would not be any armored truck deliveries on this day.

What we were not expecting was that he was heading to the apartments on Blue Bell Street and the 4Runner. This was something different. All of Batiste's previous visits to Blue Bell Street had been in the dead of night, when it was dark. But here he was, driving into the apartments at Blue Bell in the light of day.

We switched to the Blue Bell Street ATF camera hidden in our drop surveillance vehicle and watched as Batiste remotely unlocked the door of the 4Runner, got into the driver's seat, and tried to drive off.

Apparently Batiste had goofed in his vehicle maintenance protocol and the battery in the sniper vehicle didn't have enough juice to start the engine.

He needed a jump!

A short time later, coming into camera view, was the infamous Scooby-Doo van, driven by Nelson Polk!

Soon Batiste and Polk had the hoods of both the van and the 4Runner up. Someone produced a set of jumper cables and the sniper vehicle's engine was soon running.

Then, with Batiste driving the 4Runner and with Polk driving his van, they both left, moving out of the view of our hidden camera.

Bink! "Exit Blue Bell Geo Fence—Toyota 4Runner."

As we tracked the Toyota 4Runner leaving Blue Bell Street, it headed south toward Acres Homes, maybe heading to Batiste's home on Tarberry Street. Several members of the NDTU already had rolling surveillance on it, but as Batiste traveled deeper into the neighborhood, I called them off. There was not enough other vehicle traffic in the neighborhood for our undercover officers to blend in. They would be spotted.

Batiste didn't take the Toyota 4Runner back to his home. Soon it was stationary at a location on Conklin Street, a short distance from his home. After a few minutes, I did a quick drive-by at the location and saw that the 4Runner was now parked in a junk yard surrounded by a chain link fence. Within its perimeter were several decrepit vehicles, trailers, and even one large, raggedy-looking recreational motor home. Nestled deep in the yard, parked between the other vehicles and trailers, was the sniper vehicle— almost out of view from my location out in the street. All I could see of it was its roof. As I drove by, Nelson Polk had finished locking the front gate of the yard with a large padlock and chain, and was about to get into his Scooby-Doo van to drive off. Redrick Batiste sat in the passenger seat.

We didn't know why, but the bad guys had moved their sniper vehicle to another location.

We were on the phone with our special friend in CID, who told us that another pole camera had just become available. By the next morning, it was set up to keep watch over the Toyota 4Runner as it sat, hidden, in the middle of a Conklin Street junk yard.

We realized that there was a strong possibility that on the upcoming Wednesday, a few days away (November 30), the Batiste-led sniper/robbery crew would be in position at the Amegy Bank, waiting on the Loomis armored truck. Maybe this was why they had moved the 4Runner?

Our surveillance continued as we waited to see what would happen next Wednesday.

Initially my plan, "on the day," was to drive up our decoy Loomis armored truck to the Amegy's ATM. We wanted to get all the bad guys looking that way, intently focused and watching the armored truck; I wanted them to have tunnel vision. Then, when it was least expected, we were going to "shake, rattle and roll" the sniper and his observer by ramming the 4Runner with our 25,000-pound, diesel-powered, undercover Brink's armored truck. Preferably hitting the 4Runner so hard that we rolled it over on its side. If our Brink's armored truck hit the 4Runner on the rear passenger's side door, it would push the 4Runner into an opposing curb and, because of its already high center of gravity, would likely flip it over on to its side.

Then, as the bad guy sniper team in the 4Runner were experiencing this "shake, rattle and roll" and were disoriented, a tactical team composed of FBI agents and NDTU officers, who would be close behind our Brink's armored truck in unmarked vehicles, would deploy. After this planned "crash," they would be the ones to deal with the tactical problem of extracting and/or arresting the sniper and anyone else who might be in the 4Runner. There could be a shootout; after all, the sniper was a known killer with nothing to lose.

We rehearsed ad nauseam, perfecting the timing and routes that our team of agents and officers would take to correctly position themselves relative to the Toyota 4Runner, as well as the Brink's armored truck at the moment of the crash. We also planned extensively to avoid endangering any innocent citizens in the immediate area.

At the same time our Brink's undercover armored truck was ramming the sniper vehicle, our other tactical teams would take down:

- Batiste, who would be likely sitting in his parked Wrangler, in the apartment complex parking lot across the bayou from the ATM. We assumed he would be waiting, watching, and coordinating his operation, i.e., calling the shots.

- The pick-up team, who would be positioned somewhere nearby, in a still unknown vehicle. They would be poised and ready to grab the money bags from beside the body of the dead guard, after the sniper killed him.

- Any other members of the robbery crew, who might be out at the bank that day. They would be there to conduct counter surveillance on the behalf of Batiste, being on the lookout for any potential law enforcement intervention in the area. We suspected that there could be several unknown suspects performing this function and needed other task force officers to arrest them.

All of our tactical teams needed to closely coordinate their respective engagement(s) of the different elements of Batiste's robbery crew (sniper crew, shot caller, pick-up team, lookouts, etc.). Preferably, all of these engagements needed to occur at nearly the same moment. But if our timing turned out to be a bit off, then it was most important that the sniper be the first to be neutralized, before any of the other robbery crew members, including Batiste. The sniper team needed to be engaged first, because that way we at least kept the initial element of surprise there.

We perceived the sniper as the greatest threat we faced.

We had a plan to time and coordinate these simultaneous take-downs, in particular the sniper crew and Batiste, because we knew where they would be positioned. To accomplish this, after the different tactical teams were in the correct position ("last line of departure"), we would conduct a careful countdown over the radio—*ten, nine, eight, seven...*—which was monitored by everyone in the operation. That way, each respective team leader already knew in advance from their previous rehearsal(s) at what point in the countdown their team would need to leave their line of departure to arrive at their objective at the same time as the other teams. Just to ensure that our timing was correct, we all went out on Sunday to the Amegy Bank, when none of the bad guys were there. There, each team worked out its timing and again reviewed the route they were to take.

We practiced and tried to account for all the operational details of this complicated, tactical operation.

It would be probable that the bad guys would all have a line of sight to each other as well as open lines of communication. If our timing was way off, then the other unengaged members of the robbery crew would have prior warning and time to react.

We didn't want that to happen.

There was one nagging problem in my mind. We would ram the sniper vehicle hard with a large and heavy armored vehicle and try to flip it over. This pre-planned act could be construed negatively ("second-guessed") by my Command Staff or the department's lawyers in the aftermath. They might view this ramming as the use of deadly force and it might not have been necessary. Also, technically, the General Orders of the Houston Police Department prohibited the deliberate ramming of suspects' vehicles to aid in apprehension or arrest.

So, instead of taking the risk of ramming the sniper vehicle and then surrounding it with officers and agents from the FBI and NDTU, to see what the suspects inside were going to do, I began to think it would be much safer for the involved law enforcement officers and any innocent citizens in the area to neutralize the sniper while he was lying inside the back of the 4Runner. When we drove up and parked our Loomis armored truck decoy next to the ATM, the sniper would open the porthole and aim his rifle, ready to shoot the guard as he stepped out of the armored truck with the money. We would have ATF agents and other NDTU officers up on the fourth floor of the parking garage watching, with their binoculars and spotting scopes. These officers and agents would see the muzzle of the sniper's rifle if he was getting ready to shoot. If that were the case, then let's simply neutralize the sniper as a threat by using good-guy counter sniper fire from the fourth-floor parking garage.

In my mind, it was an easily articulable situation: a known serial murderer, who has a high-powered rifle in hand, is preparing to shoot (finger on the trigger), all intending to kill an innocent person.

The counter sniper option now seemed to be attractive to me, the safest and most efficient way to handle this unique tactical problem. This would also better maintain the priority of life — innocent citizens; law enforcement officers; suspects—that I firmly adhered to while conducting police tactical operations.

Captain Baimbridge disagreed with me. He was also worried about the Monday-morning quarterbacking by the department's Command Staff and lawyers. He reasoned that they might decide that because we knew our undercover police officer, safely inside the decoy Loomis armored truck, was never going to get out, he was never going to be in any imminent danger, even though we had a serial killer sniper aiming his rifle with a finger on the trigger. Captain Baimbridge thought it would be more palatable, to the politicians and to those reviewing the results of our operation afterward, if we stayed with the original ramming and overturning the sniper crew while still inside the Toyota 4Runner scenario. This way, the sniper would have the opportunity to surrender if he chose.

I liked the counter sniper plan better. I believed it was safer. But, I am a man under authority and obeyed my superiors. We agreed to disagree.

We would keep with my original plan.

Next Wednesday was soon upon us and we were ready. Early that morning, all the good guys were out in the field, in our respective positions around the Amegy Bank. Both the decoy Loomis and Brink's armored trucks were manned, with engines running. On standby was a Houston police helicopter, with the pilot and observer on the pad, waiting to launch at a moment's notice to help us. Also staged in out-of-the-way spots, outside of the Greenspoint area, were several well-trusted uniform patrol and K-9 officers, poised and ready to seal off the area around the bank as soon as we did the takedown.

We were ready!

As the hours went by, though, it soon became apparent that this particular Wednesday would not be the day. The bad guys were not ready! In fact, as best we could tell, neither Batiste, Polk, nor Hill were even at the Amegy Bank.

We watched our cameras, looking to our designated trip wire—the white Toyota 4Runner—trying to discern any activity around it at its location on Conklin Street. There was none.

Looking to the camera on Tarberry Street at Batiste's house, all was quiet there. But we noticed something unusual. Redrick Batiste's Wrangler was parked in his front yard—in the same spot where we had found it that early September morning when we were first able to get our tracking devices on it. Batiste had, since that time, pretty much always kept it parked inside his garage when he was not driving it. But now, it had been moved out of the garage sometime the night before and parked in his front yard. Why?

I made a pot of coffee and several of us continued to watch the cameras.

Late in the morning, the garage door at Batiste's residence suddenly went up. Out drove a black Jeep Cherokee. It moved off and disappeared into the neighborhood. One of our undercover officers out in the field briefly got eyes on it, from a distance, but lost it in the heavy Houston traffic.

Where did this black Jeep Cherokee come from?

Who was driving it?

We "rewound" our Tarberry Street surveillance video and found our answer. The black Jeep Cherokee had pulled into Batiste's garage late the night before. By carefully slowing down the video, we could figure out its license plate number.

The black Jeep Cherokee was a rental vehicle owned by Enterprise Rent-A-Car.

Fortunately, one of the Houston-area FBI TFOs whose specialty was auto theft investigation had a trusted contact within Enterprise Rent-A-Car; an hour later, we had a copy of the rental agreement that pertained to the Jeep Cherokee in question. The person who had rented it, the afternoon before, was a female, and with the personal information she had provided on the agreement, we soon learned all we could about her.

Amanda Morgan in our Crime Analysis Section reviewed her social media account and accessed other classified information sources. Amanda figured out that the female who had rented the black Jeep Cherokee and Redrick Batiste were "acquainted." Amanda thought it might also have been that the connection the woman and Batiste shared might have been because the woman's ex-husband had a similar world view as Redrick Batiste (hated white people and law enforcement officers).

As we had seen in the past, sometimes, when your run-of-the-mill robbery crews needed a vehicle for some future planned lick, they would have a trusted female acquaintance rent a suitable vehicle under her name. She would then deliver this same vehicle to the robbery crew for their use in a planned commercial business robbery. If later, police investigators could somehow identify this rental vehicle as having been used in a crime during the time it was rented to the female and then came to question her as to who had been using it, she could disavow all knowledge. Often this would then be an investigative dead end for the detectives.

Seeing this black Jeep Cherokee at Batiste's house and knowing a female had rented it was a big red flag to us! But, who had driven it out of Batiste's garage? Maybe it was the same woman who had rented it and there was nothing really to it. But if she had delivered the Jeep Cherokee to Batiste, for use in the upcoming Amegy Bank sniper-initiated murder/robbery, this—in my mind—would be out of Batiste's "deep-thinking" character. There was too much of a tangible link between the female acquaintance who had rented the Jeep Cherokee and Redrick Batiste. Heck, Amanda Morgan was easily able to show us that the two of them knew each other in an hour.

I doubted Redrick Batiste would leave such an obvious trail of bread crumbs for law enforcement investigators to potentially follow in his next planned armored truck robbery. If the black Jeep Cherokee was somehow identified as being a vehicle of interest and linked to being involved in a murder/robbery, then the investigative trail would lead right back to Batiste's female acquaintance who had rented it during that time. Then Batiste would have to hope and trust that this woman would keep her mouth shut and not blab when questioned by authorities. Redrick Batiste was not that stupid. Because of this, we initially felt that Redrick Batiste probably was not going to use the black Jeep Cherokee for any nefarious purpose. Apparently Redrick was quite the ladies' man and maybe she had been "visiting him," we speculated. But then again, why then had the black Jeep Cherokee been parked in his garage and not out in his driveway?

Wednesday, November 30 turned out to be just another day of surveillance for the robbery crew. We knew this because none of the main actors had been present at the bank that morning, and the 4Runner was still parked at Conklin Street. Because a sniper-initiated robbery was not immediately imminent and because it was safe to do so, we didn't cancel the regular Loomis armored truck delivery to the Amegy Bank. This delivery then occurred with no drama or interference. But, the undercover officers who were present as always, conducting surveillance at the Amegy Bank, spotted the same black Jeep Cherokee that had slipped out of Batiste's garage hours earlier. It was now parked in the apartment complex to the south of the Amegy Bank across the bayou. And sitting in its driver's seat was our buddy Redrick Batiste, who was again back at it, watching the bank's ATM.

Twice now the bad guys had seen a Loomis armored truck servicing the Amegy Bank on a Wednesday.

I suspected that someone else from Batiste's robbery crew was watching the Amegy Bank that same Wednesday morning, but we were just not able to pick him out. Maybe John Edward Scott, the other person of interest, was out there that morning. FBI Jeff had linked a cell phone to Scott communicating with other core group members of the robbery crew back on the day David Guzman was killed, the previous August. We anticipated that soon Scott would make his appearance.

But what was up with that rental vehicle, the black Jeep Cherokee?

According to the rental agreement, it was only to be rented out for a few days before it was due back to Enterprise Rent-A-Car.

Maybe it was never going to be returned and the female acquaintance who had rented it for Batiste would soon report it stolen, to cover her trail? We were not sure what to make of it. But just to be prepared, because we now had seen Batiste driving it, late that afternoon I wrote out an affidavit to obtain judicial approval to place a tracking device on it. It was probably a waste of time, though. Even if she reported it stolen after having given it to Batiste, how would we ever get our tracking devices on it? Batiste kept the black Jeep Cherokee under lock and key inside his garage when he was not driving it.

FBI Jeff called me late that evening with some good news. His T3 Affidavit had come back from Washington DC and a federal judge had already signed it. Early the next morning, the switch would be flipped. The FBI's Listening Room would be operational. We were ready to monitor all of Batiste's cell phone calls.

Jeff's wiretap was finally going up!

Maybe it would uncover some "golden nuggets" as hoped by AUSA Rick Hanes?

On the morning of December 1, 2016 the FBI's Listening Room was manned and ready.

The switch was flipped and just as soon, the calls started coming in. During the day, we listened to several relevant phone conversations between Batiste and the other core group members of the robbery crew. As we had predicted, these conversations were in a code or slang not readily understandable to the uninitiated. What further complicated the translation of this code was that the key slang words being used between the conspirators was fluid and would change in conversations, apparently at random, with a new slang word used in its place.

On the first intercepted call, FBI Jeff had a new name, another possible coconspirator to add to the names of Batiste's robbery crew. Redrick was talking to this other person cryptically about robbing armored trucks. This other person was soon identified as Bennie Charles Phillips. Phillips had a criminal record and was on parole. He would turn out to be another core member of Batiste's robbery crew whom we had previously known nothing about.

Heather and Rick were elated with the immediate success of the T3. But, there was one great concern on their part. Would they, in the future, be able to convince a jury that our "translation" of these slang/code words was correct? The defense attorneys could have a field day.

What was interesting in listening in to these initial conversations was that Polk, Hill, and Batiste still appeared to be pretty pumped up about what they had observed days earlier, when the Loomis armored truck servicing the Amegy Bank's ATM had broken down and they had watched as "all that" money was transferred into a second, functional armored truck. Batiste was heard exclaiming (rough translation) something to the effect of: "if they had been ready, they could have taken the whole load!"

We wondered then if they had "been ready," would they have gunned down the multiple guards who were transferring the money between the armored trucks? It sure sounded like it.

Also discussed, in cryptic talk, were references to the next planned sniper-initiated robbery. The concern was that the expendable "crash dummy," who was to be used in the upcoming operation—the one to jump out and grab the money bags after the guard was killed— not hesitate in fulfilling his job, as compared to the previous crash dummy who they had used in their last sniper-initiated armored truck robbery. This suspect, as we had seen on the August 29 surveillance video, had momentarily hesitated when he first approached the Wells Fargo ATM to grab the money after David Guzman was down. He had probably gotten cold feet because at that same moment he was approaching, the sniper hadn't finished his job and was still pumping rounds into David's body—making sure he was *dead, dead*—and couldn't intervene. Unlike Melvin Moore in the Chase Bank armored truck robbery on Airline Drive, who although fatally wounded by the sniper, still shot it out with the approaching pick-up team's crash dummy and foiled the attempt to steal the money he was guarding.

The slang that Batiste and the others used somewhat consistently for "armored truck" was "commissary." This was probably derived from the time these men had spent incarcerated. We figured it was "convict speak" when prisoners referred to the cafeteria or wherever they got their personal hygiene articles while in prison.

The officers and agents listening also determined that Batiste "approved of" the black Jeep Cherokee. He indicated that he thought it would work out well for whatever role he intended for it. He also referred to it as the "Go Cart." Batiste also said he wanted to "fix the peep hole on the Peckerwood," which we believed was a reference to the sniper's loop-hole cut into the rear of the Toyota 4Runner.

On another note, Batiste was heard lamenting that he had troubles sleeping at night, "just like in the other operations!" To sleep, he told of having to drink "a few drinks." One other coconspirator was heard encouraging Batiste and that he "needed to hold it together." I thought Batiste's inability to sleep might also have accounted for many of his nocturnal visits to banks and ATMs. His mind was working overtime, thinking about all the what-ifs in the next robbery/murder he was planning. Also alluded to in Batiste's conversations was his belief that the crack cocaine epidemic was actually a conspiracy by the United States government to keep African Americans "down" and in an impoverished state. Fitting in with the rumors of a possible sniper attack on Houston-area law enforcement were his conversations and evident interest in national news stories where police officers had been killed by black suspects. However, in the short time that the T3 was operating, we heard no specific information on a Batiste-led sniper attack targeting law enforcement.

Batiste also talked about how he would soon be handing out "care packages" to the other members of the crew. This resonated with us as meaning he had acquired burner phones for the core members of the crew. We had anticipated the eventual use and deployment of burner phones; in fact, we had already watched Batiste visiting a neighborhood cell phone store and suspected this was what he was up to.

We were not sure how long it would be before the bad guys switched to these burner phones and we lost our ability to listen in. There was a remedy for this eventuality, but it would be a long shot.

Batiste openly talked about an immediate "problem" and that he had spent a lot of time "wrapping his mind around it." To solve this problem, he needed a 3/32" piece of stainless-steel tubing. The acquiring of this specific diameter of tubing, in stainless steel, was important to him. We even listened as Batiste called Grainger's, a large hardware supply store chain.

There, to his relief, he found that Grainger's had the exact specification of stainless-steel tubing he needed to solve his problem. Fortunately for him, there was a Grainger's close by on the North Freeway, to the north of Greenspoint, and his problem was solved.

We were all intrigued about Batiste's immediate problem and the need for a short length of 3/32 inch stainless-steel tubing to solve it.

Maybe he needed it for some part for fabricating a homemade firearm suppressor? Big John—his eyes narrowed, forehead frowned, lips pursed, in obvious concentration—manipulated a measuring caliper to see whether a .223 or 5.56mm bullet would pass through 3/32 of an inch. It wouldn't; 3/32 of an inch converted to decimal is .093 or 2.38 in millimeter. The diameter of stainless-steel tubing that Batiste needed was way too small for a .223 or 5.56mm bullet to pass through. It was also too narrow for any known bullet to travel through.

We were stumped by the whole 3/32 inch stainless-steel tubing! But because it was important to Batiste, it was also important to us. We all kept postulating different theories about why he needed it.

Nevertheless, in just a few hours, FBI Jeff's T3 was proving to be a gold mine of information! Rick and Heather were well pleased.

In listening in on Batiste's initial conversations, we had realized that the rented black Jeep Cherokee—the Go Cart—was a significant piece of the puzzle. Not only because he was driving it, but because of the importance that Batiste was placing in it. I wanted to get a tracking device on it as soon as possible. But again, how? Batiste kept it locked up in his garage when he wasn't driving it.

We would have to try it old school, without the luxury of any middle-of-the-night operation to place tracking devices on a parked, unoccupied car. We would have to keep and maintain physical rolling surveillance on Batiste while he was driving the Cherokee, and wait for an opportunity to do so.

The NDTU then endeavored to keep and maintain our eyes on Batiste and the Cherokee from that moment of realization forward. If we lost physical rolling surveillance on it, we should eventually be able to pick it up again at one of the known locations that Batiste frequented, such as his house on Tarberry Street or the Amegy Bank itself.

The physical surveillance required to keep tabs on Batiste as he drove the Jeep Cherokee would unfortunately increase the chances of us being spotted. Was the risk worth it? I posed this question to the men and women working in the FBI's Listening Room, who were trying to correctly interpret the bad guys' cryptic conversations. The consensus was yes. The Cherokee would be used somehow in the next planned sniper attack—"Get a tracking device on it if you can!"

One of the patrol officers assigned to the North Station owned a similar year and model Jeep Cherokee. With his permission, we closely examined it. First, we wanted to know where to put our tracking devices on it if the opportunity ever arose. And the second question was could this type of vehicle be used as a sniper platform, much in the same way as the Toyota 4Runner? If the bad guys modified the Cherokee by cutting a sniper's loophole in the back tailgate, would there be enough room for someone to lie in a prone position and shoot out the back? Looking it over carefully, I didn't think so. The rear compartment on the Cherokee seemed much smaller than that of a 4Runner.

All that day and into next day (Friday), we worked to keep a cautious surveillance on the black Jeep Cherokee while Batiste drove it around the city. Sometimes we lost our eyes and had to work hard to reacquire it. We alternated small teams of undercover officers, trying to ensure that Batiste never saw the same undercover vehicle(s) for an extended time in his rearview mirror. The rule we followed was that the same undercover officer could only follow Batiste for a short period ("I have the eye"); after a few minutes, he would pull off and someone else trailing behind would pull closer and would announce over the radio, "I have the eye now." We probably had fourteen undercover officers working diligently to follow the Jeep Cherokee without being detected.

Conducting this physical surveillance had to be carefully coordinated. Even with the large numbers of undercover officers at our disposal, we had to be so cautious, so stealthy. We couldn't afford to be spotted! I expected to lose our eyes on our target at any moment, but we didn't. We managed to hang on and even if we lost him for a few minutes, someone in our team could figure out where he had gone and we would soon pick up his trail again.

This surveillance operation was one of the more risky things we had done to date in this operation. Again, it was because Redrick Batiste was so cautious, so paranoid, so constantly on the alert, always observing his environment. These factors coupled with his obvious natural intelligence all conspired to make him a formidable adversary as we tried to keep eyes on him without being compromised ourselves.

A window of opportunity briefly opened: a moment in time to put a tracker on the black Jeep Cherokee. Batiste had stopped at an area gas station to fuel up his Go Cart. After filling it up, he left it parked, unattended, by the gas pumps and walked into the service station to buy a drink. The NDTU were ready to put the tracking device on at that moment. But there was another customer nearby gassing up his vehicle, and we anxiously waited for him to finish and leave. The seconds ticked by as we watched Batiste getting in line inside the store to pay for his soda. We were too late! Just as the other customer finally finished fueling his vehicle and was pulling away, Batiste walked out of the station with his drink in hand.

But later that afternoon, we had another opportunity. Batiste stopped to eat at a seafood restaurant on North Shepherd Drive and had parked the Cherokee in the front parking lot. I sent in one of our undercover officers to watch him inside. There, my guy could text message us with regular Batiste updates. As usual, Batiste took a position in the restaurant where, while he was eating, he could monitor the front door as well as look out the front window to see the Cherokee.

Soon his food arrived, and he began eating.

We then pulled one of our larger undercover vehicles into the parking lot and slowly drove it across the front of the restaurant so it would pass between the front windows where Batiste was sitting and where the Jeep Cherokee was parked. Then, when all three were in alignment (the Jeep Cherokee, our view-blocking undercover vehicle, and the restaurant's front window), we radioed for the guy in the undercover vehicle in the parking lot acting as our smoke screen to stop momentarily. At this time, Batiste's outside view of the Jeep Cherokee was blocked by our undercover vehicle. It was only for maybe ten seconds, but it was enough time for the NDTU! John Calhoun immediately slipped under Batiste's Go Cart and was able to slap on a tracking device. It was the fastest I had ever seen John move! The FBI SWAT guys with us were pretty impressed with the operation.

We could now relax this intense, risky, rolling surveillance and mitigate our potential risk of discovery. It was such a stress relief, for me, to finally get at least one tracker on that black Jeep Cherokee. We were all able to get some sleep that night.

I assumed that Batiste would eventually instruct the female acquaintance who originally rented the Jeep Cherokee to report it stolen, before it was due to be returned to Enterprise Rent-A-Car. That was probably soon to occur. Then Batiste and/or his minions would locate other Jeep Cherokees and clandestinely remove the front license plates from them, trusting that the owners would never notice or, if they noticed, never bother to make a police report. Then they would replace the original front and back license plates on the black Jeep Cherokee with these other license plates, much like they had apparently done to the white Toyota 4Runner.

The next day, FBI Jeff called me from the Listening Room.

"Chris, I think I know why Batiste wanted a small length of 3/32" stainless-steel tubing.

He needs it to steal the Jeep Cherokee!"

I told Jeff I wasn't following him. Why did Batiste "need to steal" the Jeep Cherokee (he already had it) and why did he need the tubing?

Jeff espoused his theory:

Batiste wanted the Jeep Cherokee.

Batiste needed to create more "distance" and obscure any trail between the black Jeep Cherokee and his female acquaintance.

The female acquaintance was a weak link that might lead law enforcement investigators straight back to Batiste. If law enforcement was able to identify the black Jeep Cherokee as being used in a sniper-initiated armored truck robbery and that she had rented it, would she then keep her mouth shut?

Then Jeff explained that he had discovered that when you rent a vehicle from Enterprise Rent-A-Car, and when the keys are given to the customer—in this case, Batiste's female acquaintance—two working keys are provided. Both keys are identical and either will unlock the doors and/or turn on the engine.

To ensure that neither key is misplaced or lost, Enterprise secures them together, on a small loop of narrow-diameter, high-strength braided wire. After the wire is threaded through both keys, the two ends of the wire are then connected together with a short piece of 3/32 inch stainless-steel tubing which is then heavily crimped on either end, so neither end of the wire can be pulled out. The keys are then always together; they can't be easily separated from each other.

Apparently, Enterprise keeps both keys together on this loop of braided wire to simplify the management of the large fleet of vehicles they own. Since customers have the option of turning the rental vehicle in at a different Enterprise rental office than from the one they had originally rented from, whichever branch office one of their rental vehicle ultimately ends up at, all the keys for it are there with it.

Imagine Enterprise's vehicle key inventory headaches for its fleet. Enterprise Rent-A-Car is one of the largest rental car companies in the country, with over 9,000 offices, with many thousands of vehicles in its inventory! Say one of its rental vehicles is returned in California, but it had just originated in New York and now was being rented to another person headed to Texas. Enterprise could never be certain which branch office their rental vehicle would be at a later date, or whether it would ever make its way back to the original branch office where it had first been placed into inventory. To simplify everything, Enterprise gives all the keys belonging to a particular rental vehicle to the person who rented it and who, when finished with it, would turn the vehicle and both keys back in.

Then Jeff got to the meat.

He believed that Batiste would somehow break the Enterprise tamper-proof, wire key chain loop and remove one of the working keys or key fobs. He would then replace the one he had removed with a dummy key—a non-working key or key fob. He would then thread the braided loop of wire through the dummy key as well as the other functional key. Then re-secure the two opposite ends of the braided wire by placing either end into the ends of a new short length of 3/32 inch stainless-steel tubing. He would then crimp both ends of the tubing so neither end of the wire could be pulled out, thus replicating Enterprise's original customer "tamper-proof" key ring.

After doing this, Batiste would then possess a functional key for the black Jeep Cherokee. He would have his female acquaintance return the vehicle to Enterprise. Sometime later, when it was rented back out, if the new customer chose to use the non-functioning key and found it didn't work, they would then automatically try the other key on the key ring, which would work. If it ever came to Enterprise's attention that one key didn't work, they would assume that it was somehow defective, never realizing that their supposedly tamper-proof key ring *had* been tampered with.

This way, Batiste and/or his conspirators could then easily steal the Cherokee when it was rented out again by another unknown customer, thereby erasing the link between the female accomplice who rented it earlier and Batiste.

There was one big flaw in Jeff's theory, which up to that point made sense. How would they be able to steal the black Jeep Cherokee with the previously ill-gotten key? They would have no idea where to find it!

I discussed the issue with Jeff. I thought maybe Batiste could try to immediately steal the black Jeep Cherokee right out of the Enterprise parking lot, just as soon as his female acquaintance turned it back in. But that was risky and farfetched. Enterprise has security measures and physical barriers at its vehicle storage facilities to prevent such things from happening.

Special Agent Jeff Coughlin's voice lowered, as though he were about to divulge a secret, or maybe he was embarrassed. "Chris, I am sorry—I didn't tell you!"

I told Jeff, in jest—with maybe just a hint of sarcasm in my voice: "I know, Jeff. You're FBI, you don't tell me half the stuff I need to know!"

Then Jeff continued. "The Original Informant told me, back in September, that Batiste used his own tracking devices to steal vehicles!"

The thought of Batiste using his own vehicle tracking devices took a few seconds to sink in. I had to wrap my mind around this new criminal paradigm.

How clever!

Jeff quickly further explained to me that he had not been keeping "FBI secrets." But when he had talked to the Original Informant months before and when he had mentioned something about Red using tracking devices to steal vehicles, Jeff had all but discounted it. Jeff thought it had been some fantastical exaggeration typical of informants and had dismissed it from his mind. Jeff had never mentioned it to me—because he didn't believe it. But now, Jeff, having recalled the Original Informant's words—as incredible as it seemed—it was all starting to come together.

FBI Jeff and I then carefully walked through what we believed had occurred or what we believed would occur regarding the black Jeep Cherokee—Batiste's *Go Cart*.

Batiste had the female acquaintance, acting as his proxy, rent the Jeep Cherokee from Enterprise Rent-A-Car under her name.

After she delivered the Jeep Cherokee to him, Batiste then test drove it and determined it would be a good fit for some unknown role in a future sniper-initiated armored truck robbery.

After deciding he wanted the Jeep Cherokee, Batiste then figured out how to clandestinely "acquire" one of the two working keys that are routinely given to customers whenever Enterprise rents its vehicles.

Batiste severed or broke the Enterprise's tamper-proof key ring at the point where the two ends of its braided wire were secured by a short length of 3/32 inch stainless-steel tubing, removing one of the working keys.

Batiste would now replace one of the working Enterprise Rent-A-Car keys, which he stole, with a non-functional, lookalike dummy key so as not to arouse any suspicion with the employees at Enterprise when it was turned back in.

To do this, Batiste would carefully replicate Enterprise's standard issue, tamper-proof, braided wire, key ring with two keys on it. This was why he needed a short length of 3/32 inch stainless-steel tubing. This size of tubing was identical to the one Enterprise had used previously to secure the two ends of their braided wire key ring together.

Prior to returning the black Jeep Cherokee to Enterprise Rent-A-Car, Batiste would then mount his own tracking device on it—hiding it somewhere in or on the vehicle where it was unlikely to be discovered.

Then, by monitoring his tracking device on the Jeep Cherokee, Batiste could then set up his own electronic geo fence around the relevant

Enterprise Rent-A-Car facility. Sometime later, when his tracker sensed it was outside of the Enterprise Rent-A-Car geo fence, Batiste would receive an alert. He would then know that someone else, a complete stranger (someone with no connection potentially leading back to him) had rented the Jeep Cherokee and was driving it off.

Batiste and his conspirators could then track the black Jeep Cherokee to wherever it was now located after it had been rented out again. When it was parked and unoccupied and it was safe for them to do so, they could easily steal it via a working key, which was now in Batiste's possession.

This was probably also how the white Toyota 4Runner was stolen the year before. It was also a rental vehicle and we could not figure out how Batiste had ended up with a working electronic key fob to remotely unlock its doors as well as turn on its ignition. Mystery solved— now we knew!

But, if this was all true, was there some way we could capitalize on this information and further enhance our investigation, and increase our chances for success in any upcoming tactical operation at the Amegy Bank?

Fortunately, or maybe now unfortunately, the NDTU had placed our own tracking device on the black Jeep Cherokee. This was good in the sense now that we would know where it was at all times. But now, suppose Batiste put his own tracking device somewhere on it. Where was he going to hide it or mount it? If he decided to mount his in the same location we had mounted ours (near the muffler system), would he then find our tracking device? If he did, then our operation was over; we would be compromised. There was nothing we could do about it; we just had to cross our fingers and hope he didn't find our device when he was putting his on.

At the least, when the Cherokee was returned to Enterprise Rent-A-Car, we could be the ones to purport to be customers and rent it back out. We could then park it somewhere and document, via covert surveillance, Batiste and/or his coconspirators—or any combination thereof—stealing it. This recorded evidence would further facilitate any later prosecution by Rick or Heather in federal court.

If the Cherokee was returned, we would figure out a way to get possession of it. Hopefully in such away as not to unduly alert any of the Enterprise employees working at that office that it was undercover law enforcement renting it, or "acquiring" it. This would be important, just in case there was any Batiste insider working there we didn't know about. Fortunately, one of our FBI TFOs had good relations with a person in Enterprise Rent-A-Car's corporate management, who was willing to help us and facilitate the quiet and timely acquisition of the Jeep Cherokee when it was returned.

Our friend at Enterprise Rent-A-Car flagged the Cherokee in question, to not be rented back out, but that it be set aside for retail sale. This same person would also have both the keys and the Jeep Cherokee delivered into our possession as soon as Batiste's female acquaintance returned it to them. We would know immediately when this was about to occur because we had our tracking device on it.

Jeff was to wait for my phone call, signaling that the Jeep Cherokee was back at an Enterprise Rent-A-Car facility. Then our friend within Enterprise would be alerted. This person, who had the commensurate authority, would then make another discreet phone call to whichever Enterprise facility it was returned to and arrange for the black Jeep Cherokee to be quietly turned over into our possession, no questions asked.

Later, we would then park the Jeep Cherokee somewhere, and monitor and record to see whatever happened to it—whether Batiste and his men stole it. If they did, it would be another piece of evidence in any later prosecution. We could do this pretty easily, by using a parked and unoccupied NDTU undercover vehicle with the same hidden Rube Goldberg surveillance camera system that we had also used to monitor the 4Runner when it had still been parked at the apartments on Blue Bell Street.

But, FBI Jeff was thinking way out of the box, thinking about what we could do if we kept the Jeep Cherokee in our immediate possession for a few hours. Soon he was on the phone, calling FBI Headquarters in Washington DC.

There were still a lot of details to work out. But for now we just had to sit back and wait to see what happened—whether the Jeep Cherokee was returned to Enterprise or reported stolen by Batiste's female acquaintance.

Batiste and friends were busy. They moved the Toyota 4Runner from its Conklin Street hiding place to a small, obscure Acres Homes vehicle repair and body shop on Sandle Street.

This "business" was in a residential area and was more of an old house with many vehicles in various states of repair, all crowded onto the property. Inside a chain link fence patrolled several mangy-looking pit bulls, probably as a deterrent to keep the neighborhood crack heads at bay. As I did a drive-by, I could already see someone working at the rear of the 4Runner, doing something, but I was not sure what.

We suspected, based on the previous intercepted T3 conversation, that the "peephole fixed" reference was that Batiste wanted to modify the original sniper loophole; maybe he wanted something even stealthier. I thought he might have the original sniper's loophole in the tailgate repaired and then have a new hole cut out, relocated under the rear license plate, with some sort of spring-loaded mechanism so the license plate could be opened or shut from the inside, thereby allowing the sniper to shoot through the new loophole.

This modification would require some fabrication and mechanical ingenuity. Probably requiring the removal of the 4Runner's tailgate's internal locking mechanism, because it might block the new sniper loophole. Then the permanent welding of the tailgate shut or in the down position.

Early Friday evening, after Jeff had coordinated his end of the operation with Washington DC, I was in my office with several members of the NDTU as we carefully watched our pole camera view of Batiste's home on Tarberry Street.

Batiste was now back at home and the Jeep Cherokee was parked in his driveway, where he was cleaning it. We watched as he opened all the doors and the rear tail gate/hatch, as well as the engine compartment hood. Transfixed by the scene, we were certain that Batiste was getting the vehicle ready to turn it back in to Enterprise Rent-A-Car. But besides cleaning it, what was he doing? Most likely, we thought he was carefully and methodically looking for a place to hide his tracking device! We watched as he crawled all through the Jeep, looking into all of its nooks and crannies. Our pole camera view wasn't good enough to see him place a tracker on or in the Jeep, but I was sure that was what he was doing. Soon he had finished whatever he was up to and drove off, out of view.

I called Jeff. "Get your boys ready! I think we just watched him mount his tracking device somewhere on the Jeep Cherokee."

Maybe Redrick Batiste should have thought of mounting his tracking device underneath the Jeep Cherokee on its undercarriage. If he had and looked there, he might have found our tracking device and then would have known that law enforcement was closing in on him.

But he didn't!

Later that evening, the Jeep Cherokee was indeed returned to a Houston-area Enterprise Rent-A-Car facility. I tracked it and as soon as it arrived, even as the necessary phone calls were still being made, we raced to quietly pick it up.

Sure enough, once we arrived, a quick check of the Jeep Cherokee's two keys revealed that one of them didn't work!

Batiste had the other working key!

As soon as we knew for sure that the right black Jeep Cherokee from Enterprise Rent-A-Car was in our possession and that one key to it was a dummy, FBI Jeff made another phone call to Washington DC.

In Virginia, on the east coast of the United States, over 1,400 miles away, on standby for Jeff's green-light signal, waited several special technicians who possessed unique skill sets, as well as their highly confidential equipment. These waiting "secret squirrel" friends were assigned to the FBI's clandestine Strategic Vehicle Technologies Unit (SVTU). As soon as Jeff let them know we had the Jeep Cherokee, they were on an airplane, rolling down the runway, heading to us down in Houston, Texas.

Some valuable and expensive federal intelligence assets were being allocated to our little domestic criminal surveillance operation! I don't know who Special Agent Jeff Coughlin called in Washington DC, but I knew he had some friends in high places. In particular, well-placed federal government friends. Maybe he had made these friends when he was in the military fighting overseas in Afghanistan and Iraq? Maybe Jeff had been calling in a personal favor? I don't know.

In the meantime, we had to find a place to hide the black Jeep Cherokee. A place where Batiste and his men couldn't get to if they came to steal it that same night. As soon as we drove the Cherokee off the Enterprise Rent-A-Car parking lot, the bad guys could come looking for it.

We needed a place where our friends from Washington DC could work in secrecy on Batiste's Go Cart—where Batiste and his guys couldn't get to, a secure location, safe from prying eyes. Yet it also had to be a location that wouldn't spook Batiste when he was monitoring his tracking device to see where it was. We definitely couldn't drive the Cherokee to any police facility or to the Houston FBI Field Office.

KILLING TWO BIRDS WITH ONE STONE!

The Jeep Cherokee was driven straight from the Enterprise Rent-A-Car office to Ellington Air Force Base—or, more correctly, Ellington Field Joint Reserve Base—south of Houston. It is a secure government-guarded military facility and is also the same place where Air Force One lands, whenever the president of the United States comes to visit.

By using Ellington, we could create the illusion, from Batiste's perspective, that someone, maybe from the military or a civilian contractor, had just arrived in Houston to conduct business at the base. This imaginary person had driven the Jeep Cherokee to Ellington, where they parked it, because they would be working at the base.

As long as we had the Jeep Cherokee at Ellington Air Force Base, Batiste and his men couldn't steal it or even see it—they didn't have the proper military clearance and/or identification to get past the armed soldiers stationed at the front gate.

An unused aircraft hangar within Ellington's secure perimeter was made available to us by the nice people from the military and the Jeep Cherokee was soon parked inside it. There, Jeff and other members of our group patiently waited for the SVTU technicians to land and start doing their "thing."

Before midnight Friday, the SVTU had landed. Soon they were closely examining the Jeep Cherokee. One of the first things they did was to sweep it for bugs with one of their high-tech, Spy vs. Spy, detector device thingies. About this time, one of their technicians called me on my cell phone. I could tell he was from the East Coast because of his accent. "We found his tracking device! It was in a small black Pelican box!"

I quickly corrected him, maybe with some annoyance in my voice. "No! That's my tracking device!" The ATF tracking devices we used were all inside small black Pelican boxes, with magnets on the bottom. These Pelican boxes were made of hard plastic and were also watertight to protect the tracker's delicate electronics inside.

Then I thought better about it and politely asked the nice secret surveillance technician dude, who had just flown 1,400 miles, in the middle of a Friday night, to help us, "Where did you find 'that' tracking device?"

He responded, "On the firewall, inside of the Jeep's engine compartment." I apologized to him.

The tracking device the technicians had found was not mine. It was Redrick Batiste's. Both the good guys and bad guys were using identical-looking black Pelican boxes for their respective tracking devices, which were mounted in different locations on the Jeep Cherokee.

My tracking device, though, was still undiscovered—still where John Calhoun had slapped it on a day earlier, still underneath the frame of the Jeep Cherokee, near its muffler system. I alerted the SVTU technician that there was still yet another tracker on the Jeep Cherokee and where to find it. But it was okay—this other one was the good guy's!

We left Batiste's tracking device on the Jeep's firewall, unmolested. Many of these devices have sensors in them that can detect whether the case is opened or even if they are turned over to more than a 90-degree angle from the position wherein they had been first positioned and then activated by its owner. We couldn't touch Batiste's tracker, much less examine it for fear that he would immediately receive some tamper alert. The best we could do for the time being was to photograph it, where it sat, on the firewall.

The SVTU began taking apart the Jeep Cherokee. They then installed a hidden remote video camera which would record a view of whoever sat in its driver's seat and a live audio microphone to listen in and record conversations, as well as an FBI-issued, hard-wired GPS tracking system. Most importantly, from my perspective, they installed a "kill switch" that would enable us, if we desired, to remotely disable the engine of the Jeep Cherokee and immobilize it. No wild police pursuits with this vehicle! Lastly, the SVTU took the NDTU's tracking device from under the Jeep and carefully hid it inside the Cherokee's rear seat, where there was no chance of it being found.

Unfortunately, given the short time the SVTU had, the camera installed in the Cherokee could not be viewed live; it would have to be recovered after the sting operation to be reviewed.

It was strictly to gather evidence.

But the hidden microphone was a good idea, especially if Batiste and his crew went to burner phones. We could listen in on any conversations held within the Jeep Cherokee, maybe even both sides of the conversation, if Batiste used a speakerphone option. We would not be able to immediately listen in on the Jeep Cherokee. Using the hidden microphone amounted to a wiretap and would require another approval by a federal judge. But fortunately, this would only require an addendum to Jeff's original affidavit, explaining the situation. This work would not take nearly as long and hopefully in a few days it would be signed and the FBI's Listening Room could flip the switch and we would be listening in on conversations inside the Go Cart.

By working nonstop through the night, the SVTU guys were finished and by morning the Jeep Cherokee was all put back together. There were more "secret things" the SVTU could have done if time had permitted, but the sun was starting to rise. In the morning, as soon as possible, we wanted to drive it out of Ellington's secure perimeter, to keep up the ruse that whoever rented it had now finished their work at the airfield.

Before the SVTU technicians left, we sincerely thanked them for their help and didn't ask questions about where they were headed to next. They got back on their airplane and took off.

Redrick Batiste's Go Cart now had *three* hidden tracking devices on it (the FBI's, Batiste's, and the NDTU's), as well as a bunch of federal government-issued "non-factory standard" additions.

As the sun came up on a cold rainy Saturday morning, we drove the Jeep Cherokee out of Ellington Air Force Base and parked it in the parking lot of the Doubletree Inn at 8181 Airport Boulevard, which was close to the base. Across from the Jeep Cherokee, we parked the NDTU's infamous Silver Bullet, our silver Toyota Corolla, with its ATF hidden surveillance camera pointed straight at the Jeep Cherokee.

The trap was set. A lot of work had gone into this. Would Batiste soon go for it?

Late Saturday morning, Dave Smith and I were in the office, monitoring all of our surveillance cameras, including the one most important to us right then: the one monitoring the Jeep Cherokee as it sat in the Doubletree Inn parking lot.

An FBI agent in the Listening Room called me. Batiste had just talked to John Edward Scott, wanting him to go with him and get the Go Cart. Batiste had told Scott (in reference to our imaginary person) "he must have pulled an all-nighter at Ellington" and that the Jeep Cherokee was now parked at a hotel. As they talked, Batiste became annoyed because Scott said he couldn't go right then, because he was babysitting his kids.

We then all had to wait for Scott to get his child care/baby momma issues settled. Finally, in the early afternoon, we tracked Batiste's Wrangler headed south to the Doubletree Inn. David and I—drinking coffee to stay awake, with our feet up on our desks—watched our hidden camera as Redrick Batiste, wearing a camouflaged hoodie pulled over his head, walked up to the Jeep Wrangler, unlocked it with a remote key fob, got in and drove off, out of view.

Dave and I then tracked both the Jeep Wrangler, driven by Scott, and the Jeep Cherokee, driven by Batiste.

During their drive back to the north side of Houston, Batiste and Scott were still talking on their phones and the men and women in the FBI's Listening Room, including Captain Baimbridge, who was lending a hand, overheard Batiste serenading Scott by singing "*Merry Christmas to me! Merry Christmas to me!*" over and over again.

Redrick Batiste was a happy man that Saturday morning. His grand plan to steal the black Jeep Cherokee had gone flawlessly.

We also were happy!

Both Scott and Batiste headed straight to the apartments at 1400 Blue Bell Street where, just as the Toyota 4Runner had been, they parked the now stolen Jeep Cherokee for their future use.

I called a sleepy FBI Jeff and gave him the good news.

Redrick Batiste and his armored truck sniper crew now had two stolen vehicles at their disposal. Whatever modification the neighborhood "shade tree" mechanic shop on Sandle Street had done to the Toyota 4Runner was already completed and later that day, either Batiste or another crew member moved it back to its hiding place in the Conklin Street junk yard.

The Listening Room called with more updates on the chatter they were listening to: Batiste was again talking about handing out his "care packages" (burner phones?) to the others. If this happened, the Listening Room and Jeff's original T3 would go dark. In another phone conversation with Nelson Polk, Batiste told how they were going to hold a "scrimmage" and on Monday he wanted to "see how his players looked on the field."

We assumed next Monday, Batiste would set up his sniper crew at the Amegy Bank, along with possibly other members of his crew in a mock rehearsal for the real deal on Wednesday.

Because Monday would only be a dry run by the bad guys, we assumed that they would not be in possession of firearms, much less the sniper rifle, which we wanted so much to recover for its evidentiary value.

If the entire Batiste sniper-initiated robbery crew came out to the Amegy Bank for a scrimmage, then it would be a great opportunity for us to monitor them and confirm what we suspected. On the day, Batiste would be in the Jeep Cherokee across the bayou from the Amegy Bank in the apartment complex, acting as the shot caller, while his sniper crew would be set up and parked inside the Toyota 4Runner, a hundred yards to the east of the bank's ATM.

What we were hoping for was that by monitoring this dry run, we could identify the vehicle the bad guys would use to rush in and pick up the money bags after the guard was killed and where it would be positioned relative to the bank before the shooting. This information would be especially important to the tactical team assigned to take these suspects down, since we had no clue about which vehicle would be used, where it would be located, or who would be in it.

Monday's surveillance at the Amegy Bank might also help us figure out who the lookouts were going to be and where they would be situated.

After his conversation with Nelson Polk about the scrimmage, I watched as Batiste then met up with him at the Conklin Street junk yard and handed Polk a plastic shopping bag. The bag appeared to have several weighted items inside. From my perspective, I sensed that inside the bag where either handguns or burner phones, all to be passed out to the rest of the crew. I was leaning more toward burner phones. As soon as I saw the exchange, I was back on the phone with FBI Jeff.

"Jeff, get ready. I think Batiste is handing out the burner phones. Your T3 is about to go dark!"

That was exactly what happened! Batiste switched over to his burner phone when "talking shop" with the other core members of his crew.

Except for one oversight. Maybe because he wasn't worthy, maybe because someone miscounted, maybe because someone got cheap, or maybe because he was only to perform a secondary role as a far outer perimeter lookout on the day. But for whatever reason, John Edward Scott didn't get a burner phone like the rest of the crew. He and Batiste continued to communicate via their personal cell phones.

Jeff's T3 had almost completely gone dark, but because of Scott there was still some occasional "golden nuggets" for the Listening Room to glean. The T3 was still alive, but just barely.

Not resting on the heels of the success with our work on the Jeep Cherokee, the FBI and NDTU immediately transitioned into the one shot we had in unveiling the identity of Batiste's burner phone before the day.

Our time was running out.

We felt more and more confident that the upcoming Wednesday would finally be the day that Batiste and the rest of the armored truck sniper crew would be at the Amegy Bank en masse, ready to shoot. The tension was mounting!

Until then, we would keep pushing hard. We still wanted to keep stacking the deck in our favor. In the next day or two, if we could figure out the phone number of Batiste's burner phone, then FBI Jeff could amend his original T3 Affidavit and have it approved by a federal judge. Then the Listening Room could be fully back "up." Ideally, if all the stars lined up, by Monday we wanted to be able to listen in on both the hidden microphone inside the Jeep Cherokee as well as Batiste's new burner phone.

"Sting Ray" was the technological gadget or "surveillance miracle machine" that we had immediate access to, which might crack the code as to the identity of Batiste's burner phone. For us, in this instance, a successful operation would look something like this:

Presumably, Batiste now had his burner phone in his possession at all times. We would need him to travel to a minimum of three different physical locations, all widely separated from each other. As Batiste moved about, the NDTU would keep covert physical surveillance on him and would have to know for certain (an articulable fact) that he was physically present at these three locations. Once this occurred, trailing close behind the NDTU, would be the FBI, lugging along all their Sting Ray gizmo stuff. While the NDTU kept a close eye on Batiste, the FBI would then have to sneak up into range, into what I considered to be uncomfortably close proximity to Batiste, and then "enable" Sting Ray (push the button).

Once enabled, Sting Ray mimicked being an actual cell phone tower and would "lock on" to any cell phones that were turned on within its short operational range. Sting Ray would then record the identifiers for every cell phone within its range. These cell phones had to be turned on.

Otherwise, it was "No Bueno"!

Again, this laborious surveillance process had to be performed at a minimum of three widely different locations. Once this was accomplished, the FBI would then look for all the *common* cell phone numbers that Sting Ray had collected at *each* of these three locations.

By excluding known cell phones, like the personal phones of each member of your undercover surveillance team, as well as Batiste's known cell phone number, the one remaining cell phone number present at all three documented locations should be Batiste's burner phone!

Hopefully then, a federal judge would be sufficiently satisfied with our effort and all agog by all the FBI's Sting Ray hocus-pocus stuff and would give us permission to listen in on the conversations being held on this newly discovered cell phone, considering it was reasonable to believe it was in fact Batiste's new burner phone.

The problem we faced was that Batiste was a hard nut to crack, given his hyper-vigilance and situational awareness. We had to get him "laid down" at three different locations, without him spotting our surveillance team. But our biggest problem was the vehicle the FBI had decided to mount their mystery cell phone "uncloaking device" in!

Two young FBI agents pulled in to the back parking lot of my police station in a black Chevy Suburban, with heavily blacked-out windows. The Suburban was in immaculate condition and looked as if it had just come from participating in a presidential motorcade. It was not a good fit for sneaking around Acres Homes. But worse was that someone in the FBI had decided it would be a grand idea to mount the "guts" of Sting Ray (I am guessing the big antenna thingy) in an equally black in color, fully enclosed SNOW SKI RACK! The rack ran the length of the Suburban's roof on its centerline. These young FBI agents were pretty excited about getting to go out into the field and do real undercover secret agent stuff and equally proud that they had been entrusted to drive the Bureau's "Sting Ray Magical Mystery Machine."

I did not share their excitement and soon I was on the phone with FBI Jeff.

"Jeff, you have got to be kidding me. Have you seen this thing?"

As I talked to Jeff, I looked at the Magical Mystery Machine parked next to me, with its pair of shiny new agents sitting inside, smiling expectantly back at me.

"Jeff, for Heaven's sake. It has a snow ski rack on the top of it! What was the Bureau thinking?"

For the uninformed reader of this book, it rarely snows in Houston, Texas (it's a sub-tropical environment) and there are no hills, much less mountains, to go snow skiing on.

When "white stuff" does fall out of the sky in Houston (maybe every few years) and it then happens to lightly gather and dust the ground, there is panic among some residents of the city. This panic is mostly fed by the news media—"Some of you are going to die—take shelter immediately!" Snowfall in Houston was viewed as a harbinger to some apocalyptic event.

A snow ski rack on top of a presidential-looking black Suburban, with blacked-out windows, driving around a lower social economic Houston neighborhood might arouse considerable suspicion. To me, it looked like something that might have come straight out of the movie *Men in Black*!

Jeff was concerned also, and we came to an agreement about how we should go about deploying this thing: very, very, carefully!

Fortunately for us, the rest of the day and into the night, Redrick Batiste was a busy bee, driving to several locations, even going to the ritzy Galleria area in west Houston. Every time he stopped long enough at a location, we would try to bring up the *Men in Black* Magical Mystery Machine, slowly creeping up into range, careful to stay in Batiste's blind spot. Over the hours, we managed to do this on three different occasions and the FBI guys were confident that they had gotten all the data they needed to identify his burner phone, if he had it with him and if it was turned on.

After all the information was collected, the FBI then put all the known cell phone numbers into their computer, to exclude them from consideration and they were then left with one unknown cell phone number, which had been present at all three of the Sting Ray decoy cell phone tower locations. This number had to be Batiste's burner phone number! FBI Jeff was elated and plugged this new unknown cell phone number into the T3 Affidavit that he had already carefully drafted for just this moment. Jeff wanted to present it all along with the T3 Affidavit for the "bug" in the black Jeep Cherokee, to a federal judge, first thing Monday morning.

But the phone number to Batiste's alleged burner phone seemed odd! It had a 202 area code, which is Washington DC's. How did Batiste end up with a burner phone with a Washington DC area code? It can't be.

Something was not "computing" correctly.

Justin Williams quickly figured it out. The unknown cell phone number was emanating from the primary ATF tracking device we had put on Batiste's Jeep Wrangler. We were pinging this particular tracker hard and the way the geo location information was up-linked to us was by similar technology as used in cell phones. Each tracking device had its own cell phone number to identify itself and "talk" to its host computer.

Sting Ray was reading our tracking device and was fooled into thinking it was Batiste's burner cell phone!

All of our tracking devices had first originated from ATF Headquarters in Washington DC, where, when they were "born," they had each been assigned its own cell phone number, all with a Washington DC area code.

This could have all been a little embarrassing, wasting the time of a federal judge by asking that he or she take the time to read some hundred-page document, so we could get approval to listen in on our own tracking device.

If Batiste had his burner phone with him, it must have been turned off. FBI Jeff and I decided that to continue to follow him around with the FBI's blacked-out Chevy Suburban, with its ridiculously out-of-place snow ski rack mounted on top, was flirting with disaster. Much to the dismay of the young FBI agents helping us, they were then sent back to their office to do whatever the Bureau has rookie agents do.

We would have to be content with the bits and pieces of information we were getting when Scott and Batiste talked and hopefully by Monday afternoon, Jeff's T3 Affidavit to listen in on the hidden microphone in the Jeep Cherokee would be signed by a federal judge.

If the upcoming Wednesday was going to be the day, at least we would have these two assets in place.

CHAPTER 29

THE SCRIMMAGE AND THE FBI SAC GETS COLD FEET

Just as the agents and officers assigned to the FBI's Listening Room had discerned, on Monday morning, December 5, 2016, Batiste and some of his sniper-initiated armored truck robbery crew held a "scrimmage" (rehearsal) at the Amegy Bank in preparation for "game day," which we believed would be on the following Wednesday. We believed that Batiste believed that the regularly scheduled Loomis armored truck would arrive Wednesday to deliver monies to both the bank and to fill up its ATM in the parking lot.

In anticipation of Monday's scrimmage, undercover NDTU officers and FBI and ATF agents were also in attendance as invisible spectators, at the bank, hours before the other team arrived, waiting to watch and document the other team's practice. We were careful to remain hidden and out of sight.

Besides surveillance, we were also prepared to do a tactical intervention if warranted. Several of our officers and agents were again situated in the Amegy Bank's parking garage, where not only could they observe and report, but could also provide an overwatch capability to provide immediate counter sniper fire support. Down on the ground were numerous other undercover surveillance officers; hidden several blocks away were two heavily armed/armored React Teams of NDTU officers and FBI agents, just in case. We only anticipated having to use our React Teams if we saw the bad guys had brought their guns to the practice.

Marc Hill drove his blue Dodge Ram pickup truck to the practice session. We couldn't tell whether anyone else was in the truck with him. Redrick Batiste arrived a little later, driving his Jeep Wrangler. He might have been a little late to the practice because earlier he and Nelson Polk had dropped off the Jeep Cherokee at a local automobile window tinting business. There, an undercover NDTU officer was assigned to watch from a distance as the employees of the business began applying a dark tint to it. In the meantime, the rest of us watched as Batiste drove up to the "playing field" and went immediately to the apartment complex to the south of the Amegy Bank and parked there, positioned where he faced the ATM across the bayou. He had positioned himself just where we had anticipated.

Then, what we had all been waiting for, leaving the Conklin Street junk yard was the Toyota 4Runner, driven by Nelson Polk. As it arrived in the Greenspoint area and before it went to the Amegy Bank back parking lot, Polk slowly drove it through the wide expanse of the Greenspoint Mall's parking lot.

There in the Greenspoint Mall, I was situated with one of our emergency React Teams. From my position approximately 300 yards away, I watched the sniper vehicle drive by with my binoculars. I was trying to determine, by looking through the non-tinted front windshield of the 4Runner, whether there was anyone else sitting next to Polk. I couldn't tell.

Soon the 4Runner was inside the Amegy Bank's parking lot, and Polk drove it almost immediately underneath the officers and agents positioned above in the parking garage. Dave and Justin captured several close-up photos of the 4Runner's rear tailgate as it passed by.

Immediately, they sent the pictures to my iPhone.

The sniper porthole was gone! It had been completely repaired and repainted. The only thing we could think of was that indeed a new sniper porthole had been cut, and it was now under the rear license plate which had then been modified somehow to flip up or down, so the sniper could shoot.

Sure enough, Polk parked the Toyota 4Runner, the sniper vehicle, exactly where we had expected: in the same spot where I had tracked Batiste weeks earlier in one of his middle-of-the-night visits. Polk had parked it to the east, about 100 yards away from the ATM.

It looked to us that Batiste's designated sniper crew was now on the playing field.

Redrick Batiste must have liked what he saw. Because soon the practice was over and everyone, including Hill, left the area of the bank. Batiste followed the Toyota 4Runner back to Conklin Street, where Polk carefully again "snuggled" it among the wrecked vehicles in the junk yard. From there, Batiste picked up Polk and then they both went to retrieve the Jeep Cherokee, its window tinting job now complete. Soon the Cherokee was back in its hiding spot, parked in the parking lot of the Blue Bell Street apartments.

We never saw the bad guys with any guns and so we let the other team conduct their practice unmolested, taking careful note of all we observed.

As soon as we knew for certain that all the opposing team had left the playing field, we (ATF, FBI, and NDTU) took to the Amegy Bank and conducted yet another dress rehearsal. It was getting monotonous, but our designated tactical teams ran their routes one last time. We were still "polishing the cannonball" as best we could. Particularly of concern was the coordinating of the timing between the various teams as they made their approaches to engage the different elements of Batiste's crew at the same time.

We were now certain where both Batiste would be positioned and where his sniper team, hidden within the Toyota 4Runner, would be parked.

Although watching Batiste, Hill, and Polk had been helpful in our planning for the day and further confirmed what we had suspected, I was a little disappointed with their overall scrimmage. I was still in the dark about where the bad guys' counter surveillance would be relative to the bank and who among the crew were to be the ones to pick up the money bags. What vehicle were they going to drive; where would they be parked? These suspects, like in the other cases, were surely going to be armed, probably with handguns, and, after the sniper, were going to be our next greatest potential threat. But what about Bennie Phillips? We didn't see him at the scrimmage at all, but knew from the first intercepted T3 phone conversation he was a part of Batiste's crew. Where was he? What assignment would he have on that day? Maybe he was in the Toyota 4Runner with Polk but we just couldn't see him?

After watching the scrimmage, I thought maybe Marc Hill would be the one to drive a vehicle up to the guard's body, just after he was shot, so the designated crash dummy in the car with him could jump out and retrieve the money bag(s). I didn't think Hill would be the one to jump out considering he was too fat and presumably slow. Also, we knew there was no way Hill would be driving one of his personal vehicles up to the dead guard, unless he changed out the license plates. Or maybe Hill was just going to be a lookout for Batiste.

We were missing something! Jeff and I talked about it and decided the best we could do was have a fluid tactical plan to "fill in the dots" Wednesday morning, as to the positions and identities of the other players. I bet that these other elements of Batiste's crew would reveal themselves, for sure, once our undercover officer disguised as a guard drove up to the bank in our borrowed Loomis decoy armored truck. It would be a tight, fast-moving operation and we needed everyone involved to be totally focused and switched on. Because at the last moment, we would have to hope to identify the other suspects and the vehicles they were driving, then quickly transition and "plug in" some of our other tactical officers to engage them.

The rest of Monday passed uneventfully. A federal judge was now reviewing FBI Jeff's T3 Affidavit for the hidden microphone in the Jeep Cherokee and hopefully by Tuesday morning we would have judicial approval and could listen in on any conversations held inside it.

Behind the scenes, though, as we moved ever closer to the day, the upper administrators of the Houston Police Department, the FBI, and ATF became involved and started inserting their "two cents" into the operation—with almost disastrous results!

For much of 2016, the elected mayor of Houston, Sylvester Turner, was searching for a new chief of police for the Houston Police Department. In the running and vying with each other for this highly sought-after appointed position were several present members of the Houston Police Department's Command Staff (executive assistant chiefs and assistant chiefs).

Mayor Turner, instead of going with a known department insider, appointed an "outsider": Hubert "Art" Acevedo, who had been the chief of the Austin, Texas, Police Department. Austin is regarded in Texas as being the most "progressive" of the Texas cities, an island of liberalism in a sea of predominately much more conservative Texas cities and communities. Albeit, the big Democrat-run urban Texas cities of Houston and Dallas were not that far behind.

It would be safe to say there is little middle ground regarding Chief Acevedo's "unique" style of police administration among HPD's rank-and-file; he is detested by many and loved by some. He has a different style of leadership!

Chief Acevedo was appointed the chief of the Houston Police Department on November 30, days before our planned sting operation. He probably barely knew where to find the coffee pot, and unbeknownst to him, a unit in "his" department was about to undertake one of the most significant police tactical/sting operations in the history of the Houston Police Department.

On Monday, Captain Baimbridge requested an urgent audience with Chief Acevedo. It was probably one of the first meetings with his employees that Acevedo held in his new capacity as the chief of the Houston Police Department.

Prior to Chief Acevedo's appointment, Captain Baimbridge had tried to clue in the previous chief of police and the present Command Staff as to the seriousness and potential of the NDTU's sniper surveillance operation. But according to him, he had been met with pretty much "yawns of disinterest" or dismissive placating comments, such as "That's nice; let us know what happens!"

What was sad was that representatives from the Houston-based armored truck companies had been beseeching the Command Staff of the Houston Police Department, clamoring that the department do something about the guards who were being shot and killed in robberies. It might have been that the HPD's police administrators didn't care about the dismantling of a serial murdering robbery crew, because their consuming passion was on who among them would be the next chief of the Houston Police Department!

It must have "rocked their world" when Mayor Turner announced Art Acevedo's appointment.

Captain Baimbridge thought it wise that he fully brief the newly appointed chief of police about the NDTU's operation scheduled for Wednesday. He didn't want his new boss to be blindsided, particularly if we ended up in an officer-involved shooting of a black suspect.

To those reading this book, the notification of the chief of police prior to such a significant tactical/sting operation might seem to be a no-brainer. But for us, there was always some risk in this. As I have previously discussed, some Houston Police Department's Command Staff are bereft of real operational police tactical experience and might, after having been briefed, decide and then order an unwise or unrealistic course of action. Given the paramilitary structure of a police department, we would have to obey that order, assuming it was legal, even if the order was obviously a poor or even a dangerous one. This might have been the case with Janet Reno, the then-Attorney General of the United States, and her involvement in the disastrous raid conducted by the ATF, on the Branch Davidian compound in 1993.

But in this case, it was wise for Captain Baimbridge to thoroughly brief the new boss. He also felt that because of the pleas of these armored truck companies and the gravity of the situation and that the previous administration had ignored the situation, Chief Acevedo would be more willing to let the NDTU's sting operation take place rather than to settle for some minor criminal charge—a slap on the wrist—for Batiste or his crew.

According to Captain Baimbridge, his initial meeting with Chief Acevedo went well. The new chief was confused why a patrol division's tactical unit would be involved in such a significant surveillance operation. Chief Acevedo thought, at first, Baimbridge might have been over the CID. After all, didn't CID do these sort of things? But after careful explanation by Baimbridge about the NDTU's commercial business robbery initiative and that both HPD Homicide and the FBI had specifically sought the NDTU for assistance in the investigation, Chief Acevedo grasped the situation and gave his blessing for us to continue with the planned operation for Wednesday.

So far so good.

Unfortunately, several hours later, Assistant Chief Eisenman called Captain Baimbridge and told him that upon further consideration, Chief

Acevedo now wanted the Houston Police Department's SWAT Detail to be involved in our operation. This seems reasonable, but there were some operational issues which now arose that were not so easily settled.

In Houston, when the SWAT Detail becomes involved, they then "own the operation." Overall operational control would now rest with the captain of the SWAT Detail and they would not integrate with the NDTU. Whereas HPD SWAT was good at what they trained for and did frequently, like barricaded suspects and/or high-risk warrant service, their forte was not covert, high-risk surveillance that would also be fluid and fast-moving. Most of the SWAT personnel have never had any appreciable previous undercover or surveillance experience. The Trojan horse/tactical sting operation, scheduled for Wednesday against Batiste and his crew, was not HPD SWAT's "cup of tea."

I am not criticizing the Houston Police Department's SWAT Detail! I am just pointing out the fact that they are good at what they are trained to do, but maybe not so good at other types of police operations. Sometimes the view of the Houston police administrators is that the members of the SWAT Detail are all some sort of "supermen" and able to "perfectly" carry out any police tactical operation. This is not necessarily true.

Captain Baimbridge was concerned with the chief's order to include the SWAT Detail in our operation, this late in the game. It might be that because of the complexity of the operation and SWAT's lack of familiarity with the terrain around the Amegy Bank and all things pertaining to Batiste and his crew that they might "fumble it up."

As it turned out, he was right.

Fortunately, Captain Baimbridge was able to negotiate a compromise position between the SWAT Detail and the NDTU. I would still retain overall control of Wednesday's operation, but then once I was satisfied that all the members of the Batiste Robbery Crew were at the scene of the Amegy Bank, and knew where they were situated—when I felt that "all the stars were aligned"—then just before the combined coordinated takedown was to be initiated, I would pass operational control and responsibility over to the on-scene SWAT commander.

I hoped Tuesday would be a quiet day for all the members of the task force. That morning, we conducted one last in-depth meeting to carefully review our operational plan. Also present at the meeting with us were some agents and officers who had spent many boring hours in the Listening Room. The discussion in the meeting shifted to whether tomorrow (Wednesday) would really be the day. Some were not entirely convinced. Jessica Bruzas, who was normally quiet and reserved, and who had listened to many of the T3 conversations, looked directly at me from across the room and said quietly, "Tomorrow's the day!"

The only thing left for Tuesday was to meet with the representatives of HPD's SWAT Detail and bring them up to speed on our operation as best we could, before going "live" early the next morning.

Tuesday, though, would be anything but quiet!

There had been a storm long brewing, and it now exploded. By afternoon, the Special Agent in Charge of the FBI's Houston Division, Perrye Turner, who had been appointed by former FBI Director James Comey, "got scared" and by all appearances, in the interest of "political correctness," nearly derailed and sabotaged our entire operation!

What was worse, in my opinion, was that FBI SAC Turner also potentially endangered the lives of the Houston police officers who were to carry out the dismantling of Batiste and his crew in a few hours!

On Wednesday morning, our task force of Houston Police Department, North Division Tactical, officers, FBI and ATF agents would conduct a highly complicated sting operation and take down a sophisticated sniper-initiated armored truck robbery crew. The chance of there being a law enforcement shooting involving elements of this crew were high. Like most of the robbery crews operating on the north side of Houston, the Batiste Robbery Crew was comprised of black men. Presumably, if there was an officer-involved shooting during our tactical operation, one or more of these black male suspects would be killed or wounded. It would be a high-risk and dangerous operation.

Maybe, more importantly, in the minds of some law enforcement administrators, was the potential political fallout coming from the political left of the country, particularly those within the Black Lives Matter side of the aisle. Maybe compounding this was that Batiste was known to have ties to black liberation-type radical groups. Maybe if Batiste was killed, he would become some sort of martyr for these groups and there could be social unrest. Maybe in the minds of these law enforcement administrators/politicians, it was more important to not take the chance of antagonizing these black activists, than to bring to justice a serial murderer, who happened to be black. It didn't matter that many of the victims of this serial killer were also black! It was all about the political optics.

To those acquainted with the situation, it appeared that FBI SAC Turner (not to be confused with Houston Mayor Sylvester Turner), didn't want to get his "hands dirty" and let the FBI agents under his command participate in an operation where the shooting of a black suspect was perhaps likely.

The political optics of a law enforcement shooting involving a federal agent might not turn out to be "good press" for the FBI; the news media "spin" and resulting public perception were an unknown factor. Maybe the FBI SAC thought it better to avoid the whole situation.

Even though President Trump had been just elected into office and was viewed as pro law enforcement, the overall direction of the federal Justice Department over the previous eight years, under President Obama's administration, had not been considered "law enforcement friendly." The Justice Department was still perceived as suffering from what some considered a "hangover effect" wherein any law enforcement's usage of "righteous violence" against black suspects was viewed with great suspicion and to be avoided at all costs.

FBI SAC Turner wanted no part of Wednesday's operation! Maybe it was to ensure the image of the FBI Field Office of which he was in charge of? Maybe he thought it best that Batiste and his crew be arrested immediately for some other minor criminal charge, like Unauthorized Use of a Motor Vehicle, before the sting operation and a possible shooting of a black suspect by one of his agents? Maybe he thought if arrested for a minor charge, prior to Wednesday, Batiste and his crew might "roll over" and confess to the conspiracy to kill armored truck guards? Just like some Houston Police Department administrators, it might have been more about the political optics than protecting innocent lives or holding accountable the suspects for far greater crimes.

Arrest the suspects for whatever minor criminal offense that could be immediately proven up and be done with it!

Unfortunately for FBI SAC Turner, the United States Attorney's Office of the Southern District of Texas was more "high minded" and less concerned with issues of political correctness. The FBI SAC "demanded" that the AUSA's office (Heather and Rick) authorize arrest warrants for Batiste and maybe some of the others for "something—anything!", so that the planned Wednesday morning sting operation would not have to be undertaken. To this, the AUSA's office told FBI SAC Turner: "Nyet!" Or maybe a better translation would be "go pound sand!"

Maybe Rick and Heather were obstinate in this regard because they also wanted to permanently dismantle the Batiste Robbery Crew, hold the suspects responsible for the other murders, and bring closure to the victim's families. I had also told Rick and Heather that the upcoming sting operation, although complicated, was doable and in my view less risky than other proactive surveillance operations against robbery crews undertaken by the NDTU in the years previous.

The FBI SAC was not satisfied with the response from the AUSA's office and his next step was to meet with the new chief of police of the Houston Police Department on Tuesday afternoon.

In the office of Chief Acevedo, for a meeting to discuss the imminent sting operation, was FBI SAC Turner, Captain Baimbridge, Lieutenant Bellamy, FBI Agent Coughlin, several members of the outgoing Houston Police Department's Command Staff, and "others."

There was much discussion about the next morning's sting operation, but much to his credit, Chief Acevedo again decided that in the interest of justice to go ahead with the operation.

The Houston Police Department was still "in."

FBI SAC Turner reportedly was perceived as being the worst kind of "political hack" and while "fearful" was also an "arrogant ass" during the meeting. The FBI SAC allegedly had a "meltdown" when he couldn't dissuade Chief Acevedo and declared he was pulling "his" people out of the operation.

Chief Acevedo's response was that the Houston Police Department would go it alone, if need be!

If there was to be any gunplay, FBI SAC Turner would let the Houston Police Department be the possible bad guys and take all the risks (both political and physical). HPD would have to do all the dirty work. The FBI was washing their hands of it and would not help us in the sting operation at the Amegy Bank. All the SWAT-trained FBI agents I had been relying to help us were being pulled out.

Some in HPD viewed/view FBI SAC Turner as the worst sort of law enforcement administrator/politician and had now endangered our mission by taking out the FBI SWAT-trained agents who were so familiar with our operation. The problem was that, with now only hours to go, all the FBI agents who we had been working with and who had been well rehearsed and practiced for the operation were no longer available. It would not be possible to "spin up to speed" the Houston SWAT Detail in the hours remaining. The gap left by the departing FBI agents would be hard felt and dangerous.

I guess Jeff Coughlin saw what his boss did as a betrayal to the men and women of HPD! If the FBI pulled out, it would leave the NDTU's sting operation shorthanded of those intimately familiar with the operation, and it was too late in the game to safely bring in others to backfill the FBI vacancies.

FBI SAC Turner had just made the dismantling of the Batiste sniper-initiated robbery crew much more dangerous for HPD. But apparently he didn't care; the politics were more important.

Maybe in this meeting Agent Coughlin lost his temper and raised his voice against the head of the Houston FBI Office. Maybe Jeff did so in front of the leadership of the Houston Police Department. Maybe he embarrassed SAC Turner! A young FBI agent had called out the bureaucrat/politician head of the Houston FBI Field Office in front of Chief Acevedo.

Agent Coughlin would later suffer the wrath of the Houston FBI SAC for his impertinence.

But I know this: FBI Special Agent Jeffery Coughlin gained much respect from the members of the Houston Police Department who were in that meeting that day, including the admiration of Chief Acevedo himself!

Overall, the meeting didn't go so well.

At least I still had Dom and Big John, our ATF agents, still on board—or so I thought.

Soon after the meeting, FBI SAC Turner was on the phone with the head of the Houston ATF Office, who was about to board a flight to go on his honeymoon in Hawaii and talked him into pulling Big John and Dom out of the sting operation.

The Houston FBI and ATF administrators were really trying to cover their rear ends on this one.

I now wanted to somehow delay the implementation of the next morning's operation to have more time to backfill the void left by "our"

FBI and ATF agents. We needed more time to adequately "spin up" the Houston SWAT Detail.

But that was difficult. After well over three months of around-the-clock surveillance, we knew Batiste and his team were finally ready to go. If I delayed and didn't send in our decoy Loomis armored truck the next morning, we ran the risk of Batiste changing up bank locations or the ever-present danger of our surveillance operation finally being uncovered. All the stars were now finally aligned and a part of me didn't want to do anything that might change it!

Much more important than my concerns was that my new boss, Chief Acevedo, was fully aware of the pullout by the FBI, yet had still expressed full confidence in the NDTU. Chief Acevedo had green-lighted the next morning's operation and fully expected us to pull it off without the help of the federal government. Especially considering he had already decided to "plug in" the Houston Police Department's SWAT Detail—at literally the last minute.

That Tuesday evening, we tried as best we could to repair the damage wrought by Houston FBI SAC Turner. Over dinner, Captain Baimbridge, Lieutenant Bellamy, Lalo Torres, and I met with Lieutenant Richard Besselman and Sergeant Thomas "Tommy" Colabro from the Houston Police Department's SWAT Detail. I was still livid with the FBI SAC; he had put us in a bad position and I explained to Lieutenant Besselman that the FBI SAC had set us up for failure!

As best we could, we began explaining to Lieutenant Besselman and Tommy about the intricacies of the Batiste Robbery Crew, particularly their use of a sniper team and counter surveillance. Lieutenant Besselman, who had previously been assigned to the Narcotics Division and had a good working knowledge of surveillance operations, quickly recognized the problem(s).

For one, all the SWAT trucks were identical. They were all black Ford Expeditions, with heavily tinted windows and all black tires; if one looked closely enough, you could also see the police emergency lights mounted within, not to mention the suspicious-looking antenna arrays mounted on the roof.

He also realized that on the next morning, SWAT would not only be unable to bring any of their vehicles, but they could not even bring the "Bear" (SWAT-marked armored vehicle) anywhere near the Amegy Bank—or, for that matter, even up into Greenspoint.

Fortunately, Lieutenant Besselman had a fix for the blacked-out SWAT vehicle problem. The officer/technicians assigned to the department's Bomb Squad were each issued a large, nondescript white Ford F-250 Super Duty truck, which looked for all the world like a very non-police electricians work truck. By "borrowing" several of these vehicles from the Bomb Squad, Lieutenant Besselman figured he could load five SWAT operators into each one and still maintain a more covert profile than if they used their standard SWAT-issued vehicles. Also, instead of using the Bear, he would go with my plan of using our borrowed Brink's undercover armored truck to initiate the operation by first ramming the Toyota 4Runner with the sniper crew inside and try to flip it over. If SWAT later needed the services of their Bear "after first contact" to clean up the mess, it would be pre-positioned ahead of time at the Houston Police Academy, to the northeast of Greenspoint, maybe a ten to fifteen minute drive from the Amegy Bank. There it would be sitting, engine running, manned, ready to roll at a moment's notice.

Up in the parking garage with my guys, Dave Smith and Justin Williams, Lieutenant Besselman put two of his snipers, who would be armed with SWAT's standard fare bolt-action .308 rifles with high-powered telescopic sights. One sniper would be assigned to watch over Batiste in the Jeep Cherokee to the south and the other to cover the Toyota 4Runner to the east.

I was happy to learn that Patrick "Hootie" Straker was to be the assigned SWAT counter sniper who was to watch over the Toyota 4Runner with Batiste's sniper crew inside it. I had no doubt that if Hootie saw the armored truck sniper lining up to take a shot, before our Brink's armored truck rammed the 4Runner and *if* he felt innocent lives were in immediate danger, he would kill the sniper on his own initiative with one well-placed .308 round! It worked for me. Pat and I trusted each other. He had my back several years earlier when we were involved in taking down a homicidal suspect who we ended up having to kill.

I still thought it was a bad idea to conduct what amounted to a "ground assault" on a hidden sniper. But what do I know? I am only a police sergeant.

Following close behind the Brink's undercover armored truck would be the "electrician work trucks" with SWAT personnel all sandwiched inside. As this was happening, other "electrician trucks" with other SWAT operators would simultaneously be taking down Batiste in the Jeep Cherokee as well as the suspects in a yet unknown vehicle who we figured would be set up at the bank to pick up the money bag(s) lying next to the dead guard. Of course, we still had to figure that one out!

The great disadvantage for HPD SWAT was that none of them were familiar with the Amegy Bank or the surrounding area. There had been no time for any of them to physically go out to the area and practice their routes or to see at ground level, in real life, where they would be going or to rehearse their role in a complicated operation. It would also not be wise for any of the SWAT officers to even go to the location that night. There was always the possibility that Batiste or some of his crew might be out at the bank, also getting ready. Since they were not familiar with the "players," they might run into them and be compromised. The best HPD SWAT could do, in the time remaining, was to look at satellite overhead views of the area and "visualize." To pump as much information into the SWAT Detail about the operation, to improve our chances for success, Blake VanPelt from our Crime Analysis Section stayed up until two a.m.

with a SWAT Detail Leader, "hand feeding" him all the information we had gathered over the past three months.

Maybe an initial hindrance to effective communication between the NDTU and SWAT was that there was a long history of "very little love" between the assigned HPD SWAT Detail Leader and most members of the NDTU. Fortunately, everyone was a professional and put their personal animosities aside (for the moment) to make the best of a bad situation.

I was sure missing our FBI and ATF agents who we had been working with all this time and who knew as much as the NDTU did about Batiste and his crew.

One of the last persons I talked to that night was Jeff. He was still an angry FBI agent. For the "better good," Jeff had already made the personal, yet maybe career-wrecking decision to help us the next morning.

FBI Jeff's direct involvement in the operation was still important to any chance of our overall success. We were a sounding board for each other, and I leaned heavily on his insight into Batiste and his crew. More importantly, FBI Jeff was the federal government's case agent for the entire investigation. Assuming that in a few hours we didn't kill every member of the Batiste Robbery Crew, there would be a federal prosecution of the survivors. FBI Jeff would have to help Rick and Heather facilitate that prosecution.

But not only that, I needed FBI Jeff out at the Amegy Bank, near Batiste and the Jeep Cherokee to "command detonate" the secret FBI hidden engine kill thingy inside the Go Cart when the time came, so we didn't have a car chase.

ATF Special Agents John McDonald and Dominic Rosamilia had also come to the same conviction as FBI Jeff. Despite what the Houston ATF SAC had decreed, at the prompting of the Houston FBI SAC, both Dom and Big John were still going to help in the operation—not in a direct confrontation with Batiste or his crew, but to help in the undercover surveillance at the bank. Although, just like FBI Jeff, if the circumstances necessitated, they would be willing to "pull the trigger" and later face the wrath of their bosses—their consciences clear.

CHAPTER 30

THE DAY

At four a.m. on December 7, 2016, the NDTU was at its office, preparing for the long day ahead. The date December 7 carried a lot of symbolism for me as well as for some others. My 1970s high school NJROTC instructor was an old, grizzled, no-nonsense retired United States Navy chief petty officer. He sometimes talked about the Japanese surprise attack on Pearl Harbor on December 7, 1941. I don't know whether the old chief was actually there or not, but I suspect he lost friends on that day and he never forgot.

More personal to me was that December 7 was also the anniversary of Timothy Abernethy's murder. Many of the members of the NDTU had known and worked with Tim for years. We hadn't forgotten!

I am not superstitious, but couldn't help but notice the coincidences of these dates. I didn't bring it up with the others; I didn't have to. They all remembered Tim, but we didn't dwell on it. Everyone needed to focus on what was to occur in the next hours ahead.

Before I began our tactical briefing to the whole assembly, Captain Baimbridge called Lieutenant Bellamy, Lalo, Heath, and me to an impromptu private meeting in my office. I thought maybe my captain wanted to give some sort of police mid-manager "ill-timed, last-minute, rah-rah" speech, something a trio of tired and hardened police sergeants didn't need to hear right just then.

Instead, Captain Baimbridge wanted to pray with us and for us! He prayed for exactly what I had been praying for the past few months: that we be able to stop the killing of innocent people, bring some comfort to the families of the victims, that the perpetrators be held accountable for their crimes, and that God would protect us. I don't ever recall, in all the years before, a captain in the Houston Police Department ever praying with his subordinates.

The briefing began, the conference room was filled, and our plan was laid out.

Dave Smith, Ben LeBlanc, and Justin Williams were to be up in the parking garage with the SWAT snipers. They would identify and call out the locations and vehicle descriptions of Batiste's crew, namely: the sniper team, the shot caller, the pick-up team, and any counter surveillance.

One of the NDTU officers had already volunteered to be the "bait." Travis Curtner would wear a security guard's uniform and would drive the decoy Loomis armored truck. We felt it necessary, to keep up appearances, that he drive the normal delivery route or at least go to several banks along the normal delivery route prior to going to the Amegy Bank. FBI Jeff and I suspected that the bad guys would have surveillance set up somewhere along this route, to warn Batiste and the rest of the robbery crew when the targeted armored truck was headed to their location. If so, the best place for Batiste's lookout to be would be somewhere along the North

Freeway, which was the normal route the Loomis armored truck would take when headed to the Greenspoint area. Travis, by being our bait, would provide the diversion we needed to bring up our tactical assets from their hiding places all around Greenspoint to the "last line of departure." He would never be in any personal danger as long as he stayed in the armored truck.

Travis's call sign for this operation was "Goat Boy"—much like when hunters in India would tether a goat to a tree, as bait, then wait in a hidden blind nearby for Mr. Tiger to emerge out of the jungle, looking for an easy meal. The nickname of Goat Boy still sticks to Travis to this day.

As Travis drove the decoy Loomis armored truck up to Greenspoint, he would be covertly trailed by Big John and Dom, who would try to spot anyone following him prior to his arrival at the Amegy Bank. If so, hopefully, Big John and Dom would be able to transition from following the decoy to following and watching whoever was following and watching the decoy Loomis armored truck. That way, before the takedown, I could assign one of the non-allocated tactical teams to arrest/engage this suspect(s).

As Travis drove the decoy Loomis armored truck up to the Amegy Bank, he was to park right next to the ATM. When he did this, it was hoped that the bad guy's sniper team, shot caller, pick-up team, and the counter surveillance would watch him intently, anticipating a guard to exit the armored truck with all that money!

Once FBI Jeff and I had a firm mental picture of who all the players were and where they were positioned, and after I had allocated arrest teams for each, I would then pass operational control over to the on-scene SWAT supervisor.

The SWAT supervisor would then coordinate and order all the arrest teams, both SWAT and NDTU, to move from their hiding places, in and around the Greenspoint area, to their last line of departure, which was near the Amegy Bank itself, but still out of sight of Batiste's crew. Once this was done and everyone was in position and had checked in over the radio, the SWAT supervisor would then begin a countdown; each individual tactical team, depending on where their assigned target was located, would leave their last line of departure at the appropriate time somewhere along the countdown, so that everyone "hit" their objectives at nearly the same time. Again, a several second, early arrival bias was given to the Brink's armored truck, which we wanted to arrive just before everyone else so it could ram and flip over the Toyota 4Runner with the sniper team inside it.

Unless, of course, Pat "Hootie" Straker up in the parking garage got a "bad feeling" and killed Batiste's designated sniper beforehand.

Our Brink's 25,000 pound undercover armored truck would be driven by one of the NDTU/WET members, Jose "Z" Zapada. Before life in HPD, Jose had been a United States Marine and had driven large diesel-powered armored vehicles in the service. Since the time we had been "gifted" the Brink's armored truck months before, Jose had been practicing driving it and knew its unique handling characteristics. He drove it to the Amegy Bank during some of our practice sessions and knew exactly the route he was to take from his last line of departure to where we thought the Toyota 4Runner would be parked. He knew how fast he could safely make sharp corners and the speed he needed to get in the straightaway just before he hit the sniper vehicle to turn it over. We knew Jose to be calm, cool, and collected. This was an important assignment and because it was so critical, Steve Smith, the captain of SWAT, wanted to replace Z and have one of his guys drive the Brink's. Captain Baimbridge argued against it, citing all the reasons above. Captain Smith reconsidered, but as a compromise measure wanted one of "his" SWAT operators to ride up in the driver's compartment of the Brink's with Jose—just in case.

The placing of this unnamed SWAT operator, who until a few minutes before the operation had never been in a Brink's armored truck, would prove to be a bad idea.

The cab of this Brink's armored truck had an escape hatch built into its roof. This escape hatch is for just that: if the truck should ever overturn onto its side or the driver needs to exit post haste, then the guard/driver inside the cab can safely get out via this hatch. What none of us knew, including the SWAT supervisors, was that this unnamed SWAT operator was not going to be content to sit next to Jose inside the cab of the Brink's, safely ensconced behind all of that bulletproof glass and armor. On his own initiative, he decided that on the final run in, before the Toyota 4Runner was rammed, he would open the hatch, poke his head and shoulders out, and ride the Brink's armored truck into battle, much like General Erwin Rommel in a German Panzer tank.

Playing General Rommel Tank Commander was not part of the plan and what happened later proved why it was not wise to plug in unknown, unfamiliar, unvetted personnel into your operation at the last moment.

Following in a minute or so later, well behind the Brink's armored truck and all the tactical/arrest teams (comprised of NDTU and SWAT), would be uniformed patrol officers to establish a police presence and seal off the entire area.

A police helicopter was again placed on standby. The pilot and observer flew in from the airport and landed at the Police Academy. There they sat and would take off as soon as the order was given for the various tactical units on the ground to move up to their final point of departure, before the countdown, initiating the engagement.

As soon as the dust settled, when Batiste and the crew at the bank were taken into custody or "rendered safe" and the scene was secure, the NDTU—along with other members of the task force—would immediately transition to a long laundry list of other tasks related to the overall investigation that needed to be performed as soon as possible. These other operations were important to Rick and Heather in their federal prosecution, as well as FBI Jeff. They would have to put all the pieces together afterward and wanted no ends untied.

These tasks included:

- Execute an evidentiary search warrant at Batiste's home at 1351 Tarberry. Once the house was secured, an FBI Evidence Response Team composed of both agents and civilian support personnel would then come to the location and carefully process it for evidence.

- Execute an evidentiary search warrant of the Conklin Street junk yard, where the Toyota 4Runner had been hidden, for any evidence that might be found there.

- Execute an evidentiary search warrant of the abandoned house on Willow Street, where it was assumed that Batiste and/or others had sighted in and practiced with the sniper rifle.

- Interview the shade tree mechanics on Willow Street who had recently done work on the white Toyota 4Runner.

- Arrest Buchi Okoh. Okoh had an outstanding minor arrest warrant (unpaid traffic ticket) and taking her into custody would provide a timely opportunity for HPD Homicide investigators to interview her about the unsolved murder of her former multi-millionaire employer, Joseph Stewart of Stewart Cadillac fame.

As I finished my briefing, we all then began loading up and getting ready to head up to Greenspoint. I had told everyone to be in their respective positions an hour before the Amegy Bank was to open and well before the later window of time when Batiste and his crew believed that the regularly scheduled Loomis armored truck would arrive.

Before we left, I pulled Pat Straker aside for a private conversation. "Hootie, this sniper is a serial killer. He's going to shoot it out with us."

Pat knew what I was hinting at, knew what I was thinking. Pat responded, "No worries,

Sarge. If I have to, I will take him out before any of our guys get close to him."

I knew Pat. He wasn't lying.

As all the good guys headed up to Greenspoint, Batiste and his crew were already starting to move. In rapid succession, over fifteen minutes, my iPhone sounded incoming messages, alerting me that the tracking devices on the Jeep Wrangler, the Jeep Cherokee, and the Toyota 4Runner were outside their designated geo fences and on the move.

"Exit Tarberry Geo Fence—Jeep Wrangler."

"Enter Blue Bell Geo Fence—Jeep Wrangler."

"Exit Blue Bell Geo Fence—Jeep Cherokee."

"Exit Conklin Geo Fence—Toyota 4Runner."

Redrick Batiste drove his Jeep Wrangler straight to Blue Bell Street, where he parked it and got into the Jeep Cherokee. He then went back to his house, where he pulled into his garage.

A few minutes later, he drove back out. It was good to see that Batiste was using the Jeep Cherokee, because now the Listening Room could overhear any phone conversations he might have via the Cherokee's secret hidden microphone.

We might not have been able to crack Batiste's burner phones, but we had the next best thing!

The Toyota 4Runner was also moving. I could see the Conklin Street pole camera image well enough to identify who got into it and drove it out of the lot: Nelson Polk!

Over the next hour, we waited patiently as we tracked both the Jeep Cherokee and the Toyota 4Runner to different locations, mostly within Acres Homes. I imagined that Batiste and Polk were picking up other members of the crew and their weapons. As the time went by, some of the NDTU guys up at the Amegy Bank started getting antsy. What were Batiste and Hill up to?

Over the radio, one of them queried, "Sarge, do you want a few of us to come down there and get eyes on them?"

No, I responded; just hold your positions. "If today is the day, they will be coming to us very soon." Everybody was on pins and needles. Our radio was silent of all the normal chitchat. I had reminded everyone beforehand that communication was critical, only to "break the air" (talk on the radio) if it was of vital importance. If in doubt about the overall importance of what they wanted to say, they were to call me on my cell phone and I would then decide whether it was important enough to put out over the radio for all to hear.

I didn't know it, but scattered throughout the offices of HPD, the FBI, and ATF were uninvolved officers and agents and their supervisors huddled around radios, listening to our operation.

Ben LeBlanc, who was up in the parking garage with Justin, Dave, and the SWAT snipers, broke the air. "I have eyes on Marc Hill. He just showed up at the bank. He's driving his black Infiniti QX56. No one else is in the car with him."

The first member of Batiste's crew had just made his appearance. Hill was driving a wide, multiple-mile, circular route around the Amegy Bank, driving the roads around the bank and strip center, with monotonous regularity. He kept making a big "circle": east on the Sam Houston Parkway Service Road, south on Ronan Street, west on Benmar Drive, north on Imperial Valley Drive, and then back to the Sam Houston Parkway. After Ben's warning, I could even see Hill's black Infiniti on one of the FBI's pole camera way off in the distance every time he drove down Ronan Street.

Marc Hill was not going to be the one driving the vehicle up to the dead guard so the crash dummy could jump out and grab the money bags. He was instead running counter surveillance, making sure there was no law enforcement in the area around the bank and making sure all was clear before Batiste and the rest of the crew arrived. Sure enough, the FBI's Listening Room monitoring the hidden microphone in the Jeep Cherokee was soon reporting that Batiste had just received a call from someone and had acknowledged the caller with an affirmative response.

I am sure it was Marc Hill calling Redrick Batiste, telling him that the coast was clear; bring them up.

Soon afterward, as I watched the tracking map that showed the locations of the Toyota 4Runner and the Jeep Cherokee, they were both now headed toward Greenspoint and the Amegy Bank!

I started narrating on the radio. The next to arrive in the area was the Toyota 4Runner. I kept updating its location, until Dave and Justin got eyes on it as it slowly crept into the parking lot. With little fanfare, it pulled around to the Amegy's back parking lot and just as we expected, parked well to the east of the ATM, about 100 yards out. As I looked at the FBI pole camera, I noted that it was not parked in the exact spot I had expected. It was close but not exact. I took a screenshot of the image of the sniper vehicle and where it was parked, and sent it out on a group text for everyone to see.

Just to make sure, I broke the air on the radio and raised Jose in the Brink's armored truck. "Z, can you see your target?"

Jose Zepeda sat in the driver's seat of the Brink's armored truck as it idled, tucked away in another business parking lot only a quarter of a mile away from the Amegy Bank but out of sight from the bank. Jose was parked by another ATM, which was normally serviced by Brink's. If Hill happened to notice our Brink's armored truck, I was hoping he would think nothing of it. As it turned out, he never did!

Our Brink's armored truck was hidden in plain sight, in position, ready to go as soon as the SWAT supervisor initiated the countdown.

Again, Ben broke the air in a calm, cool, and collected voice. "I can see two suspects in the Toyota 4Runner."

It was what we had expected: one of these two suspects would be the sniper, the other an observer or driver. Our armored truck sniper team was on the field! Already, I could imagine Pat behind his .308, sighting through his scope, watching and waiting for the first indication that the opposing sniper was getting ready to shoot.

But I was the one working the throttle, setting the tempo of events. Still, many miles away to the south, Travis, driving the decoy Loomis armored truck, sat in another bank parking lot, engine running, waiting for my signal to drive toward Greenspoint and the Amegy Bank. Keeping a careful eye on him were our two faithful ATF agents.

There would not be any other armored trucks making deliveries around Houston or in Harris County this morning. FBI Jeff had made the call and all the armored truck companies in the region immediately shut down operations. The only two armored trucks on the north side of Houston were a Loomis and a Brink's, and both were being driven by undercover police officers from the Houston Police Department's NDTU.

Now, as Marc Hill in the black Infiniti continued circling the area and as the suspects in the Toyota 4Runner sat and waited, coming up and pulling into the area, like some unhurried predatory shark, was Redrick Batiste, driving the Jeep Cherokee. As we expected, he parked in the apartment parking lot, 150 yards away from the Amegy's ATM, across the bayou, behind a chain link fence.

The shot caller for the sniper-initiated armored truck robbery crew was now on the playing field and in position.

On the FBI pole camera, I could see the live image of the Jeep Cherokee with Batiste inside, while on the screen right next to it I could also see the image of the Toyota 4Runner from the other camera.

Redrick Batiste had positioned the Jeep Cherokee so that its front end was oriented toward the Amegy Bank across the bayou, but also angled to the ATM that to view it, he probably had to look through the driver's side window. But from this position, he could also view the Toyota 4Runner and most of the area around the rear of the bank through the front windshield. Batiste was in the position we had expected him to be in.

Justin was intently watching Batiste through his spotting scope and could make him out clearly as he sat in the Cherokee's driver's seat. Batiste was alone in the vehicle. Then, soon after arriving, Justin watched as he put up two large sun screens across the inside of the Cherokee's front wind-shield, which then made himself all but invisible to the guys up in the parking garage. He was careful, though, to leave a small space to still be able to view the bank and the Toyota 4Runner.

December 7, 2016 – Redrick Batiste in the stolen black Jeep Cherokee (center) in an apartment complex across a bayou from the Amegy Bank.

After Batiste had taken up his position, Lalo and Jeff drove into the same apartment complex parking lot, out of sight and behind Batiste, but close enough so Jeff could keep eyes on the Jeep Cherokee and initiate the "kill switch" when the time came.

I called FBI Jeff to review who we had in our trap:

Marc Hill (in a black Infiniti QX56) was conducting counter surveil-lance around the Amegy Bank.

Redrick Batiste (in the black Jeep Cherokee) was the shot caller and was parked in the apartment complex across the bayou from the bank.

Nelson Polk and another unknown suspect were in the Toyota 4Runner and were parked in the strip center's rear parking lot to the east of the ATM.

Still, our trap was not completely filled, and we didn't want to spring it shut until we were sure everyone was inside it. We were still missing John Scott, although maybe he was in the Toyota 4Runner with Polk? And

508

where were the bad guys who would rush in and pick up the money after the sniper killed the guard?

FBI Jeff and I continued talking to each other. I had convinced myself that John Edward Scott was in the Toyota 4Runner with Nelson Polk, and this was Batiste's sniper team. Taking out the sniper team and Batiste were the prized trophies we wanted in our trap before we sprung it, and we now had that. I would now start rolling Travis in the decoy Loomis armored truck to the Amegy Bank. It would take a while for him to get to us but once he arrived and parked the Loomis armored truck next to the Amegy's ATM, then the other members of Batiste's crew might reveal themselves.

I hung up with Jeff and was back on the radio. "Travis, you're up—start driving to the Amegy Bank!"

Goat Boy acknowledged and started heading to Greenspoint. I signaled Amanda Morgan to place an elementary school in the general area of the Amegy Bank on lockdown. Prior arrangements had been made with the school officials; we wanted to make sure the students in the school were safe once the takedown commenced.

If there had been tension before, it now increased dramatically. We were putting the bait out. It would take Travis twenty minutes to make the drive from his location to the Amegy Bank. As he drove, he was dressed just like a Loomis guard happily going about his usual rounds. The radio was quiet. The only one talking now was Big John, who, with Dom, was narrating Travis's progress as he drove the decoy as they followed a discreet distance behind.

Ten minutes later, Big John advised that Travis and the decoy Loomis armored truck were now northbound on the North Freeway. He also said that as best they could tell, no one else was following, but it was hard to tell; there were a lot of other vehicles in the area.

We waited.

FBI Jeff called me; the Listening Room had just called him with some important information.

John Scott had just called Redrick Batiste and told him, "Bentley coming your way!" A Bentley was a high-end luxury vehicle, costing from $200,000 to well over $300,000. Just like the word "commissary," it was in this case slang that they used for an armored truck.

Somewhere, Scott was watching Travis in the decoy Loomis armored truck! I advised Travis, Big John, and Dom that the bad guys were now watching them and they were still miles away, not even in the Greenspoint area yet.

Big Jon and Dom tried to pick out Scott among the vehicles driving around them as the decoy Loomis armored truck headed up the North Freeway, but weren't able to spot him. This wasn't surprising given all the heavy northbound traffic in the immediate area. It was also probable that Scott had been parked in a business parking lot along the route and when Travis drove by, he alerted Batiste.

Now we knew where Scott was (sort of) and, more importantly, where he wasn't. He was not the other unknown guy with Nelson Polk in the Toyota 4Runner!

We waited as Travis and the decoy Loomis armored truck got closer and closer to the Amegy Bank. Big John and Dom were sure that Travis was not being followed and just as he drove into the Amegy parking lot, they pulled off.

Soon, Travis parked the decoy Loomis armored truck next to the Amegy Bank's ATM.

It was normal for the armored truck crews, when pulling up to banks or ATMs, to not get out of their trucks for a few minutes. I probably had as long as ten to fifteen minutes before Batiste and the rest of his crew became antsy or suspected something was amiss.

The next two or three minutes went by slowly. Still, there was no sign of the other suspects who would rush in and pick up the money after Batiste's sniper killed the guard as he stepped out of the armored truck.

FBI Jeff called me again with an urgent update. The Listening Room had just overheard a tidbit of critical information—words spoken by Redrick Batiste in a phone conversation with John Scott. Within seconds after realizing how important the information was, they had relayed it to Jeff, who immediately called me.

With these few words, spoken by Batiste himself, everything now finally fell into place!

Batiste, sitting in a stolen Jeep Cherokee, across the bayou, all buttoned up with sunshades pulled across the front windshield, casually remarked to Scott, saying *he* was now "setting up for the shot" and also made some reference to "it's like looking through a screen door."

Redrick Batiste himself was the sniper!

December 7, 2016 – Picture of Redrick Batiste in the Jeep Cherokee as he prepares to kill yet another armored truck courier. Image taken by a hidden camera and later recovered at the conclusion of the operation.

It was not some other member of his crew. He would shoot from the Jeep Cherokee from across the bayou, through the chain link fence ("screen door") over 150 yards away from where Travis was sitting inside the decoy Loomis armored truck next to the Amegy Bank's ATM.

There was no bad guy sniper team in the Toyota 4Runner! I then realized that Nelson Polk and the other unknown person inside were the guys who would drive up to the guard after Batiste killed him and retrieve the money. Nelson Polk was the driver and the other man inside with him was their expendable crash dummy. Marc Hill and John Scott were conducting counter surveillance; Hill was close to the Amegy Bank and Scott was much farther out.

Quickly, FBI Jeff and I conferred. Everybody was in our trap except for John Scott. I deferred to Jeff. "Jeff, do you want to do it now?"

Jeff replied, "YES… We can find and arrest Scott later. LET'S DO IT!"

Carefully and deliberately, I then got on the radio channel, which was being monitored by everyone participating in the operation:

"The sniper is not in the white Toyota 4Runner! The sniper is Batiste. He is in the black Jeep Cherokee parked in the apartment complex and he's lining up for the shot at this time! The two suspects in the 4Runner are the pick-up team. They're waiting for the guard to get out of the Loomis armored truck and for Batiste to kill him."

Now what was important was that Redrick Batiste, the sniper and our greatest threat, be taken down before the other suspects—Surprise, Speed, and Violence of Action. We were having to alter our operational plan slightly just before its implementation to adapt to rapidly changing circumstances. Jose would not be able to drive the Brink's armored truck into the apartment complex where Batiste was located to ram the Jeep Cherokee. The Brink's was too large and he would not be able to navigate it through the complex to where it was parked. It was best to still go with the original plan: we knew that the suspects in the Toyota 4Runner were going to be armed, but Batiste, the sniper in the Jeep Cherokee, had to be taken out first.

I am not prone to drama. But, maybe to prompt the SWAT sniper who was watching Batiste inside the Jeep Cherokee, I again reiterated that the sniper was in the black Jeep Cherokee and to the team which was assigned to take him down: "YOU'RE GOING INTO A GUNFIGHT!"

Silently, I hoped that one of our SWAT snipers would feel legally justified and kill Redrick Batiste right then, so we didn't have to engage him in a close-quarters shootout.

The moment was at hand now that everyone involved had received the latest information. Everything was in place! The takedown was now imminent and over the radio, I passed operational control to the on-scene SWAT supervisor. As I did so, he then acknowledged that he was now in control of the operation.

What was supposed to happen now, what had been planned for and thoroughly discussed at length was that the various tactical teams would then be ordered to leave their hiding places in Greenspoint and move to their last point of departure. Once they all arrived there and confirmed they were in position, then the SWAT supervisor was to start the countdown. Then, along that same countdown, these different teams would then move out to synchronize their arrival since they were not all assembled in the same place, to not alert Marc Hill or John Scott, who were conducting counter surveillance.

Maybe it was "the fog of war" or maybe he just forgot. Instead of sticking to the plan and making an adjustment to ensure Batiste was engaged first, the SWAT supervisor, a man with a level head on his shoulders and who normally makes good decisions under pressure, said over the radio to all the waiting units: "IT'S A BUST!"

He made no directive for everyone to move up to the last point of departure. He gave no countdown! He only said, "*IT'S A BUST!*" Which, in HPD speak, means all the units were to move in immediately to make the arrest. I guess that because of the FBI SWAT "pullout" at the last minute, HPD SWAT just didn't have enough time to correctly assimilate the plan or to practice for the operation. Nor could I intervene and countermand the SWAT supervisor's order; he outranked me and it was now SWAT's operation.

Now, with the simple command over the radio of "IT'S A BUST!" and nothing else, confusion reigned. Every involved takedown team in the operation, as well as Jose driving the Brink's armored truck, started moving directly to their assigned objectives. Jose was the closest, so he would arrive first, well before any of the assigned tactical units who were not even close and who were still in their Greenspoint hiding places.

When the supervisor of HPD SWAT called "IT'S A BUST!" over the radio, there was a collective sigh of "OH NO" from every member of the NDTU as our well-planned and well-rehearsed tactical plan went to hell.

Now coming around the corner, accelerating to "ram speed" in the final straightaway, was Jose, driving that 25,000 pound Brink's armored truck, taking aim for the Toyota 4Runner. But then something else happened; suddenly the acceleration of the Brink's armored truck ceased. It started to slow down and now it sort of "rolled into" the Toyota 4Runner, instead of bowling the 4Runner over on to its side. It just sort of rocked it and put a dent in its side.

I had no way of knowing, but as Jose "floored" the accelerator of the Brink's armored truck to get enough speed to flip over the Toyota 4Runner, the unnamed SWAT officer sitting next to him decided that this was the moment to open the escape hatch atop the roof of the cab of the Brink's and look out, just like the commander of a tank. When he tried to do this, he lost his balance and his foot hit the gear shift lever inside the Brink's cab, putting the transmission into neutral! Now devoid of power, at a critical point, the Brink's armored truck coasted into the Toyota 4Runner.

The NDTUs "undercover" Brink's armored truck about to make contact with the white Toyota 4Runner. Inside the 4Runner are two members of Batiste's Robbery Crew.

When this happened, it was like throwing a rock into a hornet's nest. Soon the unknown crash dummy, as well as Nelson Polk, were abandoning ship—jumping out of the 4Runner.

More ominous was that one of these idiots had a pistol in his hand.

Up in the parking garage, 100 yards away, Dave and Pat were watching. Pat was behind his .308 rifle and Dave was laying right next to him, spotting with his binoculars. Dave called out, "*GUN!*" and Pat immediately opened fire.

A big throaty "KPOW!" reverberated and echoed throughout the Amegy parking lot.

Dave called Pat's shot: "MISS!"

As the suspect with the gun started running, Pat ran his bolt back, ejecting the fired cartridge, and slammed it back forward to chamber a live round.

Pat led the running armed suspect through his crosshairs and squeezed the trigger again.

"KPOW!"

Dave saw the impact as Pat's second shot also missed and struck an unoccupied parked car just behind his intended target.

As both suspects ran out of sight, behind a building, Pat looked down and sheepishly exclaimed, "Sorry, Dave!"

As all this was happening, Redrick Batiste still sat, seemingly unnoticed. He was now in the backseat of the Jeep Cherokee. Also, unnoticed, he had lowered the driver's side window and a sheet of black Mylar hung in its place. Batiste had been sighting his sniper rifle through a hole in the Mylar, as he had waited patiently to shoot the Loomis armored truck guard who he expected to get out at any moment.

But now with his pick-up team in the Toyota 4Runner being rammed by a Brink's armored truck and seeing Polk and the crash dummy bail out and run, while someone from somewhere was shooting at them with a big gun, Redrick Batiste moved from the rear seat of the Cherokee back into the driver's seat as he said out loud to himself, "Get out of there" and "Fuck, Fuck, Fuck!"

Already, other members of the NDTU and HPD SWAT were arriving and were rounding up Nelson Polk and the crash dummy, who, after having being rammed by a "rogue" Brink's armored truck and shot at, quickly surrendered as they saw the arriving heavily armed tactical officers coming for them.

Mark Smith had kept close eyes on Marc Hill. As all this was happening, a team of NDTU officers stopped his vehicle in a nearby parking lot and there he meekly surrendered and as Mark later explained, "He gave up like a little bitch!"

Maybe Redrick Batiste, seeing that his well-planned operation was falling apart, wanted to quietly drive out of the apartment parking lot and disappear.

But he couldn't!

As soon as Pat pulled his trigger, FBI Jeff pulled his and the engine of Batiste's Go Cart died. Batiste couldn't restart it and maybe this was why, after we reviewed the video from the hidden camera inside, he continued muttering, "*Fuck, Fuck, Fuck*" to himself as he tried in vain to restart the engine.

Maybe Batiste realized that the tables had been turned, and he was trapped!

The hunter had become the prey.

As Batiste continued to try to restart the Cherokee's engine, FBI Jeff, Lalo Torres, Lieutenant Bellamy, Captain Baimbridge, and other NDTU undercover officers hidden nearby watched and waited anxiously for the designated HPD SWAT Assault Detail to arrive and take on Batiste, as planned. They were still racing to the apartments, still in their electricians work truck, weaving in and out of traffic, even clipping a metro bus as they raced to engage the sniper.

In the complexity of the operation and with not enough time to absorb it all, HPD SWAT had been caught with their pants down and were now trying to make up for lost time.

It would not be pretty!

The tactical element of surprise had been lost and now Redrick Batiste, a cold-blooded serial killer, was fully roused and on the alert.

There would be a gunfight!

Finally, over thirty seconds after Jose had hit the 4Runner with the Brink's armored truck and Pat had tried to pick off one armed suspect in Batiste's pick-up team, the HPD SWAT Assault Team arrived to help the NDTU take down Batiste. As SWAT screeched into the apartments, they pulled up immediately behind Batiste, who was still in the driver's seat of the Jeep Cherokee, trying to restart the engine.

The takedown of Redrick Batiste was about to begin.

As soon as SWAT pulled in behind the Jeep Cherokee and as the NDTU began their approach, one SWAT operator quickly lobbed a stun grenade over the Jeep Cherokee, where it exploded on the far passenger side with a deafening roar and a blinding flash. The deployment of the stun grenade was to distract Batiste, maybe overwhelm him with the concussive loud blast as well as the bright light flash. Maybe HPD SWAT thought that by using a stun grenade, Redrick Batiste would somehow be cowed into submission.

Stun grenade deployment as the takedown of Redrick Batiste commences.

He wasn't.

As the flash bang grenade detonated, Batiste was coming out the driver's side door with his rifle in hand and he got off the first few shots. The problem for him, though, was that his .223 caliber AR-15 was configured as a sniper's rifle and had a large 3X9 variable-powered telescopic sight mounted on it. Although such a scope might be good for shooting at long range, it was actually a hindrance for fast, rapidly evolving, short-range, close quarter battle types of gunfights. Not wanting to use his scope,

Batiste instead canted his rifle to the side, so the scope would not block his view of the approaching law enforcement officers as he began shooting.

Batiste got two shots off in rapid succession. He missed both times. Unfortunately for him and fortunately for us, after firing just two rounds from his thirty-round magazine, his rifle jammed. The fired cartridge from the second round had failed to extract correctly, leaving it still in the rifle's chamber, while the bolt had continued its cycle; after stripping a third live cartridge from the top of the magazine, the bolt had then rammed this live cartridge into the back of the spent cartridge. Batiste's rifle was now hopelessly jammed and inoperable.

Maybe Redrick Batiste should have attended the Colt Armorers school for AR-15-type weapon systems like I had years earlier. If he had, then he might have known that the extractor spring in his rifle was weak and needed to be replaced.

But he didn't!

In the same split second that Batiste was shooting, he was then rapidly struck by multiple .223 rounds, fired by one of the good guys. One or more of these rounds impacted into his lower chest, and other rounds struck his hip and left leg, shattering the femur bone.

As soon as his rifle jammed, Batiste dropped it and hobbled and tried to run to the nearby chain link fence that ran along the bayou. Reaching it, he then briefly tried to climb over it to escape. His femur broken, Batiste couldn't climb over the fence, so he then tried to pull himself over by just using his arms and one good leg. As he tried desperately to get away he was then shot in the back with a Taser. Now he fell to the ground; he was quickly handcuffed behind his back, and rendered "safe."

The aftermath of the shootout a fatally wounded Redrick Batiste lies on the ground handcuffed just prior to arrival of tactical medics.

As all this transpired, Travis Curtner sat safely inside the decoy Loomis armored truck, sipping his Smoothie King protein shake, watching with a nonchalant, clinical sort of detachment as the drama unfolded.

HPD SWAT, in its operations, brings along "tactical medics" who in real life are also highly experienced medical doctors and trauma surgeons. As soon as Batiste was rendered safe, one of these tactical medics began his work to try to stabilize him for the ambulance ride downtown to the Houston Medical Center.

Even handcuffed and strapped into the ambulance's gurney, Batiste still struggled to escape. As the paramedics prepared to leave, a uniformed police officer jumped into the back to ride with them downtown, to keep an eye on our wounded prisoner.

As the tactical medic and I watched Batiste being loaded into the ambulance, I asked, "Doc, do you think he will make it?"

Doctor David Persse thought for a moment, while pulling off his bloody latex gloves, and shrugged. "Maybe. He's been shot through the liver. He's bleeding out, but he's also heading to the best trauma hospital in the country—so maybe?"

As the ambulance raced downtown, Batiste finally stopped struggling as he steadily weakened. Then, maybe in a last moment of self-reflection, he mumbled to the officer riding with him, "So this is how it feels to die!"

And then he did.

When Redrick Batiste arrived at the trauma center, the attending physicians pronounced him dead.

CHAPTER 31

THE AFTERMATH AND "AMERIKKKA IS STILL RACIST AS HELL!"

Given his association with radical black supremacy groups, I didn't identify the member of the Houston Police Department who killed Redrick Batiste for fear of any retribution on him or on his family.

As the dust settled at the scene at the Amegy Bank, it was soon swarmed by the usual news media, IAD, Crime Scene and Homicide investigators, as well as Civil Rights attorneys from the Harris County District Attorney's Office. Rick and Heather also arrived. I saw them in the distance as I was getting in my car, leaving to execute the next phase of the operation. My eyes briefly locked with Rick's and he mouthed the words *"THANK YOU!"*

As I was leaving, Chief Acevedo had also just arrived with an entourage of Command Staff members. I chuckled to myself. Two of the (old regime) assistant chiefs were scurrying to keep up with the new chief of police as he hurried around the crime scene, taking it all in. Chief Acevedo had let it be known he was "cleaning house" and would not be keeping all the old members of the Command Staff in his new administration, some of whom he was already referring to in such uncomplimentary terms such as "House Mice"—in that they were an infestation in the organization; they only take and gave nothing in return. All the present Command Staff House Mice who infested HPD would have to reapply and if not reappointed, they would have to either retire or revert to their old civil service ranks. They were panicking. Some members of the Command Staff had actually only held the rank of lieutenant before the political winds had lofted them up to much higher, well-paid positions with the resulting perks that went along with them. Now it looked like some of them were doing all they could do to impress Acevedo, by acting as if they were now interested in crime fighting or, I imagined, somehow pretending that all the while they had been an integral part of the NDTU's armored truck sniper investigation.

The second suspect in the Toyota 4Runner was identified as Trayvees Duncan-Bush. He was the crash dummy: a no-account, down-on-his-luck street punk Batiste and his crew would use and then discard. He was to jump out of the Toyota 4Runner after Nelson Polk drove him up near the dead guard's body; his only job was to grab the money bag(s) and return post haste to the Toyota 4Runner. Duncan-Bush had been promised a significant sum of money for this one simple act. When interrogated by Ben LeBlanc, he readily confessed to his role in the conspiracy. He had never worked for Batiste and his crew before and had been specifically recruited by Bennie Charles Phillips solely for this one operation. Phillips was also Duncan-Bush's "handler" and had provided a burner phone and rented a room for him at an area hotel.

The plan was that after grabbing the money bags, Duncan-Bush would jump back into the Toyota 4Runner and Polk would drive off away from the scene. Then, a short distance from the Amegy Bank, they both would abandon the Toyota 4Runner and would be picked up by Hill, making good their getaway. Batiste wanted to make sure that when the abandoned Toyota 4Runner was discovered by the police, there would be nothing to indicate that it had been used previously as a sniper platform. This was why he had taken such pains to have the sniper loophole in the back tailgate repaired or "erased." There was no sniper loophole under the license plate like I had originally conjectured. The plan to abandon the 4Runner was identical to the plan that they had carried out with the stolen Ford F-150 in their successful million-dollar armored truck robbery and murder of Alvin Kinney in 2015. And just like in 2015, they would try to get the entire money load inside the Loomis armored truck, and were not going to be content with just one or two money bags.

Bennie Phillips had been another core member of Batiste's robbery crew of which we had known nothing about until the T3 went up. Now we knew what role he played in the planned robbery/murder. Duncan-Bush also told Ben that Phillips was not at the scene of the Amegy Bank on the morning of December 7 with the others because he had a mandatory scheduled meeting with his parole officer. The NDTU arrested him (as well as John Scott) a few days later and turned them both over to the United States Marshals for their safekeeping.

Trayvees Duncan-Bush told us everything he knew. He said that he had a "bad feeling" about participating in the sniper-initiated armored truck robbery and "felt" that after fulfilling his role, the others would kill him. He said he was actually relieved when he was captured by the police! I am not sure I believe him. Supposedly Duncan-Bush had tried to back out of the December 7 operation, but had been told by Batiste "*it was too late, he knew too much!*" and "*he would have to go through with it—or else!*" We suspected that Batiste and/or the others were going to kill him later; maybe dumping his body in a Louisiana swamp to be consumed by hungry alligators. This may have been the fate of the crash dummy in the March 18 murder of Melvin Moore. And to this day, we have no idea of the identity or what happened to the designated crash dummy in the August 29 murder of David Guzman.

Eerily, Duncan-Bush recounted how Batiste always wore a full-size black mask over his face to obscure his features when Phillips brought him to meetings to lay out his role in the operation.

I am not sure why Batiste and the others didn't have the two bullet holes in the side of the Toyota 4Runner repaired, which Justin Williams had first noted months earlier. A few weeks after the sting operation at the Amegy Bank, our previous knowledge of the existence of these same bullet holes would solve yet another unsolved high-profile Houston Capital Murder.

The NDTU initiated a search warrant on the residence at 1351 Tarberry an hour after Redrick Batiste was dead. The FBI Evidence Response Team recovered many items of interest, which included several handguns, materials to make fraudulent credit cards, as well as a bundle of cash amounting to a little over $5,000 hidden in the back of the kitchen freezer.

What really stood out, though, was Batiste's homemade bomb vest, which had to be rendered safe! What was he going to use that for? And there was a black market, unregistered, suppressor (silencer) for a .223 caliber rifle. The suppressor had been damaged; it appeared that at one time it had been incorrectly mounted and thereby not perfectly aligned with the barrel of Batiste's rifle. When fired, a bullet had struck a baffle inside the suppressor (baffle strike), causing serious damage. This was probably why Batiste did not use it earlier that day. But, when had he damaged his suppressor? Was it rendered inoperable during target practice or during another attempted criminal sniper-initiated attack that we knew nothing about?

Redrick Batiste also had a shrine set up inside his house. It appeared to me to be his "altar" to the revolutionary Black Nationalism movement. The centerpiece was a picture of himself just after he had defecated and was now wiping his rectum with an American flag. Also inside the shrine were artifacts that might be construed as being associated with the original

Black Panther Party or perhaps the New Black Panther Party, such as a military camouflaged shirt, a hand grenade, and M-16 rifle (both of which were props and were inert). Printed on a piece of paper inside with his other "venerated objects" were the words *"AMERIKKKA IS STILL RACIST AS HELL!"*

The FBI Evidence Team searched Batiste's house as best they could, even using small cameras to look down into the interior walls. We were looking to recover whatever remained of the million dollars from the February 12, 2015 armored truck robbery and murder of Alvin Kinney. Except for the money bundle found in the freezer, no large amounts of cash were discovered inside the house—at least, by us! Two days later, some neighborhood crack heads were caught by patrol officers pilfering through Batiste's residence. Then, a few months after that, the house—though still vacant—was thoroughly and systematically ransacked. Even the interior walls were ripped out. Obviously someone was looking for the money. Maybe they found it?

Inside the abandoned house on Willow Street, we found many spent .223 cartridges. As we suspected, Batiste was using it to mask the sounds of gunfire from his rifle. He did so by shooting from deep within the abandoned house and out the back door, into the pasture beyond. This way, none of the neighbors in the area would be alarmed.

We also searched Redrick Batiste's Wrangler. Inside was the full-size black mask as described by Duncan-Bush. Also found was the book he had been reading when I briefly met him, in a customer waiting area some weeks earlier. The book he had been reading was titled *How Successful People Think* by John C. Maxwell.

Buchi Okoh was arrested right after Batiste was killed. She was taken into custody for her outstanding traffic ticket/warrant. She was interviewed about her knowledge regarding her boyfriend's involvement in multiple robbery killings, and about her ex-employer Joseph Stewart's murder. Okoh denied everything. To this day, I think she was lying and had to have provided information to her boyfriend to help facilitate both the home invasion and Stewart's murder. There is insufficient evidence to indict her, so she is still a free woman.

Also, while being interviewed, Okoh noted that Redrick was an angry man and was preoccupied with what was happening around the United States, specifically the shootings of unarmed black men by police. He talked of a time soon coming when he would do something about it.

The home computer recovered from 1351 Tarberry also provided more insight into Redrick Batiste's mind. He read books about the evils of white supremacy that were authored by other black men. He even wrote letters to black men who had been convicted of killing white police officers and who were now serving their life sentences in prison. Batiste would write them, telling them "he appreciated what they had done."

Batiste wanted to start a race war in America. Maybe the rumors about a sniper being used to kill a police officer at a Houston-area Black Lives Matter event was part of his plan to start the "war"? Maybe his bomb vest was also part of the plan? Maybe he had a similar motive as John Allen Muhammad, the infamous DC Sniper from October 2002.

Skip Hollandsworth, an executive editor for *Texas Monthly*, wrote a series of articles on the Redrick Batiste investigation. During his research, he interviewed several of Batiste's closest friends and family members, as well as Buchi Okoh. During these interviews, it was confirmed that Batiste did harbor strong views about racial injustice in America and ascribed to overthrowing the established order and reordering society. Skip also discovered that Redrick Batiste had written a book or a publication espousing his belief system and life experiences. He was able to get a picture of the front cover of the book or publication from a "source." The book is titled *The New America—Money, Murder, & Madness: An exclusive look into the heart of America from a free thinker*. It is dated May 5, 2016 and clearly depicted on the front cover are several pictures of Redrick Batiste. Also pictured on the front cover is the same type of mask that we found in his

Jeep Wrangler, the same mask he had used to conceal his identity when meeting with Duncan-Bush, the expendable crash dummy. We have not been able to find an actual copy of this book/publication. If so, maybe it would have shed more light into Batiste's character and motivation.

Skip and I have talked at length about what might have motivated Batiste. In his interviews with the people who knew him best, he concluded that perhaps Batiste's motivation in killing armored truck guards was out of some great frustration. As a black man, with a criminal record and without a college degree, he could not secure any bank loans. Batiste had wanted to fund his real estate and business ambitions, and by killing guards and stealing the bank's money, it was some sort of "payback" because these financial institutions were largely owned and controlled by white men.

I respectfully disagree with Skip. I believe that Batiste's primary motivation was just plain greed.

The shade tree mechanic who had "erased" the sniper loophole in the Toyota 4Runner denied knowing what it had been for, or even having performed the original work.

A few days after our Amegy Bank operation, Special Agent Coughlin was summarily involuntarily transferred out of the Violent Crime Unit by Houston FBI SAC Turner. He was then reassigned to a domestic counter-terrorism unit—which sounds cool, but it's not! It's considered drudge work by many FBI agents. It was widely viewed that Jeff was being retaliated against because he had stood up to the Houston FBI SAC in their meeting with Chief Acevedo.

Not only was he transferred, but he was also removed as the case agent for the Armored Truck Sniper investigation. The investigation was reassigned to another agent who knew nothing about it.

Jeff was pretty upset, and he didn't think he wanted to work for the FBI, given the political climate. He would resign and go work in the private sector, where he could make a lot more money. I and others talked Jeff "off the edge" and counseled him to wait a few months until he cooled down, before he made his final decision. Fortunately, the totality of the Batiste investigation would prove complex and the United States Attorney's Office (USAO) was not satisfied with the investigative effort of the FBI agent who now had the case. From what I understand, the USAO applied "friendly coercion" to FBI leadership above the Houston FBI SAC and eventually Jeff was transferred back to the Violent Crime Unit and reassigned the Armored Truck Sniper investigation.

Mark Telle, the FBI's Violent Crime Unit and Jeff's supervisor, was at the federal government's mandatory age for retirement. However, the FBI had a provision to extend employment for up to two years after mandatory retirement age, if the agent was in "good graces" and/or depending on the investigation(s) they were involved in. Instead of having his employment extended for two more years, he was told to retire by Houston FBI SAC Turner. And he did.

Jeff didn't forget about the mystery bullet holes in the side of the Toyota 4Runner! In January 2017, one evening while watching TV with his young sons, he saw a brief news story about the murder of a prominent black Houston-area businessman, who had also been a voluntary chaplain for the Fort Bend County Precinct 2 Constable's Office. Carroll Oliver was sixty-eight when he was shot down in the course of a robbery the year previous, in January 2016. He had been murdered in the parking lot of a McDonald's restaurant he owned while walking to his car to drive to the bank to deposit money. While in the parking lot, he was confronted and killed by two gunmen driving a white SUV. After killing Oliver and retrieving the bank bag, they had then escaped in the same white SUV. A year later, Oliver's murder was still unsolved and there was a great deal of community pressure on the Houston Police Department's Homicide Division to solve the case, and so anyone with any possible information about the incident was urged to contact investigators.

FBI Jeff's mind clicked when he heard "white SUV"!

The next day, he called the HPD Homicide investigator assigned to the investigation, Detective Fil Waters, for more details about Oliver's murder. According to Fil, it was a straight-up thug rip! Oliver was walking in the parking lot with the bank deposit money when two masked black males armed with handguns approached him, with guns drawn. Oliver was a fighter and immediately pulled out his own handgun (he had a concealed carry permit). The suspects opened fire and killed him. They then grabbed the bank deposit bag and fled the area in their white SUV.

Jeff was focused on the white SUV. "Fil, is there any other information about it?"

Fil Waters said he thought maybe it had been a white Chevy Tahoe, then relayed that in one surveillance video from the McDonald's parking lot, it appeared that due to the fluid nature of the confrontation, one suspect—while shooting at Oliver—may have also accidentally fired one or more handgun rounds into their own getaway vehicle, the aforementioned white SUV!

Jeff also learned that Carroll was killed by a .40 caliber bullet, which was recovered from his body at autopsy.

Fortunately, "our" white Toyota 4Runner, with the two bullet holes in it, which we had tracked for all those months and was used at the Amegy Bank the month before, was still in the possession of the FBI. Jeff had evidence technicians carefully "dissect" the bullet holes and they were able to recover one spent bullet that had buried itself deep into the vehicle's frame. It was also .40 caliber.

FBI Jeff sent the .40 caliber bullet recovered from Oliver's body and the one dug out of the Toyota 4Runner to the forensic examiners at the FBI's Firearms/Toolmarks Unit (FTU) in Washington, DC. They were a match! Both bullets had been fired from the same pistol.

The Batiste Robbery Crew had killed Houston's prominent black businessman Carroll Oliver.

Carroll Oliver was a community leader and highly thought of. So much so that Houston Mayor Sylvester Turner had dedicated a day to his memory, along with a proclamation of tribute to keep his legacy alive. It was reported that he had a "servant's heart" and his "lifelong calling was to help the poor and underprivileged." He was most recognized for giving jobs to the people in his community, especially teenagers or veterans. It was also said he often gave out free food to the homeless or those who could not afford a meal, and also granted numerous unprivileged high school students scholarships so they could pursue college.

He was so remembered for his warmth and generosity that Houston, some four years after his murder, renamed a street near one of his restaurants to "Carroll Oliver Way," dedicated to his memory.

What a loss to the community!

FBI Jeff not only solved the Carroll Oliver murder case, but he also solved the May 7, 2015 murder of Joseph Stewart. Jeff conducted additional historical analysis of Batiste's personal cell phone, which showed that on the day and approximate time that Stewart was shot and killed, Batiste's cell phone was pinging in the immediate area of the murder scene. I wouldn't be surprised to learn that someone had slipped a tracking device on Stewart's Cadillac SUV while it was parked at his dealership, to help Batiste coordinate his attack, to "hit" Stewart just as he was pulling his SUV into the garage of his upscale neighborhood.

The Original Informant who provided the initial information about "Red"—which proved to be so instrumental in our operation, but who feared becoming further involved, because Batiste's "people" would kill him—all proved warranted! Months after we killed Redrick Batiste, a black male with a pistol in hand walked up to the Original Informant, who was sitting in his car with one of his kids. The hitman shot our Original Informant thirteen times with a .380 automatic pistol! Amazingly, he proved to be hard to kill and survived, eventually making a full recovery. To this day, he still resists being placed in a witness relocation program because of all his Houston-based children. Maybe a hit had been put out on his life by those who knew Redrick Batiste and/or shared his ideology? Or maybe it was to prevent him from possibly testifying in any forthcoming federal trial against Marc Hill, Nelson Polk, Bennie Phillips, or John Scott? Then again, I am not sure that he and/or his minions didn't ransack and tear out the walls of Batiste's house looking for the million dollars, after it became public knowledge where he had lived.

It was ironic. Despite his black supremacy ideology, Redrick Batiste had no compunctions about killing other black men. Maybe Batiste's belief system was trumped by his love of money? Maybe he found it empowering and intoxicating to kill other human beings? Except for Joseph Stewart, who was white, and David Guzman, who was Hispanic, all of his other known victims were other black men. This list doesn't even include the missing crash dummies or the other suspected murders I have not documented because they are still under investigation. Maybe in the years ahead, Jeff Coughlin, Jessica Bruzas, and David Helms will be able to connect even more dots.

We had worked so hard to recover the .223 caliber sniper rifle that we were hoping to link to the murder of David Guzman. The .223 caliber AR-15 sniper rifle that we recovered at the Amegy Bank that Batiste had been using was shipped off to the FTU in Washington, DC, along with the .223 bullets recovered from inside Guzman's body.

The bullets didn't match. The bullets that killed Guzman had not been fired out of the rifle we recovered from Batiste. Or at least they hadn't been fired through the same barrel!

But, by "cracking" Batiste's personal cell phone, which we had recovered as evidence on December 7, 2016, Jeff discovered that Batiste had his own personal gunsmith! It was the same man, who months before, the NDTU had identified meeting with Batiste in a north side parking lot. Although gainfully employed as a full-time fireman, he also ran a low-profile, clandestine, gunsmithing business on the side, manufacturing and modifying AR-15 rifles!

When interviewed, the gunsmith confessed and gave up everything he knew. He told of manufacturing fully automatic AR-15s (machine guns) for Batiste, who would then sell them for profit to "unknown others." He also admitted to manufacturing the damaged rifle suppressor we had recovered at Batiste's home. Most interesting was how Batiste would contact him periodically to replace the barrel on his "personal" AR-15. This was the same one we had recovered at the Amegy Bank. Batiste was also savvy enough to make sure and specify that the rifling twist of any replacement barrels be compatible with the weight of the .223 bullets he was planning to use. Batiste always specified that he only wanted barrels installed wherein the bullet would rotate one complete turn in every seven inches of travel. He wanted to ensure optimum accuracy! Unfortunately, the gunsmith would then take the used barrels that he removed from Batiste's sniper rifle and "repurpose" them to other AR-15s he was building, and then would sell them to unknown others.

By replacing the barrel on his rifle at intervals, there would be no ballistic link or unique markings on fired and then recovered bullets, which were germane to Batiste's sniper rifle. If there had been a commonality of ballistic markings on bullets recovered from different murder victims, it might have eventually been a red flag to forensic examiners as the bodies of different murder victims were autopsied and bullets recovered. Then, maybe over months or years, someone would eventually realize that multiple murder victims had all been killed by the same weapon. This would have alerted law enforcement to a "on the loose" serial killer.

I didn't identify the gunsmith because of his cooperation in the investigation/prosecution of the core members of Batiste's crew. I imagine that when everything is all said and done, he also will be in a federal prison somewhere. We can now account for the rifle that Batiste used and that the barrels were swapped out; hence, no ballistic link between murder victims. We can also account for the origins of Batiste's rifle suppressor. But what we can't account for (and this is troublesome) is the whereabouts of the machine guns that were made by the gunsmith specifically for Batiste. There is no reason not to believe the gunsmith when he said he manufactured several for him, since he was making a statement against his prurient interest. But none of these fully automatic weapons have yet been recovered. Maybe Batiste sold them to some domestic terrorist organization with which he ideologically identified with? We don't know.

Batiste's female acquaintance who had originally rented the black Jeep Cherokee for him, to help facilitate its theft fully cooperated when interviewed and agreed to testify for the prosecution in the trial of the rest of the crew. She had some "plausible deniability" about what the Jeep Cherokee would be used for and/or that she denied having any knowledge about Batiste's intent to steal it, so she was not criminally charged. There was not enough evidence to show she was actually an accessory. She says that she "was just doing a favor for a friend." I will let the reader draw their own conclusions. I have also not identified her by name since she is a professional woman who works at a Houston-area law firm.

Batiste also trafficked young women in prostitution. Ample evidence of this was uncovered in both his personal cell phone and home computer. Maybe the young "Martin Street Girl" was being groomed to work for him as a prostitute. Maybe Batiste would eventually be advertising her on BackPage.com, a classified advertising website that specialized in the buying and selling of sex. Maybe the NDTU gave her another chance?

Some other women that Batiste might have trafficked in prostitution were also used in support roles for some of his robbery operations. One had been employed at the McDonald's restaurant where Carroll Oliver was killed; she had been in a position to know his bank deposit schedule (shades of Buchi Okoh and Joseph Stewart?). Yet another identified prostitute Batiste was pimping out was interviewed by David Helms and Jessica Bruzas about her relationship with him. This woman offered up, without being specifically asked, that she was a getaway driver for the crew in the Airline Drive sniper murder of Melvin Moore.

More federal indictments might be forthcoming and the trail is still being unraveled!

The one person we know for sure we gave another chance to was a young black man named Joshua Tyler. Joshua was the Loomis guard on Houston Route 13 and was the man who was to deliver the money to the Amegy Bank on December 7, 2016. I hope Joshua will read this book someday and come to realize the great effort undertaken by so many people to keep him alive. Yes, I agree: Black Lives Do Matter!

Joshua Tyler (left) the Loomis guard who was
targeted by Redrick Batiste and his crew.

In January 2017, a month after the Amegy Bank operation, I would retire. I had fallen into the same trap as before—a drift toward being a workaholic and neglecting my family. I had thirty-six years of service with HPD and would have a comfortable retirement. I also realized, given my conflicts with the department lawyers and Command Staff over my stance about the first priority of life should be given to innocent citizens while conducting tactical operations, that I or the NDTU would eventually be in another shooting involving black suspects. When that happened, the department lawyers and some Command Staff members would be coming after me with sharpened knives.

But before I could announce my retirement, in a big surprise, Lalo Torres announced his first! He also had enough of the internal drama within HPD and was leaving.

Lieutenant Bellamy was being promoted to captain and would soon be transferred to command his own patrol division. Captain Baimbridge was being transferred to the Tactical Operations Division, where he would be in charge of the SWAT Detail, Bomb Squad, Hostage Negotiators, and the Dive Team. Being assigned as the commander of either the Tactical Operations Division or the Homicide Division is considered to be one of the more prestigious commands any captain can hold in HPD. At least under his watch, no innocent hostages would be left to bleed out while the SWAT Detail was ordered to stand idly by.

With Lalo leaving as well as Captain Baimbridge and Lieutenant Bellamy, I couldn't—or didn't want to—leave the NDTU without someone they trusted, since all the other ones were going. So I figured I would work for a little while longer. Heath Bounds, who was burned out from running the WET for all those years, took Lalo's place. I reasoned that when Heath was fully trained up on the NDTU's commercial business robbery initiative and everything was running smooth with him and his leadership style, I would then retire in the summer of 2017. Besides, eventually the federal trial against Marc Hill, Nelson Polk, John Scott, Bennie Phillips, and Trayvees Duncan-Bush would take place, and I wanted to be available to Jeff, Rick, and Heather in case they needed me to help them in preparing for trial and/or to testify.

Into 2017, the NDTU continued dismantling commercial business robbery crews. In one case, FBI Jeff had a clue on a vehicle that was being used by a bank robbery crew and who had gotten into a shootout with an off-duty HPD Narcotics officer who happened to be in the bank when it was being robbed. Outside the bank, the Narcotics officer engaged the crew in a gunfight and shot one suspect in the chest. The entire crew made good their escape and the physical evidence at the scene suggested that the suspect who had been shot was wearing light body armor and was uninjured. After this drama, the same bank robbery crew transitioned to robbing banks in other Texas cities. In one of these other robberies, FBI Jeff was able to develop the identifiers of a vehicle they had used to help facilitate it; this bank robbery had occurred in Corpus Christi and the vehicle of interest was owned by a woman with links to the suspected ringleader of the robbery crew.

Jeff believed, as his investigation into this bank robbery crew continued, there would be enough evidence in his reactive investigation to indict the entire crew. But it would take a little time, which in federal government "speak" probably meant a few months. He called me and asked whether I would write up a vehicle tracking order and put a tracking device on her vehicle in the meantime, so that when the indictments were handed down, he would know exactly where she and her vehicle were so she could be taken into custody as soon as possible. Of course I agreed and got to work on the order. At the end of our phone conversation, Jeff mentioned, "Oh… Chris, if you ever see her vehicle leaving Houston, it probably means it's going to be used in a bank robbery somewhere in Texas!"

I wrote the order, got it signed, and in the middle of the night, Ben LeBlanc slipped under the vehicle which, of course, was parked in an apartment complex at "robbery central" in Greenspoint.

Over the weeks, we kept tabs on the vehicle, waiting for Jeff's call that the federal indictments had been handed down so we could arrest her.

One morning, Justin Williams noted that this same vehicle was heading eastbound on Interstate 10 headed to Beaumont, Texas and/or the Louisiana border. When Justin first checked, it was just then passing out of the Houston city limits.

We followed. Several hours later, as the "Snag Mike" bank robbery crew was gearing up by putting on their masks, getting their pistols and assault rifles ready to take down a Beaumont bank, they were preempted and, after much drama, were all in custody. I was glad the NDTU didn't have a shootout in a city eighty-five miles from our police station. The Command Staff would never have understood. After all, didn't they really want us doing the politically safe thing of "dope and whores" to wow the citizens about all the felony arrests being made in their neighborhoods? To this day, I don't know that the chief of police and/or his Command Staff ever knew how close an HPD DTU got into a gunfight so far from home. I guess maybe I forgot to tell them?

In April 2017, it all ended for me. I knew that the next time we had to shoot a black robbery suspect, it would be over. We instead shot three, all armed, killing one and seriously wounding the other two.

The Harris County Sheriff's Office had identified another vehicle that was being used in a string of Houston-area robberies of fast-food restaurants. One of their Robbery investigators contacted us, asking whether we could sneak into an apartment complex that same evening and put tracking devices on a stolen vehicle the crew was using. We agreed and hours later found ourselves conducting nighttime rolling surveillance on the vehicle, which was now occupied as we waited for the opportunity to put our trackers on it.

Also assisting us was a Texas DPS squad of special investigators run by Lieutenant Ralph Ohland. According to Lieutenant Ohland, when Art Acevedo was appointed to chief of the Houston Police Department, he had appealed to the governor of Texas, Greg Abbott, for state assistance in combating Houston-area violent crime. Governor Abbott had then ordered the director of the Texas DPS to do just that. One thing DPS did was to take Lieutenant Ohland's squad of experienced undercover investigators and reassign them from mid-level narcotics enforcement to doing something about Houston-area violent crime.

After being reassigned to the violent crime mission, Lieutenant Ohland had approached me and asked that I and the NDTU train him and his investigators on the tactics we had developed in dismantling commercial business robbery crews. On that night in April, the DPS squad who had only previously worked "big dope" was helping the NDTU with our rolling surveillance and in trying to get tracking devices on the targeted vehicle.

As fate would have it, in just a short time after we started the surveillance, the robbery crew was inside a restaurant that was empty of customers, holding guns to the heads of employees, trying to get into the business's safe. As we watched the robbery going down, the NDTU, as per our tactical plan, set up to arrest and confront the bad guys after the robbery as they left the restaurant to run back to their getaway car.

However, the DPS guys, seeing a robbery going down, resorted to their Narcotics training and began stacking up at the front door to the restaurant, like it was a crack house, preparing to make dynamic entry into it and confront the suspects inside. If they did that, then there would surely be a gunfight inside between the bad guys and DPS. This was something I didn't want because it would endanger innocent citizens and/or employees inside; it was better at this point to wait for the suspects to come out into the parking lot after the robbery than take the risk of a shootout inside the restaurant.

When DPS stacked up on the outside of the door of the restaurant, some of the other members of NDTU thought perhaps the DPS operators had seen something they missed and maybe the robbery suspects were now shooting or hurting the employees, which then required immediate police intervention. Seeing this, some of the NDTU began to converge on the restaurant in support of DPS.

When it was all said and done and after the last shots were fired, three armed suspects were down, while the getaway driver was arrested, uninjured.

Afterward, the scene was swarmed by the usual news media, IAD, Crime Scene and Homicide investigators, as well as Civil Rights attorneys from the Harris County District Attorney's Office. Along with Chief Acevedo were several members of his "new" Command Staff (both executive assistant chiefs and several assistant chiefs). These new Command Staff members were, mostly, more highly thought of by the rank-and-file. But, he also had retained some from the "old guard" who undoubtedly remembered my obstinate position about the priority of life to be taken during tactical operations.

This post-shooting investigation was not going well for us. From the sidelines, I could hear the "old" members of the Command Staff pumping up Chief Acevedo with comments like "This shit had to stop!" and "They are nothing but assassins!" At the scene and in the eight months following until the internal investigation was completed, both Heath and I were treated more like criminal suspects than dedicated police officers performing a difficult mission. Even though the Harris County District Attorney's Office had cleared us of any wrongdoing, the fear was we had unduly agitated the Black Lives Matter activists in Houston, by yet another shooting of black men. After all, just a few months earlier, hadn't the NDTU been responsible for killing Redrick Batiste? And it was well known that he was firmly involved in the movement.

For eight months, Heath and I were only allowed to perform administrative duties. The entire NDTU sat idle. Toward the end of that time, we were relieved of all our duties, perhaps slated for employment termination by the chief of police. If need be, the Houston Police Department would sacrifice our careers to appease the minority activists!

We were particularly incensed when Quanell X, the leader of the New Black Panther Party in Houston, a day or so after the shooting, "slipped" during a television news interview that he had communicated with a member of the Houston Police Department's Command Staff, who had provided him with some specific information about the shooting. Briefly in the days that followed, Quanell X had tried to leverage some traction among his followers about the NDTU, but it never came to fruition. With all the violent crime in Houston, most of the law-abiding citizenry were not upset that law enforcement had shot several armed robbery suspects; they applauded it. But not the politicians! Suspicion about the leak naturally fell on a certain member of Chief Acevedo's Command Staff who was seen as a thinly veiled black activist himself. It didn't help that rumors from the Harris County Sheriff's Office was that one of their Robbery investigators had overheard a phone conversation between this same Command Staff member and Quanell X—as they discussed the DPS/HPD shooting while he was at the scene.

HPD elected to release the names of the members of the NDTU who were involved in the shooting to the news media for publication. The names of the DPS who were involved were never released. After our names were made public and the inflammatory TV interview with Quanell X, which was perhaps fueled by a politically motivated member of the Houston Police Department's Command Staff, the NDTU then had to quickly take personal measures to protect the identities of our family members and any links to our home addresses. Various governmental public record information and social media accounts were scrubbed clean and additional proactive safeguards had to be undertaken. Again, it was Micah Xavier Johnson's racial hatred that had triggered the murders of five police officers in July 2016 and his connection to Quanell X that had us concerned.

Did a member of the Houston Police Department's Command Staff, a "holdover" from the old regime, who was maybe thought of highly by Houston-area black activists, who maybe Mayor Sylvester Turner had directed Chief Acevedo to retain—did this same person in a "quid pro quo" sort of relationship with Quanell X, provide confidential information about an ongoing police investigation, or even untrue inflammatory rhetoric? If it occurred, it might not have been criminal, but it was certainly unethical and contrary to the rules of the Houston Police Department. I think it happened! As far as I know, Chief Acevedo never launched an investigation into this matter. No one wanted to look under that rock. If so, it might have rocked the Houston political scene.

In contrast to the NDTU, the involved DPS Unit was given high accolades by the DPS Command Staff and reportedly by Texas Governor Abbott himself, who reviewed the night-vision video from a high-flying Black Hawk helicopter that was overhead during our operation. I think that the contrast was that the state government entity that DPS worked for was conservative/Republican while Houston was liberal/Democrat. They have markedly different views on law enforcement matters.

In the fall of 2017, it appeared that the Houston Police Department was going to fire Heath and me. Leading the charge against us were some of the usual department lawyers and old Command Staff members who Acevedo had retained. However, we also had our fans. Even one of the department's lawyers rose to our defense, as well as a new member of the Command Staff, Assistant Chief Lori Bender and the captain of the North Patrol Division, Dan Harris. Both Assistant Chief Bender and Captain Harris stepped well out of bounds in trying to shield us and their careers probably suffered because of it. Fortunately, the Houston Police Officers' Union also became heavily involved in the controversy. Their lawyer told Chief Acevedo that if any draconian action was taken against either of us, they were going to the news media and uncover the whole thing.

The issue was still the priority of life in conducting police tactical operations. If we did it my way, then there was a greater probability of shooting armed suspects. If we did it the way the administration and lawyers wanted, then there would be a high-speed vehicle pursuit and a probability of a vehicle crash and injury or death to innocent citizens. But it was hard to argue against my position because of the NDTU's success. Since we had started the initiative well before Acevedo came, the rate of commercial business robberies and murders on the Houston north side had crashed to an all-time low. It was unquantified but in doing so, how many innocent lives had the NDTU saved? Or to put it bluntly, how many innocent black lives?

In one of the high-tension recorded meetings I had with Chief Acevedo as he was deciding my fate, we argued back and forth about this priority of life. I argued for innocent citizen first; he argued that no distinction should be given or tactical operation crafted that gave priority of life to either innocent citizen, involved officers, or the armed suspects. They were all equal! At least he didn't say that the life of the armed suspect was most important! As our argument escalated and became more and more heated, seated behind the chief of police, out of his view, was the president of the Houston Police Officers' Union, who shook his head back and forth in an exaggerated motion, signaling me to stop—it wasn't an argument I would win. I was only a sergeant—a mere mortal—and he was the chief of police; I was coming dangerously close to inflaming him enough to be fired. Supposedly, Chief Acevedo had made comments earlier, that, in getting rid of employees he didn't like, he gave it as much thought as "wiping dog excrement off his boots." Almost always the department lawyers would tell these officers, after their meeting with the chief, to resign or be fired! Usually department employees who were facing his ire chose resignation. If eligible for retirement, it was important to many to do so to ensure that you went out with an "Honorable Retirement" as there were certain firearm carrying privileges that the government only gave to honorable retired law enforcement officers.

The meeting was finally adjourned until the next day, so all the lawyers could convene and discuss the issue more fully, given that the Houston Police Officers' Union was threatening to take the issue public.

The next day's meeting was held in Chief Acevedo's private office (without all the lawyers) and now his tone with Heath and me was much friendlier and conciliatory. He apologized for the inaction and ineptitude of the previous administration's Command Staff regarding our commercial business robbery initiative. He also said he knew we had "good hearts" and even started to cry and become emotional when he said it. But, without further explanation, he told me that he was reassigning me to the SWAT Detail. It was totally the prerogative of the chief of police to decide where I was assigned. I couldn't even argue that it was "negative discipline" because assignment to the SWAT Detail was considered so highly. While assigned there, my primary role was to teach others in the department as well as personnel for outside law enforcement agencies "High Risk Surveillance" and my vehicle tracking tactics.

Along with my reassignment came forth a General Order to the rest of the department that no longer would robbery crews under surveillance be arrested or taken down at the scene of the crime. Rather, a high-risk vehicle stop would be initiated after the robbery with the attendant risk of a high-speed vehicle pursuit or that the suspects, while in their getaway vehicle, be "pinned" in place, somewhere away from the scene of the robbery by use of police undercover vehicles like the LAPD SIS method. At least Chief Acevedo wasn't afraid to make a decision, even if I didn't think it was the right one.

But then again, I am only a sergeant, an expendable and easily replaceable cog in the wheel of a big-city police department.

As told to me by my lawyer, by Chief Acevedo's reassigning me to the SWAT Detail, he could keep me "safe" from the anti-police political activists because of all the bad guys I had shot or been responsible for the shooting of during my supervision, albeit in an uncommonly long career. More importantly, by taking me away from the helm of the NDTU with my rigid ideology "innocent citizen first" philosophy in concert with the chief's "no police engagement with suspects at the scene of the robbery" order ensured that, with rare exceptions, no more robbery suspects would be shot by Houston police undercover officers. It was still the same story—better to risk having a police pursuit and crash with innocent citizens than having Houston police officers shoot armed criminals. A police chase was viewed as the lesser of the two evils by the lawyers and politicians.

Some FBI upper management in Washington DC thought highly of our Armored Truck Sniper investigation. It probably would have never happened with the "Obama FBI" but in September 2018, Special Agent Jeffery Coughlin, AUSAs Heather Winter and Richard Hanes, Sergeant David Helms, Susan Cornwell (an FBI civilian analyst) as well as myself received the FBI Director's Award for Excellence.

For David Helms and me, this award was unprecedented, and it was the first time that anyone in the history of the Houston Police Department had ever been so honored to receive it. The FBI was gracious enough to fly Samantha and me to Washington, DC for a few days, where we were personally presented the award by FBI Director Christopher Wray. Of course, while in Washington, DC, we did the tourist thing and visited many of the historical sights.

Late one night, while still in Washington, DC, after the FBI ceremony, we all held a small private party at a rooftop bar atop the W Hotel, which overlooks the White House. We all reflected on the Batiste investigation. Toward the end of the party, I sensed both Jeff and Heather were somber and retrospective. I pried and learned they had both come to the same conclusion: they were young in their respective careers and now realized that there would probably never be another Armored Truck Sniper case! They had already hit their career high water marks by receiving the coveted FBI Directors Award and they thought it would all be downhill from here.

Rick and I laughed at them as we tried in vain to snatch a glimpse of Ivanka Trump down at the White House. I also marveled how just a short time before my department had been ready to eviscerate me on behalf of political correctness and now I had just received one of the highest awards that any law enforcement officer could ever strive for. How fickle the finger of fate can be!

It took until the spring of 2019 before the federal trial of Marc Hill, Nelson Polk, John Scott, and Bennie Phillips commenced. During that time, all of them, including Trayvees Duncan-Bush, were kept in the custody of the United States Marshals. None of them were given bail because the judiciary believed them to be such a dangerous threat to the community. The Justice Department had also decided not to seek out the death penalty but were instead seeking life sentences with no chance of parole for everyone involved except Duncan-Bush. I am sure, however, if Batiste himself were still alive, he would have been facing the federal death penalty, given how he was now identified as the sniper and presumed to be the trigger man in other Capital Murders.

While in custody, Marc Hill and Nelson Polk proved to be problem prisoners, with frequent outbursts during courtroom hearings, which necessitated them being forcibly removed from the courtroom. In one of his outbursts, Hill maintained that only God could judge him and intimated that the laws of the government didn't apply to him. Ultimately, both Hill and Polk elected to represent themselves and forgo any trained legal counsel. This forgoing of legal counsel was probably part of an overall strategy on their part to somehow escape from custody! They argued with the judge that because they were representing themselves, they needed to be placed on bail so they could research the case and interview witnesses for their defense. The presiding magistrate was David Hittner, a Senior United States Judge of the United States for the Southern District of Texas. Judge Hittner was my sort of judge: tough, fair, no-nonsense, with a little bit of a righteous anger. Federal prisoners hated Judge Hittner and behind his back derisively called him "Judge Hitler," which is ironic because he is Jewish and came originally from New York.

Judge Hittner was not having it and wouldn't buy into the "I need to be let out on bail so I can mount an effective defense at my trial" argument.

So Marc Hill and Nelson Polk tried yet another way to escape from federal custody!

Normally, when a defendant is kept in federal custody, his or her lawyer will bring presentable courtroom attire for their client to change into immediately prior to any court hearing held before the judge. This way, the defendant is not in court wearing a prisoner's uniform, which might be considered prejudicial. Then, immediately after the hearing and out of view of the court, the United States Marshals will make the prisoner change back into their prison uniform and their "fancy clothes" are then returned to their lawyer. Also, federal prisoners are not allowed to retain any courtroom paperwork while back in their cells and it had to be surrendered to the United States Marshals.

Varfeeta Sirleaf, Marc Hill's wife, would attend every court hearing that involved her husband and/or his nephew Nelson Polk. Sometimes in her courtroom appearances, she was also accompanied by the leader of the New Black Panthers, Quanell X. Since Nelson Polk and Marc Hill didn't want lawyers, Varfeeta Sirleaf brought them their formal courtroom clothing and shoes. She had, of course, to pass through the courthouse security protocol and metal detectors with Hill and Polk's clothing and would then pass it to the United States Marshals, who would give it to them to put on just before court.

At the conclusion of one of many pretrial hearings, after Hill and Polk had changed out of their courtroom clothing and into their prison uniforms, Nelson Polk refused to surrender the courtroom paperwork in his hand. There was a scuffle and several United States Marshals had to restrain him and physically take the paperwork from him.

Inside the paperwork that Polk possessed was found a razor blade. Someone, somehow had smuggled a weapon into the federal courthouse and it had come into Polk's possession. At the time, it was unclear how it might have happened.

Then, in March 2019, just before the trial, Varfeeta Sirleaf was again coming through the security at the federal courthouse; again she was bringing the courtroom attire for Hill and Polk. Maybe the United States Marshals already suspected her in the earlier smuggling of the razor blade incident? Maybe now they were extra diligent, because they discovered a 2.5 inch box cutter hidden in one of the shoes intended for Nelson Polk to wear while in court. Word of what happened spread through the courthouse and again Hill had another "outburst" and was forcibly removed from the courtroom.

Judge Hittner was not amused and as an added security precaution, all four prisoners, while in his court, were shackled to secure eye bolts built into the concrete floor, out of view of the jury. Also, now standing behind each prisoner, was an armed United States Marshal.

Was it Varfeeta Sirleaf's intent to smuggle weapons to Polk or Hill, so they could either take a hostage or kill a United States Marshal and then take his sidearm to facilitate their escape? I think it probable. They were that desperate and/or stupid! Some might ask, "Did Quanell X know anything prior about the smuggled weapons?" There is no evidence to suggest this.

It might be that eventually Marc Hill's wife Varfeeta Sirleaf will be prosecuted in federal court. It also might be that there is also evidence that she played a part in another murder committed by Redrick Batiste, her husband, and the rest of the crew. Maybe if she is ever indicted and to get any consideration at her sentencing, she will tell everything about everything.

The trial of Marc Hill, Nelson Polk, John Scott, and Bennie Phillips finally commenced, and a jury was seated. After more courtroom theatrics, Judge Hittner had enough of Hill and Polk and appointed defense lawyers to represent them. All four of the core members of Batiste's crew were tried together.

The trial lasted for nine days. Over those days, Rick and Heather methodically took turns laying out the prosecution's case. The T3 audio recordings, along with FBI Jeff's testimony, proved to be the most damning of the evidence against the defendants. I testified to the overall surveillance operation and how by having barrels changed on his rifle Batiste could erase any ballistic link between victims. The four lawyers for the accused could only put up a cursory defense. There was not much for them to work with. Heather did the final arguments and then the jury deliberated for a short time.

All four were found guilty as charged.

Hill, Polk, Scott, and Phillips were all convicted of Attempted Interference with Commerce by Robbery and Aiding and Abetting Discharge of a Firearm During a Crime of Violence Causing the Death of Another. These convictions were related to the sting operation we had conducted at the Amegy Bank. Ironically, the surviving core members of the crew were being held accountable for Batiste's death, even though the good guys were the ones who had killed him in a shootout. In addition, Hill and Polk were also convicted of a similar charge related David Guzman's murder.

On July 2, 2019, after listening to emotional testimony from David Guzman's family and fiancée, Judge Hittner handed down the sentencing.

Of course, Marc Hill had another outburst in court, while Nelson Polk just sat and smirked.

Judge Hittner sentenced Hill, Polk, Scott, and Phillips to life in prison plus an additional 240 months after that! Hill and Polk were also then sentenced to yet a second term of life in prison, for the role they played in the murder of David Guzman. Which, during trial, had largely been proved up by the FBI's historical cell phone traffic analysis of the cell phone calls made before, around the time and in the area of the Wells Fargo Bank on August 29, 2016 when Guzman was killed.

Unless they have successful appeals, these men will die in prison.

If possible, it got even worse for both Hill and Polk. Judge Hittner proclaimed in a loud, apoplectic voice that he was writing a letter to the federal prison system recommending that Polk be incarcerated in a maximum security federal prison, and that Hill be incarcerated in a super-maximum security (Supermax) facility for the "worst of the worst" criminals, for those prisoners who pose an extremely high threat to both national and global security. Incarceration in a Supermax usually was reserved for terrorists!

After sentencing, David Guzman's family insisted on hugging Heather, Rick, Jeff, and me to express their gratitude. I am not sure anyone had a dry eye, but then again I suffer from allergies. After meeting with Guzman's family, a court-appointed lawyer of one of the defendants approached me and wanted to shake my hand and compliment us on the great job we had done. Then he confidentially whispered to me that Redrick Batiste had been a member of Black Sovereign Nation, a black identity extremist group.

The FBI now considers these black extremists groups as a potential domestic terrorist threat.

Trayvees Duncan-Bush, the designated crash dummy who probably would have been killed later by Batiste and his crew to forever ensure his silence, pled guilty. He had helped us with our investigation and even though it imperiled his life, also agreed to testify in court against the others. He was sentenced later in a separate hearing and was facing a maximum of twenty years for his role on December 7. Judge Hittner was more than willing to give him the full measure of punishment and if he could have, even more. In a unique circumstance, Heather, the prosecutor, and Duncan-Bush's defense attorney had to work together to sway the judge to show some mercy. Heather argued successfully that "Mr. Duncan-Bush took a great risk when he got on the stand" and also tactfully reminded Judge Hittner that he had cooperated at every stage of the prosecutor's trial preparation.

Judge Hittner sentenced Duncan-Bush to 12.5 years in federal prison, then three years of supervised release after that. The judge also specified that while in prison he had to complete his high school equivalency certificate (GED). Maybe Duncan-Bush wasn't such a dummy, after all.

After being reassigned back to SWAT, my workload was a fraction of what it had been when I was directly running high-risk surveillance operations on robbery crews. It was during this time I was approached by many in the department to write and publish a book about the NDTU, high-risk surveillance, departmental intrigue and the Armored Truck Sniper investigation. But I wanted to wait until after the trial and the sentencing of the other members of Batiste's robbery crew to not possibly damage Rick or Heather's case and/or taint a perspective jury pool.

So I did!

The author just prior to his retirement (39+ years)
from the Houston Police Department.